ASSEMBLER FOR
THE IBM PC
AND PC-XT

PETER
ABEL

ASSEMBLER
FOR
THE IBM PC
AND PC-XT

a *Reston Computer Group* book
Reston Publishing Company, Inc.
a *Prentice-Hall* company
Reston, Virginia

Library of Congress Cataloging in Publication Data

Abel, Peter
   Assembler for the IBM/PC and PC-XT.

   "A Reston Computer Group book."
   1. IBM Personal Computer–Programming.   2. IBM Personal
Computer XT–Programming.   3. Assembler language
(Computer program language) I. Title.   II. Title:
Assembler for the I.B.M./P.C. and P.C.-X.T.
QA76.8.I2594A23   1983   001.64'2   83-16057
ISBN 0-8359-0153-X (pbk)
      0-8359-0110-6 (case)

©1984 by Reston Publishing Company, Inc.
         A Prentice Hall Company
         Reston, Virginia 22090

10   9   8   7   6   5   4   3   2

Interior design and production: Jack Zibulsky

The final typeset pages composed in Melior were produced on
a TyXSET 1000 system in Reston, Virginia, using a Mergenthaler
Omnitech/2100. The page proofs were produced using a Canon
LBP-10 Laser Printer. TyXSET 1000 is a trademark of TyX Corp.

IBM®, IBM® Personal Computer and IBM® PC-XT® are
registered trademarks of International Business Machines
Corporation.

Printed in the United States of America

CONTENTS

PREFACE

The origin of the microprocessor goes back to the 1960s when research designers devised the integrated circuit (IC). The designers combined various electronic components (such as capacitors and transistors) into a single component on a silicon "chip." The manufacturers set this tiny chip into a device resembling a centipede, and connected it into a functioning system. As the technology advanced in the early 1970's, designers combined components onto a single chip. The introduction of the Intel 8008 chip in a computer terminal ushered in the first generation of microprocessors.

By 1974, the 8008 had evolved into a second generation microprocessor, the 8080, offering general-purpose utility. Its success prompted other companies to manufacture 8080 processors or variations such as the Zilog Z-80.

In 1978, Intel produced the third generation of microprocessors, the 8086 processor, which not only provided some compatibility with the 8080 but also significantly advanced the design. The 8088 processor was developed as a variation of the 8086 to provide a slightly simpler design and compatibility with current input/output devices. It is the 8088 that IBM® selected in 1981 as the processor for its *personal computer*, and in 1983 for the PC-XT.®

At that time, two or three manufacturers dominated the market for microcomputers. Who would have expected that the introduction of yet another "micro" to this market would have such immediate success? Perhaps the name *IBM* has had much to do with this success, and yet the IBM Personal Computer®is a powerful, effective device. Within a year, a number of other manufacturers provided similar microcomputers that share compatiblity with the IBM PC, no doubt as an effort to share in this success. These manufacturers include Commodore, Corona, DEC, Grid, Northstar, Texas Instruments, Toshiba, Vector Graphic, Victor, Wang, and Zenith.

Intel has been further developing its microprocessors. Two coprocessors that can operate with the 8086/8088 are the 8087 Numeric Data Processor (for high-speed, high-precision scientific computations, and the 8089 Input/Output Processor (for interleaved input/output operations). A souped-up version of the 8086 is the Intel 186 that provides additional operations to the 8086/8088 instruction set. At a higher level, the Intel 286 features built in memory management. You may also see these processors referred to as iAPX 86 (8086), iAPX 88 (8088), iAPX 186, and iAPX 286, where iAPX means Intel Advanced Processor Architecture.

The amazing spread of microcomputers has also brought about a renewed interest in Assembler language. There are two main reasons for this interest. The first reason is practical: a program written in Assembler language typically requires less memory space and less execution time. The second reason is academic: a knowledge of Assembler language and its resulting machine code provides an understanding of machine architecture that no "high-level" language can possibly provide.

Everyone these days has heard of such high-level languages such as BASIC, COBOL, and FORTRAN. These languages were designed to eliminate the technicalities of a particular computer. An Assembler language however is designed for a specific computer, or perhaps more accurately, *microprocessor*. As a consequence, in order to write a program in Assembler language for your own computer, you have to know something about the computer's architecture. But don't be alarmed! This book supplies all the basic material that is required. Those requiring even more advanced material can refer to the IBM Personal Computer Technical Reference Manual.

Among the material and knowledge required for this topic are the following:

□   Access to an IBM Personal Computer or an equivalent microcomputer with compatible 8086 or 8088 architecture. The computer should have a minimum of 64K memory, and at least one diskette drive. Nice to have but not essential would be an 80-column screen, an additional 32K memory, and a second diskette drive.

□   Familiarity with the IBM Guide to Operations Manual, especially with the description of the keyboard.

□   A diskette containing the Assembler language translator.

Knowledge not required for this topic is as follows:

□   A programming language. Although such knowledge may help you grasp some programming concepts more readily, it is by no means essential.

□   Prior knowledge of electronics or circuitry. This book provides the necessary information about the Intel 8086/8088 PC architecture that you will require for Assembler programming.

What you can do once you have completed this book:

□   Understand the hardware of the Personal Computer.

□   Understand machine language code and hexadecimal format.

□   Write programs in Assembler language to handle the screen, perform arithmetic, convert between ASCII and binary formats, perform table searches and sorts, and perform disk input and output.

□   Trace machine execution as an aid in debugging.

□   Write your own macro-instructions.

□   Link together separately assembled programs.

□   Understand the steps involved in assembly, link, and execute.

OPERATING SYSTEMS

The two major operating systems available on the IBM PC and other similar 8088-based microcomputers are MS-DOS from MicroSoft (known as PC-DOS on the IBM PC) and CP/M-86 from Digital Research. Both systems have their merits and adherents. Since DOS came with the system that I and most of my acquaintances bought, I have used that system as the primary vehicle for this book.

The Assembler instruction sets for both systems are virtually identical. However, there are three main areas in which DOS and CP/M differ:

1.   Operating system commands such as "assemble" a program and "link" a program, and the support programs for linking and debugging.

2.   The special commands to the Assembler program that define special features for the language.

3.   The interface between the Assembler program and the input/output system.

I have tried to point out where the two operating systems differ. But since the suppliers are continually upgrading their versions, you should consider their manuals as the final authority.

THE APPROACH TO TAKE

This book is intended as both a tutorial and as a permanent reference. To make the most effective use of your investment in a microcomputer and software, your best approach is to work through each chapter carefully, and reread any material that is not immediately clear. Key in the example programs, assemble them, and use the DOS DEBUG program (or CP/M DDT-86) to trace execution. Work through the exercises that each chapter provides.

The first six chapters furnish the foundation material for the book and indeed for the Assembler language. After these chapters, you can begin with any of these chapters: 8, 9, 10, 12, 13, or 15. Related chapters are 6/7, 10/11, and 13/14. Chapters 18, 19, and 20 are intended as reference.

Learning Assembler and getting your programs to work is an exciting experience. You'll spend a lot of time and effort, but the rewards are sure to be great. Good luck in your efforts!

OTHER REFERENCES

Although this book is intended to stand alone, some readers may want to investigate machine language and 8086/8088 system architecture in more detail. The following books are recommended:

International Business Machines Corporation, Macro Assembler Manual, IBM Corp., Personal Computer, P.O. Box 1328, Boca Raton, Florida 33432, 1981. Provides a description of each instruction and a list of Assembler error messages. The Preface says that the manual "is a reference for experienced assembler programmers, like yourself (sic), who use the IBM Personal Computer MACRO Assembler."

_____, *Technical Reference Manual*, 1982. A stack of material on the IBM PC hardware and input/output devices. A useful reference for those inclined towards technical material.

Rector, Russell and George Alexy, *The 8086 Book*, Osborne/McGraw-Hill, Berkeley, CA, 1980. Provides material on the execution logic of each instruction and a detailed multiprocessor description.

Morse, Stephen P., *The 8086 Primer*, Hayden Book Company, Inc., Rochelle Park, New Jersey, 1980. The author was involved in the design of the 8086 and presents very readable material on why certain operations work the way they do, plus machine organization and 8086 system design.

Osborne, Adam, *An Introduction to Microcomputers*, Volume I, Osborne/McGraw-Hill, 1980. An excellent, readable introduction to the subject.

ACKNOWLEDGEMENTS

The author is grateful for the assistance and cooperation of all those who contributed suggestions and reviews, especially Sean Nelson of Easyware System Builders for technical advice. Thanks also to IBM for permission to reproduce with modifications Table B-1 in Appendix B from a publication copyrighted in 1977 by International Business Machines as IBM form number GC20-1684.

1

INTRODUCTION TO THE IBM PERSONAL COMPUTER

Objective:
To explain features of microcomputer
hardware and program organization
for the Assembler programmer.

INTRODUCTION

If you have not digested the material in the IBM Guide to Operations, then now is the time to do so. Otherwise, let's get on with the project! There are some fundamentals that you must master before progressing to Chapter 2. This material involves the organization of the computer system. The fundamental building blocks of a computer are the *bit* and the *byte*. These supply the means by which your computer can represent data and instructions in memory.

A program in machine code consists of different *Segments* for defining data, for machine instructions, and a Segment named the *Stack* that contains stored addresses. To handle arithmetic, data movement, and addressing, the computer has a number of *registers*. This chapter covers all this material so that you can get going right away in Chapter 2 on your first machine language program.

BITS'N'BYTES

The smallest unit of data in a computer is a *bit*. A bit may be magnetized as *off* so that its value is zero, or as *on* so that its value is one. A single bit doesn't provide much information, but it is surprising what a bunch of them can do!

A group of nine bits represents a *byte*, eight bits for data and one bit for "parity." The eight bits provide the basis for representing characters such as the letter "A" and the asterisk, and for binary arithmetic. For example, a representation of the on and off bits for the letter "A" is 01000001 and for the asterisk is 00101010 (you don't have to memorize such facts).

Note on parity: The parity bit assumes that the "on" bits for a byte are always an odd number. The parity bit for the letter "A" would be on and for the asterisk would be off. When an instruction references a byte in storage, the computer checks its parity. If parity is even, a bit is assumed to be "lost" and the system displays an error message. A parity error may be a result of a hardware fault or it may be nonrecurring; either way, it is a rare event. Thankfully, this is all you need to know about parity.

You may have wondered how a computer "knows" that a bit value 01000001 represents the letter "A". When you key in an "A" on the keyboard, the system accepts a signal from that particular key into a byte in memory that sets the bits to 01000001. You can move this byte about in memory as you will, and that particular value when sent to the screen or printer generates the letter "A".

For reference purposes, the bits in a byte are numbered 0 to 7 from right to left as shown for the letter "A" below:

Bit number: 7 6 5 4 3 2 1 0
Bit contents: 0 1 0 0 0 0 0 1

The number 2^{10} equals 1024, which happens to be the value "K". For example, a computer with 64K memory has 64 × 1024 bytes, or 65,536.

Since the 8088 processor in the IBM PC uses 16-bit architecture, it can access 16-bit values in both memory and its registers. A 16-bit (2-byte) field is known as a *word*. The bits in a word are numbered 0 through 15 from right to left as shown for the letters "PC" below:

Bit number: 15 14 13 12 11 10 9 8 | 7 6 5 4 3 2 1 0
Bit contents: 0 1 0 1 0 0 0 0 | 0 1 0 0 0 0 1 1

ASCII CODE

The eight data bits enable 2^8 (256) possible combinations, from all bits off, 00000000, through all bits on, 11111111. There is no requirement that the bits 01000001 must mean the letter "A". It could just as well have been any other combination of on-bits. However, for purposes of *standardization*, microcomputers typically have adopted the ASCII (American National Standard Code for Information Interchange) code. A standard code facilitates transfer of data between different computer devices. The original ASCII code of seven bits supplied 128 different characters. The 8-bit extended ASCII code that the IBM PC uses provides 256 different characters including those for special graphics.

Appendix A supplies a list of the ASCII characters. And Chapter 6 shows you how to display the entire 256 characters on your screen (well, most of them).

BINARY NUMBERS

Basically, a computer can distinguish only between 0-bit and 1-bit conditions. *Consequently, a computer works in a base-2 numbering system known as binary. In fact, a bit derives its name from "binary digit."*

A collection of binary digits (bits) can represent any value. The value of a binary number is based on the relative position of each bit and the presence of 1-bits. The following eight-bit number contains all 1-bits:

```
Position value: 128 64 32 16 8 4 2 1
On-bit:           1   1  1  1 1 1 1 1
```

The rightmost bit assumes the value 1, the next digit to the left assumes 2, the next assumes 4, and so forth. The total of the 1-bits in this case is 1 + 2 + 4 + $\cdots$ + 128, or 255 (or $2^8 - 1$).

For the binary number 01000001, the on-bits represent the values 1 plus 64, or 65. But wait! Isn't 01000001 the letter "A"? Indeed it is. Here's the part that you will have to get very clear. Bits 01000001 can represent either the number 65 or the letter "A".

☐   If your program defines a field for arithmetic purposes, then 01000001 represents a binary number equivalent to the decimal number 65.
☐   If your program defines a field meant to be descriptive such as a heading, then 01000001 represents a letter.

When you start programming, you will find this distinction quite clear.

A binary number is not limited to only eight bits. In fact, since the 8088 processor uses 16-bit architecture, it handles 16-bit numbers automatically. 2^{16} minus 1 provides values up to 65,535. And a little creative programming permits numbers up to 32 bits ($2^{32} - 1$ is 4,294,967,295) or more.

Binary Arithmetic

Your computer performs arithmetic only in binary format (some large computers also perform decimal arithmetic). This being the case, an Assembler programmer has to be familiar with binary format and arithmetic. You need to know only binary addition:

$$0 + 0 = 0$$
$$1 + 0 = 1$$
$$1 + 1 = 10$$

That's it! Now, let's add 01000001 and 00101010. The letter "A" and an asterisk? No, the number 65 and the number 42:

Binary	Decimal
01000001	65
00101010	42
01101011	107

Check that the binary sum 01101011 is actually 107. This is so much fun, let's try another one:

Binary	Decimal
00111100	60
00110101	53
01110001	113

Some of the additions cause a *carry* so that $1 + 1 = 10$, and $1 + 1 + 1 = 11$.

Negative Numbers

The preceding binary numbers are all positive values because the leftmost bit contains zero. A negative binary number contains a 1-bit in its leftmost position, but there's a "bit" more to it. A negative binary number is expressed in *two's complement notation*. That is, to represent a binary number as negative, reverse the bits and add 1. Let's use 01000001 as an example:

Number 65:	01000001
Reverse bits:	10111110
Add 1:	10111111 (equals −65)

You can add up the 1-bit values for 10111111 and you won't get 65. In fact, a binary number is known to be negative if its leftmost bit is 1. To determine the absolute value of a negative binary number, simply repeat the previous operation. Reverse the bits and add 1:

Binary value: 10111111
Reverse bits: 01000000
Add 1:   01000001   (equals +65)

Adding +65 to −65 should give a sum of zero. Let's try it:

01000001   (+65)
10111111   (−65)
─────────
(1)00000000

The eight-bit value is all zeros. The carry of the 1-bit on the left is lost. Technically, if there is a carry into the sign bit and a carry out of the sign bit, the result is correct.

Binary subtraction is a simple matter: Reverse the sign of the number being subtracted and add the two numbers. Let's subtract 42 from 65. The binary for 42 is 00101010 and its two's complement is 11010110:

65   01000001
+(−42)   11010110
─────   ──────────
23   (1)00010111

The result, 23, is correct. Once again, there was a carry into the sign bit and a carry out of the sign bit.

If the justification for two's complement notation doesn't seem immediately clear, consider the following proposition: What value would you have to add to binary 00000001 to make it equal to 00000000? In terms of decimal numbers, the answer would be -1. For binary, try 11111111, as follows:

00000001
11111111
──────────
Result: (1)00000000

Ignoring the carry (1), you can see that the binary number 11111111 is equivalent to decimal −1, and accordingly

0   00000000
−(+1)   -00000001
────   ──────────
−1   11111111

You can also see a pattern form as the binary numbers decrease in value:

+3	00000011
+2	00000010
+1	00000001
0	00000000
−1	11111111
−2	11111110
−3	11111101

In fact, in a negative binary number the *0-bits* indicate its value. Treat the positional value of each 0-bit as if it were a 1-bit, sum the values, and add 1.

You'll find this material on binary arithmetic and negative numbers particularly relevant when you get to Chapters 10 and 11 on arithmetic.

HEXADECIMAL REPRESENTATION

The letter "A" is satisfactory to represent the bit value 01000001 as long as the byte is supposed to represent an alphabetic character. But "A" is hardly suitable if 01000001 is supposed to represent a binary number. Let's say that you are viewing the contents of bytes in memory, as you'll be doing in the next chapter. You want to know the contents of four adjacent bytes (two words) that contain a binary value. Since four bytes involves 32 bits, the designers of the computer have developed a shorthand method of representing binary data. The method divides each byte in half and expresses the value of each half-byte. Assume the following four bytes:

0101	1001	0011	0101	1011	1001	1100	1110
5	9	3	5	11	9	12	14

Since there are still some numbers that require two digits, let's extend the numbering system so that 10 = A, 11 = B, 12 = C, 13 = D, 14 = E, and 15 = F. Here's the shorthand number that represents the contents of the above bytes:

59   35   B9   CE

The numbering system involves the "digits" 0 through F, and since there are 16 such digits, it is known as *hexadecimal* representation. Figure 1-1 provides the binary, decimal, and hexadecimal values of the numbers 0 through 15.

Figure 1·1 Binary, Decimal, and Hexadecimal Representation.

Binary	Decimal	Hexadecimal	Binary	Decimal	Hexadecimal
0000	0	0	1000	8	8
0001	1	1	1001	9	9
0010	2	2	1010	10	A
0011	3	3	1011	11	B
0100	4	4	1100	12	C
0101	5	5	1101	13	D
0110	6	6	1110	14	E
0111	7	7	1111	15	F

Assembler language makes considerable use of hexadecimal format. Listings of an assembled program show in hexadecimal all addresses, all machine code instructions, and the contents of all constants. Also, you will debug programs using the DOS DEBUG program, which similarly displays all addresses and contents of bytes in hexadecimal format.

Hexadecimal (or hex) format at first requires some familiarization. But once you have worked with it enough, you get quite used to it. There will be many times in fact when you'll wish for 16 fingers to help with hex addition!

Following are some simple hex arithmetic examples. Keep in mind that the hex number following hex F is 10, which is decimal value 16.

5	6	F	F	10	FF
5	7	1	F	10	1
A	D	10	1E	20	100

Note also that hex 20 equals decimal 32, hex 100 is decimal 256, and hex 1000 is decimal 4096.

Throughout this text, the expression of a hexadecimal number is normally indicated, for example, as hex 4B, a binary number as binary 01001011, and a decimal number as 75—the absence of a description assumes a decimal number. The occasional exception occurs where the base is obvious from its context.

You may sometimes need to convert a hex number to decimal and vice versa. Appendix B provides the conversion methods. Now let's examine some of the features of 8086/8088 processor design that you will need to understand for Chapter 2.

SEGMENTS

A Segment is an area of memory up to 64K bytes in length. Segments, which may be located anywhere in memory, begin on a *Paragraph* boundary, that is, at a location evenly divisible by 16.

Most programs contain at least three Segments. Although any Segment may be up to 64K bytes in size, they address as much space as necessary for execution.

The three main Segments are:

1.   *The Stack Segment.* In simple terms, the Stack contains return addresses both for your program to return to the operating system (DOS or CP/M) and for any of your own "called" subroutines to return to your main program. The Stack Segment (SS) register addresses this Segment.

2.   *The Data Segment.* The Data Segment contains any defined data, constants, and work areas that your program requires. The Data Segment (DS) register addresses this Segment.

3.   *The Code Segment.* The Code Segment contains the machine instructions that are to execute. Typically the first executable instruction is at the start of this Segment, and the operating system (DOS or CP/M) links to this location for program execution.

Figure 1-2 provides a graphic view of the SS, DS, and CS registers, although the registers and Segments are not necessarily in this sequence.

Figure 1-2 Segments and Registers.

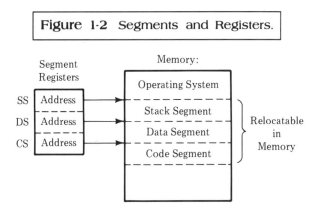

The three Segment registers contain the starting address of each Segment, and each Segment begins at a Paragraph boundary.

One other Segment register, the Extra Segment (ES) register, has specialized uses.

   Within a program, all memory locations are relative to the start of a Segment. All such locations are expressed as an *offset* from the start of a Segment. (An offset is also known as a displacement.) A two-byte (16-bit) offset can range from hex 0000 through hex FFFF, or zero through 65,535. Consequently, any memory address in a program is referenced by the address in a Segment register plus an offset. For example, the first byte of the Data Segment is at offset 00, the second byte is at offset 01, and so forth through to offset 65535.

Do you want to know how the 8086/8088 processor can address one million bytes of memory? A register provides 16 bits. Since a Segment address is always on a Paragraph boundary, the rightmost four bits of the address are zero. Now, hex FFF0 would allow addressing up to 65,520 (plus an offset). But the designers cleverly decided that there is no purpose allowing space for bits that would always be zero. An address is therefore stored in a Segment register as hex nnnn and the computer assumes that there are four more rightmost zero bits (one hex digit), as hex nnnn0. Now, hex FFFF0 allows addressing up to 1,048,560 bytes! If you are uncertain, decode each hex F as binary 1111 and add up the values for the 1-bits.

   As an example of addressing, assume that the Data Segment register contains hex 045F and an instruction references a location within the Data Segment with an offset of 0032. The actual memory location referenced is therefore the following:

DS address:	045F0
Offset:	0032
Actual address:	04622

REGISTERS

The 8086/8088 processor has 14 registers that are used to control the instruction being executed, to handle addressing of memory, and to provide arithmetic capability. Each register is one word (16 bits) in length and is addressable by name.

Four General Purpose Registers:
AX, BX, CX, and DX.

   For Assembler programming, the general purpose registers are the "workhorses." They are unique in that you can address them as a one-word or as a one-byte portion. The leftmost byte is the "high" portion and the rightmost byte is the "low" portion. For example, the AX register consists of an AH and an AL portion, and you can reference any of the three names.

The following three Assembler instructions move zeros to the AX, AH, and AL registers respectively:

MOV AX,00
MOV AH,00
MOV AL,00

1.   *The AX Register.*   The AX register is known as the "primary accumulator." It is used for all input/output operations, some "string" operations, and some arithmetic operations. For example, multiply, divide, and translate instructions assume use of the AX register. Some instructions generate more efficient code if they reference the AX.

AX: | AH | AL |

2.   *The BX Register.* The BX register is known as the "base register" since it is the only general purpose register that can be used as an "index" to extend addressing. Another common purpose is for computations.

BX: | BH | BL |

3.   *The CX Register.* The CX register is known as the "count register." It is required for controlling the number of times a loop is repeated and contains the value by which bits are shifted left or right. The CX is also used for computations.

CX: | CH | CL |

4.   *The DX Register.* The DX register is known as the "Data register" presumably because "data" begins with a "d"! Some input/output operations require its use, and multiply and divide operations that involve large values assume the DX and AX pair.

DX: | DH | DL |

Any of the general purpose registers may be used for addition and subtraction of either 8-bit or 16-bit values.

Two-Pointer Registers:
SP and BP

The two-Pointer registers, SP and BP, permit the system to access data in the Stack Segment. They may also be used (rarely) for addition and subtraction.

1.   *The SP Register.* The Stack Pointer permits implementation of a Stack in memory. This register is associated with the SS register for addressing the Stack.
2.   *The BP Register.* The Base Pointer facilitates referencing of "parameters" (data and addresses passed via the Stack).

Two-Index Registers:
SI and DI

Both of the index registers are available for extended addressing and for uoc in addition and subtraction.

1.   *The SI Register.* This register is known as the Source Index and is required for some "string" operations. In this context, the SI is associated with the DS register.
2.   *The DI Register.* This register is known as the Destination Index and is also required for some "string" operations. In this context, the DI is associated with the ES register.

Four-Segment Registers:
CS, DS, SS, and ES

The Segment registers are important in the addressing of memory. Each provides for addressing a 64K area of memory, known as the "current segment." As discussed earlier, a Segment aligns on a Paragraph boundary and its address in a Segment register omits the rightmost four bits.

1.   *The CS Register.* The Code Segment register contains the initial address of the Code Segment. This address plus the offset value in the Program Counter (PC) indicates the address of an instruction to be fetched for execution. For normal programming purposes you need not reference the CS.
2.   *The DS Register.* The Data Segment register contains the initial address of the Data Segment. In simple terms, this address plus an offset

value in an instruction causes a reference to a specific location in the Data Segment.

3.   *The SS Register.* The Stack Segment register contains the initial address of the Stack Segment.

4.   *The ES Register.* Some string operations use the Extra Segment register to handle memory addressing. In this context, the ES register is associated with the DI register. If the ES is required, an Assembler program must initialize it.

One-Instruction Pointer Register: IP

The IP register contains the offset address of the instruction that is to execute. You would not normally reference this register in a program, but you can change its value when using the DOS DEBUG program to test a program. The IP register is also known as the Program Counter (PC).

One-Flag Register

The Flag register is also known as the Status register or Program Status Word. Nine of its 16 bits are active and indicate the current status of the machine and the results of execution. Many instructions such as compare and arithmetic change the status of the flags. Briefly, the flag bits are the following:

Flag	Purpose
O (Overflow)	Indicates overflow of a high-order bit following arithmetic.
D (Direction)	Designates left or right direction for moving or comparing "string" data (data in memory that exceeds one word).
I (Interrupt)	Indicates if an interrupt is disabled.
T (Trap)	Permits CPU operation in single-step mode. The DEBUG program, for example, sets the Trap Flag so that you can step through execution one instruction at a time to examine the effect on registers and memory.
S (Sign)	Contains resulting sign of arithmetic operation (0 = plus and 1 = minus).
Z (Zero)	Indicates result of arithmetic or compare operation (0 = non-zero and 1 = zero result).

A (Auxiliary carry)	Contains a carry out of bit 3 on eight-bit data, for specialized arithmetic.
P (Parity)	Indicates parity of low-order 8 bit data operation (1 = even and 0 = odd number).
C (Carry)	Contains carries from high-order (leftmost) bit following an arithmetic operation, and contents of last bit of a shift or rotate.

You need not memorize this list. The flags that are most relevant to Assembler programming are O, S, Z, and C for compares and arithmetic, and D for direction of string operations. Later chapters contain more detail about the Flag registers.

PC ARCHITECTURE

The two main hardware elements of the IBM PC are a System Unit and a keyboard. Optional items include a display screen, diskette drives, printer, and various options for asynchronous communications and game control. The System Unit contains a System Board, power supply, and system expansion slots for up to five options.

If you open the System Unit, you can see the System Board placed horizontally at the bottom. Features of the System Board are the following:

□   The Intel 8088 microprocessor.
□   40K bytes of Read-Only Memory (ROM).
□   Up to 64K bytes of Read/Write Memory (RAM).
□   An enhanced version of the BASIC-80 interpreter.

The expansion slots provide for connecting display screens, diskette drives, communications channel, additional memory boards, and games.

The keyboard contains its own microprocessor, an Intel 8048. It performs self-testing when the power is turned on, keyboard scanning, key debounce, and buffering up to 20 key scan codes.

The brain of an IBM PC and PC-XT is the Intel 8088 microprocessor that performs all processing of instructions and data. The 8088 is a "third generation" microprocessor with 16-bit registers that can process two bytes at a time. (Second generation microprocessors such as the Z80, 8080, 6502, 6800, and 6809 have 8-bit registers that process one byte at a time.) The 8088 also provides a more advanced, versatile system and considerably more addresssable memory – up to one million bytes, as seen earlier.

The 8088 is like an 8086 but with one difference: The 8088 is limited to

8-bit (instead of 16-bit) *buses*, which provide transfers between the microprocessor, memory, and external devices. This limit means a cost in data transfer time with a gain in simplicity of design and compatibility with existing
input/output devices.

The 8086 and 8088 are partitioned into two logical units: an Execution
Unit (EU) and a Bus Interface Unit (BIU), as illustrated in Figure 1-3. The
role of the EU is to execute instructions whereas the BIU provides instructions and data to the EU. The EU contains an Arithmetic and Logic Unit
(ALU), a Control Unit (CU), and ten registers. These features provide for
instruction execution, arithmetic computation, and logic (comparison for
high, low, and equal).

Figure 1-3 8088 Execution Unit and
Bus Interface Unit.

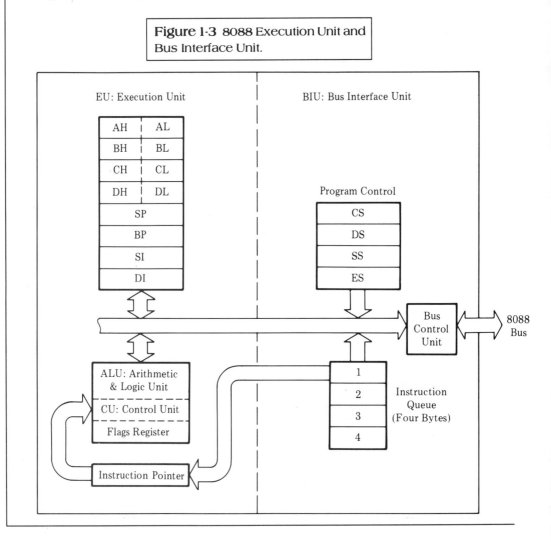

The three sections of the BIU, the Bus Control Unit, instruction queue, and the Segment registers, control three important functions. First, the BIU controls the buses that transfer data to the EU, to memory, and to external input/output devices. Second, the four Segment registers control addressing and can handle up to one million bytes of memory addressing.

The third function is instruction access. Since all program instructions are in memory, the BIU must access instructions from memory into an instruction queue. Because the queue is four bytes in size (six bytes on the 8086), the BIU is able to look ahead and *prefetch* instructions so that there is always a queue of instructions ready to execute. Note that machine instructions vary in length from one to five bytes, so that the actual number of instructions is generally fewer than four.

The EU and BIU work in parallel, with the BIU keeping one step ahead. The EU notifies the BIU if it needs access to data in memory or an I/O device. Also, the EU requests machine instructions from the BIU instruction queue. The top instruction is the currently executable one, and while the EU is occupied executing an instruction, the BIU fetches another instruction from memory. This fetching overlaps with execution and speeds up processing.

Memory

The typical microcomputer contains two types of internal memory. The first type is ROM, an acronym for "read-only memory." A ROM is a special memory chip that (as the name suggests) can only be read. Since data in a sense is permanently "burned into" the memory chip, it cannot be altered.

One main purpose of ROM is to handle start-up procedures; when you switch on the power, ROM performs various check-outs and loads into RAM (main memory) any data from a system diskette (such as DOS). For programming purposes, one feature of ROM is very important— the basic Input/Output System (BIOS) which is covered in later chapters. ("Basic" here means the conventional word, not the programming language.) ROM also handles the BASIC interpreter, cassette operating system, and patterns for graphics characters.

The type of memory with which a programmer is very much concerned is RAM, which stands for "random access memory." This acronym is rather inaccurate; a better name would be "read-write memory." In effect, RAM memory is available as a "worksheet" for temporary storage of a program and its data area for execution.

When you turn off the power, the contents of RAM are lost. Therefore, for keeping programs and data, you need separate external storage such as diskette or cassette tape. Assuming that you have the DOS diskette and a program diskette inserted, when you turn off the power, ROM causes the

DOS program to load into RAM. (Only the main part of DOS loads, not the entire set of DOS programs.) You then reply to the DOS prompt for the date and can request DOS to perform actions. One action could be to load a program from a program diskette into RAM. Since DOS does not occupy all of RAM, there is (usually) space for your program as well. Your program executes in RAM and normally produces output on the screen, printer, or diskette. When finished, you may load another program into RAM; this action overwrites the previous program, but remember that the previous one is preserved on diskette.

Memory Allocation.   The fact that a Segment can be up to 64K in size and that there are four kinds of Segments suggests that the amount of available RAM memory is 4 x 64K, or 256K. But actually there may be any number of Segments; in order to address another Segment, it is only necessary to change the address in a Segment register. This feature facilitates programs that exceed 64K bytes in size as well as *time-sharing*: loading and executing more than one program in RAM at one time.

According to the physical memory map of the original PC in Figure 1-4, the first 64K is RAM memory on the system board. The next 192K requires an expansion slot via a so-called I/O channel. The enhanced PC allows for up to 256K on the system board. Some areas are reserved, and

Figure 1-4 Physical Memory Map.

Start Address		Purpose
Dec	Hex	
Zero	0	16—64K of Read/Write Memory on System Board
64K	10000	Up to 192K Read/Write Memory in I/O Channel
256K	40000	384K Read/Write Memory Expansion in I/O Channel
640K	A0000	16K Reserved
656K	A4000	112K Graphics/Display Video Buffer
768K	C0000	192K Memory Expansion Area
960K	F0000	16K Reserved
976K	F4000	48K Base System ROM

the highest area beginning at address 976K is actually the address that the system uses for the ROM chips.

All further discussions of RAM use the general term "memory." The next chapter gets you right into entering and running a program.

Addressing.   Memory locations are numbered consecutively from 00, the lowest memory location. The processor accesses bytes or words in memory. Consider the decimal number 1025. The hex representation of this value, 0401, requires two bytes, or one word, of memory. It consists of a high-order portion ("most significant byte"), 04, and a low-order portion ("least significant byte"), 01. The system stores the bytes in a word in memory in reverse sequence: the low-order portion in the low memory address and the high-order portion in the high memory address. Assume that the processor has stored hex 0401 from a register into memory locations 5612 and 5613 as follows:

$$| 01| 04|$$
$$| \; |$$

location 5612,   location 5613.
least significant byte   most significant byte

The system expects data in memory to be in reverse sequence and processes it accordingly. Although this feature is entirely automatic, you will have to keep alert to this fact when programming and debugging Assembler programs.

KEY POINTS TO REMEMBER

☐   A single character of memory is a byte, comprised of eight data bits and one parity bit. Two adjacent bytes comprise a word.

☐   The value K equals 1024 bytes.

☐   The heart of the IBM PC is an 8088 processor. The 8088 (and 8086) can access bytes or words.

☐   The representation of character data is ASCII format.

☐   The computer distinguishes only between bits that are 0 (off) and 1 (on) and performs arithmetic only in binary format.

☐   The value of a binary number is determined by the placement of 1-bits. Thus, binary 1111 equals $2^3 + 2^2 + 2^1 + 2^0$, or 15.

☐   A negative binary number is represented by two's complement notation: Reverse the bits of its positive representation and add 1.

☐   Hexadecimal format is an important shorthand notation for representing groups of four bits. The hex digits 0-9 and A-F represent binary 0000 through 1111.

☐   Programs consist of Segments: A Stack Segment for maintaining return addresses, a Data Segment for defined data and work areas, and a Code

Segment for executable instructions. All locations in a program are relative to the start of a Segment and are expressed as an offset.

□   The 14 registers control instruction execution, addressing, arithmetic, and execution status.

□   The two types of internal memory are ROM (Read-Only Memory) and RAM (Random Access Memory, or rather Read/Write Memory).

□   The processor stores data in words in memory in reverse sequence.

QUESTIONS

1-1. Provide the ASCII bit configuration for the following one-byte characters. Use Appendix A as a guide: (a) M, (b) m, (c) ?, (d) 4.

1-2. Provide the binary bit configuration for the following numbers: (a) 7, (b) 12, (c) 19, (d) 28.

1-3. Add the following binary numbers:

(a) 00010110   (b) 00111101   (c) 00111111
    00001110   00101010   00000001

1-4. Determine the two's complement for the following binary numbers: (a) 00001011, (b) 00011110, (c) 00011001.

1-5. Determine the positive value of the following negative binary numbers: (a) 11001100, (b) 10011101, (c) 10000000.

1-6. Determine the hex representation for the following: (a) ASCII letter P, (b) ASCII number 5, (c) binary 01011100, (d) binary 01101110.

1-7. Add the following hex numbers (you may have to take off your shoes for this):

(a) 23A5   (b) 51FC   (c) 7778   (d) EABD
    0023   4   888   26C5

1-8. Determine the hex representation for the following decimal numbers. These are not ASCII numbers. Refer to Appendix B for the conversion method. You could also check your result by converting the hex to binary and adding up the 1-bits. (a) 17, (b) 34, (c) 87, (d) 255, (e) 4095, (f) 63,425.

1-9. What are the three kinds of Segments, their maximum size, and the address boundary on which they begin?

1-10. What registers can you use for the following purposes? (a) addition and subtraction, (b) counting for looping, (c) multiply and divide, (d) addressing Segments, (e) indication of a zero result, (f) address of instruction that is to execute.

1-11. What are the two main kinds of memory on the IBM PC and what is their main purpose?

2

MACHINE EXECUTION

Objective:
To introduce machine language and
the execution of a program in memory.

INTRODUCTION

The basis of this chapter is an explanation of the execution of three machine
language programs. The chapter describes how you can enter these programs directly into memory in the Code Segment area and provides an explanation of each execution step.

The first program example uses "immediate" data defined within the
instructions for loading into registers and performing arithmetic. The second
example uses data defined separately in the Data Segment. By tracing these
instructions through machine execution, you will gain great insight into the
operation of the computer and the role of the registers.

You can start right in with no prior knowledge of Assembler language or even of programming. What you need is an IBM PC (or equivalent 8086/8088-based micro) and a diskette containing the DOS or CP/M-
86 operating system.

MACHINE LANGUAGE EXAMPLE I: IMMEDIATE DATA

The purpose of this example is to illustrate a simple machine language program, how it would appear in main storage, and the effect of its execution. The following program steps are in hexadecimal format:

Instruction	Explanation
B82301	Move the value 0123 to the AX register.
052500	Add the value 0025 to the AX register.
8BD8	Move the contents of the AX register to the BX.
03D8	Add the contents of AX to BX.
8BCB	Move the contents of BX to CX.
2BC8	Subtract the contents of AX from CX.
2BC0	Subtract the contents of AX from AX (clear AX).
90	No operation (do nothing).
CB	Return to DOS Supervisor.

You may have noticed that the machine instructions vary in length: one, two, or three bytes. Also, the machine instructions appear in memory, one immediately following the other. Program execution begins with the first instruction and steps through each instruction one after another. Do not at this point expect to make much sense of the machine code itself! For example, in one case a MOV is hex B8 and in another case the MOV is hex 8B.

You can enter this program directly into memory and execute it one instruction at a time. At the same time, you can view the contents of the registers after each instruction. For CP/M users, there is a note on CP/M differences at the end of this section.

First, insert the DOS diskette into drive A. If the power is off, turn the switch on; if already on, press and hold Ctrl and Alt together and press Del. When DOS is fully loaded it responds with a prompt "A>". Key in the command DEBUG and press return. The DEBUG program now loads from diskette into main memory. When DOS has fully loaded DEBUG, the red light from the diskette drive turns off, and the prompt from DEBUG is a hyphen (−). If you want this exercise to print, turn on your printer and press Ctrl and PrtSc together.

You can now start to enter the machine language program directly by keying in the following command, including the blanks where indicated:

E CS:100 B8 23 01 05 25 00 (press return)

The command E stands for Enter. CS:100 indicates the memory address where the instructions are to be entered—100 bytes following the start of the Code Segment (this is the normal starting address for machine code under DEBUG). The E command causes each pair of hexadecimal digits to enter a byte in memory, from CS:100 through CS:105.

The next Enter command is

E CS:106 8B D8 03 D8 8B CB (return)

which enters six bytes starting at CS:106 through 107, 108, 109, 10A, and 10B. The last Enter command

E CS:10C 2B C8 2B C0 90 CB

enters six bytes starting at CS:10C through 10D, 10E, 10F, 110, and 111. You have now written and entered your first machine language program! Double-check that you have keyed in the correct values. If not, you can simply correct any command that is incorrect.

Now it's just a simple matter of executing these instructions. Figure 2-1 shows all the steps including the E commands. Your screen should display the same results as you enter each DEBUG command, although a 40-column screen will require more lines.

Key in the command R, followed by return in order to view the contents of the registers and flags. At this moment DEBUG shows the contents of the registers in hexadecimal format, for example as

AX = 0000, BX = 0000, ...

Because of differences in DOS versions, the register contents on your screen may not be identical to those shown in Figure 2-1. The IP (Instruction Pointer) register displays IP = 0100 indicating that instruction execution is to begin 100 bytes past the start of the Code Segment. (That is why you used E CS:100 to enter the start of the program.)

The Flags register in Figure 2-1 shows the following flag setting:

NV UP DI PL NZ NA PO NC

These settings mean, respectively, no overflow, up (right) direction, disable interrupt, plus sign, nonzero, no auxiliary carry, parity odd, and no carry. At this time none of these flags is important.

The R command also displays at offset 0100 the first instruction to be executed. Note that in Figure 2-1 the CS register contains CS = 049F (yours may differ) and the instruction is the following:

049F:0100   B82301   MOV AX,0123

Figure 2-1 Trace of Machine Instructions.

```
DEBUG
-E CS:100 B8 23 01 05 25 00
-E CS:106 8B D8 03 D8 8B CB
-E CS:10C 2B C8 2B C0 90 CB
-R
AX=0000  BX=0000  CX=0000  DX=0000  SP=FFF0  BP=0000  SI=0000  DI=0000
DS=049F  ES=049F  SS=049F  CS=049F  IP=0100   NV UP DI PL NZ NA PO NC
049F:0100 B82301        MOV     AX,0123
-T

AX=0123  BX=0000  CX=0000  DX=0000  SP=FFF0  BP=0000  SI=0000  DI=0000
DS=049F  ES=049F  SS=049F  CS=049F  IP=0103   NV UP DI PL NZ NA PO NC
049F:0103 052500        ADD     AX,0025
-T

AX=0148  BX=0000  CX=0000  DX=0000  SP=FFF0  BP=0000  SI=0000  DI=0000
DS=049F  ES=049F  SS=049F  CS=049F  IP=0106   NV UP DI PL NZ NA PE NC
049F:0106 8BD8          MOV     BX,AX
-T

AX=0148  BX=0148  CX=0000  DX=0000  SP=FFF0  BP=0000  SI=0000  DI=0000
DS=049F  ES=049F  SS=049F  CS=049F  IP=0108   NV UP DI PL NZ NA PE NC
049F:0108 03D8          ADD     BX,AX
-T

AX=0148  BX=0290  CX=0000  DX=0000  SP=FFF0  BP=0000  SI=0000  DI=0000
DS=049F  ES=049F  SS=049F  CS=049F  IP=010A   NV UP DI PL NZ AC PE NC
049F:010A 8BCB          MOV     CX,BX
-T

AX=0148  BX=0290  CX=0290  DX=0000  SP=FFF0  BP=0000  SI=0000  DI=0000
DS=049F  ES=049F  SS=049F  CS=049F  IP=010C   NV UP DI PL NZ AC PE NC
049F:010C 2BC8          SUB     CX,AX
-T

AX=0148  BX=0290  CX=0148  DX=0000  SP=FFF0  BP=0000  SI=0000  DI=0000
DS=049F  ES=049F  SS=049F  CS=049F  IP=010E   NV UP DI PL NZ AC PE NC
049F:010E 2BC0          SUB     AX,AX
-T

AX=0000  BX=0290  CX=0148  DX=0000  SP=FFF0  BP=0000  SI=0000  DI=0000
DS=049F  ES=049F  SS=049F  CS=049F  IP=0110   NV UP DI PL ZR NA PE NC
049F:0110 90            NOP
-T

AX=0000  BX=0290  CX=0148  DX=0000  SP=FFF0  BP=0000  SI=0000  DI=0000
DS=049F  ES=049F  SS=049F  CS=049F  IP=0111   NV UP DI PL ZR NA PE NC
049F:0111 CB            RET     L
```

☐   CS = 049F means that the start of the Code Segment is at location 049F.
The value 049F:0100 means 100 (hex) bytes following the CS address
049F.

☐   B82301 is the machine address that you entered at CS:100.

☐   MOV AX,0123 is the *symbolic Assembler instruction* for the machine
code. This is the result of an "unassembly" operation, which DEBUG

displays so that you may more easily interpret the machine instruction. In the next chapter, you will begin coding Assembler instructions exclusively. This Assembler instruction means, in effect, Move the *immediate value* 0123 into the AX register.

At this point, the MOV instruction has not executed. For this purpose, key in T (for Trace) and "return." DEBUG now displays the contents of the registers, the flags, and the next instruction that is to execute. Note that the AX register now contains 0123. The machine code was B8 (Move to AX register) followed by 2301. The operation moves the 23 to the low half (AL) of the AX register and the 01 to the high half (AH) of the AX register:

AX: |01|23|

The contents of the IP register is 0103 to indicate the location in the Code Segment of the next instruction to be executed:

049F:0103   052500   ADD   AX,0025

To execute this instruction, enter another T. The instruction adds 25 to the low half (AL) of the AX register and 00 to the high half (AH) of the AX, in effect adding 0025 to the AX. AX now contains 0148, and IP contains 0106 for the next instruction to be executed.

Key in another T command. The instruction moves the contents of the AX register to the BX register—note that BX now contains 0148. AX still contains 0148 too because the MOV operation actually *copies* the data from one location to another.

Now key in a T command to step through each remaining instruction in the program. The next instruction adds the contents of AX to BX, giving 0290 in BX. Then the program moves (copies) the contents of BX into CX, subtracts AX from CX, and subtracts AX from itself. After this last operation, the Zero Flag is changed from NZ (nonzero) to ZR (zero) to indicate that the result of the last operation was zero (subtracting AX from itself cleared it to zero).

You can also press T for the last instructions, NOP and RET, but there is no purpose going past this point. You can if you want, but you will execute instructions outside your own program (it's hard to resist!).

Do you want to view your machine language program in the Code Segment? If so, key in D for Dump as follows:

D CS:100

If your screen is 80 columns wide, DEBUG displays 16 bytes (32 hex digits) to the left of each line. To the right is the ASCII representation (if printable) of each byte (pair of hex digits). In the case of machine code, the ASCII representation is meaningless and may be ignored. Later sections discuss the right side of the dump in more detail.

The first line of the dump begins at 00 and represents the contents of locations CS:100 through CS:10F. The second line represents the contents of CS:110 through CS:11F. Although your program ends at CS:111, the Dump command automatically displays eight lines (on an 80-column screen) from CS:100 through CS:170.

Figure 2-2 shows the results of the D CS:100 command. Expect only the machine code from CS:100 through 111 to be identical to your own Dump; the bytes that follow could contain anything.

Figure 2-2 Dump of the Code Segment.

```
D CS:100
049F:0100   B8 23 01 05 25 00 8B D8-03 D8 8B CB 2B C8 2B C0   8#..%..X.X.K+H+@
049F:0110   90 CB 00 00 00 00 00 00-00 00 00 00 00 00 00 00   .K..............
049F:0120   00 00 00 00 00 00 00 00-00 00 00 00 00 00 00 00   ................
049F:0130   00 00 00 00 00 00 00 00-00 00 00 00 00 00 00 00   ................
049F:0140   00 00 00 00 00 00 00 00-00 00 00 00 00 00 00 00   ................
049F:0150   00 00 00 00 00 00 00 00-00 00 00 00 00 00 00 00   ................
049F:0160   00 00 00 00 00 00 00 00-00 00 00 00 00 00 00 00   ................
049F:0170   00 00 00 00 00 00 00 00-00 00 00 00 00 00 00 00   ................

Q
```

To terminate the DEBUG session, enter Q (for Quit). This operation returns you to DOS which displays the prompt "A>." If you printed the session, enter Ctrl/PrtSc again to terminate printing.

CP/M DIFFERENCES

The CP/M debug program DDT-86 is similar but not identical to DOS DEBUG. If you are a CP/M user, read the section on DDT-86 in your manual and compare it to the material in this chapter. The following DDT-86 commands are especially relevant:

A = Enter Assembler statements at specified locations.
D = Display memory in hex and ASCII formats.
F = Fill (enter) data.
G = Go (execute) instructions.
T = Trace.
X = Examine: display and alter flags and registers.

MACHINE LANGUAGE EXAMPLE II:
DEFINED DATA

The previous example used *immediate* values defined directly within the first two instructions (MOV and ADD). We next illustrate a similar example that *defines* the two data fields 0123 and 0025 in the Data Segment. Working through this example should give you good insight into how the computer accesses data by means of the DS register and *offset addresses*.

The present example defines data fields containing respectively the following:

DS Location	Hex value	Bytes occupied
0000	2301	0 and 1
0002	2500	2 and 3
0004	0000	4 and 5
0006	2A2A2A	6, 7, and 8

Remember that a hex character occupies a half-byte, so that, for example, 23 is stored in byte 0 (the first byte) of the Data Segment, and 01 is stored in byte 1 (the second byte).

The machine language instructions in the Code Segment that process these fields are the following:

Instruction	Explanation
A10000	Move the word (two bytes) beginning at DS location 0000 into the AX register.
03060200	Add the contents of the word (two bytes) beginning at DS location 0002 to the AX register.
A30400	Move the contents of the AX register to the word beginning at DS location 0004.
CB	Return to the DOS Supervisor.

You may have noticed that there are two Move instructions with different machine codes: A1 and A3. The actual machine code is dependent on the registers that are referenced, the number of bytes (byte or word), the direction of data transfer (from or to a register), and the reference to immediate data or memory.

Once again, you can use DEBUG to enter this program and to watch its execution. Insert the DOS diskette and enter the command DEBUG as before. When DEBUG signals its prompt, a hyphen (−), it is ready for your commands.

First key in the Enter (E) commands for the Data Segment:

E DS:00 23 01 25 00 00 00
E DS:06 2A 2A 2A

The first Enter stores the three words (six bytes) at the start of the Data Segment, DS:00. *Note that you have to enter words with the bytes reversed so that 0123 is 2301 and 0025 is 2500.* When a MOV instruction accesses these words into a register, it "unreverses" the bytes so that 2301 becomes 0123 and 2500 becomes 0025.

The second Enter command stores three asterisks (***) so that you can view them later using the Dump (D) command—the asterisks serve no purpose in the Data Segment. Now key in the instructions in the Code Segment, once again beginning at CS:100, as follows:

E CS:100 A1 00 00 03 06 02 00
E CS:107 A3 04 00 CB

These instructions are now found in memory locations CS:100 through CS:10A. You can execute these instructions just as you did earlier. Figure 2-3 shows all the steps including the E commands. Your screen should display the same results. You may want to look at the stored data in the Data Segment and the instructions in the Code Segment. Key in the Dump commands respectively:

To view the Data Segment: D DS:00 (press return)
To view the Code Segment: D:CS:100 (press return)

Compare the contents of both Segments to what you keyed in and to Figure 2-3. DS:00 through 08 and CS:100 through 10A should be identical to Figure 2-3.

Now press R to view the contents of the registers and flags, and to display the first instruction. The registers contain the same values as at the start of the first example. The displayed instruction is

049F:0100   A10000   MOV AX,[0000]

Since the CS register contains 049F, then CS:0100 contains your first instruction, A10000. DEBUG interprets this instruction as a MOV and has determined that the reference is to the first location [0000] in the Data Segment. The *square brackets* are to tell you that this reference is to a *memory address* and not an immediate value. An immediate value that would move zeros to the AX register would appear as

MOV AX,0000

```
┌─────────────────────────────────────────────────────┐
│   Figure 2-3 Trace of Machine Instructions.          │
└─────────────────────────────────────────────────────┘
```

```
DEBUG
-E DS:00 23 01 25 00 00 00      }   Enter data
-E DS:06 2A 2A 2A               }
-E CS:100 A1 00 00 03 06 02 00  }   Enter code
-E CS:107 A3 04 00 CB           }
-D DS:00
049F:0000   23 01 25 00 00 00 2A 2A-2A F0 FF 01 F7 02 04 02    #.%...***p..w...
049F:0010   F7 02 00 00 00 00 00 00-00 00 00 00 00 00 00 00    w...............
049F:0020   00 00 00 00 00 00 00 00-00 00 00 00 00 00 00 00    ................
049F:0030   00 00 00 00 00 00 00 00-00 00 00 00 00 00 00 00    ................
049F:0040   00 00 00 00 00 00 00 00-00 00 00 00 00 00 00 00    ................
049F:0050   00 00 00 00 00 00 00 00-00 00 00 00 00 20 20 20    .............
049F:0060   20 20 20 20 20 20 20 20-00 00 00 00 00 20 20 20         .....
049F:0070   20 20 20 20 20 20 20 20-00 00 00 00 00 00 00 00         ........
-R
AX=0000  BX=0000  CX=0000  DX=0000  SP=FFF0  BP=0000  SI=0000  DI=0000
DS=049F  ES=049F  SS=049F  CS=049F  IP=0100    NV UP DI PL NZ NA PO NC
049F:0100 A10000        MOV     AX,[0000]                 DS:0000=0123
-T

AX=0123  BX=0000  CX=0000  DX=0000  SP=FFF0  BP=0000  SI=0000  DI=0000
DS=049F  ES=049F  SS=049F  CS=049F  IP=0103    NV UP DI PL NZ NA PO NC
049F:0103 03060200      ADD     AX,[0002]                 DS:0002=0025
-T

AX=0148  BX=0000  CX=0000  DX=0000  SP=FFF0  BP=0000  SI=0000  DI=0000
DS=049F  ES=049F  SS=049F  CS=049F  IP=0107    NV UP DI PL NZ NA PE NC
049F:0107 A30400        MOV     [0004],AX                 DS:0004=0000
-T

AX=0148  BX=0000  CX=0000  DX=0000  SP=FFF0  BP=0000  SI=0000  DI=0000
DS=049F  ES=049F  SS=049F  CS=049F  IP=010A    NV UP DI PL NZ NA PE NC
049F:010A CB            RET     L
-D DS:00
049F:0000   23 01 25 00 48 01 2A 2A-2A F0 FF 01 F7 02 04 02    #.%.H.***p..w...
049F:0010   F7 02 00 00 00 00 00 00-00 00 00 00 00 00 00 00    w...............
049F:0020   00 00 00 00 00 00 00 00-00 00 00 00 00 00 00 00    ................
049F:0030   00 00 00 00 00 00 00 00-00 00 00 00 00 00 00 00    ................
049F:0040   00 00 00 00 00 00 00 00-00 00 00 00 00 00 00 00    ................
049F:0050   00 00 00 00 00 00 00 00-00 00 00 00 00 20 20 20    .............
049F:0060   20 20 20 20 20 20 20 20-00 00 00 00 00 20 20 20         .....
049F:0070   20 20 20 20 20 20 20 20-00 00 00 00 00 00 00 00         ........
-D CS:100
049F:0100   A1 00 00 03 06 02 00 A3-04 00 CB CB 2B C8 2B C0    !......#..KK+H+@
049F:0110   90 CB 00 00 00 00 00 00-00 00 00 00 00 00 00 00    .K..............
049F:0120   00 00 00 00 00 00 00 00-00 00 00 00 00 00 00 00    ................
049F:0130   00 00 00 00 00 00 00 00-00 00 00 00 00 00 00 00    ................
049F:0140   00 00 00 00 00 00 00 00-00 00 00 00 00 00 00 00    ................
049F:0150   00 00 00 00 00 00 00 00-00 00 00 00 00 00 00 00    ................
049F:0160   00 00 00 00 00 00 00 00-00 00 00 00 00 00 00 00    ................
049F:0170   00 00 00 00 00 00 00 00-00 00 00 00 00 00 00 00    ................
-Q
```

Now key in the DEBUG command T. The instruction MOV AX,[0000] moves the contents of the word at offset zero in the Data Segment to the

AX register. The contents are 2301, which the operation reverses in AX as 0123.

The next instruction is ADD, which you can cause to execute by keying in another T command. The operation adds the contents of the word at DS offset 0002 to the AX register. The result in the AX is now the sum of 0123 and 0025, or 0148.

The next instruction is MOV [0004],AX. Key in a T command for it to execute. The instruction moves the contents of the AX register to the word at DS offset 0004. To view the changed contents of the Data Segment, key in D DS:00. The first six bytes are

23 01 25 00 48 01

The value of 0148 that was moved from the AX register to offset 04 and 05 is reversed as 4801. Note that these hex values are represented on the right by their ASCII equivalents. For example, hex 23 generates a number (#) symbol and hex 25 generates a percent (%) symbol. The three hex 2A bytes generate asterisks (*). The left side of the dump shows the actual machine code as it appears in memory. The right side of the dump simply helps you locate alphabetic data more easily.

You can also view the contents of the Code Segment by keying in D CS:100. Finally, you can terminate the DEBUG session by entering Q (for Quit).

MACHINE ADDRESSING

To access an instruction, the processor determines its address from the contents of the CS register plus the offset in the IP register. For example, assume that the CS contains hex 04AF (actually 04AF0) and the IP contains hex 0023:

CS:	04AF0
IP:	0023
Instruction address:	04B13

Let's say that the instruction beginning at 04B13 is the following:

A11200   MOV AX,[0012]
|
location 04B13

Memory location 04B13 contains the first byte of the instruction to be accessed. The processor determines from the operation itself (A1) that the instruction is three bytes long.

To access the data item at offset [0012], the processor determines its location from the contents of the DS register (usually) plus the offset in the instruction operand. If the DS contains hex 04B1 (actually 04B10), then the actual location of the referenced data item is

DS: 04B10
Offset: 0012
Address of data: 04B22

Let's say that the contents of locations 04B22 and 04B23 are the following:

Contents: 2401
| |
Location: 04B22 04B23

The processor extracts the 24 at location 04B22 and inserts it into the AL register, and the 01 at location 04B23 into the AH register. The AX now contains 0124. As the processor fetches each byte of an instruction, it increments the IP register so that it contains the offset (0026) for the next instruction. The processor is now ready to execute the next instruction, which it derives once again from the contents of the CS (04AF0) plus the current offset in the IP (0026), in effect 04B16.

Note on 8086 Addressing

The 8086 processor operates more efficiently if an accessed word begins on an even-numbered address. If a data word, for example, begins on an even-numbered address as in the above example, the processor can access it directly into a register. But if the word begins on an odd-numbered address, the processor performs two accesses. For example, assume that an instruction has to access a word beginning at location 04B23 into the AX register:

Contents: |xx|24|01|xx|
|
Location: 04B23

The 8086 processor first accesses the bytes at 4B22 and 4B23 and delivers the byte from 4B23 to the AL register. It then accesses the bytes at 4B24 and 4B25 and delivers the byte from 4B24 to the AH register. The AX now contains 0124.

You don't have to perform any special programming for even or odd locations, nor do you even have to know whether an address is odd. The significant points are (1) the accessing operation reverses a word from memory into a register so that it resumes its correct sequence, and (2) if you have a routine that accesses memory repetitively, for efficiency you could define the data to begin at an even location.

For example, since the beginning of the Data Segment is always an even address, the first data field begins on an even number, and as long as successive data fields are defined as even-numbered words, they all begin on even addresses. For most purposes, however, the 8086 processor executes at such rapid speed that you'll never notice improvements in this efficiency.

The Assembler has an EVEN Pseudo-operation that aligns data and instructions on even memory locations.

MACHINE LANGUAGE EXAMPLE III: MEMORY SIZE DETERMINATION

You already know the amount of memory (RAM) that your computer contains. Let's see if your computer knows how much! BIOS (basic input/output system) in ROM has a routine that determines memory size. You can access BIOS through INT instructions, in this case an interrupt 12. BIOS determines memory size from base RAM (on the System Board) and from expansion slots, if any. BIOS then returns the value to the AX register in terms of 1K bytes, as the following examples show:

Memory Size	Hex Value in AX
64K	0040
96K	0060
128K	0080
256K	0100

If you have access to the IBM Technical Reference manual, you'll find the following BIOS routine for Interrupt 12H on page A-67 (of the first edition):

```
STI                          ;Interrupts back on
PUSH   DS                    ;Save Segment
MOV    AX,DATA               ;Establish addressing
MOV    DS,AX
MOV    AX,MEMORY__SIZE       ;Get value
POP    DS                    ;Recover Segment
IRET                         ;Return to caller
```

Although these instructions may not mean much at this point, don't let that stop you from executing them. Load DEBUG into memory and enter the following machine code for INT 12H and RET:

E CS:100 CD 12 CB

Now press R (and return) to display the registers and the first instruction. The AX contains 0000 and the IP contains 0100; the instruction is INT 12. Now press T (and return) repeatedly and see the following BIOS instructions execute (DEBUG shows the symbolic instructions, although it is the machine code that actually executes):

```
STI
PUSH    DS
MOV     AX,0040
MOV     DS,AX
MOV     AX,[0013]
POP     DS
IRET
```

At this point, the AX contains the size of memory. Is this value correct? Remember that it is in hexadecimal format. Now enter another T command to exit from BIOS and to return to your program. The displayed instruction is RET for the machine code CB that you entered.

If you want to reexecute these instructions, reset the IP register and trace through again. Enter R IP, enter 100, then R, and the required number of T commands, all followed by return.

KEY POINTS TO REMEMBER

DOS DEBUG and CP/M DDT-86 are powerful useful programs that you can make good use of in debugging Assembler programs. Be very careful, however, in their use, especially the Enter (E) command. Entering data at the wrong location or entering incorrect data may cause unpredictable results. You may find your screen fill up with strange characters, have your keyboard lock, or even cause DOS to interrupt DEBUG and reload itself from diskette! You are not likely to cause any damage, but you may get a bit of a surprise and will lose any data that you entered during the DEBUG session.

If you enter incorrect values in the Data Segment or Code Segment, you can correct them by reentering the E command. However, you may not have noticed the error until after beginning the Trace. You can still use E to make the changes, but you may want to begin execution back at the first instruction. No problem —just set the Instruction Pointer (IP) register to

0100. Key in the Register (R) command followed by the designated register:

R IP (followed by return)

DEBUG displays the contents of the IP and waits for an entry. Key in the value 0100 (followed by return). To check the result, key in an R command (without the IP). DEBUG displays the registers, flags, and the first instruction to be executed. You can now use T to trace through the instruction steps again.

If your program is accumulating values, you may have to clear to zero some memory locations and registers. But be sure *not* to change the contents of the CS, DS, SP, and SS registers, all of which have specific purposes.

Read the chapter in the DOS manual on DEBUG (or DDT-86 in the CP/M manual). The parts that are relevant at this time are all the introductory material and the following DEBUG commands: Dump (D), Enter (E), Hexadecimal (H), Quit (Q), Register (R), and Trace (T). You may want to scan the other DEBUG commands to see what they do, but some you may never use.

QUESTIONS

2-1. Determine the machine instruction for each of the following: (a) Move the value 5287 to the AX register. (b) Add the value 036A to the AX register.

2-2. Assume that you have entered the following E command:

E CS:100 B8 32 01 05 25 00

The hex value 32 was supposed to be 23. Code an E command to correct only the one byte that is incorrect—that is, directly change 32 to 23.

2-3. Assume that you have entered the following E command:

E CS:100 B8 03 50 05 00 20 CB

(a) What are the three instructions here? (The first example in this chapter gives a clue.) On executing this program, you discover that the AX register ends up with 7003 instead of 0370.
(b) What is the error and how would you correct it?
(c) Having corrected the instructions, you now want to reexecute the program from the first instruction. What two entries are required?

2-4. The following is a machine language program:

B0 25 D0 E0 B3 15 F6 E3 CB

The program performs the following:

☐   Moves the hex value 25 to the AL register.
☐   Shifts the contents of the AL one bit left (the result will be 4A).
☐   Moves the hex value 15 to the BL register.
☐   Multiplies AL by BL.

Use the DEBUG program to enter (E) this program beginning at CS:100. After entering the program, key in D CS:100 to view it. Then key in R and enough successive T commands to step through the program until reaching RET. At this point the AX register should contain the product 0612. Remember that these are hexadecimal values.

2-5.   Use the DEBUG program to enter (E) the following machine language program:

Data: 25 15 00 00
Machine code: A0 00 00 D0 E0 F6 26 01 00 A3 02 00 CB

The program performs the following:

☐   Moves the contents of the one byte at DS:00 (25) to the AL register.
☐   Shifts the AL contents one bit left (the result is 4A).
☐   Multiplies the AL by the one byte contents at DS:01 (15).
☐   Moves the product, 0612, from the AX to the word beginning at DS:02.

After entering the program, key in D commands to view the Data Segment and the Code Segment. Then key in R and enough successive T commands to step through the program until reaching RET. At this point, the AX register should contain the product 0612. Key in another D DS:00 and note that the product at DS:02 is stored as 1206.

3

ASSEMBLY LANGUAGE
REQUIREMENTS

Objective:
To cover the basic Assembler
coding requirements and the
steps in assembling, linking,
and executing.

INTRODUCTION

Chapter 2 showed how to key in and execute a machine language program. No doubt you were also very aware even for a small program of the difficulty in deciphering the machine code. It is questionable whether anyone seriously codes in machine language (other than patching machine code routines into high-level language programs and software applications). A higher level of coding is at the assembly level in which a programmer uses *symbolic instructions* in place of machine instructions and descriptive names for data fields and memory locations.

The symbolic instructions that are coded in Assembler language are known as the *source program*. You can enter them using DOS EDLIN, CP/M ED, or any suitable line or screen editor program. You then use the Assembler program to translate the source program into machine code, known as the *object program*. Finally, you use the DOS LINK program to complete the machine addressing for the object program, generating an *executable module*.

This chapter explains the requirements for a simple Assembler program and takes you through the steps for assembly, link, and execution.

ASSEMBLER COMMENTS

You can improve program clarity a lot by the use of *comments* throughout a program, especially in Assembler where the purpose of a set of instructions is often unclear. A comment always begins with a semicolon(;), and wherever you code it, the Assembler assumes that all characters to its right are comments. A comment may contain any printable character, including a blank.

You can insert a comment on a line by itself or following an instruction on the same line. The following two examples illustrate:

1. ; This entire line is a comment
2. ADD   AX,BX   ;Comment on same line as instruction

A comment appears only on a listing of an assembled program, and generates no machine code.

CODING FORMAT

The general format for an Assembler instruction is the following:

[name]   operation   operand(s)

A *name* (if any), *operation*, and *operand* are separated by at least one blank or tab character. There is a maximum of 132 characters on a line, although you will probably prefer to stay within 80 characters because of the screen width. Two examples follow:

Name	Oper'n	Operand	
COUNTER	DB	1	;Name, operation, one operand
	MOV	AX,0	;Operation, two operands

Name

A *name* in Assembler language can use the following characters:

Alphabetic letters:	A–Z
Digits:	0–9
Special characters:	question mark (?)
	period (.)
	at (@)
	underline (__)
	dollar ($)

The first character of a name must be an alphabetic letter or a special character. Examples of valid names are COUNT, PAGE25, and $E10. Descriptive, meaningful names are recommended. The names of registers, such as AX, DI, and AL, are reserved for referencing registers. Consequently, in an instruction such as

ADD AX,BX

the Assembler automatically knows that AX and BX refer to registers. However, in an instruction such as

MOV REGSAVE,AX

the Assembler can recognize the name REGSAVE only if you define it in the Data Segment. Table 3-1 at the end of this chapter provides a list of all the Assembler reserved words.

Operation

An *operation* tells the Assembler what action the statement is to perform. In the Data Segment, an operation defines a field, work area, or constant. In the Code Segment, an operation indicates an action such as a move (MOV) or add (ADD).

Operand

Whereas the operation specifies what action to perform, the *operand* indicates where to perform the action. In the following definition of COUNTER in the Data Segment, the operand indicates that the contents of the defined field is 0:

Name	Oper'n	Operand	
COUNTER	DB	0	;Define Byte (DB) with 0 value

In the Code Segment an operand may contain one, two, or even no entries. Following are three examples:

Oper'n	Operand	
RET		;Return, no operand
INC	CX	;Increment CX, one operand
ADD	AX,12	;Add 12 to AX, two operands

The name, operation, and operand need not begin in any specific column. However, consistently starting on the same column for these entries makes a more readable program. Also, the EDLIN line editor under DOS provides useful tab stops every eight positions.

PSEUDO-OPERATIONS

Assembler supports a number of instructions that enable you to control the way in which a program assembles and lists. These instructions, named *Pseudo-operations* (or *Pseudo-ops*), act only during the assembly of a program and generate no machine-executable code. The most common Pseudo-ops are explained in the next sections. Chapter 18 covers all of the Pseudo-ops in detail; there is too much information to cover at this point, but you can use that chapter as a reference. CP/M users should also check the section at the end of this chapter on CP/M differences.

Listing Pseudo-operations:
PAGE and TITLE

Assembler provides a number of Pseudo-operations to control the format of an assembled listing. Note that the program in Figure 3-1 is a listing of an Assembler source program but the program is not yet assembled — that's in a later section. Two Pseudo-ops that you can use in every program are PAGE and TITLE.

PAGE. At the start of a program you can designate the number of lines that are to list on a page and the maximum number of characters on a line. The Pseudo-op for this purpose is PAGE. The following example sets 60 lines per page and 132 characters per line:

> PAGE 60,132

Lines per page may range from 10 to 255, and characters per line may range from 60 to 132. Omission of a PAGE statement causes the Assembler to assume PAGE 66,80.

Assume that the line count is set to 60. When the *assembled* program has listed 60 lines, it ejects the forms to the top of the next page and increments a page count. You may also want to force a page to eject at a specific line, such as at the end of a Segment. At the required line, simply code PAGE with no operand. The assembled listing will eject automatically on encountering PAGE.

TITLE.   You can cause a title for a program to print at the top of each page using the TITLE Pseudo-op as follows:

TITLE text

As *text*, a recommended technique is to use the name of the program as catalogued on disk. For example, if the program is named ASMSORT, code that name plus a descriptive comment, all up to 60 characters in length, as follows:

TITLE ASMSORT—Assembler program to sort customer names

Assembler also supports a subtitle Pseudo-op named SUBTTL that you may find useful for very large programs that contain subprograms.

SEGMENT Pseudo-operation

A program consists of one or more *Segments*. Typically there is a Stack Segment for Stack Storage, a Data Segment for data definitions, and a Code Segment for executable code. The Assembler Pseudo-op for defining a Segment, SEGMENT, has the following format:

Name	Operation	Operand
name	SEGMENT	[options]
	•	
	•	
	•	
name	ENDS	

The Segment name must be present, must be unique, and must follow Assembler naming conventions. The ENDS statement indicates the end of a Segment and contains the *same name* as the SEGMENT statement. A SEGMENT statement may contain three types of options: alignment, combine, and class.

1. *Alignment type.* This entry indicates the boundary on which the Segment is to begin. The typical requirement is PARA for which the Segment aligns on a Paragraph boundary. The starting address is evenly divisible by 16 as in hex nnn0. Omission of an operand causes the Assembler to assume (default to) PARA.

2. *Combine type.* This entry indicates whether to combine with other Segments when "linked" after assembly (explained in a later section, Linking the Program). Types are STACK, COMMON, PUBLIC, AT expression, and MEMORY. The STACK SEGMENT is defined as follows:

name   SEGMENT   PARA STACK

     PUBLIC, COMMON, and MEMORY are used when separately assembled programs are to be combined when linked. Otherwise, a program that is not to be combined with other programs may omit this option.

3. *Class type.* This entry, enclosed in apostrophes, is used to group related Segments when linking, as follows:

name   SEGMENT   PARA STACK 'STACK'

PROC Pseudo-operation

     The Code Segment contains the executable code for a program. This Segment also contains one or more *Procedures*, defined with the PROC Pseudo-op. A Segment that contains only one Procedure would appear as follows:

Segname	SEGMENT	PARA	
Procname	PROC	FAR	One
	•		Procedure
	•		within
	•		the
	RET		Code
Procname	ENDP		Segment
Segname	ENDS		

     The Procedure name must be present, must be unique, and must follow Assembler naming conventions. The operand FAR indicates to the DOS program loader that this PROC is the entry point for program execution.

     The ENDP Pseudo-op indicates the end of a Procedure and contains the same name as the PROC statement. The RET instruction terminates processing and returns control (in this case) to DOS.

A Segment may contain more than one Procedure; Chapter 5 covers this condition.

ASSUME Pseudo-operation

The 8086/8088 processors use the SS register to address the Stack, the DS register to address the Data Segment, and the CS register to address the Code Segment. You have to tell the Assembler the purpose of each Segment. The Pseudo-op for this purpose is ASSUME, coded in the Code Segment as follows:

```
Operation    Operand
ASSUME    SS:stackname,DS:datasegname,CS:codesegname
```

For example, SS:stackname means that the Assembler is to associate the name of the Stack Segment with the SS register. The operands may appear in any sequence. The ES register may also contain an entry; if your program does not use the ES register, you may omit its reference or code ES:NOTHING.

END Pseudo-operation

As already seen, the ENDS Pseudo-op terminates a Segment, and the ENDP Pseudo-op terminates a Procedure. The entire program terminates with an END Pseudo-op as follows:

```
Operation    Operand
   END      [procname]
```

The operand may be blank if the program is not to execute—for example, you may want to assemble only data definitions, or the program is to be linked together with another (main) module. For typical programs consisting of one module, the operand contains the name of the PROC that was designated FAR.

PROGRAM INITIALIZATION

Under DOS, there are four requirements for initializing an Assembler program: (1) Notify the Assembler which Segments to associate with which segment registers; (2) Store in the Stack the address that is in the DS when the program begins execution; (3) Store in the Stack a zero address; and (4) Load the DS with the address of the Data Segment.

To exit from the program and return to DOS involves use of the RET

instruction. Figure 3-1 illustrates all of the initialization and exit requirements.

Figure 3-1 Program Initialization.

```
        CODESG  SEGMENT    PARA'CODE'
        BEGIN   PROC       FAR
1.              ASSUME     CS:CODESG,DS:DATASG,SS:STACKSG
2.              PUSH   DS             ;Store DS on stack
3.              SUB    AX,AX          ;Set AX to zero
                PUSH   AX             ;Store zero on Stack
4.              MOV    AX,DATASG      ;Store address of
                MOV    DS,AX          ; DATASG in DS
                  •
                  •
                  •
5.              RET                   ;Return to DOS
        BEGIN   ENDP
        CODESG  ENDS
                END    BEGIN
```

1. ASSUME is an Assembler Pseudo-op that notifies the Assembler that
    certain Segments are to be associated with certain segment registers,
    in this case, CODESG with CS, DATASG with DS, and STACKSG
    with SS. DATASG and STACKSG are not defined in this example,
    but would be coded as follows:

    ```
    STACKSG  SEGMENT  PARA  STACK  'Stack'
    DATASG   SEGMENT  PARA  'Data'
    ```

    By associating Segments with segment registers, the Assembler
    can determine offset addresses of items within each Segment. For
    example, each instruction in the Code Segment is a specific length.
    The first instruction is at offset 0, and if it is one byte long, the second
    instruction is at offset 2, and so forth.

2. Immediately preceding your executable program in memory is a (hex)
    100-byte area known as the Program Segment Prefix (PSP). The DOS
    loader program uses the DS register to establish the starting point of
    the PSP. Your program has to save this address by "pushing" it onto
    the Stack. Later, RET uses this address to return to DOS.

3. The system requires that the next address on the Stack is an address

of zero. For this purpose, the SUB instruction clears the AX to zero by subtracting it from itself, and PUSH stores this value on the Stack.

4. The DOS loader program has initialized the correct address of the Stack in the SS and the Code Segment in the CS. Since the loader program has used the DS for another purpose, you have to initialize the DS as shown by the two MOV instructions in Figure 3-1. A later section in this chapter, "Example Source Program II," explains the initialization of the DS is detail.

5. The RET instruction exits from your program and returns to DOS by means of the address that was pushed onto the Stack at the start (PUSH DS).

Now, even if this initialization is not clear at this point, don't despair. Every program will have virtually identical initialization steps, and you can duplicate this portion each time you code a program.

EXAMPLE SOURCE PROGRAM I

Let's combine the preceding information into a simple Assembler source program, as shown in Figure 3-2. The program consists of two Segments: a Stack Segment named STACKSG and a Code Segment named CODESG.

Figure 3-2 Assembler Source Program.

```
                page     60,132
    TITLE       EXASM1   Program depicts register operations
;-------------------------------------------------------------
    STACKSG  SEGMENT PARA STACK 'STACK'
             DB      12 DUP('STACKSEG')
    STACKSG  ENDS
;-------------------------------------------------------------
    CODESG   SEGMENT PARA 'CODE'
    BEGIN    PROC    FAR
             ASSUME  SS:STACKSG,CS:CODESG,DS:NOTHING
             PUSH    DS              ;Push DS onto stack
             SUB     AX,AX           ;Push zero address
             PUSH    AX              ;   onto stack

             MOV     AX,0123H        ;Move hex 0123 to AX
             ADD     AX,0025H        ;Add hex 25 to AX
             MOV     BX,AX           ;Move AX to BX
             ADD     BX,AX           ;Add AX to BX
             MOV     CX,BX           ;Move BX to CX
             SUB     CX,AX           ;Subtract AX from CX
             SUB     AX,AX           ;Clear AX to zero
             NOP
             RET                     ;Return to DOS
    BEGIN    ENDP                    ;End of PROC

    CODESG   ENDS                    ;End of SEGMENT
             END     BEGIN           ;End of Program
```

STACKSG contains one entry, DB (Define Byte), that defines 12 copies of the word "STACKSEG." Subsequent programs will not define the Stack this way, but when you use DEBUG to view the assembled program, the definition will help you locate the Stack.

CODESG contains the executable instructions for the program, although the first statement, ASSUME, generates no executable code. The ASSUME Pseudo-op assigns STACKSG to the SS register and CODESG to the CS register. In effect, the statement tells the Assembler that the address in the SS register is to be used for addressing STACKSG and the address in the CS register for addressing CODESG. The system loader, when loading a program from diskette into memory for execution, sets the actual addresses in the SS and CS registers. Since this program contains no defined data, it has no Data Segment, and consequently ASSUME need not assign the DS register.

The instructions following ASSUME—PUSH, SUB, and PUSH—are *standard operations to initialize the Stack* with first the current address in the DS register and second a zero address. Since the normal practice is to execute a program from DOS, these instructions facilitate the return to DOS after execution of this program. (You can also execute a program from DEBUG, although only in special cases.)

The succeeding instructions then perform the same operations as Figure 2-1 in the previous chapter when you stepped through using DEBUG.

KEYING IN THE PROGRAM

Figure 3-2 illustrates only the source code for a program that was keyed in under a line editor. At this point, you should also use the DOS EDLIN, the CP/M ED, or an equivalent editor to key in this program. If you have never used EDLIN, now is a good time to perform the exercises in the DOS manual. The name of the program is EXASM1. To activate EDLIN, insert your DOS diskette in disk drive A and a formatted dikette in drive B – you can use CHKDSK B: to make sure that it has space for this program. Key in the command

EDLIN B:EXASM1.ASM (followed by return)

DOS loads EDLIN into memory, and when ready, EDLIN displays a prompt:

New file
*_

Enter an I command to insert lines, and key in each Assembler instruction just the way you see it. Although the spacing is not important to the

Assembler, a program is more readable if you keep the name, operation, operand, and comments aligned. EDLIN has tab stops at every eight positions to facilitate aligning.

Once you have entered the program, scan the coding to ensure its accuracy. Then key in E (and return) to terminate EDLIN. You can check that the program is cataloged on disk by keying in:

DIR B: (for all files)
or DIR B:EXASM1.ASM (for one file)

For a printout of the program, turn on your printer and adjust the paper. Then press Ctrl/PrtSc and key in

TYPE B:EXASM1.ASM (return)

DOS loads the program into memory, displays the statements on the screen, and copies the screen onto the printer. (If the system displays error messages concerning the printer, check that the printer switch is on, cover panels are in place, paper is loaded, and the connecting plugs are secure.) After printing is complete, press Ctrl/PrtSc again to deactivate the printer.

As it stands, the program will not execute—you must first assemble and then link it. The next section depicts a listing of the same program after assembly and explains the steps for assembly and listing.

A minor digression: If you expect to key in a large amount of program code, a good investment is a full-screen editor, especially one that can handle a line of at least 132 columns and large-size files.

PREPARING A PROGRAM FOR EXECUTION

After keying in your source program onto disk under program.ASM, you still have two major steps before you can execute it. You must first "assemble" it and then "link edit" it. Users of BASIC will be used to executing directly on keying in a source program; however, assembly and compiler languages require a translation step and a link step.

The assembly step involves translation of source code to machine object code and generates an OBJ (object) file (or "module"). You have already seen examples of machine code in Chapter 2 and examples of source code in this chapter.

The OBJ module is almost – but not quite –in executable form. The link edit step involves converting the OBJ module to an EXE (executable) module containing machine code. The Link program is on your DOS disk and performs the following:

1. Completes any addresses that the Assembler has left empty in the OBJ module. You will see such addresses, which the Assembler lists in object code as ---- R, in may subsequent programs.

2. Combines, if requested, more than one separately assembled module into one executable program, such as two or more Assembler programs or an Assembler program with a program written in a high-level language such as Pascal or BASIC.

3. Initializes the EXE module with instructions for loading it for execution.

Once you have linked an OBJ module (one or more) into an EXE module, you may execute the EXE module any number of times. But whenever you need to make a change in the EXE module, you must correct the source program, assemble it into another OBJ module, and link the OBJ module into an EXE module. Even if initially these steps are not entirely clear, you will find that with only a little experience, the steps become automatic and eventually (believe it or not) clear.

ASSEMBLING THE PROGRAM

In order to execute an Assembler source program, you must first assemble and then link it. To assemble, insert the Assembler diskette in drive A and your program diskette containing EXASM1.ASM in drive B. (If you have only one disk drive, check the procedure in the Assembler manual.) A full command to cause assembly is the following:

ASM B:EXASM1.ASM,B:EXASM1.OBJ,B:EXASM1.LST,B:EXASM1.CRF

However, that method is too prone to keying errors. A short-cut command that allows for assembly defaults is the following:

ASM B:EXASM1,B:,B:,B:;

If you have more than 64K you can use MASM instead of ASM. The command causes the Assembler program to load from disk into memory. It then examines the operands of your ASM command:

☐   B:EXASM1 is the program on drive B that is to be assembled. Since the Assembler assumes that the file extension is ASM, you need not key it.

☐   The second B: tells the Assembler to write the machine language *object module* onto drive B under the defaulted name EXASM1.OBJ.

☐   The third B: tells the Assembler to write the assembled *listing* onto drive B under the defaulted name EXASM1.LST.

☐   The fourth B: causes the Assembler to generate a *cross-reference file* of all the names and labels in the program under the name EXASM1.CRF. Also, the entry causes the Assembler to generate line numbers on the LST file to which the CRF file refers. A cross-reference is more useful for larger programs as an aid in locating names that are to be changed.

☐   The semicolon at the end of the command tells the Assembler to ignore any further options. Actually, there are no more options, but it is a good habit to code the semicolon for other versions of the ASM or MASM command.

The above command is a convenient shortcut, but double-check the operands before pressing return! An improper command causes the Assembler to request return to DOS, and you will have to reinsert the DOS diskette to recover and then reload the Assembler.

If you do not want a listing of the assembled program or a cross-reference file, and also want to save disk space, key in

ASM B:EXASM1,B:;

The command causes the Assembler to assemble the source program and to create an OBJ file only. Neither the LST nor CRF files are produced.

The Assembler converts your source statements into machine code and displays on the screen any errors. Typical errors include a name that violates the naming convention, an operation that is spelled incorrectly (such as MOVE instead of MOV), and an operand containing a name that is not defined. For errors, the ASM version lists only an error code that is explained in the IBM Assembler manual, whereas the MASM version lists the code and the explanation. There are in total about 100 error messages.

The Assembler attempts to correct some errors, but in any event you should reload the editor, correct the source program (EXASM1.ASM), and reassemble.

Figure 3-3 provides the listing of the assembled program that the Assembler wrote on disk under the name EXASM1.LST.

Note at the top of the listing how the Assembler has acted on the PAGE and TITLE Pseudo-ops. None of the Pseudo-ops including SEGMENT, PROC, ASSUME, and END generates machine code.

The listing shows not only the original source code but also to the left the translated machine code in hexadecimal format. At the extreme left are the hex addresses of the data fields and the instructions.

The *Stack Segment* "begins" at location 0000. Actually, it loads into memory according to an address that will be in the SS register and is *offset* zero bytes from that address. The SEGMENT Pseudo-op causes alignment of an address divisible by 16 and notifies the Assembler that this is a

```
                        ┌─────────────────────────────────────────┐
                        │  Figure 3-3 Assembled Program.          │
                        └─────────────────────────────────────────┘


 offset
 address:                      page    60,132
                       TITLE   EXASM1  Program depicts register operations
 ↓        machine code:
                       ;-----------------------------------------------------------
 0000              STACKSG SEGMENT PARA STACK 'STACK'
 0000   0C [               DB      12 DUP('STACKSEG')
          53 54 41 43
          4B 53 45 47
                   ]
 0060              STACKSG ENDS
                       ;-----------------------------------------------------------
 0000              CODESG  SEGMENT PARA 'CODE'
 0000              BEGIN   PROC    FAR
                          ASSUME  SS:STACKSG,CS:CODESG,DS:NOTHING
 0000   1E                PUSH    DS              ;Push DS onto stack
 0001   2B C0             SUB     AX,AX           ;Push zero address
 0003   50                PUSH    AX              ;   onto stack

 0004   B8 0123           MOV     AX,0123H        ;Move hex 0123 to AX
 0007   05 0025           ADD     AX,0025H        ;Add hex 25 to AX
 000A   8B D8             MOV     BX,AX           ;Move AX to BX
 000C   03 D8             ADD     BX,AX           ;Add AX to BX
 000E   8B CB             MOV     CX,BX           ;Move BX to CX
 0010   2B C8             SUB     CX,AX           ;Subtract AX from CX
 0012   2B C0             SUB     AX,AX           ;Clear AX to zero
 0014   90                NOP
 0015   CB                RET                     ;Return to DOS
 0016              BEGIN   ENDP                    ;End of PROC

 0016              CODESG  ENDS                    ;End of SEGMENT
                          END     BEGIN           ;End of Program
```

Segments and groups:

	N a m e	Size	align	combine	class
CODESG		0016	PARA	NONE	'CODE'
STACKSG.		0060	PARA	STACK	'STACK'

Symbols:

	N a m e	Type	Value	Attr	
BEGIN.		F PROC	0000	CODESG	Length =0016

Warning Severe
Errors   Errors
0   0

Stack—the statement itself generates no machine code. The DB instruction, also aligned at location 0000, contains 12 copies of the word 'STACKSEG'; the machine code is indicated by hex 0C (decimal value 12) and the hex representation of the ASCII characters. (You can use DEBUG later to view the results in memory.) The Stack Segment ends at address hex 0060, which is the equivalent of decimal value 96 (12 × 8).

The *Code Segment* also "begins" at location 0000. It loads into memory according to an address that will be in the CS register and is *offset* zero bytes from that address. Since ASSUME is a Pseudo-op (a message to the Assembler), the first instruction to generate actual machine code is PUSH DS, a one-byte instruction (1E) at offset location zero. The next instruction SUB AX,AX generates a two-byte machine code (2B C0) beginning at offset location 0001. The blank space between the two bytes is for readability only. In this example, machine instructions range from one to three bytes in length.

The last statement, END, contains the operand BEGIN, which relates to the name of the PROC at offset 0000. This is the location in the Code Segment where the program loader is to begin execution.

You can print the assembled program EXASM1.LST, which has a print width of 132 positions because of the page entry. For a dot matrix printer, you can compress the print line – turn on the printer and key in the DOS command

MODE LPT1·132,6

Symbol Table

Following the program listing is a *Symbol Table*. The first part is a table of any Segments and Groups defined in the program along with their size in bytes, their alignment, and their combine class. The second part is a table of symbols—the names of data fields in the Data Segment (there are none in this example) and the names applied to instructions in the Code Segment (only one in this example).

Two-Pass Assembler

The Assembler makes two passes through the symbolic program. One of the main reasons is because of forward references – a label may be referrenced but the Assembler has not yet encountered its definition.

During pass 1, the Assembler reads the entire symbolic program and constructs a symbol table of names and labels used in the program, that is, names of data fields and program labels and their relative location in the program. Pass 1 determines the amount of code to be generated but does not generate object code. The Assembler will print a listing of the pass-1 assembly if you supply a /D parameter in the ASM command (see the Assembler manual), although there is seldom any reason to do so.

During pass 2, the Assembler uses the symbol table that it constructed in pass 1. Now that it knows the length and relative positions of each data field and instruction, it can generate the actual object code for each instruction. It then produces, if requested, the various files for OBJ, LST, and CRF.

LINKING THE PROGRAM

Once the program is free of any error messages, the next step is to link the object module. EXASM1.OBJ contains only machine code, all in hex format. Because a program can load almost anywhere in memory for execution, the Assembler may not have completed all the machine addresses. Also, there may be other (sub)programs to combine with this one. The function of the LINK program is to complete address references and to combine (if required) any other programs.

In order to link an assembled program, insert the DOS diskette in drive A and the program diskette in drive B. Key in the command LINK followed by "return." The Linker is a large program and takes a while to load into memory. It issues a series of prompts to which you are to reply:

Link prompt:	Reply:	Action:
Object Modules [.OBJ]:	B:EXASM1	Links EXASM1.OBJ
Run File [A:EXASM1.EXE]:	B:	Creates EXASM1.EXE
List File [NUL.MAP]:	CON	Creates EXASM1.MAP
LIBRARIES [.LIB]:	[return]	Defaults

The first prompt asks for the name of the object module that is to be linked and defaults to EXASM1.OBJ if the extension OBJ is omitted.

The second prompt requests the name of the file that is to execute (run) and allows a default to the filename A:EXASM1.EXE. The reply requests that LINK produce the file on drive B. The practice of supplying the same filename will simplify keeping track of all your programs.

The third prompt tells you that LINK defaults the "LIST FILE" under the name NUL.MAP (that is, no Map). The MAP file contains a map of the name and sizes of Segments and any errors that LINK has found. A typical error is failure to define a Stack Segment. The reply CON tells LINK to display this file on the screen instead of writing it on disk. Replying CON saves disk space and allows you to view the MAP immediately for errors. For this example, the MAP file contains the following:

Start	Stop	Length	Name
00000H	00015H	0016H	CODESG
00020H	0007FH	0060H	STACKSG

The reply to the fourth prompt is to press return which tells LINK to default the remaining option. A description of this option is in the DOS manual.

At this stage the only LINK error that you are likely to encounter is entering the wrong filenames. The solution is to restart with the LINK command.

EXECUTING THE PROGRAM

Having assembled and linked the program, you can now (at last!) execute it. Figure 3-4 provides a chart of the commands and steps involved in assembling, linking, and executing the program named EXASM1.

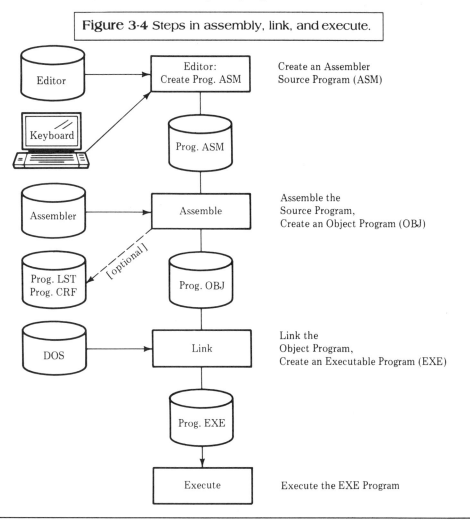

Figure 3-4 Steps in assembly, link, and execute.

Editor

Keyboard

Editor:
Create Prog. ASM

Create an Assembler
Source Program (ASM)

Prog. ASM

Assembler

Assemble

Assemble the
Source Program,
Create an Object Program (OBJ)

Prog. LST
Prog. CRF

[optional]

Prog. OBJ

DOS

Link

Link the
Object Program,
Create an Executable Program (EXE)

Prog. EXE

Execute

Execute the EXE Program

If the EXE file is in drive B, you could cause execution by entering:

B:EXASM1 or B:EXASM1.EXE

DOS assumes that the file extension is EXE and loads the file for execution. However, since this program produces no visible output, run it under DEBUG and step through with trace commands. Key in the following, including the extension EXE:

DEBUG B:EXASM1.EXE

DOS then loads DEBUG, which in turn loads the EXE program module. Once ready, DEBUG displays a hyphen (-) as a prompt. To view the Stack Segment, key in

D SS:0

This area is recognizable because of the 12 duplicated constants, STACKSEG. To view the Code Segment, key in

D CS:0

Compare the machine code to the assembled listing:

1E2BC050B823010525008BD803 ...

The immediate operands shown on the listing as 0123 and 0025 are actually in memory as, respectively, 2301 and 2500. In this case, the assembled listing does not accurately show the machine code. All two-byte (word) addresses and immediate operands are stored in machine code with the bytes reversed.

Key in R to view the registers, and step through program execution with successive T (Trace) commands. Note the effect of the two PUSH instructions on the Stack—the end (technically the top) of the Stack now contains the contents of the DS register and the zero address.

As you step through the program, take note of the contents of the registers. When you reach the RET instruction, you can terminate DEBUG with Q (QUIT).

You now have a number of files on your program diskette which you can check with the following DOS command:

DIR B:EXASM.*

The filenames that DOS lists on the screen are the following:

EXASM1.BAK   (if you used EDLIN to change EXASM1.ASM)
EXASM1.ASM
EXASM1.OBJ
EXASM1.LST
EXASM1.EXE
EXASM1.CRF

If you created EXASM1.ASM and subsequently changed it, EDLIN produces a backup copy of the original version, EXASM1.BAK, in case you change your mind. The sequence of these files may vary depending on what your diskette already contains.

No doubt you realize that if you write a number of programs you will run short of disk space. It's a good idea to use the DOS command CHKDSK regularly to check the amount of available space on diskette. You can erase OBJ, CRF, and LST (if you have a printout or don't want one) using the DOS ERASE command as follows:

ERASE B:EXASM1.OBJ, ...

You need the ASM file in case of further changes and the EXE file to execute the program. You can erase the BAK file if you are sure you no longer need it.

The next section introduces defined data and the Data Segment. A later section, "Cross-Reference File," describes the Cross-Reference Table.

EXAMPLE SOURCE PROGRAM II

The program in Figure 3-2 is unique in that it contains no defined data. Most, if not virtually all, programs contain defined constants, work areas for arithmetic computations, and areas for accepting input and writing output.

In Chapter 2, Figure 2-3, you studied a machine language program with two defined fields. In this chapter, Figure 3-5 portrays the same program, this time written in Assembler source language and for brevity, already assembled. The program introduces several new features.

The Stack Segment contains a DW (Define Word) Pseudo-op that defines 32 words, each generating an *undefined value* designated by (?). This definition of 32 words is a more realistic size for the Stack because a large program may require many "interrupts" for input/output and "calls" to subprograms, all involving use of the Stack. Further, the only reason that Figure 3-2 defined a duplicated constant, 'STACKSEG,' was to help you locate the Stack during the DEBUG session.

Suggestion: Define at least a size of 32 words for the Stack. If the size is too small, neither the Assembler nor the Linker will warn you, and the

```
┌─────────────────────────────────────────────┐
│  Figure 3-5 Assembled Program with Data Segment.  │
└─────────────────────────────────────────────┘
```

```
 1                                   page 60,132
 2                          TITLE     EXASM2  Move and Add operations

 3  ──────────────────────────────;──────────────────────────────────────────
 4   0000                     STACKSG  SEGMENT PARA STACK 'Stack'
 5   0000     20 [           DW       32 DUP(?)
 6                ????
 7            ]
 8
 9   0040                     STACKSG  ENDS
10  ──────────────────────────────;──────────────────────────────────────────
11   0000                     DATASG   SEGMENT PARA 'Data'
12   0000   00FA             FLDA     DW       250
13   0002   007D             FLDB     DW       125
14   0004   ????             FLDC     DW       ?
15   0006                     DATASG   ENDS
16  ──────────────────────────────;──────────────────────────────────────────
17   0000                     CODESG   SEGMENT PARA 'Code'
18   0000                     BEGIN    PROC    FAR
19                            ASSUME  CS:CODESG,DS:DATASG,SS:STACKSG,ES:NOTHING
20   0000   1E               PUSH    DS              ;Push DS onto Stack
21   0001   2B C0            SUB     AX,AX           ;Push zero address
22   0003   50               PUSH    AX              ;   onto Stack
23   0004   B8  ---- R       MOV     AX,DATASG       ;Set up address of DATASG
24   0007   8E D8            MOV     DS,AX           ;  in DS register
25
26   0009   A1 0000 R        MOV     AX,FLDA         ;Move 0250 to AX
27   000C   03 06 0002 R     ADD     AX,FLDB         ;Add  0125 to AX
28   0010   A3 0004 R        MOV     FLDC,AX         ;Store sum in FLDC
29   0013   CB               RET                     ;Return to DOS
30
31   0014                    BEGIN    ENDP
32   0014                    CODESG   ENDS
33                           END      BEGIN
```

```
The IBM Personal Computer MACRO Assembler


Segments and groups:

                N a m e                 Size     align    combine class

  CODESG . . . . . . . . . . . . . .  ,   0014     PARA     NONE     'CODE'
  DATASG . . . . . . . . . . . . .        0006     PARA     NONE     'DATA'
  STACKSG. . . . . . . . . . . . .        0040     PARA     STACK    'STACK'

Symbols:
                N a m e                 Type     Value    Attr

  BEGIN. . . . . . . . . . . . . . .    F PROC   0000     CODESG   Length =0014
  FLDA . . . . . . . . . . . . . . .    L WORD   0000     DATASG
  FLDB . . . . . . . . . . . . . . .    L WORD   0002     DATASG
  FLDC . . . . . . . . . . . . . . .    L WORD   0004     DATASG
```

program may "crash" in a most unpredictable way.

Figure 3-5 defines a Data Segment named DATASG in the example and beginning at offset location 0000. The Segment contains three defined values all in DW (Define Word) format. FLDA defines a word (two bytes) with the decimal value 250 which the Assembler has translated to hex 00FA (shown on the left).

FLDB defines a word with the decimal value 125, which the Assembler has translated to hex 007D. The *actual* storage values of these two constants are, respectively, FA00 and 7D00 which you can check with DEBUG.

FLDC defines a word with an unknown constant signified by (?).

The Code Segment, named CODESG in the example, contains new features concerned with the Data Segment. First, the ASSUME Pseudo-op now relates DATASG to the DS register. This program does not require the ES register, but some programmers define its use as a matter of standardization.

Second, following the PUSH, SUB, and PUSH instructions that initialize the Stack are two instructions that establish addressability for the Data Segment:

```
0004   B8 ---- R      MOV   AX,DATASG
0007   8E D8          MOV   DS,AX
```

The first MOV instruction "stores" DATASG in the AX register. Now, an instruction cannot actually store a Segment in a register – it is trying to load the address of DATASG. Note the machine code to the left:

B8 ---- R

The four hyphens mean that the Assembler cannot determine the address of DATASG; this is determined only when the object program is linked and loaded for execution. The program loader may locate a program anywhere in memory. Consequently, the Assembler has left the address open and indicated the fact with an R; the Linker is to replace (or *relocate*) the incomplete address with the actual one.

The second MOV instruction then moves the contents of the AX register to the DS register. The program now has an ASSUME that relates the DS with the Data Segment and instructions that initialize DS with the offset address of DATASG.

You may have two questions about this business. First, why not initialize the DS with one instruction as

MOV DS,DATASG ?

There is no valid instruction for a direct move from memory to the DS. Consequently, you have to code two instructions to initialize the DS.

Second, why does the program initialize the DS but not the SS or CS registers? The loader program automatically initializes the SS and CS when it loads a program for execution, but it is your responsibility to initialize the DS, and the ES if required.

While all this business may seem unduly involved, at this point you really don't have to understand it. *All subsequent programs in this text use the same standard initialization of the Stack and the Data Segment.* You simply have to reproduce this code for each of your programs. Indeed, you may want to catalog a skeleton program on diskette, and for each program, COPY it into a new name and use EDLIN or other editor to fill in the added code.

As an exercise, use your editor to create the program in Figure 3-4, assemble it, and link it. Then use DEBUG to view the Code Segment, the Data Segment, the registers, and the trace.

CROSS-REFERENCE FILE

The Assembler produces an optional Cross-Reference File that lists the program's labels, symbols, and variables. The entries are in alphabetic sequence followed by the line number in the source program where it is defined and referenced. You can request this file by a reply to the fourth prompt, assuming that the files are to be on disk B:

[M]ASM B:progname,B:,B:,B:;

After a successful assembly, enter the command

        CREF B:progname.CRF,CON
or   CREF B:progname.CRF,B:

The first example displays the cross-reference on the "console" (screen) that you can echo to your printer using Ctrl-PrtSc. The second example writes a file (another one!) onto disk under the name B:progname.REF. You can use the TYPE command to display it and Ctrl-PrtSc to print it.

Figure 3-6 contains the cross-reference for the program in Figure 3-5. Names of Segments and data items are in alphabetic sequence. The first number to the right shown as n# displays the line number where the symbol is defined in the LST program. Numbers to its right are the lines where the symbol is referenced. For example, CODESEG is defined in line 17, and is referenced in lines 19 and 32.

CP/M DIFFERENCES

CP/M-86 and DOS (PC or MS) differ in three areas: operating system commands, Assembler Pseudo-ops, and input/output requirements. This section

```
            ┌─────────────────────────────────────┐
            │  Figure 3-6 Cross-Reference Table.   │
            └─────────────────────────────────────┘

         EXASM2     Move and Add operations

     Symbol Cross Reference            (# is definition)      Cref-1

     BEGIN. . . . . . . . . . . . .      18#     31       33

     CODE . . . . . . . . . . . . .      17
     CODESG . . . . . . . . . . . .      17#     19       32

     DATA . . . . . . . . . . . . .      11
     DATASG . . . . . . . . . . . .      11#     15       19       23

     FLDA . . . . . . . . . . . . .      12#     26
     FLDB . . . . . . . . . . . . .      13#     27
     FLDC . . . . . . . . . . . . .      14#     28

     STACK. . . . . . . . . . . . .       4
     STACKSG. . . . . . . . . . . .       4#      9       19
```

examines the first two of these areas.

CP/M Operating System Commands and Formats

The Assembler source program has the name filename.A86. The command to assemble a source program under CP/M-86 is

ASM86 B:filename [options]

The optional output files that the Assembler produces are the following:

List file:	filename.LST
Object file:	filename.H86
Symbol file:	filename.SYM

Invoke the Linker program by means of

GENCMD B:filename [options]

The output from the Linker is an executable module, or "command" file:

Executable module: filename.CMD

CP/M Directives

The CP/M and DOS versions differ most in their use of Pseudo-ops. However, since they are trying to achieve the same goals, there are many similarities. Where PC-DOS uses the term Pseudo-operation, CP/M-86 and

MS-DOS use the term Directive. The following CP/M Directives are relevant to this chapter:

EJECT   Causes the Assembler listing to skip to a new page.
LIST/NOLIST   Controls listing or not listing parts of a program.
PAGESIZE n   Specifies the number of lines per page.
PAGEWIDTH n   Determines the number of characters per line.
TITLE 'title'   Allows a maximum of 30 characters for the program title.

A significant feature is that CP/M does not have an ASSUME or equivalent Directive. Under CP/M, the Directives CSEG, DSEG, ESEG, and SSEG indicate the type of Segment. As a result, the Assembler can relate the CSEG to the CS, DSEG to the DS, and SSEG to the SS register. Further, the CP/M Loader program acts differently from the DOS Loader, and the requirements for initializing Segment registers differ. For an example, see the program in Appendix E of the CP/M-86 Operating System manual. Note that the program example initializes the SS and SP registers instead of the DS, and defines the Stack as 32 bytes (16 words) as follows:

```
              RS   31   ;16-level Stack
     STACK    RB   1    ;Top of Stack
```

Other than two minor exceptions, the executable Assembler instructions are identical in both systems.

KEY POINTS TO REMEMBER

☐   Be sure to code a semicolon before comments.

☐   Terminate each Segemnt with ENDS, each Procedure with ENDP, and the program with END.

☐   In the ASSUME Pseudo-op, associate Segment registers with the appropriate Segment names.

☐   Provide at least 32 words for Stack addressing.

☐   Follow the convention for initializing the Stack with PUSH, SUB, and PUSH.

☐   Initialize the DS register with the address of the Data Segment.

☐   Double-check each command and prompt reply for [M]ASM, LINK, and DEBUG before pressing return. Be especially careful of designating drive A or B.

☐   Erase unnecessary files from your program diskettes. Use DOS CHKDSK or CP/M STAT regularly to check for available space. Also back up your program diskette regularly: keep the original diskette as your backup and the newly copied one for subsequent programming.

Table 3-1 Assembler Reserved Words.

Register Names

AH	BL	CL	DH	DS	SI
AL	BP	CS	DI	DX	SP
AX	BX	CX	DL	ES	SS
BH	CH				

Symbolic Instructions

AAA	DIV	JLE	JS	NOT	SAR
AAD	ESC	JMP	JZ	OR	SBB
AAM	HLT	JNA	LAHF	OUT	SCAS
AAS	IDIV	JNAE	LDS	POP	SHL
ADC	IMUL	JNB	LEA	POPF	SHR
ADD	IN	JNBE	LES	PUSH	STC
AND	INC	JNE	LOCK	PUSHF	STD
CALL	INT	JNG	LODS	RCL	STI
CBW	INTO	JNGE	LOOP	RCR	STOS
CLC	IRET	JNL	LOOPE	REP	SUB
CLD	JA	JNLE	LOOPNE	REPE	TEST
CLI	JAE	JNO	LOOPNZ	REPNE	WAIT
CMC	JB	JNP	LOOPZ	REPNZ	XCHG
CMP	JBE	JNS	MOV	REPZ	XLAT
CMPS	JCXZ	JNZ	MOVS	RET	XOR
CWD	JE	JO	MUL	ROL	
DAA	JG	JP	NEG	ROR	
DAS	JGE	JPE	NIL	SAHF	
DEC	JL	JPO	NOP	SAL	

Assembler Pseudo-operations

ASSUME	END	EXTRN	IFNB	LOCAL	RECORD
COMMENT	ENDIF	GROUP	IFNDEF	MACRO	REPTRD
DB	ENDM	IF	IF1	NAME	SEGMENT
DD	ENDMP	IFB	IF2	ORG	STRUC
DQ	ENDS	IFDEF	INCLUDE	PAGE	SUBTTL
DT	EQU	IFDIF	IRP	PROC	TITLE
DW	EVEN	IFE	IRPC	PUBLIC	
ELSE	EXITM	IFIDN	LABEL	PURGE	

Miscellaneous Names

BYTE	FAR	LENGTH	MOD	PRT	THIS
COMMENT	GE	LINE	NE	SEG	TYPE
CON	GT	LT	NEAR	SHORT	WIDTH
DUP	HIGH	LOW	NOTHING	SIZE	WORD
EQ	LE	MASK	OFFSET	STACK	

Note that many of these names if used to define a data field cause an Assembler error, in some cases serious. Others, although causing no error as data definition, may confuse the Assembler if used in an operand.

QUESTIONS

3-1. What operations cause the Assembler to print a heading at the top of a page of the listing and to eject to a new page?

3-2. Determine which of the following names are valid: (a) IBM_PC, (b) $25, (c) @$_X, (d) 65A9, (e) ES.

3-3. What is the purpose of each of the three Segments described in this chapter?

3-4. What are the ways to terminate coding of (a) a program, (b) a Procedure, (c) a Segment?

3-5. Distinguish between a Pseudo-operation and an instruction.

3-6. Distinguish between the purpose of RET and END.

3-7. Given the names CDSEG, DATSEG, and STKSEG for the Code Segment, Data Segment, and Stack, respectively, code the ASSUME.

3-8. Code the three instructions in the Code Segment to initialize the Stack.

3-9. Code the command to assemble a program named ASMSAMP.ASM with files LST, OBJ, and CRF. Assume that the program diskette is (a) on drive B and you have 92K, (b) on drive A and you have 64K.

3-10. Code the commands for ASMSAMP for the following:

(a) Execution through DEBUG.

(b) Direct execution.

3-11. Give the purpose of each of the following files: (a) file.ASM, (b) file.OBJ, (c) file.LST, (d) file.CRF, (e) file.MAP, (f) file.BAK, (g) file.EXE.

3-12. Code the two instructions to initialize the DS register. Assume that the name of the Data Segment is DATSEG.

3-13. Write an Assembler program for the following (see Question 2-5 for a guide):

☐   Move hex 25 (immediate value) to the AL register.

☐   Shift the AL contents one bit left (SHL).

☐   Move hex 15 (immediate value) to the BL register.

☐   Multiply AL by BL (code MUL BL).

Remember the RET. The program does not need to define or initialize a Data Segment. Remember to COPY a skeleton program and use your editor to develop the program. Assemble and link. Use DEBUG to check the Code Segment, registers, and trace.

3-14. Revise the program in Question 3-13 according to the specifications of Question 2-5:

☐   Define a one-byte field (BD) named FLD1 containing hex 25 and another DB named FLD2 containing hex 15.

□   Define a two-byte field (DW) named FLD3 with no constant.

□   Move the contents of FLD1 to the AL register and shift left one
     bit.

□   Multiply the AL by FLD2 (MUL FLD2).

□   Move the product on the AX to FLD3.

This program requires a Data Segment. You could use an editor to
modify the previous program. Assemble, link, and use DEBUG to test.

4

DATA DEFINITION

Objective:
To provide the methods of defining constants and work areas in an Assembler program.

INTRODUCTION

The entire Data Segment is reserved for constants, work areas, and input/output areas. The Assembler permits definition of fields in various lengths according to the data definition Pseudo-operation: for example, DB defines a byte and DW defines a word. A data field may contain an undefined value or it may contain a constant defined either as a character string or as a numeric value.

Another way of defining a constant is directly within an instruction operand, as an immediate value, such as

MOV AL,20H

In this case, the hex number 20 becomes part of the machine object code. An immediate value is restricted to one byte or one word, but where it can be used, it is more efficient than the use of a constant in the Data Segment.

Users of CP/M-86 should review the section CP/M-86 Differences on page 73 of this chapter.

DATA DEFINITION PSEUDO-OPERATION

The Assembler provides two ways to define data, first by means of its length and second by means of its contents. The general format for data definition is the following:

[name] Dn expression

☐ The *name* of a data field is optional (as indicated by the square brackets), but if the program references the field, it must do so by means of a name.

☐ The Pseudo-ops that define data fields are DB (byte), DW (word), DD (doubleword), DQ (quadword), and DT (tenbytes).

☐ The *expression* operand may contain either a constant expression such as

FLD1 DB 25

or a question mark to indicate an uninitialized field, as

FLDB DB ?

An expression may contain multiple constants separated by commas and limited only by the length of a line as follows:

FLD3 DB 11, 12, 13, 14, 15, 16, ...

The Assembler defines these constants in adjacent bytes. A reference to FLD3 is to the first constant, 11, and a reference to FLD3 + 1 is to the second constant, 12. (You could think of FLD3 as FLD3 + 0.) For example,

MOV AL,FLD3 + 3

loads the value 14 (hex 0E) into the AL register. The expression also permits *duplication* of constants of the general form

[name] Dn repeat-count DUP(expression) ...

The following three examples illustrate:

DW	10 DUP(?)	;Ten words, uninitialized
DB	5 DUP(14)	;Five bytes containing hex 0E
DB	3 DUP(4 DUP(8))	;Generates twelve 8's

The third example first generates four copies of the digit 8 (8888), then duplicates that value three times, giving twelve 8's in all.

An expression may contain a *character string* or a *numeric constant*.

Character Strings

A character string is used for descriptive data such as customer names and page titles. The string is contained within single quotes as 'PC' or within double qoutes as "PC". The Assembler stores charcter strings in object code as normal ASCII format.

Only DB format may define a character string that exceeds two characters. Further, only DB format stores character strings in normal left-to-right sequence. Consequently, DB is the only sensible format for defining character data. Figure 4-1 gives some examples.

Numeric Constants

Numeric constants are used for arithmetic values and for memory addresses. The constant is not stored within quotes. *The Assembler converts all numeric constants to hexadecimal and stores the bytes in object code in reverse sequence—right to left.* Following are the various numeric formats.

Decimal. This format permits the decimal digits 0 through 9 optionally followed by the letter D, as 125 or 125D. Although the Assembler allows decimal format as a coding convenience, it converts it to hex object code. Consequently, decimal 125 becomes hex 7D.

Hexadecimal. This format permits the hex digits 0 through F followed by the letter H. Since the Assembler expects that a reference beginning with a letter is a symbolic name, the first digit of a hex constant must be 0–9. Examples are 2EH and 0FFFH, which the Assembler stores respectively as 2E and FF0F—the bytes in the second example are stored in reverse sequence.

Binary. This format permits the binary digits 0 and 1 followed by the letter B. The normal use for binary format is to clearly distinguish the bit values for the Boolean instructions AND, OR, XOR, and TEST. Decimal 12, hex C, and binary 1100B all generate the same value: hex 0C or binary 00001100 depending on how you view the contents of the byte.

Octal.   This format permits the Octal digits 0 through 7 followed by the letter Q or O. An example is 253Q. Octal has specialized uses.

Decimal Scientific (Floating Point) and Hex Real.   These formats are supported only by MASM.

Be sure to distinguish between the effect of *character* and *numeric* constants. A character constant defined as DB '12' represents ASCII characters and generates hex 3132. A numeric constant defined as DB 12 generates hex 0C.

Figure 4-1 portrays the preceding data Pseudo-ops with various character strings and numeric constants. The Data Segment has been assembled in order to show the generated object code on the left.

DEFINE BYTE—DB

Of the various Pseudo-ops that define data fields, one of the most useful is DB (Define Byte). A DB *character* expression may contain a string of any length up to the end of a line. For examples, see FLD2DB and FLD7DB in Figure 4-1. Note that FLD2DB is defined to contain character value "Personal Computer." The object code shows the ASCII character for each byte; hex 20 represents a blank character.

A DB *numeric* expression may contain one or more one-byte constants. This maximum of one byte means two hex digits. The largest positive hex number is 7F; all "higher" numbers 80 through FF represent negative values. In terms of decimal numbers, the limits are + 127 and − 128.

In Figure 4-1, numeric constants are FLD3DB, FLD4DB, FLD5DB, and FLD8DB. FLD6DB depicts a mixture of numeric and string constants suitable for a *table*.

DEFINE WORD—DW

The DW Pseudo-op defines fields that are one word (two bytes) in length. A DW *character* expression is limited to two characters, which the Assembler reverses in object code such that 'PC' becomes 'CP'. For defining character strings, DW is of limited use.

A DW *numeric* expression may contain one or more one-word constants. This maximum of two bytes means four hex digits. The largest positive hex number is 7FFF; all "higher" numbers 8000 through FFFF represent negative values. In terms of decimal numbers, the limits are + 32,767 and − 32,768.

In Figure 4-1, FLD1DW and FLD2DW define numeric constants, and FLD3DW defines the operand as an address—in this case as the offset ad-

Figure 4-1 Definitions of Character String
and Numeric Values.

```
                                 page   60,132
                          TITLE   EXDEF  Assembler Define F

0000                      DATASG  SEGMENT PARA 'DATA'

                          ;                 Define Byte - DB:
                          ;                 ----------------
0000   ??                 FLD1DB  DB      ?                 ;Uninitialized
0001   50 65 72 73 6F 6E  FLD2DB  DB      'Personal Computer' ;Char. string
       61 6C 20 43 6F 6D
       70 75 74 65 72
0012   19                 FLD3DB  DB      25                ;Decimal constant
0013   19                 FLD4DB  DB      19H               ;Hex   constant
0014   19                 FLD5DB  DB      11001B            ;Binary constant
0015   01 4A 41 4E 02 46  FLD6DB  DB      01,'JAN',02,'FEB',03,'MAR'  ;Table
       45 42 03 4D 41 52
0021   31 32 33 34 35     FLD7DB  DB      '12345'           ;Numbers as chars.
0026      0A [   00   ]   FLD8DB  DB      10 DUP(0)         ;Ten zeros

                          ;                 Define Word - DW:
                          ;                 ----------------
0030   FFF0               FLD1DW  DW      0FFF0H            ;Hex constant
0032   0019               FLD2DW  DW      11001B            ;Binary constant
0034   0021 R             FLD3DW  DW      FLD7DB            ;Address as constant
0036   0001 0002 0003 0004 FLD4DW DW      1,2,3,4,5         ;Table of constants
       0005
0040      05 [   0000   ] FLD5DW  DW      5 DUP(0)          ;Five zeros

                          ;                 Define Doubleword - DD:
                          ;                 ----------------------
004A   ????????           FLD1DD  DD      ?                 ;Uninitialized
004E   43 50 00 00        FLD2DD  DD      'PC'              ;Character string
0052   39 30 00 00        FLD3DD  DD      12345             ;Decimal value
0056   11 00 00 00        FLD4DD  DD      FLD3DB - FLD2DB   ;Diff betw address
005A   0C 00 00 00 49 00  FLD5DD  DD      12,73             ;Two constants
       00 00

                          ;                 Define Quadword - DQ:
                          ;                 --------------------
0062   ????????????????   FLD1DQ  DQ      ?                 ;Uninitialized
006A   32 3C 00 00 00 00  FLD2DQ  DQ      03C32H            ;Hex constant
       00 00
0072   39 30 00 00 00 00  FLD3DQ  DQ      12345             ;Decimal constant
       00 00

                          ;                 Define Tenbytes - DT:
                          ;                 --------------------
007A   ????????????????????  FLD1DT  DT   ?                 ;Uninitialized
       ??
0084   43 50 00 00 00 00  FLD2DT  DT      'PC'              ;Character string
       00 00 00 00

008E                      DATASG  ENDS
                          END
```

```
                      Symbols-1

        Segments and groups:

                        N a m e          Size      align     combine class

        DATASG . . . . . . . . . . . . .008E      PARA      NONE      'DATA'

        Symbols:
                        N a m e          Type      Value     Attr

        FLD1DB . . . . . . . . . . . . .L BYTE    0000      DATASG
        FLD1DD . . . . . . . . . . . . .L DWORD   004A      DATASG
        FLD1DQ . . . . . . . . . . . . .L QWORD   0062      DATASG
        FLD1DT . . . . . . . . . . . . .L TBYTE   007A      DATASG
        FLD1DW . . . . . . . . . . . . .L WORD    0030      DATASG
        FLD2DB . . . . . . . . . . . . .L BYTE    0001      DATASG
        FLD2DD . . . . . . . . . . . . .L DWORD   004E      DATASG
        FLD2DQ . . . . . . . . . . . . .L QWORD   006A      DATASG
        FLD2DT . . . . . . . . . . . . .L TBYTE   0084      DATASG
        FLD2DW . . . . . . . . . . . . .L WORD    0032      DATASG
        FLD3DB . . . . . . . . . . . . .L BYTE    0012      DATASG
        FLD3DD . . . . . . . . . . . . .L DWORD   0052      DATASG
        FLD3DQ . . . . . . . . . . . . .L QWORD   0072      DATASG
        FLD3DW . . . . . . . . . . . . .L WORD    0034      DATASG
        FLD4DB . . . . . . . . . . . . .L BYTE    0013      DATASG
        FLD4DD . . . . . . . . . . . . .L DWORD   0056      DATASG
        FLD4DW . . . . . . . . . . . . .L WORD    0036      DATASG
        FLD5DB . . . . . . . . . . . . .L BYTE    0014      DATASG
        FLD5DD . . . . . . . . . . . . .L DWORD   005A      DATASG
        FLD5DW . . . . . . . . . . . . .L WORD    0040      DATASG    Length =0005
        FLD6DB . . . . . . . . . . . . .L BYTE    0015      DATASG
        FLD7DB . . . . . . . . . . . . .L BYTE    0021      DATASG
        FLD8DB . . . . . . . . . . . . .L BYTE    0026      DATASG    Length =000A
```

dress of FLD7DB. The generated object code is 0021 (the R to the right means relocatable), and a check above in the figure shows that the offset address of FLD7DB is indeed 0021.

FLD4DW defines a table of five numeric constants. Note that the object code for each constant is one word (two bytes).

For DW, DD, and DQ formats, the Assembler converts the constant to hex object code but stores it in *reverse sequence*. Consequently, the decimal vlaue 12345 converts to hex 3039 but is stored as 3930.

DEFINE DOUBLEWORD—DD

The DD Pseudo-op defines fields that are two words (four bytes) in length. A numeric expression may contain one or more constants, each with a maximum of four bytes (eight hex digits). The largest positive hex number is 7FFFFFFF; all "higher" numbers 80000000 through FFFFFFFF represent negative values. In terms of decimal numbers, these maximums are + 2,147,483,647 and − 2,147,483,648.

In Figure 4-1, FLD3DD defines a numeric constant. FLD4DD generates the numeric difference between two defined addresses; in this case, the result is the length of FLD2DB. FLD5DD defines two numeric constants.

The Assembler converts all DD numeric constants to hex but stores the object code in reverse sequence. Consequently, the decimal value 12345 converts to 00003039 but is stored as 39300000.

A DD character expression is limited to two characters. The Assembler reverses the characters and left-adjusts them in the four-byte doubleword, as shown by FLD2DD in object code.

DEFINE QUADWORD—DQ

The DQ Pseudo-op defines fields that are four words (eight bytes) in length. A numeric expression may contain one or more constants, each with a maximum of eight bytes or 16 hex digits. The largest positive hex number is 7 followed by 15 F's. As an indication of the magnitude of this number, hex 1 followed by 15 0's equals the following decimal number:

$$1,152,921,504,606,846,976$$

In Figure 4-1, FLD2DQ and FLD3DQ illustrate numeric values. The Assembler converts all DQ numeric constants to hex but stores the object code in reverse sequence as for DD and DW.

The Assembler handles DQ character strings like DD and DW.

DEFINE TENBYTES—DT

The DT Pseudo-op defines fields that are ten bytes in length. Its purpose appears to be related to "packed decimal" numeric values (discussed in Chapter 10); however, at the time of this writing DT does not translate expressions correctly under the small Assembler version.

Figure 4-1 supplies examples of DT for an uninitialized field and for a two-character constant.

Note: The "program" in Figure 4-1 contains only a Data Segment. The Assembler generated no error messages. LINK MAP displayed "Warning: No STACK Segment" and LINK displayed "There were 1 errors detected." Despite the error message, you can still use DEBUG to view the object code, as show in Figure 4-2.

The right side of the dump shows the alphabetic data such as "Personal Computer" quite clearly.

Figure 4-2 Dump of the Data Segment.

```
DEBUG B:EXDEF.EXE
-D
049F:0100  00 50 65 72 73 6F 6E 61-6C 20 43 6F 6D 70 75 74   .Personal Comput
049F:0110  65 72 19 19 19 01 4A 41-4E 02 46 45 42 03 4D 41   er....JAN.FEB.MA
049F:0120  52 31 32 33 34 35 00 00-00 00 00 00 00 00 00 00   R12345..........
049F:0130  F0 FF 19 00 21 00 01 00-02 00 03 00 04 00 05 00   p...!...........
049F:0140  00 00 00 00 00 00 00 00-00 00 00 00 00 00 43 50   ..............CP
049F:0150  00 00 39 30 00 00 11 00-00 00 0C 00 00 00 49 00   ..90..........I.
049F:0160  00 00 00 00 00 00 00 00-00 32 3C 00 00 00 00 00   .........2<....
049F:0170  00 00 39 30 00 00 00 00-00 00 00 00 00 00 00 00   ..90............
-D
049F:0180  00 00 00 00 43 50 00 00-00 00 00 00 00 00 00 00   ....CP..........
049F:0190  00 00 00 00 00 00 00 00-00 00 00 00 00 00 00 00   ................
049F:01A0  00 00 00 00 00 00 00 00-00 00 00 00 00 00 00 00   ................
049F:01B0  00 00 00 00 00 00 00 00-00 00 00 00 00 00 00 00   ................
049F:01C0  00 00 00 00 00 00 00 00-00 00 00 00 00 00 00 00   ................
049F:01D0  00 00 00 00 00 00 00 00-00 00 00 00 00 00 00 00   ................
049F:01E0  00 00 00 00 00 00 00 00-00 00 00 00 00 00 00 00   ................
049F:01F0  00 00 00 00 00 00 00 00-00 00 00 00 00 00 00 00   ................
```

Address of   Hexadecimal representation   ASCII representation
leftmost byte

IMMEDIATE OPERANDS

Figure 2-1 in Chapter 2 illustrates the use of immediate operands. The instruction

MOV AX,0123H

moves the immediate constant hex 0123 to the AX register. The three-byte object code for this instruction is B82301, where B8 means "move an immediate value to the AX register," and the following two bytes contain the value itself. Many instructions provide for two operands; the first operand may be a register or memory location, and the second operand may be an immediate constant.

The use of an immediate operand is more efficient than defining a numeric constant in the Data Segment and referencing it in the operand of the MOV, for example, as

    Data Segment: AMT1   DW   0123H
    Code Segment: MOV   AX,AMT1

Length of Immediate Operands

The length of an immediate constant is subject to the length of the first operand. For example, the following immediate operand is two bytes but the AL register is only one byte:

MOV AL,0123H (invalid)

However, if an immediate operand is shorter than the receiving operand, as

ADD AX,25H (valid),

the Assembler expands the immediate operand to two bytes, 0025 (and stores the object code as 2500).

Immediate Formats

An immediate constant may be *hex*, such as 0123H; *decimal*, such as 291 (which the Assembler converts to hex 0123); or *binary*, such as 100100011B (which converts to hex 0123).

Instructions that allow immediate operands are the following, listed by class:

Move and Compare:	MOV, CMP.
Arithmetic:	ADC, ADD, SBB, SUB.
Shift:	RCL, RCR, ROL, ROR, SHL, SAR, SHR.
Logical:	AND, OR, TEST, XOR.

Figure 4-3 portrays examples of valid immediate operands using these instructions. Later chapters explain arithmetic carry operations, shift, and logical instructions. Since the example is not intended for execution, it omits defining a Stack and initializing Segment registers.

Note: To process fields longer than two bytes, you may have to code a *loop* (Chapter 5) or use a String operation (Chapter 9).

EQU PSEUDO-OPERATION

The EQU Pseudo-op does not define a data field. Instead, it defines a value that can be used to substitute in other instructions. Assume that the following EQU instruction is coded in the Data Segment:

TIMES   EQU   10

The name, in this case TIMES, may be any acceptable Assembler name. Now whenever the word TIMES appears in an instruction or another Pseudo-

---

Figure 4-3 Immediate Operations.

```
                              page     60,132
                        TITLE  EXIMM   Example Immediate Operands

0000                    DATASG SEGMENT PARA 'DATA'
0000  ??                FLD1   DB      ?
0001  ????              FLD2   DW      ?
0003                    DATASG ENDS

0000                    CODESG SEGMENT PARA 'CODE'
0000                    BEGIN  PROC    FAR
                        ASSUME CS:CODESG,DS:DATASG

                        ;              Move & Compare Operations:
                        ;              --------------------------
0000  BB 0113                   MOV    BX,275           ;Move
0003  3C 19                     CMP    AL,19H           ;Compare

                        ;              Arithmetic Operations:
                        ;              ----------------------
0005  14 05                     ADC    AL,5             ;Add with carry
0007  80 C7 0C                  ADD    BH,12            ;Add
000A  1C 05                     SBB    AL,5             ;Sub with Borrow
000C  80 2E 0000 R 05           SUB    FLD1,5           ;Subtract

                        ;              Rotate & Shift (1 bit only):
                        ;              ----------------------------
0011  D0 D3                     RCL    BL,1             ;Rotate left/carry
0013  D0 DC                     RCR    AH,1             ;Rotate right/carry
0015  D1 06 0001 R              ROL    FLD2,1           ;Rotate left
0019  D0 C8                     ROR    AL,1             ;Rotate right
001B  D1 E1                     SAL    CX,1             ;Shift left
001D  D1 FB                     SAR    BX,1             ;Shift arith right
001F  D0 2E 0000 R              SHR    FLD1,1           ;Shift right

                        ;              Logical Operations:
                        ;              -------------------
0023  24 2C                     AND    AL,00101100B     ;AND register
0025  80 CF 2A                  OR     BH.2AH           ;OR register
0028  F6 C3 7A                  TEST   BL,7AH           ;TEST register
002B  80 36 0000 R 23           XOR    FLD1,23H         ;XOR storage

0030  CB                        RET
0031                    BEGIN  ENDP

0031                    CODESG ENDS
                        END
```

---

op, the Assembler substitutes the value 10. For example, the Assembler converts the Pseudo-op

FIELDA DB TIMES DUP(?)

to **FIELDA DB 10 DUP(?)**

An equated operand may also appear in an instruction, as in the following:

COUNTR EQU 05   ;Defined in the Data Segment

. . .

MOV CX,COUNTR   ;Defined in the Code Segment

The Assembler replaces COUNTR in the MOV instruction with the value 05, making the operand an immediate value as if it were coded as

MOV CX,05   ;Assembler substitutes 05

One advantage of EQU is that many instructions may use the value defined by COUNTR. If the value has to be changed, you need only change one instruction—the EQU. Needless to say, you can use an equated value only where a substitution makes sense to the Assembler. You can also equate symbolic names:

1. TP   EQU   TOTAL_PAY
2. MPY   EQU   MUL

The first example assumes that the program has defined TOTAL_PAY in the Data Segment. For any instruction that contains the operand TP, the Assembler replaces it with the address of TOTAL_PAY. The second example enables a program to use the word MPY in place of the regular symbolic instruction MUL. Well, you may not want to do that, but you can!

CP/M-86 DIFFERENCES

CP/M-86 uses the same data definition Directives (Pseudo-ops) as DOS, but with a few minor differences. First, CP/M Assembler does not appear to support DQ and DT Directives (no great loss). Second, whereas DOS uses a question mark (?) to signify that a field is to contain an uninitialized value, CP/M-86 uses special "reserve" Directives: RB, RW, and RS. In the following examples, the DOS version is on the left and the CP/M-86 version is on the right.

□   RB allocates one or more bytes of memory. The Assembler assumes that a reference to the named variable has the byte attribute.

	DOS		CP/M	
DB	?	RB	1	;Reserve one byte
DB	4 DUP(?)	RB	4	;Reserve 4 bytes

- RW allocates one or more words of memory. The Assembler assumes that a reference to the named variable has the word attribute.

```
DW   ?                RW   1        ;Reserve one word
DW   5 DUP(?)         RW   5        ;Reserve 5 words
```

- RS reserves any amount of storage. Presumably the area is one that you would not have to reference by name.

```
DB   50 DUP(?)        RS   50       ;Reserve 50 locations
```

KEY POINTS TO REMEMBER

- Keep names of data fields unique and descriptive. For example, a field for an employee's wage could be named EMPWAGE.
- Use DB to define character strings since this format permits strings longer than two bytes and converts them to normal left-to-right sequence.
- Be careful to distinguish between a decimal and a hex value. For example, consider the effect of adding decimal 25 and of adding hex 25:

```
              ADD AX,25        ;Adds 25
              ADD AX,25H       ;Adds 37
```

- Remember that DW, DD, DQ, and DT store a numeric value in object code with the bytes in reverse sequence.
- Use DB fields for processing a half register (AL, AH, BL, etc.) and DW for processing a full register (AX, BX, CX, etc.). Numeric fields defined as DD and DQ require special handling.
- Match immediate operands to the size of a register: a one-byte constant with a one-byte register (AL, BH) and a one-word constant with a one-word register (AX, BX).

QUESTIONS

4-1. What are the lengths in bytes of the following data Pseudo-ops: (a) DD, (b) DT, (c) DB, (d) DQ, (e) DW?

4-2. Define a character string named TITLE1 containing the constant Zolar Electronics.

4-3. Define the following numeric values in fields named, respectively, FLD1 through FLD5:

(a) A four-byte field containing the hex equivalent to decimal 130.

(b) A one-byte field containing the hex equivalent to decimal 20.

(c) A two-byte field containing an undefined value.

(d) A one-byte field containing the binary equivalent to decimal 20.

(e) A DW containing the consecutive values 15, 18, 19, 26, 40.

4-4. Show the generated hex object code for (a) DB '28' and (b) DB 28.

4-5. Determine the hex object code for (a) DB 25H, (b) DW 2573H, (c) DD 25733AH, (d) DQ 25733AH.

4-6. Code the instructions with immediate operands for the following:

(a) Store 250 in the AX.

(b) Compare FLD1 to zero.

(c) Add hex 20 to CX.

(d) Subtract hex 20 from AX.

(e) Shift FLD2 one bit left.

(f) Shift the BH register one bit right.

4-7. Key in and assemble the data fields and instructions for Questions 4-2, 4-3, and 4-6. You won't require a Stack or a Link step. Print the LST listing when the assembly is free of error messages.

5

PROGRAM LOGIC
AND ORGANIZATION

Objective:
To cover the requirements for program control (looping and jumping) and for program organization.

INTRODUCTION

Up to this chapter, program examples all executed in a straight line, with one instruction sequentially followed by another. Seldom, however, is a programmable problem that simple. Most programs consist of a number of *loops* in which a series of steps must repeat until reaching a specific requirement and various *tests* to determine which of several actions to take. A common requirement is to test a condition to determine if the program is to terminate execution.

These requirements involve a transfer of control to the address of another instruction that does not immediately follow the instruction that is currently executing. A transfer of control may be *forward* to execute a new series of steps or *backward* to reexecute the same step.

There are various instructions that transfer control from the normal sequential steps. To effect a transfer operation, these instructions cause an offset value to be added to the Instruction Pointer. Following are the four classes of transfer operations:

Unconditional Jump:	JMP	
Looping:	LOOP	
Conditional Jump:	Jnnn	(high, low, equal)
Call a Procedure:	CALL	

This chapter covers each class in detail along with program examples for each case. Note: You won't find the term "Unconditional Jump" in the manual that accompanies the Assembler program diskette. This term is commonly used in other programming languages and helps to clarify the class of operation.

THE UNCONDITIONAL JUMP: JMP

One commonly used instruction for transfering control is the jump (JMP) instruction. The jump is unconditional since the operation transfers control under all circumstances.

Figure 5-1 provides an example of a JMP instruction. The AX, BX, and CX registers are initialized to the value of 1. Then a program loop performs the following:

Add 1 to AX
Add AX to BX
Double the value in CX

The effect of repeating the loop causes AX to increase as 1, 2, 3, 4, ..., BX to increase according to the sum of the digits 1, 3, 6, 10, ..., and CX to double as 1, 2, 4, 8, ... The beginning of the loop has the label A20:—the *colon* indicates that the label is inside a Procedure (BEGIN in this case). The end of the loop contains the instruction

JMP   A20

to indicate that control is to transfer to the instruction labeled A20. Note that an address label in an instruction *operand* does not have a colon. Also, since there is no exit from this loop, processing is endless—usually not a good idea!

You can code a label either on a line with an instruction as

A20:   ADD   AX,01

```
        ┌─────────────────────────────────────────────┐
        │ Figure 5-1 Use of the JMP Instruction.      │
        └─────────────────────────────────────────────┘

                              page      65,132
                      TITLE   EXJUMP   Illustration of JMP for looping

0000                  STACKSG SEGMENT PARA STACK 'STACK'
0000      20 [  ????  ]       DW       32 DUP(?)
0040                  STACKSG ENDS

0000                  CODESG  SEGMENT PARA 'CODE'
0000                  BEGIN   PROC     FAR
                              ASSUME   CS:CODESG,SS:STACKSG
0000   1E                     PUSH     DS
0001   2B C0                  SUB      AX,AX
0003   50                     PUSH     AX

0004   B8 0001                MOV      AX,01      ;Init'ze AX,
0007   BB 0001                MOV      BX,01      ;        BX, &
000A   B9 0001                MOV      CX,01      ;      CX to 1
000D                  A20:
000D   05 0001                ADD      AX,01      ;Add 1 to AX
0010   03 D8                  ADD      BX,AX      ;Add AX to BX
0012   D1 E1                  SHL      CX,1       ;Double CX
0014   EB F7                  JMP      A20        ;Jump to A20 instr'n
0016                  BEGIN   ENDP

0016                  CODESG  ENDS
                              END      BEGIN
```

or on a separate line as

A20:

ADD   AX,01

In both cases, the address of A20 references the first byte of the ADD instruction. Technically, the colon in A20: gives the label the NEAR attribute. Consequently, A20: must be within -128 to $+127$ bytes of the JMP instruction. In this example, A20 is -7 bytes from the JMP. You can confirm this distance by examining the object code for the JMP: EBF7. EB is the machine code for a near JMP and F7 is a negative offset value. The JMP operation adds the F7 to the Instruction Pointer which contains the offset of the instruction following the JMP, namely 0016:

Instruction Pointer:	16
JMP offset:	F7
Transfer address:	(1)0D

Since an offset is one byte, the one-bit overflow is dropped, and the jump address becomes 0D. And if you check the program listing for the offset address of A20:, guess what?—000D. Conversely, the operand for a forward JMP will be a positive value.

As a useful experience, key in the program, assemble it, and link it. No Data Segment is required, since immediate operands generate all the data. Trace the EXE module with DEBUG for a number of iterations. Once AX contains eight, BX and CX will have been incremented respectively to hex 24 (decimal 36) and hex 80 (decimal 128).

THE LOOP INSTRUCTION

The JMP instruction in Figure 5-1 causes a routine to loop endlessly. But a more likely situation is for a routine to loop a specified number of times or until a particular value is reached. The Assembler LOOP instruction serves this purpose; it requires that an initial value is stored in the CX register. For each iteration, LOOP automatically deducts 1 from the CX register; if CX is nonzero, control jumps to the operand address, and if zero, control drops through to the following instruction.

Figure 5-2 illustrates use of the LOOP instruction. The program performs the same operation as Figure 5-1 except that the routine terminates after ten loops. A MOV instruction initializes CX with the value 10. Since LOOP must use the CX, this program now uses DX in place of CX for doubling the initial value 1. The LOOP instruction replaces JMP A20, and for efficiency INC AX replaces ADD AX,01.

```
                       ┌──────────────────────────────────────────┐
                       │ Figure 5-2 Use of the LOOP Instruction.  │
                       └──────────────────────────────────────────┘

                            page      65,132
                     TITLE   EXLOOP    Illustration of LOOP for looping

0000                 STACKSG SEGMENT PARA STACK 'STACK'
0000     20 [ ???? ]         DW       32 DUP(?)
0040                 STACKSG ENDS

0000                 CODESG  SEGMENT PARA 'CODE'
0000                 BEGIN   PROC    FAR
                             ASSUME  CS:CODESG,SS:STACKSG
0000   1E                    PUSH    DS
0001   2B C0                 SUB     AX,AX
0003   50                    PUSH    AX

0004   B8 0001               MOV     AX,01      ;Init'ze AX,
0007   BB 0001               MOV     BX,01      ;      BX, &
000A   BA 0001               MOV     DX,01      ;      DX to 1
000D   B9 000A               MOV     CX,10      ;Init'ze no. of loops
0010                 A20:
0010   40                    INC     AX         ;Add 1 to AX
0011   03 D8                 ADD     BX,AX      ;Add AX to BX
0013   D1 E2                 SHL     DX,1       ;Double DX
0015   E2 F9                 LOOP    A20        ;Decr CX, loop if nonzero
0017   CB                    RET                ;Terminate
0018                 BEGIN   ENDP

0018                 CODESG  ENDS
                             END     BEGIN
```

Just as for JMP, the distance from the end of the LOOP instruction to the address of A20 is added to the Instruction Pointer. *This distance must be within −128 to +127 bytes.*

It is recommended that you modify your copy of Figure 5-1 for these changes and assemble and link it. Then trace the program under DEBUG for the entire ten loops. Once CX is reduced to zero, the contents of AX, BX, and DX are, respectively, hex 0B, 42, and 400. The RET instruction then terminates execution of this program.

There are two variations of the LOOP instruction: LOOPE and LOOPNE. Both operations decrement the CX by 1. LOOPE (or LOOPZ) transfers to the operand address if the CX is not zero and the zero condition is set (ZF = 1). LOOPNE (or LOOPNZ) transfers if the CX is not zero and the nonzero condition is set (ZF = 0).

FLAGS REGISTER

Much of the remaining material in this chapter requires a more detailed knowledge of the Flags register. The Flags register contains 16 bits that various instructions set to indicate the status of an operation. On some systems, the Flags register is known as the Status Register or the Program Status Word. The Flags register contains the following nine used bits (an asterisk indicates an unused bit):

Bit no.:	15	14	13	12	11	10	9	8	7	6	5	4	3	2	1	0
Flag:	*	*	*	*	O	D	I	T	S	Z	*	A	*	P	*	C

CF (Carry Flag). Contains "carries" (0 or 1) from the high-order bit following arithmetic operations and some shift and rotate operations (Chapter 10).

PF (Parity Flag). A check of the low-order eight bits of data operations. An odd number of data bits sets the flag to 0 and an even number to 1—not to be confused with the parity bit and seldom of concern for conventional programming.

AF (Auxiliary Carry Flag). Set to 1 if arithmetic causes a carry out of bit 3 (fourth from the right) of a register one-byte operation. This flag is concerned with arithmetic on ASCII and packed-decimal fields (Chapter 11).

ZF (Zero Flag). Set as a result of arithmetic or compare operations. *Unexpectedly, a nonzero result sets it to 0 and a zero result sets it to 1.* However, the setting, if not apparently correct, is logically correct: 0 means no (the result is not equal to zero) and 1 means yes (the result equals zero). JE and JZ test this flag.

SF (Sign Flag). Set according to the sign (high-order or leftmost bit) after an arithmetic operation: positive sets to 0 and negative sets to 1. JG and JL instructions test this flag.

TF (Trap Flag). You have already set this flag when you entered the T command in DEBUG. When set, the Trap Flag causes the processor to execute in single-step mode, that is, one instruction at a time under user control.

IF (Interrupt Flag). When 0 all interrupts are disabled, and when 1 all interrupts are enabled.

DF (Direction Flag). Used by String operations to determine the direction of data transfer. When 0 the operation increments the SI and DI registers causing left-to-right data transfer; when 1 the operation decrements the SI and DI causing right-to-left data transfer (Chapter 9).

OF (Overflow Flag). Indicates a carry into and out of the high-order (leftmost) sign bit following a signed arithmetic operation (Chapter 10).

As an example, the CMP instruction compares two operands and affects the AF, CF, OF, PF, SF, and ZF flags. However, you do not have to test these flags individually. The following tests if the BX register contains a zero value:

```
        CMP BX,00            ;Compare BX to zero
        JZ   B50             ;Jump to B50 if zero
        • (action if nonzero)

        •
B50:    • • •                ;Jump point if BX zero
```

If the BX contains zero, CMP sets the ZF to 1 and may or may not change other flags. The JZ (Jump if Zero) instruction tests only the ZF flag. Since ZF contains 1 (meaning a zero condition), JZ transfers control (jumps) to the address indicated by operand B50.

CONDITIONAL JUMP INSTRUCTIONS

An earlier example explains how the LOOP instruction decrements and tests the CX register; if the register now contains nonzero, the instruction transfers control to the operand address. In effect, the transfer occurs depending on a certain condition. The Assembler supports a wide variety of conditional jump instructions that transfer control depending on settings in the Flags register. For example, you can compare two fields and then jump according to flag values.

In Figure 5-2, you could replace the LOOP instruction with two instructions, one which decrements CX and the other a conditional jump:

Use of LOOP	Use of Conditional Jump
LOOP A20	DEC CX
	JNZ A20

The two instructions on the right perform exactly what LOOP does: Decrement the CX by 1 and jump to A20 if CX is nonzero. DEC also sets the Zero Flag in the Flags register either to zero or nonzero. JNZ then tests the setting of the Zero Flag. In this example, LOOP, although it has limited uses, is more efficient than the two instructions DEC and JNZ.

Just as for the JMP instruction, the distance from the end of the JNZ instruction to the address of A20 is added to the Instruction Pointer. *This distance must be within −128 to +127 bytes.*

Signed and Unsigned Data

Distinguishing the purpose of conditional jumps may help clarify their use. Basically, you can determine which instruction to use by the type of data on which you are performing a comparison or arithmetic: unsigned or signed. An *unsigned* data field treats all bits as data bits; typical examples are character strings such as names and addresses and numeric values such as customer numbers. A *signed* data field treats the leftmost bit as a sign, where 0 is positive and 1 is negative. Many numeric values may be either positive or negative.

As an example, assume that the AX contains 11000110 and the BX contains 00010110. The instruction

CMP   AX,BX

compares the contents of the AX to the BX. As unsigned data, the AX value is larger; as signed data, the AX value is smaller.

Jumps Based on Unsigned Data

Symbol	Description	Flags Tested
JE/JZ	Jump Equal or Jump Zero	ZF
JNE/JNZ	Jump Not Equal or Jump Not Zero	ZF
JA/JNBE	Jump Above or Jump Not Below/Equal	CF, ZF
JAE/JNB	Jump Above/Equal or Jump Not Below	CF
JB/JNAE	Jump Below or Jump Not Above/Equal	CF
JBE/JNA	Jump Below/Equal or Jump Not Above	CF, AF

You can express each test in one of two symbolic codes. For example, JB and JNAE generate the same object code. However, you will probably find a positive test such as JB easier to understand than a negative test such as JNAE.

Jumps Based on Signed Data

Symbol	Description	Flags Tested
JE/JZ	Jump Equal or Jump Zero	ZF
JNE/JNZ	Jump Not Equal or Jump Not Zero	ZF
JG/JNLE	Jump Greater or Jump Not Less/Equal	ZF, SF, OF
JGE/JNL	Jump Greater/Equal or Jump Not Less	SF, OF
JL/JNGE	Jump Less or Jump Not Greater/Equal	SF, OF
JLE/JNG	Jump Less/Equal or Jump Not Greater	ZF, SF, OF

The jumps for testing equal/zero (JE/JZ) and for not equal/zero (JNE/JNZ) are included in both lists for unsigned and signed data. An equal/zero condition occurs regardless of the presence of a sign.

Special Arithmetic Tests

Symbol	Description	Flags Tested
JS	Jump Sign (negative)	SF
JNS	Jump No Sign (positive)	SF
JC	Jump Carry (same as JB)	CF
JNC	Jump No Carry	CF
JO	Jump Overflow	OF
JNO	Jump No Overflow	OF
JP/JPE	Jump Parity Even	PF
JNP/JPO	Jump Parity Odd	PF

One other conditional jump, JCXZ, tests if the contents of the CX register is zero. This instruction need not be placed immediately following an arithmetic or compare operation. One use for JCXZ could be at the start of a loop to ensure that the CX actually contains a nonzero value.

Don't expect to memorize all these instructions! For unsigned data all you need to remember is whether you want to jump if equal, above, or low. For *signed* data remember that a jump is on equal, greater, or less. The jumps for testing the Carry, Overflow, and Parity flags have unique purposes. In any event, choose the symbolic code carefully. The Assembler translates symbolic to object code regardless of which instruction you use, but, for example, JAE and JGE, although apparently similar, do not test the same flags.

CALL AND PROCEDURES

Up to this point, our Code Segments have consisted of only one Procedure, coded as follows:

$$\text{BEGIN} \quad \text{PROC} \quad \text{FAR}$$
$$\bullet$$
$$\bullet$$
$$\text{BEGIN} \quad \text{ENDP}$$

The operand FAR informs the system that this address is the entry point for program execution, whereas the ENDP Pseudo-op defines the end of the Procedure. A Code Segment, however, may contain any number of Procedures all distinguished by PROC and ENDP. A typical organization could appear as shown in Figure 5-3. Note the following features:

CODESG	SEGMENT	PARA
BEGIN	PROC	FAR
	•	
	•	
	CALL	B10
	CALL	C10
	RET	
BEGIN	ENDP	
B10	PROC	NEAR
	•	
	•	
	RET	
B10	ENDP	
C10	PROC	NEAR
	•	
	•	
	RET	
C10	ENDP	
CODESG	ENDS	
	END	BEGIN

Figure 5-3 Called Procedures

☐ The PROC Pseudo-ops for B10 and C10 contain the operand NEAR to indicate that these Procedures are within the current Code Segment. Since omission of the NEAR operand causes the Assembler to default to NEAR, many subsequent examples omit this operand.

☐ Each Procedure has a unique name and contains its own ENDP for termination.

☐ To transfer control, the Procedure BEGIN contains two CALL instructions:

CALL B10

CALL C10

The effect of executing the first CALL is that program control transfers to the Procedure B10 and begins its execution. Reaching the RET instruction then causes control to return to the instruction immediately following CALL B10. The second CALL performs similarly—it transfers control to C10, executes its instructions, and returns by means of the RET.

Figure 5-4 Effect of Execution on the Stack.

```
                                  page      65,132
                          TITLE   CALLPROC Calling Procedures

0000                      STACKSG SEGMENT PARA STACK 'STACK'
0000       20 [  ????  ]          DW      32 DUP(?)
0020                      STACKSG ENDS
                          ;-------------------------------------
0000                      CODESG  SEGMENT PARA 'CODE'
0000                      BEGIN   PROC    FAR
                                  ASSUME  CS:CODESG,SS:STACKSG
0000       1E                     PUSH    DS
0001       2B C0                  SUB     AX,AX
0003       50                     PUSH    AX
0004       E8 0008 R              CALL    B10         ;Call B10
0007       CB                     RET                 ;Terminate
0008                      BEGIN   ENDP
                          ;-------------------------------------
0008                      B10     PROC
0008       E8 000C R              CALL    C10         ;Call C10
000B       C3                     RET                 ;Return to
000C                      B10     ENDP                ;  caller
                          ;-------------------------------------
000C                      C10     PROC
000C       C3                     RET                 ;Return to
000D                      C10     ENDP                ;  caller
                          ;-------------------------------------
000D                      CODESG  ENDS
                                  END     BEGIN
```

□   RET always returns to the original calling routine. BEGIN calls B10 and C10 which therefore return to BEGIN. DOS "called" BEGIN, and its RET instruction returns control to DOS.

The use of Procedures can enable you to better organize your program into logical routines that contain related logic. Also, operands for a CALL do not have to be within − 128 and + 127 bytes.

Technically, you can transfer control to a NEAR Procedure by means of a jump instruction or even by normal in-line code. For example, if B10 did not contain a RET instruction, then instructions would execute through B10 and drop directly into C10. In fact, if C10 did not contain a RET, the program would execute past the end of C10 into whatever instructions happen to be there (if any), with unpredictable results. *It is recommended that only CALL instructions transfer control to Procedures.*

STACK SEGMENT

Up to this point, the only operations involving the Stack have been the two PUSH instructions at the start of the Code Segment that facilitate return to DOS when the program terminates. Consequently, these programs needed to define only a very small Stack. However, CALL automatically pushes onto the Stack the offset address of the following instruction. In the called Procedure, the RET instruction uses this address for returning to the calling Procedure and automatically pops the Stack. Because of this feature, you must ensure that a RET matches its original CALL. Also, a called Procedure can CALL another Procedure which in turn can CALL yet another Procedure. The Stack must be large enough to contain the pushed addresses. All this turns out to be easier than it first appears, and a Stack definition of 32 words is ample for most of our purposes.

Stacks are also known as "pushdown lists." Certain instructions— PUSH, PUSHF, CALL, INT, and INTO—save a return address or the contents of the Flags register by pushing them onto the Stack. Other instructions— POP, POPF, RET, and IRET— return the address or Flags by popping them off the Stack. On entry to a program, the system sets the following register values:

DS and ES: Address of the Program Segment Prefix (a hex 100-byte area that precedes your executable program module).

CS: Address of the entry point to your program, the first executable instruction.

IP: Zero.

SS: Address of the Stack Segment.

SP: Offset to the top of the Stack. For example, if you define the Stack as 32 words (64 bytes) as

DW   32 DUP(?)

the SP contains 64, or hex 40.

Let's trace a simple program through its execution. Assume that our skeleton program contains instructions shown in Figure 5-4.

The first PUSH decrements the SP by 2 and stores the DS (containing 049F in this example) at the top of the Stack, at 4B00 + 3E. The second PUSH decrements the SP by 2 and stores the AX containing 0000 on the Stack at 4B00 + 3C. CALL B10 decrements the SP and stores the offset address of the following instruction (0007) in the Stack at 4B00 + 3A. CALL C10 decrements the SP and stores the offset address of the following instruction (000B) in the Stack at 4B00 + 38.

On return from C10, the RET instruction pops the address (000B) from the Stack at 4B00 + 38, inserts it in the IP, and increments the SP by 2. There is now an automatic return to offset 000B in the Code Segment, in B10.

The RET at the end of the B10 Procedure pops the address (0007) from the Stack at 4B00 + 3A, inserts it into the IP, and increments the SP by 2. There is now an automatic return to offset 0007 in the Code Segment. At 0007, the program terminates its execution with a FAR return.

The following shows the effect on the Stack as each instruction executes. You could also trace this program using DEBUG. In this example, 04B0:0000 is the bottom of the Stack and 04B0:0040 is the top of the Stack. The example shows only Stack locations 0034 through 003F and the contents of the SP:

Operation		Stack						SP
On entry,	initially:	0000	0000	0000	0000	0000	0000	0040
PUSH DS	(push 049F)	0000	0000	0000	0000	0000	9F04	003E
PUSH AX	(push 0000)	0000	0000	0000	0000	0000	9F04	003C
CALL B10	(push 0007)	0000	0000	0000	0700	0000	9F40	003A
CALL C10	(push 000B)	0000	0000	0B00	0700	0000	9F40	0038
RET	(pop 000B)	0000	0000	0000	0700	0000	9F40	003A
RET	(pop 0007)	0000	0000	0000	0000	0000	9F40	003C
Stack offset:		0034	0036	0038	003A	003C	003E	

Note two points: First, words in memory contain the bytes in reverse sequence, such that 0007 becomes 0700. Second, if you use DEBUG to view the Stack, notice that it stores other values including the contents of the IP for its own purposes.

PROGRAM: EXTENDED-MOVE OPERATIONS

Previous programs moved immediate data into a register, moved data from defined memory to a register, moved register contents to memory, and moved the contents of one register to another. In all cases, data length was limited to one or two bytes, and no operation moved data from one memory area directly to another memory area. It is possible to move data that exceeds two bytes, and this section explains this process. It is also possible to move data from one memory area directly to another, but this process is covered in Chapter 9 on String operations.

In Figure 5-5, the Data Segment contains three nine-byte fields defined as NAME1, NAME2, and NAME3. The object of the program is to move NAME1 to NAME2 and to move NAME2 to NAME3. Since these fields are nine bytes in length, more than a simple MOV instruction is required. The program contains a number of new features.

Figure 5-5 Extended Move Operations

```
          page    65,132
TITLE   EXMOVE  Extended Move operations
;--------------------------------------------------------------
STACKSG SEGMENT PARA STACK 'STACK'
        DW      32 DUP(?)
STACKSG ENDS
;--------------------------------------------------------------
DATASG  SEGMENT PARA 'DATA'
NAME1   DB      'ABCDEFGHI'
NAME2   DB      'JKLMNOPQR'
NAME3   DB      'STUVWXYZ*'
DATASG  ENDS
;--------------------------------------------------------------
CODESG  SEGMENT PARA 'CODE'
BEGIN   PROC    FAR
        ASSUME  CS:CODESG,DS:DATASG,SS:STACKSG,ES:DATASG
        PUSH    DS
        SUB     AX,AX
        PUSH    AX
        MOV     AX,DATASG
        MOV     DS,AX
        MOV     ES,AX
        CALL    B10MOVE          ;Call Jump routine
        CALL    C10MOVE          ;Call LOOP routine
        RET                      ;Terminate processing
BEGIN   ENDP

;       Extended Move using Jump-on-Condition:
;       --------------------------------------
B10MOVE PROC
        LEA     SI,NAME1         ;Init'ze address of NAME1
        LEA     DI,NAME2         ;   & NAME2
        MOV     CX,09            ;Init'ze to Move 9 chars
B20:
        MOV     AL,[SI]          ;Move from NAME1
        MOV     [DI],AL          ;Move to NAME2
        INC     SI               ;Incr next char in NAME1
        INC     DI               ;Incr next pos'n in NAME2
        DEC     CX               ;Decr loop count
        JNZ     B20              ;Count not zero? Yes, loop
        RET                      ;Count = 0, return to
B10MOVE ENDP                     ;   caller

;       Extended Move using LOOP:
;       ------------------------
C10MOVE PROC
        LEA     SI,NAME2         ;Init'ze address of NAME2
        LEA     DI,NAME3         ;   & NAME3
        MOV     CX,09            ;Init'ze to Move 9 chars
C20:
        MOV     AL,[SI]          ;Move from NAME2
        MOV     [DI],AL          ;Move to NAME3
        INC     DI               ;Incr next char of NAME2
        INC     SI               ;Incr next pos'n of NAME3
        LOOP    C20              ;Decr count, loop nonzero
        RET                      ;Count = 0, return to
C10MOVE ENDP                     ;   caller
;--------------------------------------------------------------
CODESG  ENDS
        END     BEGIN
```

The Procedure BEGIN initializes the Segment registers and then calls B10-MOVE and C10MOVE. B10MOVE moves the contents of NAME1 to NAME2. Since the operation moves one byte at a time, the routine begins with the leftmost byte of NAME1 and loops to move the second byte, the third byte, and so on, as follows:

```
NAME1:   A   B   C   D   E   F   G   H   I
         |   |   |   |   |   |   |   |   |
NAME2:   J   K   L   M   N   O   P   Q   R
```

Because the routine has to step through NAME1 and NAME2, it initializes the CX register to 9 and uses the index registers, SI and DI. Two LEA instructions load the offset addresses of NAME1 and NAME2 into the SI and DI registers as follows:

```
LEA   SI,NAME1      ;Load offset addresses
LEA   DI,NAME2      ;  of NAME1 and NAME2
```

Using the addresses in the SI and DI registers, a looping routine moves the first byte of NAME1 to the first byte of NAME2. Note that the brackets around SI and DI in the MOV operands means that the instruction is to use the address in that register for the memory location to be moved. Thus,

```
MOV   AL,[SI]
```

means: Use the address in SI (which is NAME1) and move the referenced byte to the AL register. And the instruction

```
MOV   [DI],AL
```

means: Move the contents of the AL to the address referenced by DI (which is NAME2).

The next instructions increment the SI and DI registers. If CX is non-zero, the routine loops back to B20. And since SI and DI have been incremented by 1, the next MOV references NAME1 + 1 and NAME2 + 1. The loop continues in this fashion until it has moved NAME1 + 8 to NAME2 + 8.

The Procedure C10MOVE is similar to B10MOVE with two exceptions. It moves NAME2 to NAME3 and uses LOOP instead of DEC/JNZ.

Suggestion: Key in the program, and then assemble, link, and trace it using DEBUG. Note the effect on NAME2, NAME3, the registers, the Instruction Pointer, and the Stack.

BOOLEAN OPERATIONS: AND, OR, XOR, TEST

Boolean logic is important in circuitry design and has a parallel in programming logic. The programming instructions for Boolean logic are AND, OR, XOR, and TEST. These instructions are useful in clearing and setting bits and in handling ASCII data for arithmetic purposes (Chapter 11). All of these instructions process one byte or one word in a register or in memory.

They match the bits of the two referenced operands and set the CF, OF, PF, SF, and ZF flags (AF is undefined).

AND: If the matched bits are both 1, the result is 1; all other conditions result in 0.

OR: If either of the matched bits is 1, the result is 1; if both are 0, the result is 0.

XOR: If one matched bit is 0 and the other 1, the result is 1; if the matched bits are the same (both 0 or both 1), the result is 0.

TEST: Acts like AND—sets the flags but does not change the bits.

The following AND, OR, and XOR instructions use the same bit values:

	AND	OR	XOR
	0101	0101	0101
	0011	0011	0011
Result:	0001	0111	0110

For the following unrelated examples, assume that the AL contains 1100 0101 and that the BH contains 0101 1100:

1.	AND	AL,BH	;Sets AL to 0100 0100
2.	OR	BH,AL	;Sets BH to 1101 1101
3.	XOR	AL,AL	;Sets AL to 0000 0000
4.	AND	AL,00	;Sets AL to 0000 0000
5.	AND	AL,0FH	;Sets AL to 0000 0101

Examples 3 and 4 portray ways of clearing a register to zero. Example 5 zeros the left four bits of the AL. You can also use these instructions to process bytes and words in memory.

The TEST instruction acts like AND but only sets Flags. Following are some examples:

1.	TEST	BL,11110000B	;Any of leftmost bits
	JNZ	• • •	; in BL nonzero?
2.	TEST	AL,00000001B	;Does the AL contain
	JNZ	• • •	; an odd number?
3.	TEST	DX,0FFH	;Does the DX contain
	JZ	• • •	; a zero value?

The NOT Instruction   Another related instruction, NOT, simply reverses the bits in a byte or word in a register or memory—0's become 1's and 1's become 0's. For example, if the AL contains 1100 0101, then the instruction NOT AL changes the AL to 0011 1010. Flags are unaffected. Note that NOT is not the same as changing a value from positive to negative and vice versa, which involves reversing the bits and adding 1 (see Negative Numbers in Chapter 1). The instruction that performs this operation is NEG.

PROGRAM: CHANGING LOWERCASE TO UPPERCASE

There are various reasons for converting between uppercase and lowercase letters. For example, you may have received a data file created by a micro that processes only uppercase letters. Or a program has to allow for users to enter commands either as uppercase or lowercase (such as YES or yes) and converts to uppercase for testing it. Uppercase letters, A through Z, are hex 41 through 5A, and lowercase letters, a through z, are hex 61 through 7A. The only difference is that bit 5 is 0 for upppercase and 1 for lowercase, as the following shows:

	Bit:	76543210		Bit:	76543210
Letter A:		01000001	Letter Z:		01011010
Letter a:		01100001	Letter z:		01111010

The program in Figure 5-6 converts the contents of a data field, TITLEX, from lowercase to uppercase, beginning at TITLEX + 1. The Procedure named B10CASE initializes the BX with the address of TITLEX + 1. It then uses the address in the BX to move each character starting at TITLEX + 1 to the AH. If the value is between hex 61 and 7A, an AND instruction

AND   AH,11011111B

sets bit 5 to 0. All characters other than a through z remain unchanged. The routine then moves the changed character back to TITLEX, increments the BX for the next character, and loops.

Used this way, the BX register acts as an index register for addressing memory locations. The SI and DI may also be used for this purpose.

SHIFTING AND ROTATING

The shift and rotate instructions are part of the computer's "logical" capability. The instructions have the following features:

```
                    Figure 5-6 Changing Lowercase to Uppercase

                              page      65,132
                       TITLE  CASE      Change lowercase to upper case
                       ;------------------------------------------------
0000                   STACKSG SEGMENT PARA STACK 'STACK'
0000      20 [  ????  ]        DW      32 DUP(?)
0040                   STACKSG ENDS
                       ;------------------------------------------------
0000
                       DATASG  SEGMENT PARA 'DATA'
0000 43 68 61 6E 67 65 TITLEX  DB      'Change to uppercase letters'
     20 74 6F 20 75 70
     70 65 72 63 61 73
     65 20 6C 65 74 74
     65 72 73
001B                   DATASG  ENDS
                       ;------------------------------------------------
0000                   CODESG  SEGMENT PARA 'CODE'
0000                   BEGIN   PROC    FAR
                               ASSUME  CS:CODESG,SS:STACKSG,DS:DATASG
0000 1E                        PUSH    DS
0001 2B C0                     SUB     AX,AX
0003 50                        PUSH    AX
0004 B8  ---- R                MOV     AX,DATASG
0007 8E D8                     MOV     DS,AX
0009 E8 000D R                 CALL    B10CASE         ;Call convert routine
000C CB                        RET                     ;End processing
000D                   BEGIN   ENDP
                       ;------------------------------------------------
000D                   B10CASE PROC    NEAR
000D B9 001F                   MOV     CX,31           ;No. chars to change
0010 8D 1E 0001 R              LEA     BX,TITLEX+1     ;1st char to change
0014                   B20:
0014 8A 27                     MOV     AH,[BX]         ;Char from TITLEX
0016 80 FC 61                  CMP     AH,61H          ;Is it
0019 72 0A                     JB      B30             ;  lower
001B 80 FC 7A                  CMP     AH,7AH          ;  case
001E 77 05                     JA      B30             ;  letter?
0020 80 E4 DF                  AND     AH,11011111B    ;Yes - convert
0023 88 27                     MOV     [BX],AH         ;Restore in TITLEX
0025                   B30:
0025 43                        INC     BX              ;Set for next char
0026 E2 EC                     LOOP    B20             ;Loop 31 times
0028 C3                        RET
0029                   B10CASE ENDP
                       ;------------------------------------------------
0029                   CODESG  ENDS
                               END     BEGIN
```

- Reference a byte or a word.
- Reference a register or memory.
- Shift/rotate left or right.
- Shift/rotate up to 8 bits if a byte and up to 16 bits if a word.
- Shift/rotate logically (unsigned) or arithmetically (signed).

□   A shift value of 1 can be coded as an immediate operand; a value greater than 1 must be contained in the CL register.

Shifting

The bit that is shifted off enters the CF Flag. The shift instructions are

SHR	;Shift unsigned right
SHL	;Shift unsigned left
SAR	;Shift arithmetic right
SAL	;Shift arithmetic left

The following related instructions illustrate the SHR instruction:

```
MOV   CL,03           ;    AX:
MOV   AX,10110111B    ; 10110111
SHR   AX,1            ; 01011011
SHR   AX,CL           ; 00001011
```

The first SHR shifts the contents of the AX one bit to the right. The shifted 1-bit now resides in the CF Flag and a 0-bit is filled to the left in the AX. The second SHR shifts the AX three more bits. The CF Flag contains successively 1, 1, then 0, and three 0-bits are filled to the left in the AX.

Notice the effect of using SAR for arithmetic shifts:

```
MOV   CL,03           ;    AX:
MOV   AX,10110111B    ; 10110111
SAR   AX,1            ; 11011011
SAR   AX,CL           ; 11111011
```

The SAR operation differs from SHR in one important way: SAR uses the sign bit to fill leftmost vacated bits. In this way, positive and negative values retain their sign. In the above example, the sign is a 1-bit.

Left shifts always fill 0-bits to the right. As a result, SHL and SAL are identical.

Note that left shifts are especially useful for doubling values and right shifts for halving values. Halving odd numbers such as 5 and 7 always generates a smaller value (2 and 3, respectively) and sets the CF Flag to 1. Also, if you have to shift two bits, coding two shift instructions is more efficient than initializing the CL and coding one shift.

Rotating

For rotate instructions, the bit that is shifted off rotates to fill the vacated bit position. The rotate instructions are the following:

ROR	;Rotate right
ROL	;Rotate left
RCR	;Rotate with carry right
RCL	;Rotate with carry left

The following related instructions demonstrate the effect of using ROR:

MOV	CL,03	;	BX:
MOV	BX,10110111B	; 10110111	
ROR	BX,1	; 11011011	
ROR	BX,CL	; 01111011	

The first ROR rotates the rightmost 1-bit of the BX to the leftmost vacated position. The second ROR rotates the three rightmost bits.

The RCR and RCL instructions cause the CF Flag to participate. The shifted off bit moves into the CF, and the CF bit moves into the vacated bit position.

CP/M-86 DIFFERENCES

The only executable instructions in Assembler that differ under CP/M-86 are two minor variations of JMP and CALL. You can denote a short jump (within −128 and +127 bytes) by JMPS. This instruction generates a one-byte machine operand. A far jump to another Segment involves JMPF.

The other difference involves a far CALL to another Segment ("intersegment CALL") using CALLF and returning with RETF. Chapters 16 and 18 cover the use of multiple Segments and linking.

The area in which CP/M-86 and DOS differ most is Directives. Since CP/M-86 Assembler has no PROC Directive, you can code subroutines without PROC as follows:

	CALL	D10SUBR2	;Call subroutine
	•		
	•		
D10SUBR:	•		;Subroutine
	•		
	RET		;Return to caller

PROGRAM ORGANIZATION

Once you are familiar with the basic rules for data definition and the instruction set, you can typically use the following steps in writing an Assembler program.

1.   Have a clear idea of the problem that the program is to solve.
2.   Sketch out your ideas in general terms. First, plan the overall logic. For example, if a problem is to test multibyte move operations such as in Figure 5-5, start by defining the fields to be moved. Then plan the strategy for the Code Segment: a routine for initialization, a routine to use a Conditional Jump, and a routine to use a LOOP. The main logic routine could contain

> Initialize Stack and Segment registers
> Call Jump Routine
> Call Loop Routine
> Return

The Jump Routine could be planned as

> Initialize registers for count, addresses of names
> Loop: Move one character of name
> Increment for next characters of names
> Decrement count: If nonzero, Loop
>   If zero, Return

The Loop Routine could be sketched in a similar way. The above is a kind of pseudo-code that many programmers use to plan a program. Others use flowcharts and decision tables.

3.   Organize the program into logical units, such that related routines are done together. A Procedure that is about 25 lines (the size of the screen) is easier to debug.
4.   Use example programs as a guide. Attempts to memorize all the technical material and code "off the top of the head" often results in more program bugs (and who needs even more?).
5.   Use comments to clarify what a Procedure is supposed to accomplish, what arithmetic and comparison operations are performing, and what a seldom-used instruction is doing. (A good example of the latter is the XLAT instruction which you code with no operands.)
6.   For keying in the program, use a catalogued skeleton program that you can copy into a newly named file.

The remaining programs in this text make considerable use of the LEA instruction, the SI and DI index registers, and called Procedures. Having covered the basics of Assembler, you are now in a position for more advanced and realistic programming. Chapter 6 introduces some interesting features: displaying messages on the screen and accepting input from the keyboard.

KEY POINTS TO REMEMBER

☐ Labels within Procedures such as B20: require colons to indicate a NEAR label. Omission of the colon causes an assembly error.

☐ Labels for Conditional Jump and LOOP instructions must be within −128 to +127 bytes. The operand generates one byte of object code. Hex 01 to 7F covers the range from decimal +1 to +127, and hex FF to 80 covers the range from −1 to −128. Since machine instructions vary in length from one to four bytes, the limit is not obvious, but about two screens full of source code is a practical guide.

☐ For using the LOOP instruction, initialize the CX with a positive number. LOOP checks for only a zero value, so if CX is negative, the program will continue looping.

☐ When an instruction sets a flag, the flag remains set until another instruction changes it. For example, you could perform an arithmetic operation that sets flags and if the operation is immediately followed by MOV instructions, the flags remain unchanged. However, to minimize bugs, code a Conditional Jump instruction immediately following the instruction that set the flag.

☐ Select the appropriate Conditional Jump instructions depending on whether the operation processes signed or unsigned data.

☐ Always CALL a Procedure, and always include RET for returning. A called Procedure may call other Procedures, and if you follow the conventions, RET will cause the correct address in the Stack to pop.

☐ Be careful when using indexed operands. In the following moves,

```
MOV    AX,SI
MOV    AX,[SI]
```

the first MOV moves the contents of the SI register. The second MOV uses the offset address in the SI to access memory.

☐ Use shift instructions to double and halve values, but be sure to select the appropriate instruction for unsigned and signed data.

QUESTIONS

5-1. What is the maximum number of bytes that a near JMP, a LOOP, and a Conditional Jump instruction may jump? What characteristic of the operand causes this limit?

5-2. A JMP instruction begins at hex location 0438. Determine the transfer address based on the following object code for the JMP operand: (a) 25, (b) 7A, (c) D3.

5-3. Code a routine using LOOP that calculates the Fibonacci series: 1, 1, 2, 3, 5, 8, 13, ... (each number is the sum of the preceding two numbers). Set the limit for 12 loops. Assemble, link, and use DEBUG to trace.

5-4. Assume that AX and BX contain signed data and that CX and DX contain unsigned data. Determine the CMP (where necessary) and Conditional Jump instructions for the following:

(a) Does the CX value exceed the DX?

(b) Does the AX value exceed the BX?

(c) Does the CX contain zero?

(d) Was there an overflow?

(e) Is the AX equal to or smaller than the BX?

(f) Is the CX equal to or smaller than the DX?

5-5. In the following, what flags are affected and what would they contain?

(a) An overflow occurred.

(b) A result is negative.

(c) A result is zero.

(d) Processing is in single-step mode.

(e) A string data transfer is to be right to left.

5-6. Refer to Figure 5-4. What would be the effect on program execution if the Procedure BEGIN did not contain a RET?

5-7. What is the difference between coding a PROC operand with FAR and with NEAR?

5-8. What are the ways in which a program can begin executing a Procedure?

5-9. In a program, A10 calls B10, B10 calls C10, and C10 calls D10. Other than the initial return address to DOS, how many addresses does the Stack contain?

5-10. Assume that the DX contains 1110 0011 and that a location named BOOLA contains 0111 1001. Determine the effect on the DX for the following: (a) XOR DX,BOOLA (b) AND DX,BOOLA (c) OR DX,BOOLA (d) AND DX,00000000B (e) XOR DX,11111111B.

5-11. Revise the program in Figure 5-6 as follows: (a) define the contents of TITLEX as uppercase letters; (b) convert uppercase to lowercase.

5-12. Assume that the BX contains binary 10111001 and the CL contains 03. Determine the contents of the BX after the following unrelated instructions: (a) SHR BX,1 (b) SHR BX,CL (c) SHL BX,CL (d) SHL BL,1 (e) ROR BX,CL (f) ROR BL,CL (g) SAL BH,1.

6

SCREEN PROCESSING I:
BASIC FEATURES

Objective:
To cover the requirements for
displaying information on the screen
and accepting input from the
keyboard.

INTRODUCTION

Up to this point, programs have processed data that is defined within an
instruction operand (immediate data) or in the Data Segment. The number
of practical applications for programs that process only defined data is few
indeed. Most programs require data from an input device, such as a terminal
or a diskette. Further, a program must provide answers in a useful format.
For example, output may be on a printer or on a screen, or on a diskette if it
is to be preserved. For the screen and keyboard, all data is in ASCII format.

In Assembler, the INT (Interrupt) instruction performs input and output. There are various requirements for telling the system whether processing is to be input or output, and on what device. This chapter covers the
basic requirements for displaying information on the screen and for accepting input from the keyboard.

The material in this chapter is suitable for both black and white (BW)
and color video monitors. Chapter 7 covers more advanced screen-handling

features and the use of color for graphics display. Users of CP/M should examine the section CP/M DIFFERENCES near the end of this chapter.

THE INTERRUPT INSTRUCTION: INT

You can perform all required screen/keyboard operations by the use of an INT 10H instruction that transfers control directly to BIOS. However, to facilitate some of the more complex operations, there is a higher level of interrupt, INT 21H, that transfers control to DOS. For example, input from the keyboard requires a count of the characters entered, a check against a maximum number of characters, and a check for the return character. The DOS INT 21H operation handles much of this additional processing and then transfers automatically to BIOS.

The INT instruction interrupts the processing of a program, transfers to DOS or to BIOS for specified action, and returns to the program to continue processing. Most often, an interrupt is to perform an input or output operation. All interrupts require a trail for exiting from your program and for returning. For this purpose, INT performs the following:

☐ Decrements the Stack Pointer by 2 and pushes the Flags register onto the Stack.
☐ Clears the TF and IF flags.
☐ Decrements the Stack Pointer by 2 and pushes the CS register onto the Stack.
☐ Decrements the Stack Pointer by 2 and pushes the Instruction Pointer onto the Stack.
☐ Causes the required operation to be performed.
☐ Pops the registers off the Stack and returns to the instruction following the INT.

This process is entirely automatic, and your only concern is to ensure that the Stack Segment is large enough for the necessary pushing and popping.

The two types of interrupts that this chapter covers are the BIOS operation INT 10H for all screen and keyboard processing and the DOS operation INT 21H for displaying output and accepting input.

SETTING THE CURSOR

The screen is a grid of addressable locations and the cursor can be set at any of them. A typical video monitor, for example, has 25 rows (numbered 0 to 24) and 80 columns (numbered 0 to 79). Some examples of cursor locations follow:

Location	Decimal format Row	Column	Hex format Row	Column
Upper left corner	00	00	00	00
Upper right corner	00	79	00	4F
Center of screen	12	39/40	0C	27/28
Lower left corner	24	00	18	00
Lower right corner	24	79	18	4F

You can use INT 10H to set the cursor at any location on the screen or to clear all or any portion of the screen. The following example sets the cursor to row 05 and column 12:

```
MOV   AH,02      ;Request set cursor
MOV   BH,00      ;Screen #0
MOV   DH,05      ;Row to 05
MOV   DL,12      ;Column to 12
INT   10H        ;Interrupt -- exit to BIOS
```

The value 02 in the AH notifies BIOS to set the cursor. The row and column must be in the DX register, and the screen (or "page") number, normally 0, is in the BH. The content of the other registers is not important. You could also set the row and column with one MOV instruction using an immediate hex value as

MOV DX,050CH.

CLEARING THE SCREEN

Typically, prompts and commands stay on the screen until scrolled up and off. When your program starts executing, you may want the screen cleared. You can clear beginning at any location and ending at any higher numbered location. Insert the starting row/column in the DX, the value 07 in the BH, and 0600H in the AX. The following example clears the entire screen:

```
MOV   AX,0600H   ;AH 06 (scroll), AL 00 (full screen)
MOV   BH,07      ;Normal attribute (black & white)
MOV   CX,0000    ;Upper left row/col
MOV   DX,184FH   ;Lower right row/col
INT   10H        ;Interrupt - - exit to BIOS
```

This operation *scrolls* the full screen to blank; the next chapter describes scrolling in more detail. If by mistake you set the lower right location higher than hex 184F, the operation wraps around the screen and clears some locations twice. Although the action causes no harm, it does involve more execute time.

DISPLAYING ON THE SCREEN

A program often has to display messages indicating completion or errors detected or prompts to the user requesting data or action to take. This process, as shown next, requires defining a prompt message in the Data Segment, setting the AH register to 09, and issuing a DOS INT 21H instruction. The operation recognizes the end of a message by a dollar sign ($) delimiter, as shown next:

```
DATASEG    SEGMENT   PARA
NAMPRMP    DB        'Customer name?','$'
             •
             •
DATASEG    ENDS

;------------------------------------------------
CODESEG    SEGMENT   PARA
           LEA       DX,NAMPRMP      ;Load address of prompt
           MOV       AH,09           ;Set display function
           INT       21H             ;DOS Interrupt
```

The dollar sign delimiter can be coded inside the prompt as 'Customer name?$', immediately following as shown above, or on the next line of code as DB '$'.

The LEA instruction loads the address of NAMPRMP into the DX register. This address enables BIOS to locate the information that is to display. Technically, LEA loads the offset address of NAMPRMP, and BIOS uses the address in the DS register plus the DX (DS:DX) for the actual memory address.

PROGRAM: DISPLAYING THE ASCII CHARACTER SET

Most of the 256 ASCII characters are represented by a symbol that can display on the video screen. Hex 00 and FF have no symbol and display as blank, although the true ASCII blank character is hex 20.

The program in Figure 6-1 displays the entire range of ASCII characters. The program calls three Procedures: B10CLR, C10SET, and D10DISP. B10CLR clears the screen and C10SET initializes the cursor to 00,00. Procedure D10DISP displays the contents of CTR which is initialized to hex 00 and is successively incremented for each display until reaching hex FF.

Figure 6-1 Displaying the ASCII Character Set.

```
           page      60,132
  TITLE    EXALLASC Display all ASCII characters 00-FF
  STACKSG  SEGMENT PARA STACK 'STACK`
           DW        32 DUP(?)
  STACKSG  ENDS

  DATASG   SEGMENT PARA 'DATA'
  CTR      DB        00,'$'
  DATASG   ENDS

  CODESG   SEGMENT PARA 'CODE'
  BEGIN    PROC    FAR
           ASSUME  CS:CODESG,DS:DATASG,SS:STACKSG,ES:NOTHING
           PUSH    DS
           SUB     AX,AX
           PUSH    AX
           MOV     AX,DATASG
           MOV     DS,AX

           CALL    B10CLR          ;Clear screen
           CALL    C10SET          ;Set cursor
           CALL    D10DISP         ;Display chars
           RET
  BEGIN    ENDP
  ;                 Clear screen:
  ;                 ------------
  B10CLR   PROC
           MOV     CX,0000         ;Upper left location
           MOV     DX,184FH        ;Lower right location
           MOV     BH,07
           MOV     AX,0600H
           INT     10H
           RET
  B10CLR   ENDP
  ;                 Set cursor to 00,00:
  ;                 -------------------
  C10SET   PROC
           MOV     DX,0000
           MOV     BH,00
           MOV     AH,02
           INT     10H
           RET
  C10SET   ENDP
  ;                 Display ASCII characters:
  ;                 ------------------------
  D10DISP  PROC
           MOV     CX,256          ;Init'ze for 256 iterations
           LEA     DX,CTR          ;Init'ze address of CTR
  D20:
           MOV     AH,09           ;Display ASCII char
           INT     21H
           INC     CTR             ;Increment CTR
           LOOP    D20.            ;Decr CX, loop if nonzero
           RET                     ;Terminate
  D10DISP  ENDP
  ;
  CODESG   ENDS
           END     BEGIN
```

The only problem is that the characters between hex 08 and hex 0D are special "forms control characters" for backspacing, and so forth, that cause the cursor to move. If you use Ctrl/PrtSc for a printout, these characters also cause some printer movement. *Suggestion:* Reproduce the program as it stands, assemble it, and link it. Then run it by keying in the name of the EXE module, such as B:ASCII.EXE. (If you run the program under DEBUG, the trace follows the INT instructions through BIOS.)

On the screen output, the first line begins with a blank character (hex 00), two "happy faces" (hex 01 and 02), and then a heart, a diamond, and a club (hex 03, 04, and 05). Hex 07 causes the buzzer to sound. Hex 06 would have been a spade but the control characters hex 08 through 0D erased it. In fact, hex 0D caused a "carriage return" to the start of the next line. The musical note is hex 0E. The characters above hex 7F include graphics symbols.

You can change the program to bypass the control characters. The following section of code bypasses all characters between hex 08 and 0D; you may want to experiment with bypassing only, say, hex 08 (backspace) and 0D (carriage return).

```
          CMP   CTR,08H   ;Lower than 08?
          JB    D30       ;Yes -- accept
          CMP   CTR,0DH   ;Lower/equal 0D?
          JBE   D40       ;Yes -- bypass
    D30:
          MOV   AH,09     ;Display < 08
          INT   21H       ;    and > 0D
    D40:
          INC   CTR
```

Like living dangerously? Before running this revised version, press Ctrl/PrtSc to print the characters. Most printers will reproduce many of the special characters as blank.

ACCEPTING INPUT FROM THE KEYBOARD

If a program displays a message or a prompt, then to receive a reply from the keyboard, the program must supply another interrupt. The procedure is similar to that for displaying output. However, the input area requires additional definitions. First, the operation needs to know the maximum length of the input reply. The purpose is to warn users who key in a reply that is too long; the operation sounds the buzzer and will not accept additional characters. Second, the input operation returns the length in bytes of the reply. Although this feature is trivial for YES and NO type of replies, it is very useful for replies with variable length such as names, and programs in this book make much use of it.

Basically, the input area is a *parameter list* containing specified fields that the INT operation is to process. The following defines a parameter list in the Data Segment for an input area that is suitable for the ASM Assembler and will also work for the MASM version. LABEL is a Pseudo-op with the type attribute of BYTE.

```
NAMEPAR   LABEL   BYTE        ;Start of parameter list
MAXLEN    DB      20          ;Max length of input name
ACTLEN    DB      ?           ;Actual length
NAMEFLD   DB      20 DUP(' ') ;Name entered from keyboard
          DB      '$'         ;Input delimiter
```

MASM can also use the STRUC Pseudo-op to define a parameter list as a Structure. However, since references to names defined within a Structure require special addressing, our discussion will delay this topic until Chapter 18, "Assembler Pseudo-op Reference."

In a parameter list, all of the names may be any valid Assembler label. You have to load the address of the parameter list (NAMEPAR in the example) into the DX register, move the value 10 (hex 0AH) into the AH register, and issue an INT 21H as follows:

```
MOV   AH,0AH         ;Request input function
LEA   DX,NAMEPAR     ;Load address of para list
INT   21H            ;Interrupt
```

The INT operation waits for the user to enter characters and checks that the number of characters entered does not exceed the maximum in the parameter list (20 in the example). The user signals the end of an entry by pressing the return key (hex 0D). This return character also enters the input field (named NAMEFLD in the examples). Therefore, if you key in a name such as WALDO (return), the parameter list will appear as follows:

```
decimal: | 20 |  5 | W | A | L | D | O | # |    |    |    |    | ...
hex:     | 14 | 05 | 57| 41| 4C| 44| 4F| 0D| 20 | 20 | 20 | 20 | ...
```

The operation delivers the length of the input name, 5, into the second byte of the parameter list, named ACTLEN in the examples. The return character is at NAMEFLD+5. The # symbol here is to indicate this character, although hex 0D has no printable symbol. Since the maximum length of 20 includes the hex 0D, the actual name may be only 19 characters long.

The next sections discuss a few features about the input field to keep in mind when programming.

Clearing the Return Character

You can use an input value for various purposes, such as printing on reports, storing in a table, or writing on disk. For these purposes, you may have to replace the return character (hex 0D) with a blank (hex 20). The position of the return character is somewhere in NAMEFLD. The field containing the actual length, ACTLEN, provides its relative position, at NAMEFLD + 5. You can move this length into the BX register and use the BX for indexing the address of NAMEFLD as follows:

```
MOV    BH,00                ;Set BX
MOV    BL,ACTLEN            ;  to 00 05
MOV    NAMEFLD[BX],20H      ;Clear ret char to blank
```

The third MOV instruction involves moving a blank (hex 20) to the address specified in the first operand: the address of NAMEFLD plus the contents of BX, in effect, NAMEFLD + 5. Another way to code this instruction is

```
MOV    NAMEFLD[BX],' '    ;Clear ret char to blank
```

You could use this technique to move any character. For example, if you want to replace the return character with the bell character (hex 07) so that the buzzer sounds when you display the name, code the following:

```
MOV    NAMEFLD[BX],07H
```

Entering Only the Return Character

If you key in a name that exceeds the maximum in the parameter list, the buzzer sounds and the operation will accept only the return character. But what happens if you key in no name but only the return character? In this case, the operation accepts the return character and inserts a length of zero in the parameter list, as follows:

Parameter list (hex): |14|00|0D|...

This feature is useful where a program loops repetitively accepting names. On a prompt for name, to signify the end of input data, a user can simply press return. The program compares for a zero length and jumps to another routine if the length is zero, as follows:

```
CMP    ACTLEN,00              ;No name entered?
JZ     label                 ;Yes - - jump elsewhere
```

Clearing the Input Field

The preceding examples initialized NAMEFLD with blanks. Once you reply, however, the name replaces the blanks, and these characters remain in NAMEFLD until other characters replace them. Assume the following successive input after clearing the return character:

Input	NAMEPAR (hex)											
1. WALDO	14	05	57	41	4C	44	4F	20	20	20	20	...	20
2. MARTINEZ	14	08	4D	41	52	54	49	4E	45	5A	20	...	20
3. JONES	14	05	4A	4F	4E	45	53	20	45	5A	20	...	20

The name MARTINEZ replaces the shorter name WALDO. However, since the name JONES is shorter than MARTINEZ, it replaces MARTI and the return character (cleared to blank) replaces the N. The remaining letters, EZ, still follow JONES. Therefore, it is a useful practice to clear NAMEFLD prior to prompting for a name as follows:

```
        MOV    CX,20                  ;Init'ze for 20 loops
        MOV    SI,0000                ;Start position for name
B30:
        MOV    NAMEFLD[SI],20H        ;One blank to name
        INC    SI                     ;Incr for next char
        LOOP   B30                    ;20 times
```

Instead of the SI register, you could use DI or BX. A more efficient method that moves a *word* of two blanks requires only ten loops. The problem is that NAMEFLD is defined as DB (byte). Consequently, you have to override this length with a WORD and PTR (pointer) operand as the following indicates:

```
        MOV    CX,10                  ;Init'ze for 10 loops
        LEA    SI,NAMEFLD             ;Init'ze start of name
B30:
        MOV    WORD PTR[SI],2020H     ;Two blanks to name
        INC    SI                     ;Incr 2 positions
        INC    SI                     ;    in name
        LOOP   B30                    ;Loop 10 times
```

Interpret the MOV at B30 as Move a blank word to where the address in the SI register points. This example uses an LEA instruction to initialize and uses a slightly different method for the MOV at B30 because you cannot code an instruction such as

MOV WORD PTR[NAMEFLD],2020H   ;Invalid

PROGRAM: ACCEPTING AND DISPLAYING NAMES

The program in Figure 6-2 combines all the preceding material. The example requests that the user enter a name, then displays the name on the center of the screen and rings the bell. The program continues accepting and displaying names in this fashion until the user replies to a prompt with just the return key.

The only new material is in the Procedure E10CENT that determines the location on row 12 for centering the name. Assume that an input name is DAN SMITH. The "actual length" delivered to the parameter list is 09. The fifth character (S) is to be centered on row 12 at column 40. The starting position on the row is calculated by the following two steps:

1. Divide the length 09 by 2 = 4
2. Subtract this value from 40 = 36

Set the cursor at row 12, column 36. The name appears on the screen as follows:

Row 12:   DAN   SMITH
            | |
Column: 36   40

The SHR instruction shifts the length 09 one bit to the right, effectively dividing it by 2. Bits 00001001 become 00000100. The NEG instruction reverses the sign, changing +4 to −4. ADD adds the value 40, giving the starting position, 36, in the DL register for the column.

Note that the program could eliminate the Procedure F10CLNM for blanking the name. Replace the instruction following A30: that inserts the bell (07) character with a dollar delimiter character:

MOV   NAMEFLD[BX],'$'

The Procedure E10CENT will then display the name only up to the delimiter.

Figure 6-2 Accepting and Displaying Names.

```
          page     60,132
TITLE     CTRNAME  Accept input names & center on screen

STACKSG SEGMENT PARA STACK 'STACK'
          DW       32 DUP(?)
STACKSG ENDS
;----------------------------------------------------------
DATASG  SEGMENT PARA 'DATA'
NAMEPAR LABEL    BYTE                ;Start of Name parameter list
MAXNLEN DB       20                  ;Max. length of name
ACTNLEN DB       ?                   ;No. chars entered
NAMEFLD DB       20 DUP(' '),'$'     ;Name & delimiter

PROMPT  DB       'Name?','$'
DATASG  ENDS
;----------------------------------------------------------
CODESG  SEGMENT PARA 'CODE'
BEGIN     PROC    FAR
          ASSUME  CS:CODESG,DS:DATASG,SS:STACKSG,ES:DATASG
          PUSH    DS
          SUB     AX,AX
          PUSH    AX
          MOV     AX,DATASG
          MOV     DS,AX
          MOV     ES,AX
          CALL    Q10CLR
A20LOOP:
          MOV     DX,0000             ;Set cursor to 00,00
          CALL    Q20CURS
          CALL    B10PRMP             ;Display prompt
          CALL    D10INPT             ;Provide for input of name
          CALL    Q10CLR
          CMP     ACTNLEN,00          ;No name? (indicates end)
          JNE     A30
          RET                         ;If so, return to DOS
A30:
          MOV     BH,00               ;Replace return char (0D)
          MOV     BL,ACTNLEN          ; with bell (07)
          MOV     NAMEFLD[BX],07H
          CALL    E10CENT             ;Center & display name
          CALL    F10CLNM             ;Clear name
          JMP     A20LOOP
BEGIN     ENDP
;                  Display prompt:
;                  --------------
B10PRMP PROC     NEAR
          LEA     DX,PROMPT
          MOV     AH,09               ;Request display
          INT     21H
          RET
B10PRMP ENDP

;                  Accept input of name:
;                  --------------------
D10INPT PROC     NEAR
          LEA     DX,NAMEPAR
          MOV     AH,0AH              ;Request input
          INT     21H
          RET
D10INPT ENDP
```

```
;                        Center & display name:
;                        ----------------------
E10CENT PROC    NEAR
        MOV     DL,ACTNLEN        ;Locate center column:
        SHR     DL,1              ;  Divide length by 2
        NEG     DL                ;  Reverse sign
        ADD     DL,40             ;  Add 40
        MOV     DH,12             ;Center row
        CALL    Q20CURS           ;Set cursor
        MOV     AH,09
        LEA     DX,NAMEFLD        ;Display name
        INT     21H
        RET
E10CENT ENDP
;                        Clear name:
;                        ----------
F10CLNM PROC    NEAR
        MOV     CX,20             ;Init'ze 20 loops
        MOV     SI,0000
F20:
        MOV     NAMEFLD[SI],20H   ;Store blank
        INC     SI                ;Increment next pos'n
        LOOP    F20
        RET
F10CLNM ENDP
;                        Clear screen:
;                        ------------
Q10CLR  PROC    NEAR
        MOV     AX,0600H          ;Request scroll screen
        MOV     BH,07             ;Normal
        MOV     CX,0000           ;From 00,00
        MOV     DX,184FH          ;To 24,79
        INT     10H               ;Call BIOS
        RET
Q10CLR  ENDP
;                        Set cursor row/col according to DX:
;                        ----------------------------------
Q20CURS PROC    NEAR
        MOV     AH,02             ;Request set cursor
        MOV     BH,00             ;Page #0
        INT     10H               ;Call BIOS
        RET
Q20CURS ENDP

CODESG  ENDS
        END     BEGIN
```

CP/M DIFFERENCES

Intel reserves interrupt 224 for CP/M-86 to enter BDOS (Basic Disk Operating System). Although there are technical differences, the CP/M operation is similar to DOS INT 21H. You have to insert a function code in the CL register, as well as values in the DL or DX depending on the operation.

Display a String on the Screen

The display operation is similar to its DOS counterpart. Define a string to be displayed in the Data Segment and follow its definition with a dollar sign ($). Load the address of the string in the DX register.

```
            MOV    CL,09H            ;Request display
            LEA    DX,MESSGE         ;Address of message
            INT    224               ;Call BDOS
            •
            •
            •
  MESSGE    DB     'CP/M-86 Display'
            DB     '$'
```

Accept Input From the Keyboard

The input operation is also similar to its DOS counterpart. Define an input area with a byte that contains the maximum length of the input string, then a byte that the operation fills to indicate the actual number of bytes entered, and an area for the input string itself.

```
            MOV    CL,0AH            ;Request keyboard input
            LEA    DX,INNAME         ;Address of input area
            INT    224               ;Call BDOS
            •
            •
            •
  INNAME    DB     20                ;Max. length of input
  ACTLEN    RB                       ;Actual length of input
  NAMEFLD   RB     20                ;The input string
```

Other CP/M operations are available in Appendix D of the manual. You should also examine the ESC instruction codes in Appendix F that handle control of the cursor. For example, the ESC operation to clear the screen is ESC E.

KEY POINTS TO REMEMBER

☐   INT 10H is the instruction that links to BIOS for keyboard and display operations. INT 21H is a special DOS operation that handles some of the complexity of input/output.

☐   Be consistent in using hex notation. For example, INT 21 is not the same as INT 21H.

☐   Be careful to enter the correct values in the AX, BX, CX, and DX registers depending on the video operation.

☐   When using INT 21H be sure to define a delimiter ($) immediately following the input or output field. Be careful when clearing the field not to clear the delimiter as well. A missing delimiter on a display operation can cause spectacular effects on the screen!

☐   For input, define the parameter list carefully. The INT 21H operation expects the first byte to contain a maximum value and automatically inserts an actual value in the second byte.

QUESTIONS

6-1. A 40-column screen has columns numbered 0 through 39. What is the hex value for 39?

6-2. Code the instructions to set the cursor to row 15, column 5.

6-3. Code the instructions to clear the screen beginning at row 10, column 0, through row 20, column 79.

6-4. Code the Data Segment and Code Segment to display a message "What is the Date (mm/dd/yy)?." Follow the message with a buzzer sound and a delimiter.

6-5. Code the Data Segment and Code Segment to accept the data from the keyboard according to the format in Question 6-4.

6-6. Key in the program in Figure 6-2 with the following changes:

(a) Instead of clearing the input name field to blank, set it to hex B2's.

(b) Instead of row 12, center at row 10.

(c) Instead of clearing the entire screen, clear only rows 0 through 10. Assemble, link, and test.

7

SCREEN PROCESSING II:
ADVANCED FEATURES

Objective:
To cover the more advanced
features of screen handling,
including scrolling, reverse video,
blinking, and color graphics.

INTRODUCTION

Chapter 6 introduced some of the basic features concerned with screen handling. This chapter provides all the more advanced features related to scrolling the screen and setting an *attribute byte* for underlining, blinking, and high intensity. Other advanced features include *graphics mode* on color monitors.

The material in the first section on BIOS interrupt 10 is suitable for both monochrome and color displays. The chapter then introduces the use of color for both text (normal character display) and for graphics. Users of monochrome displays can skip this section entirely.

A Motorola 6485 CRT Controller controls both the monochrome and the color/graphics adapter. However, the two adapters are different and fit into their own expansion slot.

Monochrome Display

The monochrome display supports 4K bytes of memory (display buffer) starting at address hex B0000. This memory provides for:

☐   2K bytes of 25 rows and 80 columns of characters.
☐   2K bytes for an attribute for each character that specifies reverse video, blinking, high intensity, and underlining.

Color/Graphics Display

The color/graphics display supports 16K bytes of memory (display buffer) starting at address hex B8000. This display can operate in either color or BW. Color/graphics display also has modes for *text* display (normal ASCII characters) and for *graphics*.

The 16K byte display buffer provides for screen "pages" numbered 0 through 3 for an 80-column screen and 0 through 7 for a 40-column screen. The normal default page number is 0, but you may format any of the pages in memory. This feature enables you to display one screen while formatting another screen internally. In this way, you can flip/flop pages for simulating motion and for animation. A later section, COLOR/GRAPHICS, covers color video and graphics in detail.

Users of CP/M should examine Appendix F of their manual for the use of the ESC instruction to set colors.

ATTRIBUTE BYTE

An attribute byte for both monochrome and color (in text, not graphics mode) determines the characteristics of each displayed character. The attribute byte provides the following features:

Bit no.:	7	6	5	4	3	2	1	0
Attribute:	BL	R	G	B	I	R	G	B
		Background				Foreground		

The letters RGB each represent a bit position and technically stand for red, green, and blue for a color monitor. Bit 7 (BL) sets blinking, and bit 3 (I) sets high intensity. For normal purposes, on an IBM monochrome monitor, the foreground is green and the background is black, although this chapter will refer to the display as black and white (BW). You may combine these attributes to modify them as follows:

Function	Background RGB	Foreground RGB
Nondisplay	000	000
Underline (not for color)	000	001
Normal video: white on black	000	111
Reverse video: black on white	111	000

Color monitors do not provide for underlining; instead, the bit value selects the blue color as foreground, thereby displaying blue on black. Let's examine some typical attributes:

Binary	Hex	Effect
0000 0000	00	No display (for secret passwords?)
0000 0111	07	Normal white on black
1000 0111	87	Normal white on black, blinking
0000 1111	0F	White on black, intense
0111 0000	70	Reverse black on white
1111 0000	F0	Reverse black on white, blinking

These attributes are valid for character display in both monochrome and color. A later section in this chapter, "Color/Graphics," explains how to select specific colors. You can generate a screen attribute through INT 10H instructions with the BL containing the required attribute and the AH containing either 06 (scroll up), 07 (scroll down), 08 (read attribute/character), or 09 (write attribute/character). If you happen to set the attribute to hex 00, the character doesn't display at all – a most disconcerting situation! When a program sets an attribute, it remains set until another operation changes it.

BIOS INTERRUPT 10

INT 10H facilitates full screen handling. Insert in the AH register a code that determines the function of the interrupt as follows:

AH = 00: Set Mode.   This is an operation that you could use if you have a color monitor and switch between text and graphics, or if you are writing software for unknown video monitors. You can first use the BIOS INT 11H operation to determine the device attached to the system; the operation returns a value to the AX and bits 5 and 4 indicate the video mode:

> 00—Unused
> 01—40 × 25 BW using a color card
> 10—80 × 25 BW using a color card
> 11—80 × 25 BW using a BW card

Having determined the video mode, you can set the mode for the program using INT 10H with the AH set to 00 and the AL set as follows:

0	40 x 25 BW
1	40 x 25 color text
2	80 x 25 BW (standard monochrome)
3	80 x 25 color text
4	320 x 200 color graphics
5	320 x 200 BW graphics
6	640 x 200 BW graphics

The following example sets the video mode:

```
MOV   AH,00        ;Request set mode
MOV   AL,03        ;80 x 25 color text
INT   10H          ;Call BIOS
```

AH = 01: Set Cursor Type.   The cursor is not part of the ASCII character set. The computer maintains its own hardware for its control, and there are special INT operations for its use. The normal cursor symbol is similar to an underline or break character. You can use INT 10H to adjust its size vertically. Set the CH (bits 4-0) for the top ("start scan line") and the CL (bits 4-0) for the bottom ("end scan line"). You can adjust the size between the top and bottom; for example, to enlarge the cursor from its top position (0) to its bottom position (12):

```
MOV   AH,01        ;Request set type
MOV   CH,00        ;Start scan line
MOV   CL,12        ;End scan line
INT   10H          ;Call BIOS
```

The cursor now blinks as a solid rectangle. You can adjust its size anywhere between these bounds, such as 04/08, 03/10, and so forth. The cursor remains at this type until another operation changes it. You can return it to its normal setting using 11/12.

AH = 02: Set Cursor Position.   This is an important operation for cursor control. Set the AH to 02, the BH to page number, and the DX to row/column:

```
MOV   AH,02        ;Request move cursor
MOV   BH,00        ;Page #0
MOV   DX,row/col   ;Row and column
INT   10H          ;Call BIOS
```

AH = 03: Read the Current Cursor Location.   A program can determine the present location of the cursor as follows:

```
MOV   AH,03        ;Request cursor location
MOV   BH,00        ;Set page #0
INT   10H          ;Call BIOS
```

AH = 04: Read Light Pen Position.   For use with graphics, this operation returns the following:

AH   = 0 if the light pen switch is not down or not triggered,
            or 1 if valid
BX   = pixel column
CH   = raster line
DH/DL   = row/column of light pen position

AH = 05: Select an Active Page.   For color text mode, set a new page as follows:

```
MOV   AH,05        ;Request
MOV   AL,page#     ;page no.
INT   10H          ;Call BIOS
```

AH = 06: Scroll Up the Screen.   When a program displays down the screen past the bottom, the next line wraps around to start at the top. But even if the interrupt operation specifies column 0, the new lines are indented, and succeeding lines display from this column. When these lines pass the bottom of the screen, they also resume at the top, but are further indented. By this point, the screen contents are badly skewed. An operation to clear the screen may still leave the cursor indented. The solution is to "scroll" the screen.

Earlier you used code 06 to clear the screen. Setting the AL to 00 causes a scroll up of the entire screen, effectively clearing it to blank. Inserting a nonzero value in the AL causes that number of lines to scroll up. Top lines scroll off and blank lines appear at the bottom. The following instructions scroll up the entire screen one line:

```
MOV   AX,0601H     ;Scroll up one line
MOV   BH,07        ;Normal video attribute
MOV   CX,0000      ;From 00,00
MOV   DX,184FH     ;to 24,79
INT   10H          ;Call BIOS to scroll
```

To change the scroll to any value, simply insert the value in the AL. The BH contains the attribute for normal or reverse video, blinking, and so forth. The CX and DX registers permit scrolling any portion of the screen.

AH = 07: Scroll Down the Screen.   Scrolling down the screen causes the bottom lines to scroll off and blank lines to appear at the top. Set the AH to 07 and set the other registers just as for code 06, scroll down.

Scrolling up and down the screen is particularly useful for screen editing and word-processing programs.

AH = 08: Read Attribute/Character at Current Cursor Position.   Use the following instructions to read both character and attribute:

```
MOV   AH,08        ;Request read attrib/char
MOV   BH,00        ;Page #0
INT   10H          ;Call BIOS
```

The operation returns the character in the AL and its attribute in the AH. Since this operation reads one character at a time from the keyboard, you will have to code a loop to read more than one character.

AH = 09: Write Attribute/Character at Current Cursor Position.   Here's a fun operation: Use it to display characters with blinking, reverse video, and all that, as follows:

```
MOV   AH,09              ;Request display
MOV   AL,char-to-display
MOV   BH,page#           ;Page # (for color text)
MOV   BL,attribute       ;Attribute
MOV   CX,repetition      ;No. of repeated chars.
INT   10H                ;Call BIOS
```

The entry in the AL is the single character that is to display; to display more than one requires a loop. The entry in the CX determines the number of times to repetitively display the character in the AL. The operation does not advance the cursor. For example, to display five blinking hearts with reverse video, code

```
MOV   AH,09        ;Request display
MOV   AL,03H       ;Heart
MOV   BH,00        ;Page #0
MOV   BL,0F0H      ;Blink reverse video
MOV   CX,05        ;Five times
INT   10H          ;Call BIOS
```

To display a prompt or message, code a routine that sets the CX to 01 and loops to move one character at a time into the AL. But you won't be able to use the CX for a countdown of the loop. Also, when displaying each character, you have to advance the cursor to the next column (code 02). The program in Figure 7-1 in the next section provides an example.

AH = 10: Write a Character at the Current Cursor Position. The only difference between code 10 and code 09 is that code 10 does not set the attribute.

```
MOV   AH,10            ;Request write
MOV   AL,char          ;Character to display
MOV   BH,page#         ;Page # (for color text)
MOV   CX,repetition    ;No. of repeated chars.
INT   10H              ;Call BIOS
```

For most write purposes, the DOS operation INT 21H is more convenient.

AH = 11, 12, 13, and 14: Graphics Operations. A later section, "Color/ Graphics," covers these operations in detail.

PROGRAM: BLINKING, REVERSE VIDEO, AND SCROLLING

The program in Figure 7-1 accepts names from the keyboard and displays them on the screen. This program, however, displays the prompt with underlining, accepts the name normally, and displays the name at column 40 on the same row with blinking and reverse video. Following is somewhat the format, although the publishers inform me that they cannot get the printing to blink:

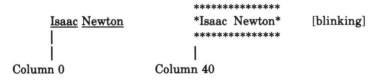

In order to control cursor placement, the program defines ROWCTR for the row and COLCTR for the column. For each new prompt it increments ROWCTR by 1. It uses COLCTR for moving the cursor horizontally when displaying the prompt and the name (INT 10H does not automatically advance the cursor). The program displays down the screen until it reaches row 20. From that point, it begins scrolling up one line for each additional prompt.

Figure 7-1 Blinking, Reverse Video, and Scrolling.

```
          page      60,132
TITLE     NMSCROLL Reverse video, blinking, and scrolling

STACKSG  SEGMENT PARA STACK 'STACK'
         DW       32 DUP(?)
STACKSG  ENDS

DATASG   SEGMENT PARA 'DATA'
NAMEPAR  LABEL    BYTE                  ;Start of Name parameter list
MAXNLEN  DB       20                    ;Max. length of name
ACTNLEN  DB       ?                     ;No. chars entered
NAMEFLD  DB       20 DUP(' '),'$'  ;Name

COLCTR   DB       00
COUNT    DB       ?
PROMPT   DB       'Name?','$'
ROWCTR   DB       00
DATASG   ENDS

CODESG   SEGMENT PARA 'CODE'
BEGIN    PROC     FAR
         ASSUME   CS:CODESG,DS:DATASG,SS:STACKSG,ES:DATASG
         PUSH     DS
         SUB      AX,AX
         PUSH     AX
         MOV      AX,DATASG
         MOV      DS,AX
         MOV      ES,AX
         CALL     Q10CLR
A20LOOP:
         MOV      COLCTR,00             ;Set column to 0
         CALL     Q20CURS
         CALL     B10PRMP               ;Display prompt
         CALL     D10INPT               ;Provide for input of name
         CMP      ACTNLEN,00            ;No name? (indicates end)
         JNE      A30
         CALL     Q10CLR                ;If so, clear screen,
         RET                            ;   terminate
A30:
         CALL     E10DISP               ;Display name
         JMP      A20LOOP
BEGIN    ENDP
;                 Display prompt:
;                 --------------
B10PRMP  PROC     NEAR
         LEA      SI,PROMPT             ;Set address of prompt
         MOV      COUNT,05
B20:
         MOV      AH,09                 ;Display code
         MOV      AL,[SI]               ;Get name character
         MOV      BH,00                 ;Page#
         MOV      BL,01H                ;Underline attribute
         MOV      CX,01                 ;One character
         INT      10H                   ;Display

         INC      SI                    ;Next char in name
         INC      COLCTR                ;Next column
         CALL     Q20CURS
         DEC      COUNT                 ;Countdown
         JNZ      B20                   ;Loop n times
         RET
```

```
                INT     10H
                RET
B10PRMP ENDP
;                       Accept input of name:
;                       ---------------------
D10INPT PROC    NEAR
                LEA     DX,NAMEPAR
                MOV     AH,0AH
                INT     21H
                RET
D10INPT ENDP
;                       Display name with blinking reverse video:
;                       ----------------------------------------
E10DISP PROC    NEAR
                LEA     SI,NAMEFLD      ;Initialize name
                MOV     COLCTR,40       ;Set screen column
E20:
                CALL    Q20CURS         ;Set cursor
                MOV     AH,09
                MOV     AL,[SI]         ;Get character
                MOV     BH,00
                MOV     BL,0F0H         ;Blink reverse video
                MOV     CX,01           ;One character
                INT     10H
                INC     SI              ;Next character in name
                INC     COLCTR          ;Next screen column
                DEC     ACTNLEN         ;Countdown name length
                JNZ     E20             ;Loop n times

                CMP     ROWCTR,20       ;Near bottom screen?
                JB      E30             ;No
                MOV     AX,0601H        ;Yes -
                MOV     BH,07           ;   scroll up
                MOV     CX,0000         ;   one
                MOV     DX,184FH        ;   line
                INT     10H
                MOV     ROWCTR,19
E30:    INC     ROWCTR
                RET
E10DISP ENDP
;                       Clear screen:
;                       ------------
Q10CLR  PROC    NEAR
                MOV     CX,0000
                MOV     DX,184FH
                MOV     BH,07
                MOV     AX,0600H
                INT     10H
                RET
Q10CLR  ENDP
;                       Set cursor row/col:
;                       ------------------
Q20CURS PROC    NEAR
                MOV     AH,02
                MOV     BH,00
                MOV     DH,ROWCTR
                MOV     DL,COLCTR
                INT     10H
                RET
Q20CURS ENDP

CODESG  ENDS
        END     BEGIN
```

For input, the Procedure D10INPT still uses the DOS operation INT 21H. To substitute with BIOS INT 10H, you would no longer require a parameter list. Instead:

1. Initialize a counter for the address of the input name and a counter for name length.
2. Execute an INT 10H with 08 in the AH and 00 in the BH. The operation returns each character to the AL.
3. If the AL does not contain the return character and the counter is at its maximum, ring the bell and exit.
4. Move the AL to the name field.
5. If the AL contains the return character, exit.
6. Increment the counter and the address of the name field.
7. Advance the cursor one column.
8. Loop back to point 2.

At the end of the loop, the name field contains the name and return character, and the counter contains the number of characters entered. Perhaps you would prefer to use INT 21H instead!

COMMENTS ON DISPLAYING

An inspection of the 256 ASCII characters reveals a lot of special characters used for graphics display. You can make good use of these characters for programs that display prompts, menus, and logos, and couple these with the screen display attribute. For example, you can draw a rectangle with solid lines using these characters:

Hex	Character
DA	Top left corner angle
BF	Top right corner angle
C0	Bottom left corner angle
D9	Bottom right corner angle
C4	Solid horizontal line
B3	Solid vertical line

The following code uses INT 10H to draw a solid horizontal line 25 positions long:

```
MOV   AH,09        ;Request display
MOV   AL,0C4H      ;Solid line
MOV   BH,00        ;Page #0
```

```
MOV    BL,0FH        ;Intense attribute
MOV    CX,25         ;25 repetitions
INT    10H           ;Call BIOS
```

Remember that the cursor does not advance. To draw a vertical line involves a loop that advances the cursor down one line and writes the hex B3 character. The "dots on" characters for shaded areas can also be very useful:

Hex	Character
B0	One-quarter dots on (light)
B1	One-half dots on (medium)
B2	Three-quarter dots on (dark)

You may also want to examine INT 16H in Chapter 17 on BIOS regarding checking if such keyboard entries as insert status, caps lock, and alt shift are pressed. You can derive many good ideas from examining the displays of professionally designed software, or, better yet, let your imagination dream up some original ideas.

COLOR/GRAPHICS

There are at least three types of video monitors used to display color graphics (in order of increasing cost and quality):

1. An unmodified color television. This is the common home TV set that many people use with their computer simply because it is available.
2. A composite video monitor. This type accepts a combined color signal without the radio frequency modulation used for its transmission over the airwaves and provides a superior image.
3. An RGB monitor. This type accepts three input signals that are sent to three separate electron guns – red, green, and blue, for each of the primary additive colors. Although more expensive, an RGB monitor provides the best quality image.

The color/graphics monitor adapter can operate a variety of BW or color monitors. There are three video interfaces: a composite video port, a direct drive port, and an interface for a user-supplied RF monitor. There are 16K bytes of color display memory beginning at address hex B8000, with 8K available for the characters and 8K for their attributes. When operating in 80 x 25 format, the adapter can store four pages of display screen; when operating in 40 x 25 format, the adapter can store eight pages. You can then display one page while processing another page.

The adapter has two basic modes of operation: *text* (or alphanumeric) and *graphics*, with additional modes possible between the two basic modes.

The normal default mode is text. You can set graphics mode or return to text mode using BIOS interrupt INT 10H:

Set 80 x 25 color text: Set medium resolution graphics:

MOV AH,00	MOV AH,00
MOV AL,03	MOV AL,04
INT 10H	INT 10H

TEXT (ALPHANUMERIC) MODE

Text mode is for normal processing of letters and numbers on the screen. Processing in text mode is similar for both BW and color; the main difference is the underline attribute.

The color/graphics adapter supports two text formats. The first format is suitable for color TV's and composite monitors and provides 25 rows of 40 columns. The second format is suitable for RGB monitors and supports 25 rows of 80 columns. When using text mode, you have access to the same 256 extended ASCII character set as the monochrome adapter. Each character can be one of 16 colors, and its background can be one of eight colors. You can also select one of 16 colors for the border.

Colors

The three basic colors are red, green, and blue. You can combine these to form a total of eight colors (including black and white), and can set high intensity for a total of 16 colors:

I R G B		I R G B	
0 0 0 0	black	1 0 0 0	gray
0 0 0 1	blue	1 0 0 1	light blue
0 0 1 0	green	1 0 1 0	light green
0 0 1 1	cyan	1 0 1 1	light cyan
0 1 0 0	red	1 1 0 0	light red
0 1 0 1	magenta	1 1 0 1	light magenta
0 1 1 0	brown	1 1 1 0	yellow
0 1 1 1	white	1 1 1 1	high-intensity white

Foreground (the actual displayed character) can consist of all 16 colors. Background to a displayed character can consist of only the first eight colors. Note that if foreground and background are the same color, the displayed character is invisible. You can also use the attribute byte to cause the foreground character to blink.

Attribute Byte

Text mode involves use of the attribute byte discussed earlier. In the following picture of the attribute byte, RGB means, respectively, red, green, and blue, BL means blinking, and I means high intensity:

Bit no.:	7	6	5	4	3	2	1	0
Attribute:	BL	R	G	B	I	R	G	B
		Background				Foreground		

Blinking and intensity apply to foreground. The following are some typical attributes:

Bit:	7	6	5	4	3	2	1	0		
	BL	R	G	B	I	R	G	B	Hex	
	0	0	0	0	0	0	0	0	00	Black on black
	0	0	0	0	0	0	0	1	01	Blue on black
	0	0	0	1	0	1	0	0	14	Red on blue
	0	0	1	0	0	0	1	1	23	Cyan on green
	0	1	1	1	1	1	0	1	7D	Light magenta on white
	1	0	1	0	1	0	0	0	A8	Gray on green, blinking

You can use the attribute byte the same way as was shown for a BW monitor. For example, to display five asterisks as light green on magenta, blinking:

```
MOV   AH,09        ;Request display
MOV   AL,'*'       ;Asterisk
MOV   BH,00        ;Page #0
MOV   BL,0DAH      ;Color attribute
MOV   CX,05        ;Five times
INT   10H          ;Call BIOS
```

GRAPHICS MODE

The color/graphics adaptor has three resolutions, low, medium, and high, although ROM supports only two of them. Note that this mode offers direct access to only the first (bottom) 128 characters using INT 1FH. This interrupt points to hex 0007C, a 1K area that defines the top 128 characters, eight bytes per character.

For color patterns, graphics mode uses *pixels* (picture elements, also known as pels) to generate color patterns. You might be warned that the use of Assembler for graphics, although efficient, is tedious, and you may want to consider a high-level language for this feature.

1.   Low Resolution. This mode, not supported by ROM, provides a display of 100 rows of 160 pixels (that is, four bits per pixel). Each can consist of the standard 16 colors as described in the preceding section, "Colors."

   To produce this mode, you have to directly address the Motorola 6845 CRT Controller. The two ports are hex 3D4 and 3D5.

2.   Medium Resolution. This mode provides 200 rows of 320 pixels. Each byte represents four pixels (that is, two bits per pixel). This is the normal mode for color graphics.

3.   High Resolution. This mode provides 200 rows of 640 pixels. Since it requires the full 16K bytes of color/graphics storage, high resolution graphics can support only BW. Each byte represents eight pixels (that is, one bit per pixel) providing for 0 (black) and 1 (white).

The mapping of graphics bytes to video scan lines is the same for both medium- and high-resolution graphics.

MEDIUM-RESOLUTION MODE

Under medium resolution, each byte represents four pixels, numbered 0 through 3, as follows:

```
byte:     |C1  C0|C1  C0|C1  C0|C1  C0|
pixel:       0      1      2      3
```

At any given time there are four available colors numbered 0 through 3. The reason for only four colors is because a two-bit pixel provides for four bit combinations: 00, 01, 10, and 11. You can choose as color 00 any one of the 16 available colors, and choose as colors 01, 10, and 11 any one of two three-color palettes:

C1	C0	Palette 0	Palette 1
0	0	background	background
0	1	green	cyan
1	0	red	magenta
1	1	brown	white

Use INT 10H to select a color palette and the background. Thus, if you choose background color yellow and palette 0 above, available colors are yellow, green, red, and brown. A byte consisting of the pixel value 10101010 would display as all red. If you choose background color blue and palette 1, available colors are blue, cyan, magenta, and white. A byte consisting of pixel value 00011011 displays blue, cyan, magenta, and white.

BIOS Interrupt 10 for Medium-Resolution Graphics

For medium-resolution graphics, you can set the color palette and display a graphics character using INT 10H. A code in the AH register determines the operation.

AH = 11: Set Color Palette. The BL value determines the purpose of the BH register:

> BL = 00   Select the background color according to the BH.
> BL = 01   Select the palette according to the BH.

The BH contains either the background color (1 of 16, hex 0-F) or the palette (0 or 1). The following provides an example:

```
MOV   AH,11      ;Request color
MOV   BL,01      ;Select palette
MOV   BH,00      ;   #0 (green, red, brown)
INT   10H        ;Call BIOS
```

If you use code 11 while in text mode, the value set for palette color 0 determines the border color. If you want to keep the same palette, you need set it only once. But once you change palette, the whole screen changes to that color combination.

AH = 12: Write Dot. You can display a selected color (background and palette) using code 12 in the AH register as follows:

```
MOV   AH,12          ;Request write dot
MOV   AL,color       ;color
MOV   CX,column      ;column
MOV   DX,row         ;row
INT   10H            ;Call BIOS
```

AH = 13: Read Dot.   You may want to read a dot to determine its color value. Set the DX to the row, the CX to the column, and the AH to hex 13. The INT 10H operation then returns the dot to the AL.

AH = 14: Write Teletype.   For this operation, set the AH to hex 14, the character to be written in the AL, the foreground color in the BL, and the display page number in the BH.

KEY POINTS TO REMEMBER

☐   Monochrome display supports 4K bytes of memory, 2K of which are available for characters and 2K for an attribute for each character.

☐   Color display supports 16K bytes and can operate in color or BW. You can also process in either text mode for normal character display or in graphics mode.

☐   The 16K memory for color display permits storing additional "pages" or "screens." There are four pages for 80-column screens and eight pages for 40-column screens.

☐   The attribute byte is available for both monochrome display and for color display in text mode. The attribute provides for blinking, reverse video, and high intensity. For color/text, the RGB bits enable you to select colors but no underlining.

☐   BIOS INT 10H provides the interrupt for full-screen processing such as setting mode, setting the cursor location, scrolling the screen, reading from the keyboard, and writing characters.

☐   Graphics mode provides for low resolution (not supported by ROM), medium resolution (for normal color graphics), and high resolution (for BW graphics).

☐   A pixel (picture element) consists of a specified number of bits:

Resolution	Bits	Colors
Low	4	16
Medium	2	4 at one time
High	1	BW only

☐   Under medium-resolution graphics you can select 4 colors of which one is any of the 16 available colors and the other 3 are from a color palette.

□ If your program displays down the screen, scroll up before it reaches the bottom.

□ When using the attribute for blinking and reverse video, watch out for resetting it to normal.

□ For INT 10H operations that read and write, remember to advance the cursor.

QUESTIONS

7-1. Provide the screen attributes for the following: (a) blinking underline, (b) normal intensity, (c) reverse video intensity.

7-2. Code the following routines:

(a) Set the mode for 80-column BW;

(b) Set the cursor type for start line 5 and end line 12;

(c) Scroll up the screen 10 lines;

(d) Display ten blinking "dots" with one-half dots on.

7-3. Under text mode, how many colors are available for background and for foreground?

7-4. Provide the attribute bytes in binary for the following: (a) light cyan on magenta, (b) yellow on brown, (c) gray on red, blinking.

7-5. Explain the reason for the number of colors available under low-, medium-, and high-resolution graphics.

7-6. Code the instructions for displaying five diamond characters in text mode with light red on magenta.

7-7. Code the instructions for selecting background color blue in graphics mode.

7-8. Code the instructions to read a dot from row 12, column 13, in graphics mode.

8

PRINTING

Objective:
To describe the requirements for
printing in Assembler language.

INTRODUCTION

Compared to screen and disk handling, printing is at first glance a simple process. There are only a few operations involved, all done either through DOS INT 21H or through BIOS INT 17H. The commands to the printer include form feed, line feed, and carriage return. A printer may accept all of the ASCII characters for printing, but treats many of them such as hex 00 and hex FF values as blank. So without a graphics printer, all the happy faces, hearts, and clubs that you send may appear as blank.

One classification of printers is according to their print quality: dot matrix or letter-quality. A *dot matrix printer* produces symbols as patterns of tiny dots in a defined box, or matrix. The IBM matrix printer and Epson MX-80 and MX-100 provide a matrix of nine rows of seven dots each. Generally, the more dots in the matrix, the better is the image resolution. These printers can provide normal, compressed, or expanded characters.

More advanced matrix printers can produce dot graphics, slanted printing, and emphasized and double-strike symbols.

The more expensive *letter-quality printer* typically uses a replaceable daisy-wheel or thimble element providing excellent quality of type and variety of font styles. Many letter-quality printers can print 10, 12, or 15 characters per inch and provide proportional spacing, underlining, shadowing, and bold printing. But where a dot matrix printer can be doctored to produce virtually any character, a letter-quality printer is restricted to the characters on the daisy-wheel or thimble.

Another classification of printer is according to its interface: parallel or serial. A *parallel printer* accepts data from the processor several bits at a time (for example, eight), and accordingly is faster but more complex than a serial printer. The IBM PC is designed for a parallel interface. Parallel dot matrix printers include Epson MX-80 and MX-100 and the IBM PC matrix printer (which has an Epson printer mechanism); parallel letter-quality printers include NEC 3550 Spinwriter and F10 StarWriter.

A *serial printer* accepts data from the processor one bit at a time. To support a serial printer, an IBM PC requires installation of a serial interface. However, many software packages for the PC assume a parallel printer.

Many printers have a memory buffer that can hold a full line of print. This feature facilitates bidirectional printing. If that is not enough, printers accept either even parity, odd parity, or no parity bit at all. Sometimes between the processor and printer there is a breakdown in communications. The printer must understand a signal from the processor; for example, to eject to a new page, to feed one line down a page, and to tab across a page. The processor also must understand a signal from the printer; for example, that the printer is busy or it is out of paper (some printers have a spring-loaded switch to indicate no paper).

Unfortunately, there are many types of printers that respond differently to signals from a processor. Many software specialists have found that interfacing their programs to printers is often their most difficult task. If you have unusual problems, check with your dealer.

Users of CP/M-86 should examine Appendix D of their manual regarding interrupt 224 for printing.

PRINT CONTROL CHARACTERS

The standard characters that control printing include the following:

Decimal	Hex	Function
08	08	Backspace
09	09	Horizontal tab
10	0A	Line feed (advance one line)

11	0B	Vertical tab
12	0C	Form feed (advance to next page)
13	0D	Carriage return (return to left margin)

HORIZONTAL TAB. Horizontal tab (hex 09) works only on printers that have the feature and the printer tabs set up. Otherwise, the printer ignores the command. You can print blank spaces to get around an inability to tab.

LINE FEED. Use the line feed (hex 0A) for advancing a single line, and two successive line feeds for double-spacing.

FORM FEED. Initializing the paper when you power up the printer determines the starting position for the top of a page. The default length for a page is 11 inches. Neither the processor nor the printer automatically checks for the bottom of a page. If your program continues printing down a page, it will eventually print over the page perforation and onto the top of the next page. You can control paging by counting the lines as they print, and on reaching the maximum for a page (such as 50 lines), execute a form feed (hex 0C); then reset the line count to 0 or 1.

Many printers have a buffer to store full lines for bidirectional printing. At the end of printing, deliver a command such as line feed or form feed to force printing the last line still in the buffer. The use of form feed at the end of a program run is a good idea to facilitate tearing off the last page of a report.

PRINTING USING DOS INT 21

To print using DOS interrupt 21H, insert 05 in the AH register, the character that you want to print in the DL register, and issue an INT 21H command as follows:

```
MOV   AH,05      ;Print function
MOV   DL,char    ;Character to print
INT   21H        ;Call DOS
```

These instructions are adequate for sending print control characters. However, printing typically involves a full or partial line of text and requires stepping through a line formatted in the Data Segment.

The following section of code illustrates printing a line. It first initializes the address of HEADG in the SI register and sets the CX to the length of HEADG. The loop at P20 moves each character successively from HEADG and sends it to the printer. Note that the first character in HEADG is a form feed and the last two characters are line feeds. As a result, the heading prints at the top of a new page and is followed by a double space.

```
HEADG      DB        0CH,'Industrial Bicycle Mfrs',0AH,0AH
             .
             .
P10PRNT    PROC      NEAR
           LEA       SI,HEADG      ;Init'ze address &
           MOV       CX,26         ; length of heading
P20:
           MOV       AH,05         ;Request to print
           MOV       DL,[SI]       ;Char from heading
           INT       21H           ;Call DOS
           INC       SI            ;Next char in heading
           LOOP      P20
           RET
P10PRNT    ENDP
```

If the printer power is not turned on, DOS returns the message

Out of paper

repetitively. If you turn on the power, the program begins printing correctly. You can also press Ctrl/Break to cancel the program.

PROGRAM: PRINTING WITH PAGE OVERFLOW AND HEADINGS

Figure 8-1 demonstrates the use of DOS for printing. The program is similar to the one in Figure 7-1 that accepts names from the keyboard and displays them down the screen. This program, however, directs the names to the printer. Each printed page contains a heading followed by a double space and the entered names in the following format:

> List of Employee Names   Page 01
>
> Claude Anderson
> Janet Brown
> David Clark
> ...

The program counts each line printed and, on reaching the "bottom" of a page, ejects the forms to the top of the next page. Major Procedures are the following:

B10PRMP	Prompts for a name from the keyboard.
D10INPT	Accepts a name.
E10PRNT	If at the end of a page, calls M10PAGE; Prints the name (its length is based on the actual length in the input parameter list.

M10PAGE	Advances to a new page;
	Prints the heading;
	Resets the line count and adds to the page count.
N10LINE	Common routine—handles line feeds.
P10OUT	Common routine—handles actual request to print.

At the beginning of execution, it is necessary to print a heading, but not necessary to eject to a new page. At this point PAGECTR is still set at its initial 01 value; M10PAGE therefore bypasses the form feed if PAGECTR contains 01.

Placing the test for end of page before (rather than after) printing a name ensures that the last page will have at least one name under the title. PAGECTR is defined as

$$\text{PAGECTR} \quad \text{DB} \quad \text{'01'}$$

and generates an ASCII number, hex 3031. The routine in M10PAGE increments PAGECTR by 1 so that it becomes progressively 3032, 3033, and so forth. The value is valid up to 3039 and then becomes 303A, which would print as a colon (:). If the rightmost byte of PAGECTR contains hex 3A, the routine changes it to hex 30 and adds 1 to the leftmost byte. Hex 303A would become 3130, or 10.

Why not define PAGECTR as a binary value? If the program did this, the arithmetic would be easier, but printing of a character requires an ASCII value. For example, for page 1, binary 00000001 represents a "happy face." The program would have to convert binary numbers to ASCII, such as hex 01 to 3031 (but that's a topic for Chapter 11).

Figure 8-1 Printing with Page overflow and Headings.

```
          page    60,132
TITLE   PRTNAME  Accept input names & print

STACKSG SEGMENT PARA STACK 'STACK'
        DW       32 DUP(?)
STACKSG ENDS

DATASG  SEGMENT PARA 'DATA'
NAMEPAR LABEL    BYTE                  ;Start of Name parameter list
MAXNLEN DB       20                    ;Max. length of name
ACTNLEN DB       ?                     ;No. chars entered
NAMEFLD DB       20 DUP(' '),'$' ;Name & delimiter

ENDPAGE EQU      13                    ;Page limit
HEADG   DB       'List of Employee Names    Page
```

```
        LINECTR DB      01
        PAGECTR DB      '01'
        PROMPT  DB      'Name?','$'
        DATASG  ENDS

        CODESG  SEGMENT PARA 'CODE'
        BEGIN   PROC    FAR
                ASSUME  CS:CODESG,DS:DATASG,SS:STACKSG,ES:DATASG
                PUSH    DS
                SUB     AX,AX
                PUSH    AX
                MOV     AX,DATASG
                MOV     DS,AX
                MOV     ES,AX
                CALL    Q10CLR          ;Clear screen
                CALL    M10PAGE         ;Page heading
        A20LOOP:
                MOV     DX,0000         ;Set cursor to 00,00
                CALL    Q20CURS
                CALL    B10PRMP         ;Display prompt
                CALL    D10INPT         ;Provide for input of name
                CALL    Q10CLR
                CMP     ACTNLEN,00      ;No name? (indicates end)
                JNE     A30
                MOV     DL,0CH          ;If so,
                CALL    P10OUT          ;   form feed
                RET                     ;   return to DOS
        A30:
                CALL    E10PRNT         ;Prepare printing
                JMP     A20LOOP
        BEGIN   ENDP
        ;               Display prompt:
        ;               --------------
        B10PRMP PROC    NEAR
                LEA     DX,PROMPT
                MOV     AH,09           ;Request display
                INT     21H
                RET
        B10PRMP ENDP

        ;               Accept input of name:
        ;               --------------------
        D10INPT PROC    NEAR
                LEA     DX,NAMEPAR
                MOV     AH,0AH          ;Request input
                INT     21H
                RET
        D10INPT ENDP
        ;               Prepare for printing name:
        ;               -------------------------
        E10PRNT PROC    NEAR
                CMP     LINECTR,ENDPAGE ;End of page?
                JB      E20             ;No - bypass
                CALL    M10PAGE         ;Yes - print heading
        E20:
                SUB     CH,CH           ;Set no. chars
                MOV     CL,ACTNLEN      ;   to print
```

```
            LEA      SI,NAMEFLD       ;Init'ze addr of name
E30:
            MOV      DL,[SI]          ;Char from name
            CALL     P10OUT           ;Print char
            INC      SI               ;Next char in name
            LOOP     E30
            CALL     N10LINE          ;Line feed
            RET
E10PRNT ENDP
;                    Page heading routine:
;                    --------------------
M10PAGE PROC         NEAR
            CMP      PAGECTR,'0'      ;First page?
            JNE      M20
            CMP      PAGECTR+1,'1'
            JE       M30              ;Yes - no form feed
M20:
            MOV      DL,0CH           ;Form feed
            CALL     P10OUT
            MOV      LINECTR,01       ;Reset line count
M30:
            LEA      SI,HEADG         ;Address of heading
            MOV      CX,34            ;Length of heading
M40:
            MOV      DL,[SI]          ;Char from heading
            CALL     P10OUT
            INC      SI               ;Next char in heading
            LOOP     M40
            INC      PAGECTR+1        ;Add to page count
            CMP      PAGECTR+1,3AH    ;Page no. = hex 3A?
            JNE      M50              ;No  - bypass
            MOV      PAGECTR+1,30H    ;Yes - Set to
            INC      PAGECTR          ;  ASCII 10
M50:
            CALL     N10LINE          ;Line feed
            CALL     N10LINE          ;  twice
            RET
M10PAGE ENDP
;                    Line feed routine:
;                    -----------------
N10LINE PROC         NEAR
            MOV      DL,0AH           ;Line feed
            CALL     P10OUT
            INC      LINECTR          ;Add to line count
            RET
N10LINE ENDP
;                    Print character in DL:
;                    ---------------------
P10OUT  PROC         NEAR
            MOV      AH,05            ;Request print
            INT      21H
            RET
P10OUT  ENDP
;                    Clear screen:
;                    ------------
Q10CLR  PROC         NEAR
```

```
                MOV     AX,0600H        ;Request scroll screen
                MOV     BH,07           ;Normal
                MOV     CX,0000         ;From 00,00
                MOV     DX,184FH        ;To 24,79
                INT     10H             ;Call BIOS
                RET
        Q10CLR  ENDP
        ;                       Set cursor row/col:
        ;                       -------------------
        Q20CURS PROC    NEAR            ;DX already set
                MOV     AH,02           ;Request set cursor
                MOV     BH,00           ;Page #0
                INT     10H             ;Call BIOS
                RET
        Q20CURS ENDP

        CODESG  ENDS
                END     BEGIN
```

PRINTING USING BIOS INT 17

BIOS interrupt 17H provides for three different operations specified in the AH register:

AH = 0:   This operation causes printing and allows for three printers, numbered 0, 1, and 2 (0 is the standard default).

```
        MOV   AH,00        ;Request print
        MOV   AL,char      ;Character to be printed
        MOV   DX,00        ;Select printer #0
        INT   17H          ;Call BIOS
```

If the operation cannot print the character, it sets the AH register to 01.

AH = 1:   Initialize the printer port as follows:

```
        MOV   AH,01        ;Request initialize port
        MOV   DX,00        ;Select printer port #0
        INT   17H          ;Call BIOS
```

You could use this operation to set the printer to the top-of-page position, although most printers do this automatically when turned on.

AH = 2:   Read the printer port status as follows:

```
MOV    AH,02          ;Request read port
MOV    DX,00          ;Select printer port #0
INT    17H            ;Call BIOS
```

The purpose of AH = 1 and AH = 2 is to determine the status of the printer. The operations set the AH bits to 1 as follows:

Bit:	Cause:
7	Busy
6	Acknowledge
5	Out of paper
4	Selected
3	Input/output error
0	Time out

Printer "errors" are bit 5 (out of paper) and bit 3 (input/output error). If the printer is already switched on, the operation returns hex 90, or binary 10010000 – the printer is "busy" and it is "selected." This condition is valid. If the printer is not switched on, the operation returns hex B0, or binary 10110000, indicating "Out of paper."

When the program runs, if the printer is not initially turned on, BIOS is unable to return a message automatically – your program is supposed to test and act upon the printer status. If your program does not check the status, your only indication is the cursor blinking away merrily. If you turn on the printer at this point, some of the output data is lost. Consequently, before print operations using BIOS, check the port status; if there is an error, display a message. Note that the DOS operation performs this checking automatically, although its message "Out of paper" applies to various conditions.

PROGRAM: PRINTING WITH BIOS

Figure 8-2 demonstrates the use of BIOS for printing. The program defines PRLINE1 containing a line feed command followed by a company title, then PRLINE2 containing a line feed followed by an address. The last command, form feed, clears the last line still in the printer buffer and ejects the forms to the next page.

The program is organized as follows:

☐   B10TST requests the cursor location from BIOS and saves it in ROWCOL (used in E10MSSG). The routine then tests the printer status; if not ready, it calls E10MSSG to print a message at the same row/column until the printer is ready.

- □ C10PRT requests printing of PRLINE1, PRLINE2, and the final form feed.
- □ D10OUT performs the actual call to BIOS to print.
- □ E10MSSG sets the cursor according to ROWCOL and displays the message "Printer not ready."

Figure 8-2 Printing with BIOS.

```
            page     60,132
TITLE    PRBIOS  Print Using BIOS INT 17H
STACK    SEGMENT PARA STACK 'Stack'
         DW      32 DUP(?)
STACK    ENDS

DATA     SEGMENT PARA 'Data'
PRLINE1  DB      0AH                ;Line feed
         DB      'MacroSoftware Corporation'
PRLINE2  DB      0AH                ;Line feed
         DB      '    Belleview, Wash.'
FORMFD   DB      0CH                ;Form feed
MSSGE    DB      'Printer not ready','$'
ROWCOL   DW      ?
DATA     ENDS

CSEG     SEGMENT PARA 'Code'
BEGIN    PROC    FAR
         ASSUME  CS:CSEG,DS:DATA,SS:STACK,ES:DATA
         PUSH    DS
         SUB     AX,AX
         PUSH    AX
         MOV     AX,DATA
         MOV     DS,AX
         CALL    B10TST             ;Call test status
         CALL    C10PRT             ;Call print routine
         RET
BEGIN    ENDP
;                Printer status routine:
;                -----------------------
B10TST   PROC    NEAR
         MOV     AH,03              ;Request
         MOV     BH,00              ; cursor
         INT     10H                ; location
         MOV     ROWCOL,DX          ; & save it
B20:
         MOV     AH,02              ;Test printer status
         MOV     DX,00
         INT     17H
         TEST    AH,00101001B       ;Ready?
         JZ      B30                ; yes
         CALL    E10MSSG            ; no - message
         JMP     B20
B30:
         RET
B10TST   ENDP
;                Initialize print:
;                -----------------
C10PRT   PROC    NEAR
```

```
                LEA     SI,PRLINE1      ;Init'ze print line #1
                MOV     CX,26           ;# chars to print
                CALL    D100UT

                LEA     SI,PRLINE2      ;Init'ze print line #2
                MOV     CX,21           ;# chars to print
                CALL    D100UT

                LEA     SI,FORMFD       ;Form feed
                MOV     CX,01
                CALL    D100UT
                RET
C10PRT  ENDP
;                       Perform print:
;                       --------------
D100UT  PROC    NEAR
                MOV     DX,0000         ;Printer #0
D20:
                MOV     AH,00           ;Request print
                MOV     AL,[SI]         ;Char from line
                INT     17H             ;Call BIOS
                INC     SI              ;Next address in line
                LOOP    D20
                RET
D100UT  ENDP
;                       Status message routine:
;                       -----------------   ----
E10MSSG PROC    NEAR
                MOV     AH,02           ;Set cursor
                MOV     BH,00
                MOV     DX,ROWCOL
                INT     10H

                LEA     DX,MSSGE        ;Display message
                MOV     AH,09H
                INT     21H
                RET
E10MSSG ENDP

CSEG    ENDS
        END     BEGIN
```

The program sets the cursor at a specific location so that the warning message appears to display in the same positions on the screen. Now if the printer is initially switched off, the message displays repetitively. When the printer is switched on, the message no longer displays and printing begins normally with no loss of data.

At any time, a printer may run out of forms or may be inadvertently switched off. Consequently, if you are writing a program to be used by others, include a status test before every attempt to print.

KEY POINTS TO REMEMBER

☐ The printer displays only ASCII characters.
☐ Before attempting to print, turn on the power and have the printer loaded with an adequate supply of paper.

□　On completion of printing, use a line feed or form feed to clear the printer buffer.

□　DOS provides a message if there is a printer error, but BIOS returns only a status code. When using BIOS INT 17H, check the printer status before printing.

QUESTIONS

8-1. Code a program using DOS INT 21H for the following requirements:

(a) Eject the forms to the next page.

(b) Print your name.

(c) Perform a line feed and print your address.

(d) Perform a line feed and print your city/state.

(e) Eject the forms.

8-2. Revise Question 8-1 for using BIOS INT 17H. Include a test for printer status.

8-3　Revise Question 8-1 so that the program performs (b), (c), and (d) five times.

9

STRING INSTRUCTIONS

Objective:
To explain the special String
instructions used to process data
that exceeds one word in length.

INTRODUCTION

Instructions to this point have handled only one byte or one word at a time. It is often necessary, however, to move or compare data fields that exceed one word. For example, you may want to compare descriptions or names in order to sort them into ascending sequence. Fields of this length are known as *String data* and may be either character or numeric. For processing String data, the Assembler provides five String instructions (also known as "string primitives"):

MOVS	Moves one byte or one word from one memory location to another memory location.
LODS	Loads from memory one byte into the AL or one word into the AX register.
STOS	Stores the AL or AX registers into memory.
CMPS	Compares two memory locations of one byte or one word.
SCAS	Compares the contents of the AL or AX to a memory location.

An associated instruction, the REP prefix, causes the above String instructions to perform repetitively through a specified String length.

FEATURES OF STRING OPERATIONS

You can code each String instruction so that it specifies a byte or word operation: that is, the instruction will repeatedly process one byte or one word at a time. For example, you could select a byte instruction for a string with an odd number of bytes, and a word instruction for an even number of bytes. The following indicates the registers implied for each String instruction and the one-byte and one-word versions. DI and SI are assumed to contain addresses:

Instruction	Implied Operands	Byte	Word
MOVS	DI,SI	MOVSB	MOVSW
LODS	AH,SI or AX,SI	LODSB	LODSW
STOS	DI,AH or DI,AX	STOSB	STOSW
CMPS	SI,DI	CMPSB	CMPSW
SCAS	DI,AL or DI,AX	SCASB	SCASW

For example, the MOVS instruction requires coded operands, but for MOVSB and MOVSW you omit the operands, as REP MOVSB. This instruction assumes that the DI and SI contain offset addresses that reference memory (use LEA for this purpose), and that each repeated move is one byte.

Offset addresses in the SI and DI registers require a related Segment register. The SI register is normally associated with the DS (Data Segment) register, as DS:SI. The DI register is always associated with the ES (Extra Segment) register, as ES:DI. Consequently, MOVS, STOS, CMPS, and SCAS require that you initialize the ES register, usually with the address of the Data Segment.

REP: REPEAT STRING PREFIX

You may have noticed that the String instructions reference only one byte or one word. The REP prefix provides for repeated execution of a String instruction. REP is coded immediately before the String instruction, for example as REP MOVSB. REP requires an initial value in the CX register. It executes the String instruction, decrements the CX, and repeats this operation until CX is zero. In this way, you can handle strings of virtually any length.

The Direction Flag determines the direction of a repeated operation:

□ For left to right, use CLD to set the DF Flag to 0.

□ For right to left, use STD to set the DF Flag to 1.

The following example moves the 20 bytes of STRING1 to STRING2. Assume that both the DS and ES are initialized with the address of the Data Segment.

```
STRING1   DB         20 DUP('*')
STRING2   DB         20 DUP(' ')
          . . .
          CLD                         ;Clear DF Flag
          LEA        SI,STRING1       ;Init'ze sending address
          LEA        DI,STRING2       ;Init'ze receiving name
          MOV        CX,20            ;Init'ze for 20 bytes
          REP  MOVSB                  ;Move STRING1 to STRING2
```

Following execution, CMPS and SCAS also set Status Flags so that the operation can terminate immediately on finding a specified condition. The variations of REP for this purpose are the following:

REP   Repeat the operation until CX equals zero.

REPZ or REPE   Repeat the operation while the ZF (Zero) Flag indicates equal/zero. Terminate when the ZF indicates not equal/zero or CX equals zero.

REPNE or REPNZ   Repeat the operation while the ZF Flag indicates not equal/zero. Terminate when the ZF indicates equal/zero or CX equals zero.

MOVS: MOVE STRING

Earlier, Figure 5-5 illustrated moving a nine-byte field. The operation involved three instructions for initialization and five for looping. The MOVS instruction combined with a REP prefix can move any number of characters more efficiently.

For the *receiving* string, the Segment register is the ES and the offset register is the DI. For the *sending* string, the Segment register is the DS and the offset register is the SI. As a result, at the start of the program, initialize the ES register along with the DS register, and prior to executing the MOVS, use LEA to initialize the DI and SI registers.

Depending on the DF Flag, MOVS increments or decrements the DI and SI registers by 1 for a byte and by 2 for a word.

In Figure 9-1, the first Procedure, C10MVSB, uses MOVSB to move a ten-byte field, NAME1, one byte at a time to NAME2. The first instruction, CLD, clears the Direction Flag to zero so that the operation will process left to right. (The DF Flag is normally zero at the start of execution, but CLD is coded here as a wise precaution.)

The two LEA instructions load the SI and DI registers respectively with the offset addresses of NAME1 and NAME2. Note that since earlier instructions initialized the DS and ES registers with the address of DATASG, the segment/offset addresses are correct for ES:DI and DS:SI. A MOV instruction initializes CX with 10 (the length of NAME1 and NAME2). The instruction REP MOVSB now performs the following:

□   Moves the leftmost byte of NAME1 (addressed by ES:DI) to the leftmost byte of NAME2 (addressed by DS:SI).
□   Increments DI and SI by 1 for the next bytes to the right.
□   Decrements CX by 1.
□   Repeats this operation, ten loops in all, until CX becomes zero.

Note that because the Direction Flag is zero and MOVSB increments DI and SI, each iteration processes one byte farther to the right, as NAME1 + 1 to NAME2 + 1, and so on. If the DF Flag is 1, MOVSB would decrement DI and SI, causing processing from right to left. But in that case, you would have to initialize the SI and DI registers with NAME1 + 9 and NAME2 + 9, respectively.

The next Procedure in Figure 9-1, D10MVSW, uses MOVSW to move a word at a time. Since MOVSW increments the DI and SI registers by 2, the operation requires only five loops. But if processing is right to left, initialize the SI with NAME1 + 8 and the DI with NAME2 + 8.

LODS: LOAD STRING

LODS "loads" the AL with a byte or the AX with a word from memory. The memory address is subject to the DS:SI registers (although you can override the SI). Depending on the DF Flag, the operation also increments or decrements the SI register.

Since one LODS operation fills the register, there is no practical use for the REP prefix. For normal purposes, a simple MOV instruction is adequate. But MOV generates three bytes of machine code whereas LODS generates only one (although you do have to initialize the SI register). You could use LODS where you want to step through a string one byte or word at a time examining successively for a particular value.

```
┌─────────────────────────────────────────────┐
│  Figure 9-1 Use of String Operations.        │
└─────────────────────────────────────────────┘
```

```
            page     65,132
TITLE     EXSTRG   Tests of String Operations
STACKSG SEGMENT PARA STACK 'STACK'
            DW       32 DUP(?)
STACKSG ENDS
;----------------------------
DATASG  SEGMENT PARA 'DATA'
NAME1     DB       'Assemblers'
NAME2     DB       10 DUP(' ')
NAME3     DB       10 DUP(' ')
DATASG  ENDS
;----------------------------
CODESG  SEGMENT PARA 'CODE'
BEGIN     PROC     FAR
            ASSUME   CS:CODESG,DS:DATASG,SS:STACKSG,ES:DATASG
            PUSH     DS
            SUB      AX,AX
            PUSH     AX
            MOV      AX,DATASG
            MOV      DS,AX
            MOV      ES,AX

            CALL     C10MVSB            ;MVSB subroutine
            CALL     D10MVSW            ;MVSW subroutine
            CALL     E10LODS            ;LODS subroutine
            CALL     F10STOS            ;STOS subroutine
            CALL     G10CMPS            ;CMPS subroutine
            CALL     H10SCAS            ;SCAS subroutine
            RET
BEGIN     ENDP
;                  Use of MOVSB:
;                  ------------
C10MVSB PROC
            CLD
            LEA      SI,NAME1
            LEA      DI,NAME2
            MOV      CX,10              ;Move 10 bytes,
            REP MOVSB                   ;  NAME1 to NAME2
            RET
C10MVSB ENDP
;                  Use of MOVSW:
;                  ------------
D10MVSW PROC
            CLD
            LEA      SI,NAME2
            LEA      DI,NAME3
            MOV      CX,05              ;Move 5 words,
            REP MOVSW                   ;  NAME2 to NAME3
            RET
D10MVSW ENDP

;                  Use of LODSW:
;                  ------------
E10LODS PROC
            CLD
            LEA      SI,NAME1           ;Load 1st word of NAME1
            LODSW                       ;  into AX reg.
            RET
E10LODS ENDP
```

```
;                       Use of STOSW:
;                       ------------
F10STOS PROC
        CLD
        LEA     DI,NAME3
        MOV     CX,05
        MOV     AX,2020H        ;Move blanks
        REP STOSW               ;  to NAME3
        RET
F10STOS ENDP
;                       Use of CMPSB:
;                       ------------
G10CMPS PROC
        CLD
        MOV     CX,10
        LEA     SI,NAME1
        LEA     DI,NAME2
        REPE CMPSB              ;Compare NAME1:NAME2
        JNE     G20             ;Not equal?
        MOV     BH,01
G20:
        MOV     CX,10
        LEA     SI,NAME2
        LEA     DI,NAME3
        REPE CMPSB              ;Compare NAME2:NAME3
        JE      G30             ;Equal?
        MOV     BL,02
G30:    RET
G10CMPS ENDP
;                       Use of SCASB:
;                       ------------
H10SCAS PROC
        CLD
        MOV     CX,10
        LEA     DI,NAME1
        MOV     AL,'m'          ;Scan NAME1
        REPNE SCASB             ;  for 'm'
        JNE     H20             ;Not found?
        MOV     AH,03
H20:    RET
H10SCAS ENDP

CODESG  ENDS
        END     BEGIN
```

In Figure 9-1, the Procedure E10LODS depicts the LODSW instruction. The example processes only one word and inserts the first byte of NAME1 in the AL register and the second byte in the AH (that is, reversed), so that the AX contains sA.

STOS: STORE STRING

STOS "stores" the contents of the AL or AX register into a byte or word in memory. The memory address is always subject to the ES:DI registers. Depending on the DF Flag, STOS also increments or decrements the DI register, by 1 for a byte and by 2 for a word.

A practical use of STOS with a REP prefix is to initialize a data area to any specified value. For example, you could clear an input or print area to blank.

In Figure 9-1, the Procedure F10STOS depicts the STOSW instruction. The operation repeatedly stores hex 2020 (blanks) five times through NAME3. The operation stores the AL in the first byte and the AH in the next byte (that is, reversed). On termination, the DI register contains the address of NAME3 + 10.

CMPS: COMPARE STRING

CMPS compares the contents of one memory location (addressed by DS:SI) to another memory location (addressed by ES:DI). Depending on the DF Flag, CMPS also increments or decrements the SI and DI registers, by 1 for a byte and by 2 for a word. CMPS sets the AF, CF, OF, PF, SF, and ZF Flags. When combined with a REP prefix, CMPS can successively compare any number of bytes or words.

Consider the comparison of two strings containing JEAN and JOAN. A comparison from left to right one byte at a time causes the following:

> J : J   Equal
> E : O   Unequal (E is low)
> A : A   Equal
> N : N   Equal

A comparison of the entire four bytes ends with a comparison of N to N: equal/zero. Now since the two names are not "equal," the operation should terminate as soon as it finds an unequal condition. *For this purpose, REP has a variation, REPE, which repeats the operation as long as the comparison is equal, or until the CX register equals zero.* The coding for repeated one-byte compares is as follows:

> REPE CMPSB

In Figure 9-1, the Procedure G10CMPS consists of two examples using CMPSB. The first example compares NAME1 to NAME2. Earlier, MOVSB moved the contents of NAME1 to NAME2. Therefore, the CMPSB operation continues for the entire ten bytes and results in an equal/zero condition: the SF Flag is 0 (positive) and the ZF Flag is 1 (for zero).

The second example compares NAME2 to NAME3. Earlier, STOSW stored blanks in NAME3. Therefore, the CMPSB operation terminates after comparing the first byte and results in a high/unequal condition: the SF Flag is 0 (positive) and the ZF Flag is 0 (for nonzero).

The first example results in equal/zero and moves 01 to the BH register. The second example results in unequal and moves 02 to the BL register. If you use DEBUG to trace the instructions, at the end of G10CMPS the BX register should contain 0102.

Warning! These examples use CMPSB to compare one byte at a time. If you use CMPSW to compare a *word* at a time, then initialize CX to 5. But that's not the problem. When comparing words, CMPSW reverses the bytes. For example, let's compare the name SAMUEL to ARNOLD. For the initial comparison of words, instead of comparing SA to AR, the operation compares AS to RA. So, instead of higher, the result is lower – and incorrect. CMPSW works correctly only if the compared strings contain numeric data defined as DW, DD, or DQ.

SCAS: SCAN STRING

SCAS differs slightly from CMPS because it scans a string for a specified byte or word value. SCAS compares the contents of a memory location (addressed by ES:DI) to the AL or AX register. Depending on the DF Flag, SCAS also increments or decrements the DI register, by 1 for a byte and by 2 for a word. SCAS sets the AF, CF, OF, PF, SF, and ZF Flags. When combined with the REP prefix, SCAS can scan any string length.

SCAS would be particularly useful for a text-editing application where the program has to scan for punctuation such as periods, commas, and blanks.

In Figure 9-1, the Procedure H10SCAS scans NAME1 for the lowercase letter m. Since the SCASB operation is to continue scanning while the comparison is *not equal* or until the CX is zero, the REP prefix is REPNE:

REPNE SCASB

Since NAME1 contains "Assemblers," SCASB finds an equal on the fifth compare. If you use DEBUG to trace the instructions, at the end of H10SCAS you will see that the AH register contains 03 to indicate that an "m" was found. The REP SCASB operation has also decremented the CX from 10 to 06.

SCASW scans for a word in memory that matches the word in the AX register. If you used LODSW or MOV to transfer a word into the AX register, the first byte will be in the AL and the second byte in the AH. Since SCAS compares the bytes in reversed sequence, the operation works correctly.

SCAN AND REPLACE

You may also want to replace a specific character with another character, for example, to clear editing characters such as paragraph and end-of-page symbols from a document. The following partial program scans STRING for an ampersand (&) and replaces it with a blank. If SCASB locates an ampersand, it terminates the operation. In this example there is an ampersand at STRING + 8, where the blank is to be inserted. The SCASB operation will have incremented the DI register to STRING + 9. Decrementing DI by 1 provides the correct address for the blank replacement character.

```
STRLEN  EQU     15                      ;Length of STRING
STRING  DB      'The time&is now'
        ...
        CLD
        MOV     AL,'&'                  ;Search character
        MOV     CX,STRLEN               ;Length of STRING
        LEA     DI,STRING               ;Address of STRING
        REPNE SCASB                     ;Scan
        JNZ     K20                     ;Found?
        DEC     DI                      ;Yes -- adjust address
        MOV     BYTE PTR[DI],' '        ;Replace with blank
K20:    RET
```

ALTERNATE CODING

If you code explicitly with a byte or word instruction such as MOVSB or MOVSW, the Assembler assumes the correct length and does not require operands. For instructions such as MOVS, which do not indicate byte or word, you must indicate the length in the operands. For example, if FLDA and FLDB are defined as byte (DB), then the instruction

REP MOVS FLDA,FLDB

implies a repeated move of the byte beginning at FLDB to the byte beginning at FLDA. You could also code the instruction as

REP MOVS ES:BYTE PTR[DI],DS:[SI]

However, you must still load the DI and SI registers with the addresses of FLDA and FLDB.

DUPLICATING A PATTERN

The STOS instruction is useful for setting an area according to a specific byte or word value. For repeating a pattern that exceeds a word, you can use the MOVS instruction with a minor modification. Let's say that you want to set a display line to the following pattern:

***   ***   ***   ***   ***
  _ _   _ _   _ _   _ _   _ _ . . .

Rather than define the entire pattern repetitively, you need only the first six bytes. The definition appears immediately before the display line, and the required coding is as follows:

```
PATTERN   DB    '***   '
                     _ _
DISLINE   DB    42 DUP(?)
          .
          .
          .
          CLD
          LEA   SI,PATTERN
          LEA   DI,DISLINE
          MOV   CX,21
          REP   MOVSW
```

The MOVSW operation begins by moving the first word of PATTERN (**) to the first word of DISLINE, then the second (*_), and third (_ _) words:

PATTERN   DISLINE

Now watch what happens. At this point the DI register contains the address of DISLINE + 6. The SI contains the address of PATTERN + 6, which is also the address of DISLINE. The operation now starts automatically duplicating the pattern by moving the first word of DISLINE to DISLINE + 6, DISLINE + 2 to DISLINE + 8, DISLINE + 4 to DISLINE + 10, and so forth. Eventually the pattern is duplicated through to the end of DISLINE:

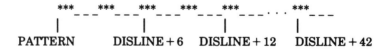

PATTERN   DISLINE + 6   DISLINE + 12   DISLINE + 42

You can use this technique to duplicate any pattern any number of times. The only requirement is that the pattern must be located *immediately* before the receiving field.

PROGRAM: RIGHT-ADJUSTING ON THE SCREEN

The program in Figure 9-2 illustrates most of the material described in this chapter. The Procedures perform the following:

B10INPT Accepts names up to 30 characters in length at the top of the screen.

D10SCAS Uses SCASB to scan the name and bypasses any input containing an asterisk.

E10RGHT Uses MOVSB to right-adjust the names to the right of the screen, one under the other, as follows:

> ALFRED SMITH
> TED JONES
> JOAN WILLINGDON

Note that the length in ACTNLEN in the input parameter list is used to calculate the rightmost character of a name.

F10CLNM Uses STOSW to clear the name in memory.

> **Figure 9-2** Right-adjusting on the Screen.

```
          page    60,132
TITLE     EXRIGHT Right-adjusting displayed names
;------------------------------------------------
STACKSG SEGMENT PARA STACK 'STACK'
          DW      32 DUP(?)
STACKSG ENDS
;------------------------------------------------
DATASG  SEGMENT PARA 'DATA'
NAMEPAR LABEL   BYTE              ;Name parameter list
MAXNLEN DB      31                ;Max. length
ACTNLEN DB      ?                 ;No. chars entered
NAMEFLD DB      31 DUP(' '),'$'   ;Name
;
PROMPT  DB      'Name?',,'$'
NAMEDSP DB      31 DUP(' '),'$'
ROWCTR  DB      00
DATASG  ENDS
;------------------------------------------------
CODESG  SEGMENT PARA 'CODE'
BEGIN   PROC    FAR
          ASSUME  CS:CODESG,DS:DATASG,SS:STACKSG,ES:DATASG
          PUSH    DS
          SUB     AX,AX
          PUSH    AX
          MOV     AX,DATASG
          MOV     DS,AX
          MOV     ES,AX
          MOV     DX,184FH
          CALL    Q10CLR
A20LOOP:
          SUB     DX,DX             ;Set cursor 00,00
          CALL    Q20CURS
          CALL    B10INPT           ;Provide for input of name
          MOV     DX,0020H          ;Clear name on screen
          CALL    Q10CLR
          TEST    ACTNLEN,0FFH      ;No name? (indicates end)
          JNZ     A30
          RET
```

```
        A30:
                CALL      D10SCAS           ;Scan for asterisk
                CMP       AL,'*'            ;Found?
                JE        A20LOOP           ;  Yes - bypass
                CALL      E10RGHT           ;Right-adjust name
                CALL      F10CLNM           ;Clear name
                JMP       A20LOOP
        BEGIN   ENDP
        ;                 Prompt for input:
        ;                 ----------------
        B10INPT PROC
                LEA       DX,PROMPT         ;Display prompt
                MOV       AH,09
                INT       21H
                LEA       DX,NAMEPAR        ;Accept input
                MOV       AH,0AH
                INT       21H
                RET
        B10INPT ENDP
        ;                 Scan name for asterisk:
        ;                 ----------------------
        D10SCAS PROC
                CLD
                MOV       CX,30             ;Set 30-byte scan
                LEA       DI,NAMEFLD
                MOV       AL,'*'
                REPNE SCASB                 ;Asterisk found?
                JE        D20               ;  Yes - exit
                MOV       AL,' '            ;  No - clear * in AL
        D20:    RET
        D10SCAS ENDP
        ;                 Right-adjust & display name:
        ;                 ---------------------------
        E10RGHT PROC
                STD
                SUB       CH,CH
                MOV       CL,ACTNLEN        ;Length in CX for REP
                LEA       SI,NAMEFLD        ;Calc rightmost
                ADD       SI,CX             ;  position
                DEC       SI                ;  of input name
                LEA       DI,NAMEDSP+30     ;Right pos'n of display name
                REP MOVSB                   ;Move string right to left
                MOV       DH,ROWCTR         ;Set row &
                MOV       DL,49             ;  column for cursor
                CALL      Q20CURS
                MOV       AH,09
                LEA       DX,NAMEDSP        ;Display name
                INT       21H
                INC       ROWCTR
                RET
        E10RGHT ENDP
        ;                 Clear displayed name:
        ;                 --------------------
        F10CLNM PROC
                CLD
                MOV       CX,15             ;Clear 15 words
                MOV       AX,2020H
                LEA       DI,NAMEDSP
                REP STOSW
                RET
        F10CLNM ENDP
        ;                 Clear screen (DX already set):
        ;                 ------------
        Q10CLR  PROC
                SUB       CX,CX
                MOV       BH,07
                MOV       AX,0600H
                INT       10H
                RET
        Q10CLR  ENDP
        ;                 Set cursor row/col (DX already set):
        ;                 ------------------
        Q20CURS PROC
                SUB       BH,BH
                MOV       AH,02
                INT       10H
                RET
        Q20CURS ENDP

        CODESG  ENDS
                END       BEGIN
```

KEY POINTS TO REMEMBER

☐ For the String instructions MOVS, STOS, CMPS, and SCAS, be sure to initialize the ES register.

☐ Be sure to clear (CLD) or set (STD) the Direction Flag depending on the direction of processing.

☐ Double-check initialization of the DI and SI registers. For example, MOVS implies operands DI,SI whereas CMPS implies operands SI,DI.

☐ Initialize the CX register according to the number of bytes or number of words being processed.

☐ For normal processing, use REP with MOVS and STOS, and use a modified REP (REPE or REPNE) with CMPS and SCAS.

☐ Watch out for CMPSW and SCASW, which reverse the bytes in compared words.

☐ Where you want to process right to left, watch out for addressing beginning at the rightmost byte of a field. If the field is NAME1 and is ten bytes long, then for processing bytes, the load address for LEA is NAME + 9. For processing words, however, the load address for LEA is NAME + 8 because the String operation initially accesses NAME + 8 and NAME + 9.

QUESTIONS

9-1. Key in, assemble, and link the program in Figure 9-1. Be sure to initialize the ES register. Use DEBUG to trace through the Procedures and note the contents of the Data Segment and registers. As an experiment, for MOVSB and MOVSW change the operation to move from right to left. Also, change H10SCAS to scan NAME1 for the word "mb."

9-2. Assume the following data definitions:

```
DATASG   SEGMENT  PARA
TITLE1   DB       'ACME DIRIGIBLE CORP.'
PRTLINE  DB       20 DUP(' ')
```

Code the following related questions using String operations:

(a) Move TITLE1 to PRTLINE left to right.

(b) Move TITLE1 to PRTLINE right to left.

(c) Load the third and fourth bytes of TITLE1 into the AX.

(d) Store the AX beginning at PRTLINE + 5.

(e) Compare TITLE1 to PRTLINE (they will be unequal).

(f) Scan TITLE1 for a blank character and if found move it to the BH register.

9-3. Recode H10SCAS in Figure 9-1 so that the operation scans NAME1 for "er." If you check NAME1 you will see that the pairs of bytes form the following words: |As|se|mb|le|rs|. The characters "er" do not appear as a word. Two possible solutions are:

(a) Use SCASW twice. The first SCASW begins at NAME1 and the second SCASW begins at NAME1 + 1.

(b) Use SCASB and on finding an "e" compare the following byte for an "r."

9-4. Define a field containing hex 03, hex 04, hex 05, and hex 20. Duplicate this field 20 times and display the result on the screen.

10

ARITHMETIC I: PROCESSING BINARY DATA

Objective:
To cover the requirements for addition, subtraction, multiplication, and division of binary data.

INTRODUCTION

A microcomputer performs only binary (base 2) arithmetic. It is important to remember this fact because we are accustomed to decimal (base 10) arithmetic. Further, 16-bit registers impose limitations on the size of fields and require special treatment for large values. (Luckily, the 8086/8088 processors use 16-bit architecture, because 8-bit registers involve even more serious restrictions.)

This chapter covers addition, subtraction, multiplication, and division and the use of unsigned and signed data. The chapter also provides many examples and warnings of various pitfalls for the unwary traveler in the realm of the microprocessor.

Chapter 11 proceeds with special requirements involved with converting between binary and ASCII data formats.

ADDITION AND SUBTRACTION

The instructions ADD and SUB simply add and subtract designated bytes and words that contain binary data. Indeed, only an add operation is required internally since the computer performs subtraction by means of two's complement methodology: Reverse the bits of operand 2, add 1, and add to operand 1. Other than this latter step, the processing of ADD and SUB are identical.

Figure 10-1 furnishes examples of ADD and SUB instructions. Both can process a byte or a word. The Procedure B10ADD uses ADD to process bytes and the Procedure C10SUB uses SUB to process words. The examples depict all five possibilities:

> Add/sub register to register
> Add/sub memory to register
> Add/sub register to memory
> Add/sub immediate to register
> Add/sub immediate to memory

Note that there is no direct memory-to-memory operation. You can handle this situation by using a register. The following example adds WORD1 to WORD2, both defined as DW:

```
MOV   AX,WORD1
ADD   AX,WORD2
MOV   WORD2,AX
```

Figure 10-1 Examples of ADD and SUB.

```
          page    60,132
TITLE     EXADD   Example ADD and SUB operations
;------------------------------------------------
STACKSG SEGMENT PARA STACK 'STACK'
        DW      32 DUP(?)
STACKSG ENDS
;------------------------------------------------
DATASG  SEGMENT PARA 'DATA'
BYTE1   DB      64H
BYTE2   DB      40H
BYTE3   DB      16H
WORD1   DW      4000H
WORD2   DW      2000H
WORD3   DW      1000H
DATASG  ENDS
;------------------------------------------------
CODESG  SEGMENT PARA 'CODE'
BEGIN   PROC    FAR
        ASSUME  CS:CODESG,DS:DATASG,SS:STACKSG
```

```
                    PUSH      DS
                    SUB       AX,AX
                    PUSH      AX
                    MOV       AX,DATASG
                    MOV       DS,AX
                    CALL      B10ADD             ;Call Add routine
                    CALL      C10SUB             ;Call Subtract routine
                    RET
         BEGIN      ENDP
         ;                    Examples of ADD bytes:
         ;                    --------------------
         B10ADD     PROC
                    MOV       AL,BYTE1
                    MOV       BL,BYTE2
                    ADD       AL,BL              ;reg-to-reg
                    ADD       AL,BYTE3           ;memory-to-reg
                    ADD       BYTE1,BL           ;register-to-memory
                    ADD       BL,10H             ;immediate-to-reg
                    ADD       BYTE1,25H          ;immediate-to-memory
                    RET
         B10ADD     ENDP
         ;                    Examples of SUB words:
         ;                    --------------------
         C10SUB     PROC
                    MOV       AX,WORD1
                    MOV       BX,WORD2
                    SUB       AX,BX              ;reg-from-reg
                    SUB       AX,WORD3           ;memory-from-reg
                    SUB       WORD1,BX           ;reg-from-memory
                    SUB       BX,1000H           ;immediate-from-reg
                    SUB       WORD1,256H         ;immediate-from-memory
                    RET
         C10SUB     ENDP

         CODESG     ENDS
                    END       BEGIN
```

Overflows

In all arithmetic operations you have to be alert for overflows. A byte provides a maximum of only a sign bit plus seven data bits, or -128 to +127. Consequently, an arithmetic operation can easily exceed the capacity of a one-byte register. For example, a sum in the AL register that exceeds its capacity does not automatically overflow into the AH register. Assume that the AL register contains hex 70. The effect of

ADD   AL,10H

generates a sum of hex 80 in the AL. But the operation also sets the Overflow Flag to overflow and the Sign Flag to negative. The reason? Hex 80, or binary 10000000, is a negative number. Instead of +128, the sum is -128. Since the problem is that the AL register is too small, the sum should be in the AX register. In the following example, the CBW (Convert Byte to Word) instruction extends the hex 70 in the AL into hex 0070 in the AX by propagating the sign bit (0) through the AH. The ADD generates the correct result in the AX: hex 0080, or +128:

```
        CBW                 ;Extend AL to AH
        ADD    AX,10H    ;Add to AX
```

But even a full word allows only a maximum of a sign bit plus 15 data bits, or -32,768 to +32,767. Our next step is to examine how to handle numbers that exceed this maximum.

Multiword Addition

Obviously, a maximum of only +32,767 in a register would rather restrict a computer's usefulness in handling arithmetic. Let's examine two ways to perform multiword arithmetic. The first is very simple and specific, whereas the second is more sophisticated and general.

In Figure 10-2, D10DWD illustrates a simple way of adding one pair of words (WORD1A and WORD1B) to a second pair (WORD2A and WORD2B) and storing the sum in a third pair (WORD3A and WORD3B). The operation first adds the rightmost words, just as you would add manually (that is, if you have 16 fingers):

WORD1B	BC62
WORD2B	553A
Total	1119C

Figure 10-2 Multiword Addition.

```
            page     60,132
TITLE     EXDBADD  Example ADD Doubleword Operations
;***********************************************
STACKSG  SEGMENT  PARA STACK 'STACK'
            DW       32 DUP(?)
STACKSG  ENDS
;***********************************************
DATASG   SEGMENT  PARA 'DATA'
WORD1A   DW       0123H
WORD1B   DW       0BC62H
WORD2A   DW       0012H
WORD2B   DW       553AH
WORD3A   DW       ?
WORD3B   DW       ?
DATASG   ENDS
;***********************************************
CODESG   SEGMENT  PARA 'CODE'
BEGIN    PROC     FAR
            ASSUME   CS:CODESG,DS:DATASG,SS:STACKSG
            PUSH     DS
            SUB      AX,AX
            PUSH     AX
            MOV      AX,DATASG
```

```
                    MOV     DS,AX
                    CALL    D10DWD           ;Call 1st ADD
                    CALL    E10DWD           ;Call 2nd ADD
                    RET
       BEGIN        ENDP
       ;                    Example of ADD doublewords:
       ;                    --------------------------
       D10DWD       PROC
                    MOV     AX,WORD1B        ;Add rightmost word
                    ADD     AX,WORD2B
                    MOV     WORD3B,AX
                    MOV     AX,WORD1A        ;Add leftmost word
                    ADC     AX,WORD2A        ;  with carry
                    MOV     WORD3A,AX
                    RET
       D10DWD       ENDP
       ;                    Generalized ADD operation:
       ;                    --------------------------
       E10DWD       PROC
                    CLC                      ;Clear carry flag
                    MOV     CX,02            ;Set loop count
                    LEA     SI,WORD1B        ;Leftmost word of DWORD1
                    LEA     DI,WORD2B        ;Leftmost word of DWORD2
                    LEA     BX,WORD3B        ;Leftmost word of sum
       E20:
                    MOV     AX,[SI]          ;Move word to AX
                    ADC     AX,[DI]          ;Add with carry to AX
                    MOV     [BX],AX          ;Store word
                    DEC     SI               ;Adjust addresses for
                    DEC     SI               ;  next word to left
                    DEC     DI
                    DEC     DI
                    DEC     BX
                    DEC     BX
                    LOOP    E20              ;Repeat for next word
                    RET
       E10DWD       ENDP

       CODESG       ENDS
                    END     BEGIN
```

Note that the sum, hex 1119C, exceeds the capacity of the register. The
overflow digit causes the Carry Flag to be set to 1. Next, the example adds
the word at the left. In this case, however, instead of ADD, the example
uses ADC (Add With Carry). The instruction adds the two values, and if
the Carry Flag is already set, adds 1 to the sum:

WORD1A	0123
WORD2A	0012
Plus carry	1
Total	0136

By tracing the arithmetic using DEBUG, you will see this sum, 0136,
in the AX register, and the reversed values 3601 stored in WORD3A and
9C11 in WORD3B.

In Figure 10-2, E10DWD provides an approach to adding values of any length. The example begins with the rightmost words of the fields to be added. The first loop adds the rightmost words and the second loop adds the leftmost words. Note that since the second loop is to process the words to the left, the addresses in the SI, DI, and BX registers must be decremented by 2. Two DEC instructions perform this operation for each register. (The instruction

SUB reg,02

would clear the Carry Flag and would cause an incorrect answer.)

Because of the loop, there is only one add instruction, ADC. At the start, a CLC (Clear Carry) instruction ensures that the Carry Flag is initially clear. For this method to work, ensure that (1) the words are defined adjacent to each other, (2) processing is from right to left, and (3) the CX register is initialized to the number of words to be added.

For multiword subtraction, the instruction equivalent to ADC is SBB (Subtract With Borrow). Simply replace ADC with SBB in the E10DWD Procedure.

UNSIGNED AND SIGNED DATA

Some numeric fields are *unsigned*; examples include a customer number and a memory address. Some numeric fields are supposed to be always positive; examples include rate of pay, day of the month, and the value of pi. Other numeric fields are *signed* because the contents may be positive or negative. Examples include customer balance owing (which could be negative if overpaid) and an algebraic number.

For unsigned data, all bits are intended to be data bits. Instead of + 32,767, a register could contain + 65,535. For signed data, the leftmost bit is a sign bit. The ADD and SUB instructions do not distinguish between unsigned and signed data, and indeed simply add and subtract the bits. The following depicts adding two binary numbers. The top number contains a 1-bit to the left. For unsigned data, the bits represent 249, but for signed data the bits represent -7:

	Unsigned	Signed
11111001	249	-7
00000010	2	$+2$
11111011	251	-5

The result of adding in binary is the same for unsigned and for signed. However, the bits in the unsigned field represent + 251, whereas the bits in the signed field represent -5. In effect, the contents of a field mean anything you want.

A *carry* occurs where there is a carry into the sign bit. An *overflow* occurs where a carry into the sign bit does not carry out, or a carry out has no carry in. Where a carry occurs on unsigned data, the result is invalid:

	Unsigned	Signed	CF	OF
11111100	252	− 4		
00000101	5	+ 5		
00000001	1	1	1	0
	(invalid)			

Where an overflow occurs on signed data, the result is invalid:

	Unsigned	Signed	CF	OF
01111001	121	+ 121		
00001011	11	+ 11		
10000100	132	− 124	0	1
		(invalid)		

And the same add operation may cause both a carry and an overflow:

	Unsigned	Signed	CF	OF
11110110	246	− 10		
10001001	137	− 119		
01111111	127	+ 127	1	1
	(invalid)	(invalid)		

MULTIPLICATION

For multiplication, the MUL instruction handles unsigned data and the IMUL (Integer Multiplication) instruction handles signed data. As the programmer, you have control over the format of data that you process and the responsibility of selecting the appropriate instruction. The two basic multiplication operations are the following:

1. *Byte Times Byte.* The multiplicand is in the AL register and the multiplier is a byte in memory or a register. After multiplication, the product is in the AX register. The operation ignores and erases any data that is already in the AH register.

AH	AL		AX
Before:	Mult'd	After:	Product

2. *Word Times Word.* The multiplicand is in the AX register and the multiplier is a word in memory or a register. After multiplication, the product is a doubleword that requires two registers: The high order (leftmost) portion is in the DX and the low order (rightmost) portion is in the AX. The operation ignores and erases any data that is already in the DX register.

	AX		DX	AX
Before:	Multiplicand	After:	High product	Low product

The operand of MUL and IMUL references only the multiplier. Assume the following instruction:

MUL   MULTR

☐   If MULTR is defined as DB, the operation assumes AL times byte.
☐   If MULTR is defined as DW, the operation assumes AX times word.

When the multiplier is in a register, the length of the register determines the type of operation. The following illustrate:

```
MUL CL    ;1-byte multiplier: multiplicand in AL, product in AX
MUL BX    ;1-word multiplier: multiplicand in AX, product in DX:AX
```

Unsigned Multiplication: MUL

The MUL instruction multiplies unsigned data. In Figure 10-3, C10MUL gives three examples of multiplication:

Byte times byte
Word times word
Word times byte

The first MUL example multiplies hex 80 (128) and hex 40 (64). The product in the AX register is hex 2000 (8,192).

The second MUL example generates hex 1000 0000 in the DX:AX registers.

The third MUL example involves word times byte and requires extending BYTE1 to a word. Since the values are supposed to be *unsigned*, the example assumes that leftmost bits in the AH register are to be zero. (The problem with using CBW is that the leftmost bit of the AL could be 0 or 1.) The product in the DX:AX is hex 0040 0000.

Figure 10-3 Unsigned and Signed Multiplication

```
        page    60,132
TITLE   EXMULT  Examples of MUL & IMUL operations
;********************************************
STACKSG SEGMENT PARA STACK 'Stack'
        DW      32 DUP(?)
STACKSG ENDS
;********************************************
DATASG  SEGMENT PARA 'Data'
BYTE1   DB      80H
BYTE2   DB      40H
WORD1   DW      8000H
WORD2   DW      2000H
DATASG  ENDS
;********************************************
CODESG  SEGMENT PARA 'Code'
BEGIN   PROC    FAR
        ASSUME  CS:CODESG,DS:DATASG,SS:STACKSG
        PUSH    DS
        SUB     AX,AX
        PUSH    AX
        MOV     AX,DATASG
        MOV     DS,AX
        CALL    C10MUL          ;Call MUL routine
        CALL    D10IMUL         ;Call IMUL routine
        RET
BEGIN   ENDP
;               Examples of MUL:
;               ---------------
C10MUL  PROC
        MOV     AL,BYTE1        ;byte x byte
        MUL     BYTE2           ;  product in AX

        MOV     AX,WORD1        ;word x word
        MUL     WORD2           ;  product in DX:AX

        MOV     AL,BYTE1        ;byte x word
        SUB     AH,AH           ;  extend multiplicand in AH
        MUL     WORD1           ;  product in DX:AX
        RET
C10MUL  ENDP
;               Examples of IMUL:
;               ----------------
D10IMUL PROC
        MOV     AL,BYTE1        ;byte x byte
        IMUL    BYTE2           ;  product in AX

        MOV     AX,WORD1        ;word x word
        IMUL    WORD2           ;  product in DX:AX

        MOV     AL,BYTE1        ;byte x word
        CBW                     ;  extend multiplicand in AH
        IMUL    WORD1           ;  product in DX:AX
        RET
D10IMUL ENDP

CODESG  ENDS
        END     BEGIN
```

Signed Multiplication: IMUL

The IMUL (Integer Multiplication) instruction multiplies signed data. In Figure 10-3, D10IMUL uses the same three examples as C10MUL, replacing MUL with IMUL.

The first IMUL example multiplies hex 80 (a negative number) by hex 40 (a positive number). The product in the AX register is hex E000. Note that using the same data, MUL generated a product of hex 2000, so you can see the difference in using MUL and IMUL. MUL treats hex 80 as $+128$ whereas IMUL treats hex 80 as -128. The product of -128 times $+64$ is $-8,192$, which equals hex E000. (Try converting hex E000 to bits, reverse the bits, add 1, and add up the bit values.)

The second IMUL example multiplies hex 8000 (a negative value) times hex 2000 (a positive value). The product in the DX:AX registers is hex F000 0000 and is the negative of the product that MUL generated.

The third IMUL example requires extending BYTE1 to a word in the AX. Since the values are supposed to be *signed*, the example uses CBW to extend the leftmost sign bit into the AH register: hex 80 in the AL becomes hex FF80 in the AX. Since the multiplier, WORD1, is also negative, the product should be positive. And indeed it is: hex 0040 0000 in the DX:AX – the same result as MUL, which assumed it was multiplying two positive numbers.

In effect, if the multiplicand and multiplier have the same sign bit, MUL and IMUL generate the same result. But if the multiplicand and multiplier have different sign bits, MUL produces a positive product and IMUL produces a negative product.

You may find it worthwhile to use DEBUG to trace these examples.

Efficiency.   If you multiply by a power of 2 (2, 4, 8, etc.), it is more efficient simply to shift left the required number of bits. A shift greater than 1 requires the shift value in the CL register. In the following examples, assume that the multiplicand is in the AL or AX:

Multiply by 2:   SHL AL,1   Multiply by 4:   MOV   CL,2
                                               SHL   AX,CL

Multiword Multiplication

Conventional multiplication involves multiplying byte by byte or word by word. As already seen, the maximum signed value in a word is $+32,767$. Multiplying larger values involves some additional steps. The approach is to multiply each word separately and to add each product to a sum. Consider the following multiplication in decimal format:

$$
\begin{array}{r}
1365 \\
\times\,12 \\
\hline
2730 \\
1365 \\
\hline
16380
\end{array}
$$

What if decimal arithmetic could multiply only two-digit numbers? You could multiply the 13 and the 65 by 12 separately, as follows:

$$
\begin{array}{r}
13 \\
\times\,12 \\
\hline
26 \\
13 \\
\hline
156
\end{array}
\qquad
\begin{array}{r}
65 \\
\times\,12 \\
\hline
130 \\
65 \\
\hline
780
\end{array}
$$

Next, add the two products; but remember, since the 13 is at the 100's position, its product is actually 15600:

$$
\begin{array}{r}
15600 \\
+\,780 \\
\hline
16380
\end{array}
$$

Basically, an Assembler program uses the same technique, except that the data consists of words (four digits) in hexadecimal format.

Doubleword by word. In Figure 10-4, E10XMUL gives an example of multiplying a doubleword by a word. The multiplicand, MULTCND, consists of two words containing, respectively, hex 3206 and 2521. The reason for defining two DW's instead of a DD is to facilitate addressing for MOV instructions that move words to the AX register. The multiplier, MULTPLR, contains hex 6400. The field for the generated product, PRODUCT, provides for three words. The first MUL operation multiplies MULTPLR and the right word of MULTCND; the product is hex 0E80 E400, stored in PRODUCT+2 and PRODUCT+4. The second MUL multiplies MULTPLR and the left word of MULTCND; the product is hex 138A 5800. The routine adds the two products as follows:

Product 1:	0000 0E80 E400
Product 2:	138A 5800
Total:	138A 6680 E400

Figure 10-4 Multiword Multiplication.

```
            page    60,132
    TITLE   EXDWMUL - Multiplication of Doublewords
;**********************************************
STACKSG SEGMENT PARA STACK 'Stack'
        DW      32 DUP(?)
STACKSG ENDS
;**********************************************
DATASG  SEGMENT PARA 'Data'
MULTCND DW      3206H
        DW      2521H
MULTPLR DW      6400H
        DW      0A26H
PRODUCT DW      0
        DW      0
        DW      0
        DW      0
DATASG  ENDS
;**********************************************
CODESG  SEGMENT PARA 'Code'
BEGIN   PROC    FAR
        ASSUME  CS:CODESG,DS:DATASG,SS:STACKSG
        PUSH    DS
        SUB     AX,AX
        PUSH    AX
        MOV     AX,DATASG
        MOV     DS,AX
        CALL    E10XMUL         ;Call 1st mult
        CALL    Z10ZERO         ;Clear product
        CALL    F10XMUL         ;Call 2nd mult
        RET
BEGIN   ENDP
;               Doubleword x word:
;               ------------------
E10XMUL PROC
        MOV     AX,MULTCND+2    ;Multiply right word
        MUL     MULTPLR         ;  of multiplicand
        MOV     PRODUCT+4,AX    ;Store product
        MOV     PRODUCT+2,DX

        MOV     AX,MULTCND      ;Multiply left word
        MUL     MULTPLR         ;  of multiplicand
        ADD     PRODUCT+2,AX    ;Add to stored product
        ADC     PRODUCT,DX
        RET
E10XMUL ENDP
;               Doubleword x doubleword:
;               ------------------------
F10XMUL PROC
        MOV     AX,MULTCND+2    ;Multiplicand word-2
        MUL     MULTPLR+2       ;  x multiplier word-2
        MOV     PRODUCT+6,AX    ;Store product
        MOV     PRODUCT+4,DX

        MOV     AX,MULTCND+2    ;Multiplicand word-2
        MUL     MULTPLR         ;  x multiplier word-1
        ADD     PRODUCT+4,AX    ;Add to stored product
        ADC     PRODUCT+2,DX
        ADC     PRODUCT,00      ;Add any carry
```

```
                MOV     AX,MULTCND      ;Multiplicand word-2
                MUL     MULTPLR+2       ;  x multiplier word-2
                ADD     PRODUCT+4,AX    ;Add to stored product
                ADC     PRODUCT+2,DX
                ADC     PRODUCT,00      ;Add any carry

                MOV     AX,MULTCND      ;Multiplicand word-1
                MUL     MULTPLR         ;  x multiplier word-1
                ADD     PRODUCT+2,AX    ;Add to product
                ADC     PRODUCT,DX
                RET
F10XMUL ENDP
;                       Clear product area:
;                       -------------------
Z10ZERO PROC
                MOV     PRODUCT,0000
                MOV     PRODUCT+2,0000
                MOV     PRODUCT+4,0000
                MOV     PRODUCT+6,0000
                RET
Z10ZERO ENDP

CODESG  ENDS
        END     BEGIN
```

Since the first ADD instruction may cause a carry, the second add is ADC (Add with Carry). Because of the reversed storage method of the 8086/8088 microprocessors, PRODUCT will actually contain 8A13 8066 00E4. Note that the routine requires that the first word of PRODUCT must initially contain zero.

Doubleword by doubleword. Multiplying two doublewords involves the following four multiply operations:

Multiplicand		Multiplier
word 2	×	word 2
word 2	×	word 1
word 1	×	word 2
word 1	×	word 1

Each product in the DX and AX is added to the appropriate word in the final product. In Figure 10-4, F10XMUL gives an example. MULTCND contains hex 3206 2521, MULTPLR contains hex 6400 0A26, and PRODUCT provides for four words.

Although the logic is similar to multiplying doubleword by word, this problem requires an additional feature. Following the ADD/ADC pair is another ADC that adds 0 to PRODUCT. The first ADC itself could cause a carry which subsequent instructions would clear. The second ADC therefore adds 0 if there is no carry and adds 1 if there is a carry. The final ADD/ADC pair does not require an additional ADC; since PRODUCT is large enough for the final generated answer, there is no final carry.

The final product is 138A 687C 8E5C CCE6, stored in PRODUCT with the bytes reversed. Try tracing this example under DEBUG!

SHIFTING THE DX:AX REGISTERS

If you want to shift a product in the DX:AX registers to the left or right, the following routines could be useful. You could contrive a more efficient method, but these examples are generalized for any number of loops (and shifts) in the CX register. Note that shifting off a 1-bit sets the Carry Flag.

Shift Left 4 Bits

```
         MOV    CX,04              ;Init'ze 4 loops
C20:     SHL    DX,1               ;Shift DX
         SHL    AX,1               ;Shift AX
         ADC    DX,00              ;Add AX carry, if any
         LOOP   C20                ;Repeat
```

Shift Right 4 Bits

```
         MOV    CX,04              ;Init'ze 4 loops
D20:     SHR    AX,1               ;Shift AX
         SHR    DX,1               ;Shift DX
         JNC    D30                ;If DX carry,
         OR     AH,10000000B       ;   insert 1-bit in AH
D30:     LOOP   D20                ;Repeat
```

Following is a more efficient method for left shifting that does not require looping. This example stores a shift factor in the CL register. As it stands, the example is specific to a 4-bit shift but could be adapted to other shifts.

```
         MOV    CL,04          ;Set shift
         SHL    DX,CL          ;Shift DX left 4 bits
         MOV    BL,AH          ;Store AH in BL
         SHL    AX,CL          ;Shift AX left 4 bits
         SHR    BL,CL          ;Shift BL right 4 bits
         OR     DL,BL          ;Insert BL 4 bits in DL
```

DIVISION

For division, the DIV instruction handles unsigned data and the IDIV instruction handles signed data. You have the responsibility of selecting the appropriate instruction. The two basic divide operations are the following:

1. *Byte into Word.* The dividend is in the AX register and the divisor is a byte in a register or in memory. After division, the remainder is in the AH and the quotient is in the AL register. Since a one-byte quotient is very small—a maximum of +255 (hex FF) if unsigned and +127 (hex 7F) if signed—this operation is of limited use.

2. *Word into Doubleword.* The dividend is in the DX:AX pair and the divisor is a word in a register or memory. After division, the remainder is in the DX and the quotient is in the AX register. The quotient of one word allows a maximum of +32,767 (hex FFFF) if unsigned and +16,383 (hex 7FFF) if signed.

The operand of DIV and IDIV references the divisor. Assume the following instruction:

DIV   DIVISOR

☐   If DIVISOR is defined as DB, the operation assumes byte into word.
☐   If DIVISOR is defined as DW, the operation assumes word into doubleword.

If you divide 13 by 3, the result is 4 and 1/3. The quotient is 4 and the true remainder is 1. Note that a hand calculator (and a BASIC program for that matter) would deliver a quotient of 4.333... . The value consists of an integer portion (4) and a fractional portion (.333). The values 1/3 and .333 are fractions whereas the 1 is a remainder.

Unsigned Division: DIV

The DIV instruction divides unsigned data. In Figure 10-5, D10DIV gives four examples of division:

Byte into word
Byte into byte
Word into doubleword
Word into word

The first DIV example divides hex 2000 (8092) by hex 80 (128). The remainder in the AH is 00 and the quotient in the AL is hex 40 (64).

The second DIV example requires extending BYTE1 to a word. Since the value is supposed to be unsigned, the example assumes that leftmost bits in the AH register are to be zero. The remainder in the AH is hex 12 and the quotient in the AL is hex 05.

The third DIV example generates a remainder in the DX of hex 1000 and a quotient in the AX of hex 0080.

The fourth DIV requires extending WORD1 to a doubleword in the DX register. After the divide, the remainder in the DX is hex 0000 and the quotient in the AX is hex 0002.

Figure 10-5 Unsigned and Signed Division

```
            page    60,132
TITLE    EXDIV    Examples of DIV & IDIV operations
; ================================================
STACKSG SEGMENT PARA STACK 'Stack'
         DW       32 DUP(?)
STACKSG ENDS
; ================================================
DATASG   SEGMENT PARA 'Data'
BYTE1    DB       80H
BYTE3    DB       16H
WORD1    DW       2000H
WORD2    DW       0010H
WORD3    DW       1000H
DATASG   ENDS
; ================================================
CODESG   SEGMENT PARA 'Code'
BEGIN    PROC     FAR
         ASSUME   CS:CODESG,DS:DATASG,SS:STACKSG
         PUSH     DS
         SUB      AX,AX
         PUSH     AX
         MOV      AX,DATASG
         MOV      DS,AX
         CALL     D10DIV          ;Call DIV routine
         CALL     E10IDIV         ;Call IDIV routine
         RET
BEGIN    ENDP
;                  Examples of DIV:
;                  ---------------
D10DIV   PROC
         MOV      AX,WORD1        ;word / byte
         DIV      BYTE1           ;  rmdr:quot in AH:AL
         MOV      AL,BYTE1        ;byte / byte
         SUB      AH,AH           ;  extend dividend in AH
         DIV      BYTE3           ;  rmdr:quot in AH:AL

         MOV      DX,WORD2        ;doubleword / word
         MOV      AX,WORD3        ;  dividend in DX:AX
         DIV      WORD1           ;  rmdr:quot in DX:AX
```

```
                MOV     AX,WORD1        ;word / word
                SUB     DX,DX           ;   extend dividend in DX
                DIV     WORD3           ;   rmdr:quot in DX:AX
                MOV     BYTE1,01
                MOV     AX,1234H
                IDIV    BYTE1
                RET
D10DIV          ENDP
;                       Examples of IDIV:
;                       ----------------
E10IDIV         PROC
                MOV     AX,WORD1        ;word / byte
                IDIV    BYTE1           ;   rmdr:quot in AH:AL
                MOV     AL,BYTE1        ;byte / byte
                CBW                     ;   extend dividend in AH
                IDIV    BYTE3           ;   rmdr:quot in AH:AL

                MOV     DX,WORD2        ;doubleword / word
                MOV     AX,WORD3        ;   dividend in DX:AX
                IDIV    WORD1           ;   rmdr:quot in DX:AX
                MOV     AX,WORD1        ;word / word
                CWD                     ;   extend dividend in DX
                IDIV    WORD3           ;   rmdr:quot in DX:AX
                RET
E10IDIV         ENDP

CODESG          ENDS
                END     BEGIN
```

Signed Division: IDIV

The IDIV (Integer Divide) instruction divides signed data. In Figure 10-5, E10IDIV uses the same four examples as D10DIV, replacing DIV with IDIV.

The first IDIV example divides hex 2000 (positive) by hex 80 (negative). The remainder in the AH is hex 00 and the quotient in the AL is hex C0 (-64). Note that DIV using the same data caused a quotient of $+64$.

The results in hex of the remaining three IDIV examples are as follows:

IDIV Example	Remainder	Quotient
2	EE (-18)	FB (-5)
3	1000 (4096)	0080 (128)
4	0000	0002

Only Example 4 produces the same answer as DIV. In effect, if the dividend and divisor have the same sign bit, DIV and IDIV generate the same result. But if the the dividend and divisor have different sign bits, DIV generates a positive quotient and IDIV generates a negative quotient.

You may find it worthwhile using DEBUG to trace these examples.

Efficiency. If you divide by a power of 2 (2, 4, etc.), it is more efficient simply to shift right the required number of bits. In the following examples, assume that the dividend is in the AX register:

Divide by 2:   SHR   AX,1   Divide by 4:   MOV   CL,2
                                               SHR   AX,CL

Overflows and Interrupts

It is certainly easy to cause an overflow using DIV and especially IDIV! An interrupt occurs, and, at least with the system used during testing of these programs, the results are unpredictable. The operation assumes that the quotient will be significantly smaller than the original dividend. Dividing by zero will always cause an interrupt. But dividing by 1 generates a quotient that is the same as the dividend and could easily cause an interrupt.

There is one rule that you can apply. If the divisor is a byte, its contents must be less than the left byte (AH) of the dividend; if the divisor is a word, its contents must be less than the left word (DX) of the dividend. Here's an illustration using a divisor of 1, although other values could serve:

Divide operation:	Dividend	Divisor	Quotient
Word by byte:	0123	01	(1)23
Doubleword by word:	0001 4026	0001	(1)4026

In both cases, the quotient exceeds its available space. You may be wise to include a test prior to a DIV or IDIV operation. In the first example following, assume that DIVBYTE is a one-byte divisor and that the dividend is already in the AX. In the second example, DIVWORD is a one-word divisor and the dividend is in the DX:AX.

Word by Byte	Doubleword by Word
CMP AH,DIVBYTE	CMP DIVWORD
JNB overflow-rtne	JNB overflow-rtne
DIV DIVBYTE	DIV DIVWORD

For IDIV, the logic should account for the fact that either dividend or divisor could be negative. Since the absolute value of the divisor must be smaller, you could temporarily set negative values to positive (using the NEG instruction).

Division by Subtraction

If you find that a quotient is too large for the divisor, you could perform successive subtraction. That is, subtract the divisor from the dividend, increment a quotient value by 1, and continue subtracting until the dividend is less than the divisor. In the following example, the dividend is in the AX and the divisor is in the BX, and the quotient is developed in the CX:

```
        SUB   CX,CX          ;Clear quotient
C20:    CMP   AX,BX          ;If dividend < divisor,
        JB    C30            ; then exit
        SUB   AX,BX          ;Subtract div'r from div'd
        INC   CX             ;Add 1 to quotient
        JMP   C20
C30:    RET                  ;Quotient in CX, rmdr in AX
```

At the end of the routine, the CX contains the quotient and the AX contains the remainder. The example is intentionally primitive to demonstrate the technique. If the quotient is in the DX:AX, make the following two additions:

1.   At C20, compare AX to BX only if DX is zero.
2.   After the SUB instruction, insert SBB DX,00.

Note: If the quotient is very large and the divisor is small, there could be thousands of loops!

There is one minor problem remaining: It is all very well to perform arithmetic on binary data that the program itself defines. However, most data enters a program from an external device. Now, if the device is disk or tape, arithmetic data may already be in binary format. But data entered from a terminal is in ASCII format. Although ASCII data is fine for displaying and printing, for arithmetic it requires special adjusting. But that's the topic for the next chapter.

INTEL 8087 NUMERIC DATA PROCESSOR

Need more mathematical punch? Adjacent to the 8088 processor is an empty socket reserved for an Intel 8087 Numeric Data Processor. This is a coprocessor that can operate in conjunction with an 8088 (or 8086) and has its own instruction set and floating-point hardware for performing such operations as exponential, logarithmic, and trigonometric functions. The 8087 contains eight 80-bit floating-point registers that can represent numeric values up to 10 to the 400th power. Its mathematical processing is rated at about 100 times faster than an 8086 (which in turn outperforms an 8088!).

The 8088 requests a specific operation and delivers numeric data to the 8087, which performs the operation and returns the result. Since there is little software available for the 8087 at the time of this writing, you may have to do most of your own programming for it.

KEY POINTS TO REMEMBER

☐ Watch out especially when using one-byte accumulators. The maximum signed values are +127 and -128.

☐ For multiword addition, use ADC to account for any carry from a previous ADD. If the operation is performed in a loop, use CLC to initialize the Carry Flag to zero.

☐ Select MUL or DIV for unsigned data, and IMUL and IDIV for signed data.

☐ For division, be especially careful of overflows. If there is any chance of a zero divisor, be sure to test for the condition. Also, the divisor must be greater than the contents of the AH register (if a byte) or the DX register (if a word).

☐ For multiplying or dividing by powers of 2, use shifting for efficiency. For right shifts, use SHR for unsigned fields and SAR for signed fields. For left shifts, SHL and SAL act identically.

☐ Be alert for Assembler defaults. For example, if FACTOR is defined as DB, then MUL FACTOR assumes the multiplicand is the AL, and DIV FACTOR assumes the dividend is the AX. If FACTOR is a DW, then MUL FACTOR assumes the multiplicand is the AX, and DIV FACTOR assumes the dividend is the DX:AX.

QUESTIONS

Questions refer to the following data:

```
FIELDA   DW   0148H
         DW   2316H
FIELDB   DW   0237H
         DW   4052H
```

10-1. Code the instructions to add:

(a) The word FIELDA to the word FIELDB.

(b) The doubleword beginning at FIELDA to the doubleword at FIELDB.

10-2. Explain the effect of the following instructions:

```
STC
MOV   BX,FIELDA
ADC   BX,FIELDB
```

10-3. Code the instructions to multiply (MUL):

   (a) The contents of the word FIELDA by the word FIELDB.

   (b) The doubleword beginning at FIELDA by the word FIELDB.

10-4. Other than a zero divisor, what divisors will cause an overflow error?

10-5. Code the instructions to divide (DIV):

   (a) The contents of the word FIELDA by 25.

   (b) The doubleword beginning at FIELDA by the word FIELDB.

10-6. Refer to the section Shifting the DX:AX Registers. The second part contains a more efficient method of shifting left four bits. Revise the example for a right shift of four bits.

11

ARITHMETIC II: PROCESSING ASCII AND BCD DATA

Objective:
To examine ASCII and BCD data formats and to cover conversions between these formats and binary.

INTRODUCTION

For efficiency, the computer performs only binary arithmetic. As seen in Chapter 10, this format represents no major problems as long as the program itself defines the data. For most purposes, new data enters a program from a terminal. This data is in the form of ASCII characters, in base-10 format. Similarly, the display of answers back on the screen must be ASCII. To demonstrate the difference between data formats, the number 23 in binary is 00010111, which is hex 17. In ASCII, each character requires a full byte, and the ASCII number 23 internally is hex 3233.

The purpose of this chapter is to cover the techniques of converting ASCII data into binary in order to perform arithmetic, and converting the binary results back into ASCII for viewing. The program at the end of this chapter combines most of the material from the chapters up to this point.

If you have programmed in a high-level language such as BASIC or Pascal you are used to the compiler accounting for decimal positions. However, a computer does not recognize a decimal point in an arithmetic field. In fact, a binary value has no provision for inserting a decimal point; if anything, it requires a *binal* point. Consequently, you as the programmer have to fully account for the placement of decimal or binal points.

ASCII FORMAT

The data that you enter through a terminal is in ASCII format. Consequently, if you enter an alphabetic value such as SAM, its representation in memory is hex 53414D. The representation of a numeric value such as 1234 is hex 31323334. For most purposes, the format of an alphabetic entry such as a person's name or a stock item description remains unchanged in a program. But if you want to perform arithmetic on the numeric value hex 31323334, it requires special treatment.

Now, it is possible to perform arithmetic directly on ASCII numbers. You may have already noticed the following Assembler instructions that adjust ASCII numbers:

AAA (ASCII Adjust for Addition)
AAD (ASCII Adjust for Division)
AAM (ASCII Adjust for Multiplication)
AAS (ASCII Adjust for Subtraction)

These instructions are all coded without operands and automatically adjust the AX register. The "adjust" occurs because the ASCII value represents a so-called "unpacked" base-10 number but the computer performs base-2 arithmetic.

ASCII Addition

Consider the effect of adding the ASCII numbers 8 and 4:

Hex Representation:
38
34
––
6C

The sum hex 6C is neither an ASCII value nor a true binary value. However, ignore the leftmost 6 and add 6 to the rightmost hex C: hex C plus 6 = hex 12 – the correct answer in terms of decimal numbers. Well, that's a little oversimplified, but it does indicate the way in which AAA performs an adjustment.

As an example, assume that the AX contains hex 0038 and the BX

Figure 11-1 ASCII Addition.

```
          page    60,132
TITLE    ASCADD  Adds ASCII numbers
;------------------------------------------------
STACKSG SEGMENT PARA STACK 'Stack'
        DW       32 DUP(?)
STACKSG ENDS
;------------------------------------------------
DATASG  SEGMENT PARA 'Data'
ASC1    DB       '578'
ASC2    DB       '694'
ASC3    DB       '0000'
DATASG  ENDS
;------------------------------------------------
CODESG  SEGMENT PARA 'Code'
BEGIN   PROC     FAR
        ASSUME   CS:CODESG,DS:DATASG,SS:STACKSG
        PUSH     DS
        SUB      AX,AX
        PUSH     AX
        MOV      AX,DATASG
        MOV      DS,AX
        CALL     B10ADD           ;Call Add routine
        RET
BEGIN   ENDP
;                Add ASCII numbers:
;                -----------------
B10ADD  PROC
        CLC
        LEA      SI,ASC1+2        ;Init'ze ASCII numbers
        LEA      DI,ASC2+2
        LEA      BX,ASC3+3
        MOV      CX,03            ;Init'ze 3 loops
B20:
        MOV      AH,00            ;Clear AH
        MOV      AL,[SI]          ;Load ASCII byte
        ADC      AL,[DI]          ;Add (with carry)
        AAA                       ;Adjust for ASCII
        MOV      [BX],AL          ;Store sum
        DEC      SI
        DEC      DI
        DEC      BX
        LOOP     B20              ;Loop 3 times
        MOV      [BX],AH          ;At end, store carry
        RET
B10ADD  ENDP

CODESG  ENDS
        END      BEGIN
```

contains hex 0034. The 38 and 34 represent two ASCII bytes that are to be added. Addition and adjustment are as follows:

```
ADD   AL,BL        ;Add hex 34 to 38
AAA                ;Adjust for ASCII add
```

The AAA instruction checks the rightmost hex digit (four bits) of the AL register. If the digit is between A and F or the AF Flag is 1, the operation adds 6 to the AL register, adds 1 to the AH register, and sets the AF and CF Flags to 1. In all cases, AAA clears to zero the leftmost hex digit of the AL. The result in the AX of the above is:

After the ADD: 006C
After the AAA: 0102

If you want to restore the ASCII representation, simply insert 3's in the leftmost bytes as follows:

```
OR      AX,3030H        ;Result now 3132
```

All that is very well if you want to add one-byte numbers. Addition of multibyte ASCII numbers requires a loop that processes from right to left (low order to high order) and accounts for carries. Figure 11-1 gives an example of adding two three-byte ASCII numbers into a four-byte sum. Following are several important points:

- ☐ The routine uses ADC for addition because any add may cause a carry that should be added to the next (left) byte. A CLC initializes the CF Flag to zero.
- ☐ A MOV instruction clears the AH register on each loop because each AAA may add 1 to the AH. ADC, however, will account for any carry. *Note:* The use of XOR or SUB to clear the AH would change the CF Flag.
- ☐ When looping is complete, the routine moves the AH (containing either 00 or 01) to the leftmost byte of the sum.
- ☐ At the end, the sum is 01020702. The routine did not use OR after AAA to insert leftmost 3's because OR sets the CF Flag and changes the effect for the ADC instructions. One solution to save the Flag settings is to push (PUSHF) the Flags register, execute the OR, and then pop (POPF) the Flags to restore the Flag settings:

```
ADC     AL,[DI]         ;Add with carry
AAA                     ;Adjust for ASCII
PUSHF                   ;Save the Flags
OR      AL,30H          ;Insert ASCII 3
POPF                    ;Restore Flags
MOV     [BX],AL         ;Store sum
```

The instructions LAHF (Load AH with Flags) and SAHF (Store AH in

Flag Register) could replace the PUSHF and POPF instructions respectively. LAHF loads the AH register with the SF, ZF, AF, PF, and CF Flags; SAHF stores the AH contents back into the specific Flags. This example, however, already uses the AH register for arithmetic overflows. Another solution to insert ASCII 3's is to loop through the sum in memory and OR each byte with hex 30.

ASCII Subtraction

The AAS (ASCII Adjust for Subtraction) instruction works in a similar fashion to AAA. The AAS instruction checks the rightmost hex digit (four bits) of the AL register. If the digit is between A and F or the AF Flag is 1, the operation subtracts 6 from the AL, subtracts 1 from the AH, and sets the AF and CF Flags. For all cases, AAS clears to zero the leftmost hex digit of the AL.

In the following two examples, assume that ASC1 contains hex 38 and ASC2 contains hex 34:

Example 1		AX	AF	Example 2		AX	AF
MOV	AL,ASC1	;0038		MOV	AL,ASC2	;0034	
SUB	AL,ASC2	;0004	0	SUB	AL,ASC1	;00FC	1
AAS		;0004	0	AAS		;FF06	1

In Example 1, AAS does not need to make an adjustment. In Example 2, since the rightmost digit is hex C, AAS subtracts 6 from the AL, 1 from the AH, and sets the AF and CF Flags. The answer, which should be -4, is hex FF06, the 10's complement of -4.

ASCII Multiplication

The AAM (ASCII Adjust for Multiplication) instruction corrects the result of multiplying ASCII data in the AX register. However, the data must first be cleared of 3's in the leftmost hex digits and accordingly is not a true ASCII value (the IBM manual uses the term "unpacked decimal"). For example, the ASCII number 31323334 as unpacked decimal is 01020304. Further, because the adjustment is only one byte at a time, you can multiply only one-byte fields and have to code the operation as a loop.

AAM divides the AL by 10 (hex 0A) and stores the quotient in the AH and the remainder in the AL. For example, suppose the AL contains hex 35 and the CL contains hex 39. The following multiplies the contents of the AL by the CL and converts the result to ASCII format:

```
                                                    AX:
      AND    CL,0FH      ;Convert CL to 09
      AND    AL,0FH      ;Convert AL to 05        0005
      MUL    CL          ;Mult AL by CL           002D
      AAM                ;Convert to unpacked dec 0405
      OR     AX,3030H    ;Convert to ASCII        3435
```

Figure 11-2 ASCII Multiplication.

```
            page    60,132
TITLE    ASCMUL  Multiplies ASCII numbers
;-------------------------------------------------
STACKSG SEGMENT PARA STACK 'Stack'
        DW      32 DUP(?)
STACKSG ENDS
;-------------------------------------------------
DATASG  SEGMENT PARA 'Data'
MULTCND DB      '3783'
MULTPLR DB      '5'
PRODUCT DB      5 DUP(0)
DATASG  ENDS
;-------------------------------------------------
CODESG  SEGMENT PARA 'Code'
BEGIN   PROC    FAR
        ASSUME  CS:CODESG,DS:DATASG,SS:STACKSG
        PUSH    DS
        SUB     AX,AX
        PUSH    AX
        MOV     AX,DATASG
        MOV     DS,AX
        CALL    C10MULT         ;Call Multiply routine
        RET
BEGIN   ENDP
;               Multiply ASCII numbers:
;               ----------------------
C10MULT PROC
        MOV     CX,04           ;Init'ze 4 loops
        LEA     SI,MULTCND+3
        LEA     DI,PRODUCT+4
        AND     MULTPLR,0FH     ;Clear ASCII 3
C20:
        MOV     AL,[SI]         ;Load ASCII character
        AND     AL,0FH          ;Clear ASCII 3
        MUL     MULTPLR         ;Multiply
        AAM                     ;Adjust for ASCII
        ADD     AL,[DI]         ;Add to
        AAA                     ;  stored
        MOV     [DI],AL         ;  product
        DEC     DI
        MOV     [DI],AH         ;Store product carry
        DEC     SI
        LOOP    C20             ;Loop 4 times
        RET
C10MULT ENDP

CODESG  ENDS
        END     BEGIN
```

The MUL operation generates 45 (hex 002D) in the AX. AAM then divides this value by 10, generating a quotient of 04 in the AH and a remainder of 05 in the AL. The OR instruction then converts the unpacked decimal value to ASCII format.

Figure 11-2 depicts multiplying a four-byte multiplicand by a one-byte multiplier. Since AAM can accommodate only one-byte operations, the routine steps through the multiplicand one byte at a time, from right to left. The final product is 0108090105.

If the multiplier is greater than one byte, you will have to provide for yet another loop that steps through the multiplier. It may be simpler to convert the ASCII data to binary format (see the later section, "Conversion of ASCII to Binary Format").

ASCII Division

The AAD (ASCII Adjust for Division) instruction provides a correction of an ASCII dividend *prior* to dividing. However, you must first clear the leftmost 3's from the ASCII fields to create "unpacked decimal." AAD allows for a two-byte dividend in the AX. Assume that the AX contains the ASCII value 3238 and the divisor, 37, is in the CL. The following performs the adjustment and the division:

			AX
AND	CL,0FH	;Convert to unpacked	
AND	AX,0F0FH	;Convert to unpacked	0208
AAD		;Convert to binary	001C
DIV	CL	;Divide by 7	0004

The AAD operation multiplies the AH by 10 (hex 0A), adds the product 20 (hex 14) to the AL, and clears the AH. The result, 001C, is the hex representation of decimal 28. The divisor can be only a single byte containing 01 to 09.

Figure 11-3 allows for dividing a one-byte divisor into a four-byte dividend. The routine steps through the dividend from left to right. The remainders stay in the AH register so that AAD will adjust it in the AL. The final quotient is 00090204 and the remainder in the AH is 02.

If the divisor is greater than one byte, you will have to provide for yet another loop to step through the divisor. Better yet, see the later section, "Conversion of ASCII to Binary Format."

BINARY CODED DECIMAL (BCD) FORMAT

In the preceding example of ASCII division, the quotient was 00090204. If you were to compress this value keeping only the right digit of each byte, the value would be 0924. This latter value is known as binary coded decimal (BCD) format (also known as "packed") and contains only the decimal digits 0 through 9. The BCD length is one-half the ASCII length. Note, however, that the decimal number 0924 is in base 10; converted to base 16 (hexadecimal) it would appear as hex 039C.

Figure 11-3 ASCII Division.

```
                page     60,132
TITLE     ASCDIV  Divides ASCII numbers
;-----------------------------------------------
STACKSG SEGMENT PARA STACK 'Stack'
        DW       32 DUP(?)
STACKSG ENDS
;-----------------------------------------------
DATASG  SEGMENT PARA 'Data'
DIVDND  DB       '3698'
DIVSOR  DB       '4'
QUOTNT  DB       4 DUP(0)
DATASG  ENDS
;-----------------------------------------------
CODESG  SEGMENT PARA 'Code'
BEGIN   PROC     FAR
        ASSUME   CS:CODESG,DS:DATASG,SS:STACKSG
        PUSH     DS
        SUB      AX,AX
        PUSH     AX
        MOV      AX,DATASG
        MOV      DS,AX
        CALL     D10DIV              ;Call Divide routine
        RET
BEGIN   ENDP
```

```
;                       Divide ASCII numbers:
;                       --------------------
D10DIV    PROC
          MOV     CX,04               ;Init'ze 4 loops
          SUB     AH,AH               ;Clear left byte of dividend
          AND     DIVSOR,0FH          ;Clear divisor of ASCII 3
          LEA     SI,DIVDND
          LEA     DI,QUOTNT
D20:
          MOV     AL,[SI]             ;Load ASCII byte
          AND     AL,0FH              ;Clear ASCII 3
          AAD                         ;Adjust for divide
          DIV     DIVSOR              ;Divide
          MOV     [DI],AL             ;Store quotient
          INC     SI
          INC     DI
          LOOP    D20                 ;Loop 4 times
          RET
D10DIV    ENDP

CODESG    ENDS
          END     BEGIN
```

You can perform addition and subtraction on BCD data. For this purpose, there are two adjustment instructions:

DAA (Decimal Adjustment for Addition)

DAS (Decimal Adjustment for Subtraction)

Once again, you have to process the fields one byte at a time. The example program in Figure 11-4 converts two ASCII numbers to BCD format and adds the BCD numbers. The Procedure B10CONV converts ASCII to BCD. Processing, which is from right to left, could just as easily process left to right. Also, processing words is easier than bytes because you need two ASCII bytes to generate one BCD byte. This technique does require that the length of the ASCII field is an even number.

Figure 11-4 BCD Conversion and Arithmetic.

```
           page       60,132
TITLE      BCDARITH Converts ASCII numbers to BCD and adds
;-------------------------------------------------
STACKSG SEGMENT PARA STACK 'Stack'
        DW       32 DUP(?)
STACKSG ENDS
;-------------------------------------------------
DATASG  SEGMENT PARA 'Data'
ASC1    DB       '057836'
ASC2    DB       '069427'
BCD1    DB       '000'
BCD2    DB       '000'
BCD3    DB       4 DUP(0)
DATASG  ENDS
;-------------------------------------------------
CODESG  SEGMENT PARA 'Code'
BEGIN   PROC     FAR
        ASSUME   CS:CODESG,DS:DATASG,SS:STACKSG
        PUSH     DS
        SUB      AX,AX
        PUSH     AX
        MOV      AX,DATASG
        MOV      DS,AX

        LEA      SI,ASC1+4       ;Init'ze for ASC1
        LEA      DI,BCD1+2
        CALL     B10CONV         ;Call Convert routine
        LEA      SI,ASC2+4       ;Init'ze for ASC2
        LEA      DI,BCD2+2
        CALL     B10CONV         ;Call Convert routine
        CALL     C10ADD          ;Call Add routine
        RET
BEGIN   ENDP
;                 Convert ASII to BCD:
;                 -------------------
B10CONV PROC
        MOV      CL,04           ;Shift factor
        MOV      DX,03           ;No. of words to convert
B20:
        MOV      AX,[SI]         ;Get ASCII pair
        XCHG     AH,AL
        SHL      AL,CL           ;Shift off
        SHL      AX,CL           ;  ASCII 3's
        MOV      [DI],AH         ;Store BCD digits
        DEC      SI
```

```
                    DEC    SI
                    DEC    DI
                    DEC    DX
                    JNZ    B20
                    RET
        B10CONV ENDP
        ;                  Add BCD numbers:
        ;                  ---------------
        C10ADD  PROC
                    XOR    AH,AH              ;Clear AH
                    LEA    SI,BCD1+2          ;Init'ze
                    LEA    DI,BCD2+2          ; BCD
                    LEA    BX,BCD3+3          ; addresses
                    MOV    CX,03              ;3 byte fields
                    CLC
        C20:
                    MOV    AL,[SI]            ;Get BCD1
                    ADC    AL,[DI]            ;Add BCD2
                    DAA                       ;Decimal adjust
                    MOV    [BX],AL            ;Store in BCD3
                    DEC    SI
                    DEC    DI
                    DEC    BX
                    LOOP   C20                ;Loop 3 times
                    RET
        C10ADD  ENDP

        CODESG  ENDS
                    END    BEGIN
```

The Procedure C10ADD adds the BCD numbers. The final total is 127263.

CONVERSION OF ASCII TO BINARY FORMAT

Performing arithmetic in ASCII or BCD formats is suitable only for short fields. For most arithmetic purposes, it is more practical to convert into binary format. In fact, it is easier to convert from ASCII directly to binary rather than convert from ASCII to BCD to binary.

The conversion method is based on the fact that the ASCII number is in base 10 and the computer performs arithmetic only in base 2. The conversion procedure is as follows:

1. Start with the rightmost byte of the ASCII number and process from right to left.
2. Strip out the 3's from the left hex digit of the ASCII byte.
3. Multiply the ASCII digits progressively by 1, then 10, then 100 (hex 1, A, 64), and so forth, and sum the products.

For example, assume conversion of the ASCII number 1234:

	Decimal	Hexadecimal
4 × 1 =	4	4
3 × 10 =	30	1E
2 × 100 =	200	C8
1 × 1000 =	1000	3E8
Total:		04D2

Try checking that hex 04D2 really equals decimal 1234. In Figure 11-5, B10ASBI illustrates conversion of an ASCII number 1234 to binary. The example assumes that the length of the ASCII number, 4, is stored in ASCLEN. This field could be in the parameter list used as input from the terminal. For initialization, the address of the ASCII field, ASCVAL-1, is in the SI register and the length is in the BX register. The instruction at B20 that moves the ASCII byte to the AL register

$$\text{MOV} \quad \text{AL,[SI+BX]}$$

uses the address of ASCVAL-1 plus the contents of the BX register (4), or ASCVAL + 3 (initially the rightmost byte of ASCVAL). Each iteration of the loop decrements BX by 1 and references the next byte to the left. Note that for this addressing you can use BX but not CX, and consequently cannot use the LOOP instruction. Also, each iteration multiplies MULT10 by 10 giving a multiplier of 1, 10, 100, and so forth. The routine is coded for clarity; for efficiency, the multiplier could be stored in the SI or DI register.

Figure 11-5 Conversion of ASCII and Binary Formats.

```
           page    60,132
TITLE      EXCONV  Conversion of ASCII & Binary formats
; --------------------------------------------------------
STACKSG SEGMENT PARA STACK 'Stack'
        DW      32 DUP(?)
STACKSG ENDS
; --------------------------------------------------------
DATASG  SEGMENT PARA 'Data'
ASCVAL  DB      '1234'
BINVAL  DW      0
ASCLEN  DW      4
MULT10  DW      1
DATASG  ENDS
; --------------------------------------------------------
CODESG  SEGMENT PARA 'Code'
BEGIN   PROC    FAR
        ASSUME  CS:CODESG,DS:DATASG,SS:STACKSG
        PUSH    DS
        SUB     AX,AX
        PUSH    AX
        MOV     AX,DATASG
        MOV     DS,AX
```

```
                CALL    B10ASBI         ;Call Convert ASCII
                CALL    C10BIAS         ;Call Convert Binary
                RET
BEGIN   ENDP
;                       Convert ASCII to binary:
;                       ------------------------
B10ASBI PROC
                MOV     CX,10           ;Mult factor
                LEA     SI,ASCVAL-1     ;Address of ASCVAL
                MOV     BX,ASCLEN       ;Length of ASCVAL
B20:
                MOV     AL,[SI+BX]      ;Select ASCII char.
                AND     AX,000FH        ;Remove 3-zone
                MUL     MULT10          ;Multiply by 10 factor
                ADD     BINVAL,AX       ;Add to binary
                MOV     AX,MULT10       ;Calculate next
                MUL     CX              ;  10 factor
                MOV     MULT10,AX
                DEC     BX              ;Last ASCII char?
                JNZ     B20             ;  no - continue
                RET
B10ASBI ENDP

;                       Convert binary to ASCII:
;                       ------------------------
C10BIAS PROC
                MOV     CX,0010         ;Divide factor
                LEA     SI,ASCVAL+3     ;Address of ASCVAL
                MOV     AX,BINVAL       ;Get binary field
C20:
                CMP     AX,0010         ;Value < 10?
                JB      C30             ;  yes - exit
                XOR     DX,DX           ;Clear upper quotient
                DIV     CX              ;Divide by 10
                OR      DL,30H
                MOV     [SI],DL         ;Store ASCII char.
                DEC     SI
                JMP     C20
C30:
                OR      AL,30H          ;Store last quotient
                MOV     [SI],AL         ;  as ASCII char.
                RET
C10BIAS ENDP

CODESG  ENDS
        END     BEGIN
```

CONVERSION OF BINARY TO ASCII FORMAT

In order to print or display an arithmetic result, you have to convert it into
ASCII format. The operation involves reversing the previous step: Instead of
multiplying, simply divide the binary number by 10 (hex 0A) successively
until the result is less than 10. The remainders, which can be only 0 through
9, generate the ASCII number. As an example, let's convert hex 4D2 back
into decimal format:

	Quotient	Remainder
A⟌4D2	7B	4
A⟌7B	C	3
A⟌C	1	2

Since the quotient, 1, is now less than hex A, the operation is complete. The remainders along with the last quotient form the ASCII result, from right to left, as 1234. It is now a simple matter of storing these digits in memory with the ASCII 3's, as 31323334.

In Figure 11-5, C10BIAS gives an example of converting binary hex 4D2 (as calculated in B10ASBI) to ASCII 1234. You may find it useful if not downright entertaining to reproduce this program and trace its execution step by step.

The next section combines the material from this and preceding chapters.

SHIFTING AND ROUNDING

Suppose that you are rounding a product to two decimal places. If the product is 12.345, then add 5 to the unwanted decimal position and shift right one digit as follows:

$$
\begin{array}{ll}
\text{Product:} & 12.345 \\
\text{Add 5:} & \underline{+5} \\
\text{Rounded product:} & 12.350 = 12.35 \\
\end{array}
$$

If the product is 12.3455, add 50 and shift two digits, and if the product is 12.34555, add 500 and shift three digits:

$$
\begin{array}{ll}
12.3455 & 12.34555 \\
\underline{+50} & \underline{+500} \\
12.3505 = 12.35 & 12.35055 = 12.35 \\
\end{array}
$$

Further, a number with six decimal places requires adding 5000 and shifting four digits, and so forth. Now, since data representation on the computer is binary, 12.345 appears as hex 3039. Adding 5 to 3039 gives 303E, or 12350 in decimal format. So far, so good. But *shifting* one binary digit results in hex 181F, or 6175 — indeed, the shift simply halves the value. What we require is a shift that is equivalent to shifting right one decimal digit. You can accomplish this shift by dividing by 10, or hex A:

Hex 303E divided by hex A = 4D3, or decimal 1235

Conversion of hex 4D3 to an ASCII number gives 1235. Now just insert a decimal point in the correct position, 12.35, and you can display a rounded and shifted value.

In this fashion you can round and shift any binary number. For three decimal places, add 5 and divide by 10; for four decimal places, add 50 and divide by 100. Perhaps you have noticed a pattern: The rounding factor (5, 50, 500, etc.) is always one-half the value of the shift factor (10, 100, 1000, etc.).

Of course, the decimal point in a binary number is implied and is not normally physically present.

PROGRAM: CONVERTING HOURS AND RATE FOR CALCULATING WAGE

The program in Figure 11-6 allows users to enter hours worked and rate of pay for employees and displays the calculated wage. For brevity, the program omits some error checking. The Procedures are as follows:

B10INPT   Accepts hours and rate of pay from the terminal. These values may contain a decimal point.

D10HOUR   Initializes conversion of ASCII hours to binary.

Figure 11-6 Displaying Employee Wages.

```
          page     60,132
     TITLE   SCREMP  Enter hours & rate, display wage
     ; --------------------------------------------------
     STACKSG SEGMENT PARA STACK 'Stack'
             DW      32 DUP(?)
     STACKSG ENDS
     ; --------------------------------------------------
     DATASG  SEGMENT PARA 'Data'
     HRSPAR  LABEL   BYTE              ;Hours parameter list:
     MAXHLEN DB      6                 ;----- --------- ----
     ACTHLEN DB      ?
     HRSFLD  DB      6 DUP(?), '$'

     RATEPAR LABEL   BYTE              ;Rate parameter list:
     MAXRLEN DB      6                 ;---- --------- ----
     ACTRLEN DB      ?
     RATEFLD DB      6 DUP(?), '$'
```

```
              MESSG1   DB       'Hours worked? ','$'
              MESSG2   DB       'Rate of pay?  ','$'
              MESSG3   DB       'Wage = '
              ADJUST   DW       ?
              ASCWAGE  DB       10 DUP(30H),'$'
              ASCHRS   DB       0
              ASCRATE  DB       0
              BINVAL   DW       00
              BINHRS   DW       00
              BINRATE  DW       00
              DECIND   DB       00
              MULT10   DW       01
              NODEC    DW       00
              ROWCTR   DB       00
              SHIFT    DW       ?
              TENWD    DW       10
              DATASG   ENDS
              ; --------------------------------------------
              CODESG   SEGMENT  PARA 'Code'
              BEGIN    PROC     FAR
                       ASSUME   CS:CODESG,DS:DATASG,SS:STACKSG,ES:DATASG
                       PUSH     DS
                       SUB      AX,AX
                       PUSH     AX
                       MOV      AX,DATASG
                       MOV      DS,AX
                       MOV      ES,AX
                       CALL     Q10CLR          ;Clear screen
              A20LOOP:
                       CALL     B10INPT         ;Accept hours & rate
                       CMP      ACTHLEN,00      ;End of input?
                       JE       A30
                       CALL     D10HOUR         ;Convert hours to binary
                       CALL     E10RATE         ;Convert rate to binary
                       CALL     F10MULT         ;Calc wage, round
                       CALL     G10WAGE         ;Convert wage to ASCII
                       CALL     K10DISP         ;Display wage
                       JMP      A20LOOP
              A30:
                       CALL     Q10CLR
                       RET                      ;Return to DOS
              BEGIN    ENDP
              ;                 Input hours & rate:
              ;                 ------------------
              B10INPT  PROC
                       SUB      DL,DL
                       CALL     Q20CURS         ;Set cursor
                       LEA      DX,MESSG1       ;Prompt for hours
                       MOV      AH,09
                       INT      21H
                       LEA      DX,HRSPAR       ;Accept hours
                       MOV      AH,0AH
                       INT      21H
                       CMP      ACTHLEN,00      ;No hours? (indicates end)
                       JNE      B20
                       RET                      ;If so, return to A20LOOP
              B20:;
                       MOV      DL,25
                       CALL     Q20CURS
                       LEA      DX,MESSG2       ;Prompt for rate
                       MOV      AH,09
                       INT      21H
                       LEA      DX,RATEPAR      ;Accept rate
```

```
                    MOV       AH,0AH
                    INT       21H
                    RET
B10INPT ENDP
;                             Process hours:
;                             --------------
D10HOUR PROC
                    MOV       NODEC,00
                    MOV       CL,ACTHLEN
                    SUB       CH,CH
                    LEA       SI,HRSFLD-1     ;Set right pos'n
                    ADD       SI,CX           ; of hours
                    CALL      M10ASBI         ;Convert to binary
                    MOV       AX,BINVAL
                    MOV       BINHRS,AX
                    RET
D10HOUR ENDP
;                             Process rate:
;                             ------------
E10RATE PROC
                    MOV       CL,ACTRLEN
                    SUB       CH,CH
                    LEA       SI,RATEFLD-1    ;Set right pos'n
                    ADD       SI,CX           ; of rate
                    CALL      M10ASBI         ;Convert to binary
                    MOV       AX,BINVAL
                    MOV       BINRATE,AX
                    RET
E10RATE ENDP
;                             Multiply, round, & shift:
;                             -------------------------
F10MULT PROC
                    MOV       CX,05
                    LEA       DI,ASCWAGE      ;Set ASCII wage
                    MOV       AX,3030H        ; to 30's
                    CLD
                    REP STOSW

                    MOV       SHIFT,10
                    MOV       ADJUST,00
                    MOV       CX,NODEC
                    CMP       CL,06           ;If more than 6
                    JA        F40             ; decimals, error
                    DEC       CX
                    DEC       CX
                    JLE       F30             ;Bypass if 0, 1, 2 decs
                    MOV       NODEC,02
                    MOV       AX,01
F20:
                    MUL       TENWD           ;Calculate shift factor
                    LOOP      F20

                    MOV       SHIFT,AX
                    SHR       AX,1            ;Calculate round value
                    MOV       ADJUST,AX
F30:
                    MOV       AX,BINHRS
                    MUL       BINRATE         ;Calculate wage
                    ADD       AX,ADJUST       ;Round wage
                    ADC       DX,00
                    CMP       DX,SHIFT        ;Product too large
                    JB        F50             ; for DIV?
```

```
F40:
            SUB       AX,AX
            JMP       F70
F50:
            CMP       ADJUST,00         ;No shift required?
            JZ        F80
            DIV       SHIFT             ;Shift wage
F70:        SUB       DX,DX             ;Clear remainder
F80:        RET
F10MULT     ENDP
;                     Convert to ASCII:
;                     ----------------
G10WAGE     PROC
            LEA       SI,ASCWAGE+7      ;Set decimal pt.
            MOV       BYTE PTR[SI],'.'
            ADD       SI,NODEC          ;Set right start pos'n
G30:
            CMP       BYTE PTR[SI],'.'
            JNE       G35               ;Bypass if at dec pos'n
            DEC       SI
G35:
            CMP       DX,00             ;If DX:AX < 10,
            JNZ       G40
            CMP       AX,0010           ;  operation finished
            JB        G50
G40:
            DIV       TENWD             ;Remainder is ASCII digit
            OR        DL,30H
            MOV       [SI],DL           ;Store ASCII character
            DEC       SI
            SUB       DX,DX             ;Clear remainder
            JMP       G30
G50:
            OR        AL,30H            ;Store last ASCII
            MOV       [SI],AL           ;  character
            RET
G10WAGE     ENDP
;                     Display wage:
:                     ------------
K10DISP     PROC
            MOV       DL,50
            CALL      Q20CURS
            INC       ROWCTR
            MOV       CX,09
            LEA       SI,ASCWAGE
K20:                                    ;Clear leading zeros
            CMP       BYTE PTR[SI],30H
            JNE       K30               ;  to blanks
            MOV       BYTE PTR[SI],20H
            INC       SI
            LOOP      K20
K30:
            LEA       DX,MESSG3         ;Display
            MOV       AH,09
            INT       21H
            RET
K10DISP     ENDP
;                     Convert ASCII to binary:
;                     -----------------------
M10ASBI     PROC
            MOV       MULT10,0001
            MOV       BINVAL,00
```

```
                MOV     DECIND,00
                SUB     BX,BX
        M20:
                MOV     AL,[SI]         ;Get ASCII character
                CMP     AL,'.'          ;Bypass if dec pt.
                JNE     M40
                MOV     DECIND,01
                JMP     M90
        M40:
                AND     AX,000FH
                MUL     MULT10          ;Multiply by factor
                ADD     BINVAL,AX       ;Add to binary
                MOV     AX,MULT10       ;Calculate next
                MUL     TENWD           ;   factor x 10
                MOV     MULT10,AX
                CMP     DECIND,00       ;Reached decimal pt?
                JNZ     M90
                INC     BX              ;   yes - add to count
        M90:
                DEC     SI
                LOOP    M20

                CMP     DECIND,00       ;End of loop
                JZ      M100            ;Any decimal pt?
                ADD     NODEC,BX        ;   yes - add to total
        M100:   RET
        M10ASBI ENDP
        ;                       Clear screen:
        ;                       ------------
        Q10CLR  PROC    NEAR
                MOV     AX,0600H
                MOV     BH,07
                SUB     CX,CX
                MOV     DX,184FH
                INT     10H
                RET
        Q10CLR  ENDP
        ;                       Set cursor acc'g to DX:
        ;                       ----------------------
        Q20CURS PROC    NEAR
                MOV     AH,02
                SUB     BH,BH
                MOV     DH,ROWCTR
                INT     10H
                RET
        Q20CURS ENDP

        CODESG  ENDS
                END     BEGIN
```

E10RATE   Initializes conversion of ASCII rate to binary.

F10MULT   Performs the multiplication, rounding, and shifting. A wage with
          zero, one, or two decimal places does not require rounding or shifting.
          A limitation is in allowing up to only six decimal places in wage,
          although that is certainly more than would reasonably be required.

G10WAGE   Inserts the decimal point, determines the right position to begin stor-
           ing ASCII characters, and converts the binary wage to ASCII.

K10DISP   Clears leading zeros to blank and displays the wage.

M10ASBI   Converts ASCII to binary (a common routine for hours and for rate)
           and determines the number of decimal places in the entered value.

Limitations. One limitation in the program mentioned earlier is a total of six decimal places. Another limitation is the magnitude of the wage itself and the fact that shifting involves dividing by a multiple of 10 and converting to ASCII involves dividing by 10. If hours and rate contain a total that exceeds six decimal places or if the wage exceeds about 655,350, the program clears the wage to zero. In practice, a program would print a warning message or would contain subroutines to overcome these limitations.

Error Checking. A program designed for users other than the programmer not only should produce warning messages, but also should validate hours and rate. The only valid characters are numbers 0 through 9 and one decimal point. For any other character, the program should display a message and return to the input prompt. A useful instruction for validating is XLAT, which Chapter 12 covers.

Negative Values. Some applications involve negative amounts, especially for reversing and correcting entries. You could allow a minus sign preceding a value, such as -12.34, or following the value, such as $12.34-$. The program could check for a minus sign during conversion to binary. You may want to leave the binary number as positive and simply set an indicator to record the fact that the amount is negative. When the arithmetic is complete, the program, if required, can insert a minus sign in the ASCII field.

If you want the binary number to be negative, convert the ASCII input to binary as usual. Then use the NEG instruction to change the sign of the binary field. But watch out for using IMUL and IDIV to handle signed data. For rounding, subtract 5 instead of add 5.

Test your program thoroughly for all possible conditions: zero value, extreme high and low values, and negative values.

KEY POINTS TO REMEMBER

☐   An ASCII field requires one byte for each character. If the field contains only digits 0 through 9, then converting the high-order ASCII 3's to 0's causes the field to contain "unpacked decimal." Compressing the digits to two digits per byte causes the field to contain "packed decimal."

☐ After an ASCII add, adjust the answer with AAA; after an ASCII subtract adjust the answer with AAS.

☐ Before an ASCII multiplication, convert the multiplicand and multiplier to "unpacked decimal" by clearing the leftmost hex 3's. After the multiplication adjust the product with AAM.

☐ Before an ASCII divide, (1) convert the dividend and divisor to "unpacked decimal" by clearing the leftmost hex 3's, and (2) adjust the dividend with AAD.

☐ For most arithmetic purposes, convert ASCII numbers to binary. When converting from ASCII to binary format, check that the ASCII characters are valid: 30 though 39, decimal point, and possibly a minus sign.

QUESTIONS

11-1. Assume that the AX contains ASCII 9 and the CX contains ASCII 7. Explain the exact results of the following unrelated operations:

    (a) ADD   AX,33H   (b) ADD   AX,CX
           AAA   AAA

    (c) SUB   AX,CX   (d) SUB   AX,0DH
           AAS   AAS

11-2. An "unpacked decimal" field named UNDEC contains hex 01020702. Code a loop that will cause its contents to be proper ASCII 31323732.

11-3. A field named ASCX contains the ASCII value 313733 and another field named ASCY contains 35. Code the instructions to multiply the ASCII numbers and to store the product in ASCPRD.

11-4. Use the same field as Question 11-3 to divide ASCX by ASCY and store the quotient in ASCQNT.

11-5. Provide the manual calculations for the following:

(a) Convert ASCII 53682 to binary (show in hex).

(b) Convert the hex value back to ASCII.

11-6. Code and run a program that determines the computer's memory size (INT 12H – see Chapter 2), converts the size to ASCII format, and displays it on the screen as follows:

Memory size is nnn bytes

12

TABLE PROCESSING

Objective:
To cover the requirements for defining tables, for performing table searches, and for sorting table entries.

INTRODUCTION

Many program applications require a tabular arrangement of data. These tables may include, for example, names, descriptions, quantities, and prices. The definition and use of tables involves no new Assembler instructions. Indeed, it is simply a matter of technique and of applying what you have already learned.

This chapter begins by defining some example tables that are intended mainly as a guide. You will doubtless encounter unique requirements that involve other situations. Further, since techniques for table searching are subject to the way in which the tables are defined, many variations of table search are possible.

DEFINING TABLES

In order to facilitate table searching, most tables are defined methodically. That is, each entry is in the same format (character or numeric), the same length, and in either ascending or descending order.

One example of a table that you have been using all along is the definition of the Stack, a table of 32 uninitialized words:

> STACK   DW   32 DUP(?)

The following two tables initialize character and numeric values respectively:

> MONTAB DB   'JAN', 'FEB', 'MAR', ..., 'DEC'
> EMPTAB DB   102, 108, 109, 112, 113, 120, ...

MONTAB defines an alphabetic abbreviation of the months, and EMPTAB defines a table of employee numbers. A table may also contain a mixture of numeric and character values, provided that the numeric values are consistent and the character values are consistent. In the following table of stock items, each numeric entry (stock number) is two digits (one byte) and each character entry (stock description) is nine bytes:

> STOKTAB DB   20,'Computers',22, 'Printers ',23,'Diskettes'

For added clarity, you may even code the table entries vertically:

> STOKTAB   DB   20, 'Computers'
>   DB   22, 'Printers '
>   DB   23, 'Diskettes'

Now that's the way to define tables; let's examine different ways to use them in a program.

DIRECT TABLE ACCESSING

Suppose that a terminal user enters a numeric month such as 08 and a program is to convert the month, 03, to alphabetic, March. The routine to perform this conversion involves defining a table of alphabetic months, all of equal length. Since the longest name is September, the length is 9, as in the following definition:

```
          MONTAB   DB   'January  '
                   DB   'February '
                   DB   'March    '
                        •
                        •
                        •
```

The entry 'January' is at MONTAB + 0, 'February' is at MONTAB + 9, and 'March' is at MONTAB + 18. To locate month 03, the program has to perform the following steps:

1.   Convert the entered month from ASCII 33 to binary 03.
2.   Deduct 1 from the month: 03 − 1 = 02.
3.   Multiply the month by 9: 02 x 9 = 18.
4.   Add this product to the address of MONTAB; the result is the address of the required description: MONTAB + 18.

Figure 12-1 provides an example of a direct access of a table of the months' names, although for brevity the descriptions are three rather than nine characters long. The entered month is defined as MONIN; assume that a routine has requested a user to enter an ASCII month number into this location.

Figure 12-1 Direct Table Addressing.

```
          page    66,132
TITLE     DIRECT  Direct table access
; ----------------------------------------------------
STACKSG SEGMENT PARA STACK 'Stack'
        DW        32 DUP(?)
STACKSG ENDS
; ----------------------------------------------------
DATASG   SEGMENT PARA 'Data'
THREE    DB      3
MONIN    DB      '11'
ALFMON   DB      '???','$'
MONTAB   DB      'JAN','FEB','MAR','APR','MAY','JUN'
         DB      'JUL','AUG','SEP','OCT','NOV','DEC'
DATASG   ENDS
; ----------------------------------------------------
CODESG   SEGMENT PARA 'Code'
BEGIN    PROC    FAR
         ASSUME  CS:CODESG,DS:DATASG,SS:STACKSG,ES:DATASG
         PUSH    DS
         SUB     AX,AX
         PUSH    AX
         MOV     AX,DATASG
         MOV     DS,AX
```

```
                MOV      ES,AX
                CALL     C10CONV            ;Convert to binary
                CALL     D10LOC             ;Locate month
                CALL     F10DISP            ;Display alpha month
                RET
BEGIN    ENDP
;                        Convert ASCII to binary:
;                        ------------------------
C10CONV  PROC
                MOV      AH,MONIN           ;Set up month
                MOV      AL,MONIN+1
                XOR      AX,3030H           ;Clear ASCII 3's
                CMP      AH,00              ;Month 01-09?
                JZ       C20                ;  Yes - bypass
                SUB      AH,AH              ;  No  - clear AH,
                ADD      AL,10              ;  correct for binary
C20:     RET
C10CONV  ENDP
;                        Locate month in table:
;                        ----------------------
D10LOC   PROC
                LEA      SI,MONTAB
                DEC      AL                 ;Correct for table
                MUL      THREE              ;Mult AL by 3
                ADD      SI,AX
                MOV      CX,03              ;Init'ze 3-char move
                CLD
                LEA      DI,ALFMON
                REP MOVSB                   ;Move 3 chars
                RET
D10LOC   ENDP
;                        Display alpha month:
;                        -------------------
F10DISP  PROC
                LEA      DX,ALFMON
                MOV      AH,09
                INT      21H
                RET
F10DISP  ENDP

CODESG   ENDS
         END      BEGIN
```

The technique is direct table accessing. Since the algorithm directly calculates the required table address, the program does not have to search through the table.

Although direct table addressing is very efficient, it works only when the entries have consecutive organization. That is, you could design such a table if the entries are in order of 1, 2, 3, ..., or 106, 107, 108, ..., or even 5, 10, 15, ... You don't usually have such a neat arrangement of table entries. The next section examines tables that do not have consecutive organization and the special requirements for table searching.

TABLE SEARCHING

Not all tables lend themselves to consecutive organization. Some tables consist of entries that have no apparent pattern of numbers. A typical example is a table of stock items with numbers such as 134, 138, 141, 239, and 245. Another type of table contains ranges of values such as an income tax table. The following sections will examine these types – tables with unique entries and tables with ranges – and the requirements for table searching.

Tables with Unique Entries

The stock item numbers for most firms are often not in consecutive order. Numbers tend to be grouped by category, with a leading number to indicate furniture or appliance, or to indicate department number. Also, over time, numbers are deleted and others are added. As a result, you will have to attach a stock number to its particular description (and unit price, if required). Stock items and descriptions could be defined in separate tables, as:

```
STOKNOS   DB    '101','107','109', ...
STOKDCR   DB    'Excavators','Processors','Assemblers', ...
```

or in the same table, as:

```
STOKTAB   DB    '101','Excavators'
          DB    '107','Processors'
          DB    '109','Assemblers'
          ...
```

The program in Figure 12-2 defines the stock table and performs a table search. The table contains six pairs of item numbers and descriptions. The search loop in C10SRCH begins comparing the input stock number, STOKNIN, to the first stock number in the table. If the comparison is unequal, the routine adds to the table address in order to compare to the next table stock number. If the comparison is equal, the routine at C30 extracts the description from the table and stores it in DESCRN.

The search loop performs a maximum of six compares. If the required item number is not in the table, the program calls an error routine that would display an error message.

Note that table initialization contains an instruction that moves STOKNIN to the AX. Although STOKNIN is defined as 3233, the MOV instruction loads the AX with 3332. Since the table entries are not reversed, following the MOV is an XCHG instruction that "unreverses" the two bytes as 3233. When the CMP instruction compares the AX to a table entry, it compares first the rightmost bytes and then the leftmost bytes. Consequently, a test for equal is valid, but a high or low test would not give valid results. To

Figure 12-2 Table Searching.

```
          page    60,132
TITLE   TABSRCH Table Search
; ---------------------------------------------
STACKSG SEGMENT PARA STACK 'STACK'
        DW      32 DUP(?)
STACKSG ENDS
; ---------------------------------------------
DATASG SEGMENT  PARA 'DATA'
STOKNIN DW      '23'
STOKTAB DB      '05','Excavators'
        DB      '08','Lifters   '
        DB      '09','Presses   '
        DB      '12','Valves    '
        DB      '23','Processors'
        DB      '27','Pumps     '
DESCRN  DB      10 DUP(?)
DATASG  ENDS
; ---------------------------------------------
CODESG  SEGMENT PARA 'CODE'
BEGIN   PROC    FAR
        ASSUME  CS:CODESG,DS:DATASG,SS:STACKSG,ES:DATASG
        PUSH    DS
        SUB     AX,AX
        PUSH    AX
        MOV     AX,DATASG
        MOV     DS,AX
        MOV     ES,AX
        CALL    C10SRCH         ;Call Search routine
        RET
BEGIN   ENDP
;               Search routine:
;               --------------
C10SRCH PROC
        MOV     CX,06           ;No. of entries
        MOV     AX,STOKNIN      ;Get stock#
        XCHG    AL,AH
        LEA     SI,STOKTAB      ;Init'ze table address
C20:
        CMP     AX,[SI]         ;Stock# : Table
        JE      C30             ;Equal - exit
        ADD     SI,12           ;Not equal - increment
        LOOP    C20
        CALL    R10ERR          ;Not in table
        RET
C30:
        MOV     CX,05           ;Length of descr'n
        LEA     DI,DESCRN       ;Addr of descr'n
        INC     SI
        INC     SI              ;Extract description
        REP MOVSW               ;  from table
        RET
C10SRCH ENDP
;               Display error message:
R10ERR  PROC
;       ...
        RET
R10ERR  ENDP

CODESG  ENDS
        END     BEGIN
```

compare for high or low, omit the XCHG instruciton, MOV the table entry to, say, the BX, and then compare the AX to the BX as follows:

```
          MOV   AX,STOKNIN
          LEA   SI,STOKTAB
   C20:
          MOV   BX,[SI]
          CMP   AX,BX
          JA or JB ...
```

In a program of this nature, another table could define unit prices. The program could locate the item in the table, calculate selling price, (quantity times unit price), and display the description and selling price.

In Figure 12-2, the item number is two characters and the description is ten characters. Programming detail would vary for different number of entries and different lengths of entries. For example, if you compare three byte fields, you could use REPE CMPSB, although the instruction also involves use of the CX register.

Tables with Ranges

Income tax provides a typical example of a table with ranges of values. Assume the following table of taxable income, rates, and correction factors for the IRS of Bulgonia:

Taxable Income	Rate	Correction Factor
0-1000.00	.10	0.00
1000.01-2500.00	.15	050.00
2501.01-4250.00	.18	125.00
4250.01-6000.00	.20	260.00
6000.01 and over	.23	390.00

The tax table is "progressive" in that the rates increase as taxable income increases. The entries in the taxable income table contain the high amount for each step:

        TAXTAB DD   100000, 250000, 425000, 600000, 999999

The program has to perform a search of the table by comparing the taxpayer's taxable income to the table's taxable income:

         Low or equal: Use the associated rate and correction factor.
                High: Increment for the next entry in the table.

The tax deduction is calculated as (taxpayer's taxable income × table rate) − correction factor.

TABLE SEARCHING USING STRING COMPARES

If item numbers exceed two bytes, you can use REPE CMPS for the compare operation. Assume that the stock item table from Figure 12-2 is revised for a three-byte item number. If STOKNIN is the first field in the Data Segment and STOKTAB is next, they could appear in memory as follows:

```
Data:      |123|035Excavators|038Lifters  |049Presses  |. . .
            |   |   |          |   |        |   |
Address:   00  03  06         16  19       29  32
```

The program in Figure 12-3 defines STOKTAB, including a last entry with '999' to force termination of the search. The search routine compares the contents of each table entry to STOKNIN as follows:

Table Entry	STOKNIN	Result of Compare
035	123	Low: check next entry
038	123	Low: check next entry
049	123	Low: check next entry
102	123	Low: check next entry
123	123	Equal: entry found

Note that the CMPSB operation in Figure 12-3 compares byte for byte as long as the bytes are equal and automatically increments the SI and DI registers.

Figure 12-3 Table Search Using CMPSB.

```
            page      60,132
TITLE   STRSRCH Table Search Using CMPSB
; ------------------------------------------------------------
STACKSG SEGMENT PARA STACK 'STACK'
        DW        32 DUP(?)
STACKSG ENDS
; ------------------------------------------------------------
DATASG SEGMENT  PARA 'DATA'
STOKNIN DB        '123'
STOKTAB DB        '035','Excavators'      ;Start of table
        DB        '038','Lifters   '
        DB        '049','Presses   '
        DB        '102','Valves    '
        DB        '123','Processors'
        DB        '127','Pumps     '
        DB        '999', 10 DUP(' ')      ;End of table
DESCRN  DB        10 DUP(?)
```

```
DATASG   ENDS
; --------------------------------------------------------
CODESG   SEGMENT PARA 'CODE'
BEGIN    PROC    FAR
         ASSUME  CS:CODESG,DS:DATASG,SS:STACKSG,ES:DATASG
         PUSH    DS
         SUB     AX,AX
         PUSH    AX
         MOV     AX,DATASG
         MOV     DS,AX
         MOV     ES,AX
         CALL    C10SRCH         ;Call Search routine
         RET
BEGIN    ENDP
;                Search routine:
;                --------------
C10SRCH  PROC
         CLD
         LEA     SI,STOKTAB      ;Init'ze table address
C20:
         MOV     CX,03           ;Set to compare 3 bytes
         LEA     DI,STOKNIN      ;Init'ze stock# address
         REPE CMPSB              ;Table ; Stock#
         JE      C30             ;Equal - exit
         JA      C40             ;High  - not in table
         ADD     DI,CX           ;Add CX value to offset
         ADD     SI,10           ;Next table item
         JMP     C20
C30:
         MOV     CX,05           ;Set to move 5 words
         LEA     DI,DESCRN       ;Init'ze addr of descr'n
         REP MOVSW               ;Move descr'n from table
         RET
C40:
         CALL    R10ERR          ;Not in table
         RET
C10SRCH  ENDP
;                Error routine:
;                -------------
R10ERR   PROC
;                Display error message
         RET
R10ERR   ENDP

CODESG   ENDS
         END     BEGIN
```

The CX is initialized to 03, and the initial offset addresses in the SI and DI registers are 03 and 00, respectively. A comparison of the first table entry (035:123) causes termination after one byte; the SI contains 04, the DI contains 01, and the CX contains 02. For the next compare, the SI should contain 16 and the DI 00. Correcting the DI address simply involves reloading the address of STOKNIN. For the address of the table entry that should be in the SI, however, the increment depends on whether the comparison ends after one, two, or three bytes. The CX register contains the number of the remaining uncompared bytes, in this case, 02. Adding the CX value plus the length of the stock description gives the offset of the next table item as follows:

Address in SI after CMPSB	04
Add CX	02
Add length of description	10
Next table offset address	16

Since the CX contains the number of the remaining uncompared bytes (if any), the arithmetic works for all cases: termination after 1, 2, or 3 compares. On an equal compare, the CX contains 00 and the SI is already incremented to the address of the required description.

THE TRANSLATE (XLAT) INSTRUCTION

The XLAT instruction translates the contents of a byte into another predefined value. One purpose of XLAT is to validate the contents of fields. Or, if you were transferring data between your PC and an IBM mainframe, you could use XLAT to translate bytes between ASCII format and EBCDIC format.

As a simple example, let's convert ASCII numbers 0 through 9 into EBCDIC. Since representation of ASCII is 30-39 and EBCDIC is F0-F9, you could make the change with an OR operation. However, let's also convert all other characters to EBCDIC blank, hex 40. You have to define the translate table to account for all 256 possible characters, with the EBCDIC codes inserted in the ASCII positions:

```
XLTAB    DB    47 DUP(40H)                        ;EBCDIC blanks
         DB    0F0H,0F1H,0F2H,0F3H, ...,0F9H      ;EBCDIC 0-9
         DB    199 DUP(40H)                       ;EBCDIC blanks
```

XLAT requires the address of the table in the BX register and the byte to be translated (let's name it ASCNO) in the AL register. The following performs the initialization and translation:

```
LEA    BX,XLTAB
MOV    AL,ASCNO
XLAT
```

XLAT uses the AL value as an offset address, in effect, the address in the BX plus the offset in the AL. If ASCNO contains 00, for example, the table address would be XLTAB+0, and XLAT would replace the 00 in the AL with hex 40 from the table. If ASCNO contains hex 32, the table address is XLTAB+50. This position contains hex F2 (EBCDIC 2), which XLAT inserts in the AL register.

The partial program in Figure 12-4 expands this example to convert ASCII decimal point (2E) and minus sign (2D) to EBCDIC (4B and 60, respectively) and to loop through a six-byte field. Initially, ASCNO contains -31.5 followed by a blank, or hex 2D33312E3520. At the end of the loop, EBCNO should contain hex 60F3F14BF540.

Figure 12-4 Conversion of ASCII to EBCDIC.

```
          page    60,132
TITLE   EXLATE  Translate ASCII to EDCDIC
; ------------------------------------------------
STACKSG SEGMENT PARA STACK 'Stack'
        DW      32 DUP(?)
STACKSG ENDS
; ------------------------------------------------
DATASG  SEGMENT PARA 'Data'
ASCNO   DB      '-31.5 '
EBCNO   DB      6 DUP(' ')
XLTAB   DB      45 DUP(40H)
        DB      60H, 2DH
        DB      5CH
        DB      0F0H,0F1H,0F2H,0F3H,0F4H,0F5H,0F6H,0F7H,0F8H,0F9H
        DB      199 DUP(40H)
DATASG  ENDS
; ------------------------------------------------
CODESG  SEGMENT PARA 'Code'
BEGIN   PROC    FAR
        ASSUME  CS:CODESG,DS:DATASG,SS:STACKSG,ES:DATASG
        PUSH    DS
        SUB     AX,AX
        PUSH    AX
        MOV     AX,DATASG
        MOV     DS,AX
        MOV     ES,AX
        CALL    C10XLAT            ;Call Translate routine
        RET
BEGIN   ENDP
;               Translate routine:
;               -----------------
C10XLAT PROC
        LEA     SI,ASCNO          ;Address of ASCNO
        LEA     DI,EBCNO          ;Address of EBCNO
        MOV     CX,06             ;Length
        LEA     BX,XLTAB          ;Address of table
C20:
        MOV     AL,[SI]           ;Get ASCII character
        XLAT                      ;Translate
        MOV     [DI],AL           ;Store in EBCNO
        INC     SI
        INC     DI
        LOOP    C20               ;Repeat 6 times
        RET
C10XLAT ENDP

CODESG  ENDS
        END     BEGIN
```

PROGRAM: DISPLAYING HEX AND ASCII

You may find the program in Figure 12-5 worth duplicating. The program displays all (well, almost all) the ASCII symbols as well as their hex values. For example, the ASCII symbol for hex 53 is the letter S, which the program displays as 53 S. The full display appears on the screen as a 16 by 16 matrix:

00 10 20 30 40 50 60 70 80 90   A0 B0 C0 D0 E0 F0

.   .   .   .

.   .   .   .

.   .   .   .

0F 1F 2F 3F 4F 5F 6F 7F 8F 9F   AF BF CF DF EF FF

An example of a partial row is the following:

. . . 2A * 3A : 4A J 5A Z 6A j 7A z . . .

Displaying the ASCII symbols is no problem – Figure 6-1 has already done that. However, displaying the hex value as ASCII is more involved. For example, to display as ASCII, you have to convert hex 00 to hex 3030, hex 01 to hex 3031, and so forth.

Figure 12-5 Displaying Hex and ASCII.

```
                page    60,132
        TITLE   ASCHEX  Conversion of all ASCII characters to hex
        ; --------------------------------------------------------
        STACKSG SEGMENT PARA STACK 'Stack'
                DW      32 DUP(?)
        STACKSG ENDS
        ; --------------------------------------------------------
        DATASG  SEGMENT PARA 'Data'
        CHARX   DB      ?,?,' ','$'
        HEXCTR  DB      00,'$'
        ROWCTR  DB      01
        COLCTR  DB      00
        XLATAB  DB      30H,31H,32H,33H,34H,35H,36H,37H,38H,39H
                DB      41H,42H,43H,44H,45H,46H
        DATASG  ENDS
        ; --------------------------------------------------------
        CODESG  SEGMENT PARA 'Code'
        BEGIN   PROC    FAR
                ASSUME  CS:CODESG,DS:DATASG,SS:STACKSG,ES:DATASG
                PUSH    DS
                SUB     AX,AX
                PUSH    AX
                MOV     AX,DATASG
                MOV     DS,AX
                MOV     ES,AX
                CALL    Q10CLR          ;Clear screen
        A20LOOP:
                CALL    Q20CURS         ;Set cursor
```

```
                CALL    C10HEX                  ;Translate & display
                CALL    D10DISP                 ;Display counter
                CMP     HEXCTR,0FFH             ;Last hex value (FF)?
                JE      A50                     ;  yes - terminate
                INC     HEXCTR                  ;  no  - incr next hex
                JMP     A20LOOP
        A50:    RET
        BEGIN   ENDP
        ;
        C10HEX  PROC    NEAR
                MOV     CL,04                   ;Set shift value
                MOV     AH,00
                MOV     AL,HEXCTR               ;Get hex pair
                SHR     AX,CL                   ;Shift off right hex digit
                LEA     BX,XLATAB               ;Set table address
                XLAT                            ;Translate hex
                MOV     CHARX,AL                ;Store left char

                MOV     AL,HEXCTR
                SHL     AX,CL                   ;Shift off left digit
                SHR     AL,CL
                XLAT                            ;Translate hex
                MOV     CHARX+1,AL              ;Store right char

                LEA     DX,CHARX                ;Display 2 chars
                MOV     AH,09
                INT     21H
                RET
        C10HEX  ENDP
        ;               Display counter:
        ;               ----------------
        D10DISP PROC    NEAR
                CMP     HEXCTR,08H              ;Lower than 08?
                JB      D20                     ;  yes - ok
                CMP     HEXCTR,0DH              ;Lower/equal 0D?
                JBE     D40                     ;  yes - bypass
        D20:
                LEA     DX,HEXCTR               ;Display counter
                MOV     AH,09
                INT     21H
        D40:    RET
        D10DISP ENDP
        ;               Clear screen:
        ;               -----------
        Q10CLR  PROC    NEAR
                MOV     CX,0000
                MOV     DX,184FH
                MOV     BH,07
                MOV     AX,0600H
                INT     10H
                RET
        Q10CLR  ENDP
        ;               Set cursor:
        ;               ----------
        Q20CURS PROC    NEAR
                MOV     DH,ROWCTR               ;Set cursor according
                MOV     DL,COLCTR               ;  to row/col
                MOV     BH,00
                MOV     AH,02
                INT     10H
```

```
                    CMP     ROWCTR,16        ;Row 16 (bottom)?
                    JNE     Q30              ;  no - bypass
                    MOV     ROWCTR,00        ;  yes - set row = 00
                    ADD     COLCTR,05        ;  & move over column
            Q30:
                    INC     ROWCTR           ;Add 1 to row
                    RET
            Q20CURS ENDP

            CODESG  ENDS
                    END     BEGIN
```

The program initializes HEXCTR to 00. Either of the hex digits may range from 0 to F. The Procedure C10HEX splits HEXCTR into its two hex digits. For example, assume that HEXCTR contains hex 4F. The routine extracts the hex 4 and uses its value for a translate operation against XLATAB. The value returned to the AL is hex 34. The routine then extracts the hex F and translates it to hex 46. The result, hex 3446, displays as 4F.

There are a number of reasons for converting hex to ASCII. Both DEBUG and the Assembler (in the LST file) display ASCII characters that represent hex object code.

There are also numerous other ways of converting hex digits to ASCII characters, and you may want to experiment with shifting and comparing.

PROGRAM: SORTING TABLE ENTRIES

Often an application requires sorting data in a table into ascending or descending sequence. For example, a user may want a list of stock descriptions in ascending sequence, or a list of salesmen's total sales in descending sequence. Typically, the data in the table is not defined as in previous examples, but is loaded from a terminal or disk. Let's make a clear distinction: this chapter covers sorting of table entries; a different application that involves sorting of disk records can be much more complex.

There are a number of table sort routines varying from not efficient but clear to efficient but obscure. The sort routine this section describes is fairly efficient and should serve for most table sorting. Now you possibly will not be doing a lot of table sorting, and even the least efficient routine will seem to execute at the speed of light. Also, the objective of this book is to explain Assembler, not sort, techniques.

The general approach is to compare a table entry to the entry immediately following. If the compare is high, exchange the entries. Continue in this fashion comparing entry 1 to entry 2, entry 2 to entry 3, to the end of the table, exchanging where necessary. If you made any exchange, repeat the entire process from the start of the table, comparing entry 1 to entry 2.

If you made no exchanges, the table is in sequence and you can terminate the sort.

A more formal presentation follows. Assume that Swap is a field that indicates whether an exchange was made (YES) or not made (NO).

G10:   Initialize address of last entry in table
G20:   Set Swap to NO
        Initialize address of start of table
G30:   Table entry > next entry?
            Yes: Exchange entries
                 Set Swap to YES
            Increment for next entry in table
            At end of table?
                No: Jump to G30
                Yes: Does Swap = YES?
                         Yes: Jump to G20 (repeat sort)
                         No: End of sort

The program in Figure 12-6 allows for a user to enter up to 30 names on a terminal. When all the names are entered, the program sorts the names into ascending sequence and displays the sorted names on the screen.

Figure 12-6 Sorting a Table of Names.

```
          page   60,132
TITLE     NMSORT  Sort of names entered from terminal
; --------------------------------------------------
STACK     SEGMENT PARA STACK 'Stack'
          DW      32 DUP(?)
STACK     ENDS
; --------------------------------------------------
DATASG  SEGMENT PARA 'Data'
NAMEPAR LABEL   BYTE                ;Start of Name parameter list
MAXNLEN DB      21                  ;Max. length of name
ACTNLEN DB      ?                   ;No. chars entered
NAMEFLD DB      21 DUP(' ')         ;Employee name
        DB      '$'                 ;Name delimiter

MESSG1  DB      'Employee name?', '$'
NAMETAB DB      30 DUP(20 DUP(' ')) ;Name table
NAMESAV DB      20 DUP(?)
SWAPPED DB      00
ENDADDR DW      ?
NAMECTR DB      00
DATASG  ENDS
; --------------------------------------------------
CODESG  SEGMENT PARA 'Code'
BEGIN   PROC    FAR
        ASSUME  CS:CODESG,DS:DATASG,SS:STACK,ES:DATASG
        PUSH    DS
        SUB     AX,AX
        PUSH    AX
        MOV     AX,DATASG
```

```
            MOV     DS,AX
            MOV     ES,AX
            CLD
            LEA     DI,NAMETAB
A20LOOP:
            CALL    B10READ         ;Accept name
            CMP     ACTNLEN,00      ;End of names?
            JZ      A30
            CMP     NAMECTR,30      ;30 names entered?
            JE      A30
            CALL    C10BLNK         ;Blanks to right of entered name
            CALL    D10STOR         ;Store entered name in table
            JMP     A20LOOP
A30:
            CALL    Q10CLR          ;End of input
            CMP     NAMECTR,01      ;One or no name entered?
            JBE     A40             ; yes - exit
            CALL    G10SORT         ;Sort stored names
            CALL    K10DISP         ;Display sorted names
A40:        RET
BEGIN       ENDP
;                   Accept name as input:
;                   ---------------------
B10READ PROC
            CALL    Q10CLR          ;Clear screen
            SUB     DX,DX           ;Set cursor to 00,00
            CALL    Q20CURS
            LEA     DX,MESSG1       ;Display prompt
            MOV     AH,09
            INT     21H
            LEA     DX,NAMEPAR      ;Accept name
            MOV     AH,0AH
            INT     21H
            RET
B10READ ENDP
;                   Clear characters after name:
;                   ----------------------------
C10BLNK PROC
            MOV     BH,00
            MOV     BL,ACTNLEN      ;Get count of chars in name
            MOV     CX,21
            SUB     CX,BX           ;Calc remaining length in name
C20:
            MOV     NAMEFLD[BX],' ' ;Clear to blank
            INC     BX
            LOOP    C20
            RET
C10BLNK ENDP
;                   Store name in table:
;                   --------------------
D10STOR PROC
            INC     NAMECTR         ;Add to number of names
            CLD
            LEA     SI,NAMEFLD
            MOV     CX,10
            REP MOVSW               ;Move Name to table
            RET
D10STOR ENDP
;                   Sort names in table:
;                   --------------------
G10SORT PROC
            SUB     DI,40           ;Set up stop address
            MOV     ENDADDR,DI
G20:
            MOV     SWAPPED,00      ;Set up start
            LEA     SI,NAMETAB      ; of table
G30:
            MOV     CX,20           ;Length of compare
            MOV     DI,SI
```

```
                ADD     DI,20           ;Next name for compare
                MOV     AX,DI
                MOV     BX,SI
                REPE CMPSB               ;Compare name to next
                JBE     G40             ;- No exchange
                CALL    H10XCHG         ;- Exchange
        G40:
                MOV     SI,AX
                CMP     SI,ENDADDR      ;End of table?
                JBE     G30             ;No - continue
                CMP     SWAPPED,00      ;Any swaps?
                JNZ     G20             ;Yes - continue
                RET                     ;End of sort
        G10SORT ENDP
        ;               Exchange table entries:
        ;               ----------------------
        H10XCHG PROC
                MOV     CX,10
                LEA     DI,NAMESAV
                MOV     SI,BX
                REP MOVSW                ;Move lower item to save

                MOV     CX,10
                MOV     DI,BX
                REP MOVSW                ;Move higher item to lower

                MOV     CX,10
                LEA     SI,NAMESAV
                REP MOVSW                ;Move save to higher item
                MOV     SWAPPED,01      ;Signal that exchange made
                RET
        H10XCHG ENDP

        ;               Display sorted names:
        ;               --------------------
        K10DISP PROC
                LEA     SI,NAMETAB
        K20:
                LEA     DI,NAMEFLD      ;Init'ze start of table
                MOV     CX,10
                REP MOVSW
                LEA     DX,NAMEFLD
                MOV     AH,09
                INT     21H             ;Display
                DEC     NAMECTR         ;Last name?
                JNZ     K20
                RET
        K10DISP ENDP
        ;               Clear screen:
        ;               ------------
        Q10CLR  PROC
                SUB     CX,CX
                MOV     DX,184FH
                MOV     BH,07
                MOV     AX,0600H
                INT     10H
                RET
        Q10CLR  ENDP
        ;               Set cursor:
        ;               ----------
        Q20CURS PROC
                SUB     BH,BH
                MOV     AH,02
                INT     10H
                RET
        Q20CURS ENDP

        CODESG  ENDS
                END     BEGIN
```

TYPE, LENGTH, AND SIZE

The Assembler supplies a number of special operators that you may find useful. For example, the length of a table may change from time to time and you may have to modify the program for the new definition and for routines that check for the table end. But the use of the TYPE, LENGTH, and SIZE operators can enable you to reduce the number of instructions that have to be changed.

Assume the following definition of a table:

TABLEX DW   10 DUP(?)

The program can use the TYPE operator to determine the definition (DW in this case), the LENGTH operator to determine the DUP factor (10), and the SIZE operator to determine the number of bytes (10 x 2, or 20). The following examples illustrate all three operators:

```
MOV     AX,TYPE TABLEX        ;AX = 0002
MOV     BX,LENGTH TABLEX      ;BX = 000A (10)
MOV     CX,SIZE TABLEX        ;CX = 0014 (20)
```

You can now use the values that LENGTH and SIZE return in order to terminate a table search or a sort. For example, if the SI register contains the incremented address of a table search, test it using

CMP   SI,SIZE TABLEX

Chapter 18, "Assembler Pseudo-ops," describes TYPE, LENGTH, and SIZE in detail.

KEY POINTS TO REMEMBER

☐ For most purposes, define tables with related entries that are the same length and data format. However, it is possible to define a table with variable-length entries. A special "delimiter" character such as hex 00 could follow each entry, and hex FF could distinguish the end of the table. However, you have to be sure that no byte within an entry contains the bit configuration of a delimiter. For example, an arithmetic binary amount can contain any possible bit configuration. For the table search, use the SCAS instruction.

☐ Design tables based on their data format. For example, entries may be character or numeric and one, two, or more bytes each. It may be more practical to define two tables: one, for example, for item numbers that are three bytes long, and another for unit prices that are one word. The search could increment the address of the item number table by 3 and the address of the price table by 2. Or, keep a count of the number of loops; on finding an equal item multiply the count by 2 (SHL one bit), and use this value as an offset to the address of the price table. (Actually, initialize the count to -1.)

□   Remember that DB permits numeric values with a maximum of 256 and that a numeric DW reverses the bytes. Also, CMP and CMPSW assume that words are reversed.

□   If a table is subject to frequent changes or if several programs reference it, store the table on disk. An updating program can handle changes to the table. Any program can load the table from disk and the programs need not be changed.

□   Be especially careful coding a sort routine. *Recommendation:* Use a trace to test the sort because a minor coding error can cause unpredictable results.

QUESTIONS

12-1. Define a table that contains the names of the days of the week, beginning with Sunday.

12-2. Given that Sunday equals 1, code the instructions that directly access the name from the table defined in Question 12-1. Use any suitable names.

12-3. Define three separate related tables that contain the following data:

(a) Item numbers 08, 12, 15, 22, 25.

(b) Item descriptions Videotape, Receivers, Modems, Keyboards, Diskettes.

(c) Item prices 13.95, 72.25, 90.67, 65.80, 3.85

12-4. Code a program that allows a user to enter item number (ITEMIN) and quantity (QTYIN) from the keyboard. Using the tables defined in Question 12-3, include a table search routine using ITEMIN to locate an item number in the table. Extract description and price from the tables. Calculate value (quantity times price), and display description and value back on the screen.

12-5. Using the description table defined in Question 12-3, code the following:

(a) A routine that moves the contents of the table to another (empty) table;

(b) A routine that sorts the contents of this new table into ascending sequence.

13

DISK PROCESSING I:
INTRODUCTION

Objective:
To examine the basic programming
requirements for creating and
reading files on diskette.

INTRODUCTION

Diskette is a popular storage medium for data that is to be kept (more or less) permanently. In order to process files, it is useful to be familiar with disk organization. A single side of a diskette contains 40 concentric tracks, numbered 00 through 39 (see Figure 13-1). Each track is formatted into eight sectors (numbered 1 through 8) of 512 bytes each, providing a total of 512 x 40 x 8 or 163,840 bytes on a side. DOS 2.0 also provides for nine sectors (numbered 1 through 9), giving 184,320 bytes per side.

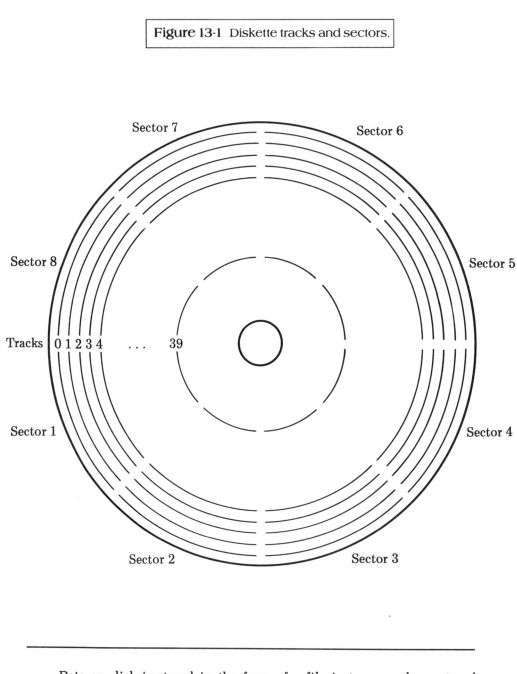

Figure 13-1 Diskette tracks and sectors.

Data on disk is stored in the form of a file just as you have stored Assembler programs. Although there is no restriction on the kind of data that you may keep in a file, a typical user file would consist of records for customers, for inventory supplies, or for name and address lists. Each record contains information about a particular customer or inventory item. Within a file, all records are the same length and format. A record contains one or more fields. A customer file, for example, could consist of records that contain such fields as customer number, customer name, and balance owing. These records would be in ascending sequence by customer number as follows:

Processing of diskettes under DOS involves definition of a File Control Block (FCB) that defines the file and records. You define the FCB in the Data Segment and provide its address to DOS for all disk input/output operations. No new Assembler instructions are required.

There are also a number of special interrupt codes for handling input/output processing. Writing a file requires that it first be "created" so that DOS can generate an entry in the disk Directory. On completion of writing all the records, the program must "close" the file so that DOS can complete the Directory. Reading a file requires that it first be "opened" to ensure that the file exists. Because records are fixed length and because of the design of the DOS directory, you may process a disk file either sequentially or randomly.

Note: The term "cluster" denotes one sector of data on single-sided drives and an adjacent pair of sectors on dual-sided drives.

To get started with program examples as soon as possible, this chapter first describes the organization of the disk Directory. It then covers certain essentials for defining the FCB. You will then examine the requirements for creating a disk file defined as "sequential" and for reading this file sequentially. For those interested in more technical material, later sections discuss diskette formats. Chapter 14 explains the requirements for processing records randomly.

You should also be aware that there is more than one level of disk accessing. The method that supports use of the Directory and "blocking" and "unblocking" of records is by means of DOS interrupt 21H. The next lower level, also via DOS, is by means of interrupts 25H and 26H but involves absolute addressing of disk sectors. The next lower level is via BIOS interrupt 13H, which requires direct addressing of track and sector numbers. The two DOS methods perform some preliminary processing before linking to BIOS. Since the first method supports the most features, this chapter covers it first.

For CP/M users, interrupt 224 is similar to DOS INT 21H. For technical differences, check Appendix D of your manual for CP/M-86 functions 12 through 52.

THE DIRECTORY

In order to account for the information stored on disk, DOS reserves certain sectors for its own purposes. A formatted one-sided disk with eight sectors per track contains the following:

Track 0, sector 1	The boot record
Track 0, sectors 2-3	The File Allocation Table (FAT)
Track 0, sectors 4-7	The Directory
Track 0, sectors 8 and on	Data files

For dual-sided diskettes, the Directory requires three additional sectors: side 0, track 0, sector 8 and side 1, track 0, sectors 1-2. Data begins at side 1, track 0, sector 3 through sector 8. The system stores records next on side 0, track 1, then side 1, track 1, then side 0, track 2, and so forth. This feature of filling data on opposite tracks before proceeding to the next track reduces disk head motion and is also the method used on hard disk.

If you use FORMAT /S to format a diskette, then DOS modules occupy the following space:

Single-sided diskettes

IBMBIO.COM:	Track 0, sector 8 through track 1, sector 3
IBMDOS.COM:	Track 1, sector 4 through track 2, sector 8

Dual-sided diskettes

IBMBIO.COM:	Side 1, track 0, sectors 3-6.
IBMDOS.COM:	Side 1, track 0, sectors 7-8, then side 0, track 1, sectors 1-8, and side 1, track 1, sectors 1-4.

Diskettes formatted with nine sectors per track require two sectors for each FAT.

All files begin on a sector boundary even if the file is less than 512 bytes (or multiple of 512). For all files on a diskette DOS constructs a Directory in track 0, sectors 4-7. Each Directory entry describes the name, date, size, and disk location of a file. There is provision for 64 entries and therefore 64 files. The Directory entries for both PC-DOS and MS-DOS have the following format:

Byte	Purpose
0–7	Filename as designated in the program that created the file. Under DOS 2.0, the first byte can also indicate file status: hex 00 means that the file has never been used and hex E5 means that the file has been deleted.

8–10	Filename extension.

11   File attribute defining the type of file:
         Hex 00—a normal file
         Hex 01—under DOS 2.0, a file that can only be read
         Hex 02—a "hidden" file
         Hex 04—a DOS system file
         Hex 08, 10, 20—see the DOS 2.0 manual

12–21   Reserved for DOS.

22–23   Time of day when the file was created or last updated, stored in binary as

$$|hhhhhmmmmmmsssss|$$

24-25   Date when the file was created or last updated. The date is compressed into two bytes in binary format as

$$|yyyyyyym|mmmddddd|$$

         where year begins at 1980 and can be 0-119, month can be 1-12, and day can be 1-31. The bytes are stored in reversed sequence.

26-27   Starting cluster of the file. On one-sided diskettes, the number is relative to track 0, sector 6; therefore track 0, sector 6, is relative cluster 000, and sector 7 is relative cluster 001. (If you check the layout of track 0, you will see that these sectors are actually part of the Directory.) If the first data file begins at track 0, sector 8 (with no DOS COM modules), it begins at relative cluster 002. However, for this calculation, you will have to check the number of your DOS version.

28-31   File size in bytes. When you create a file, DOS calculates and stores its size in this field.

FILE CONTROL BLOCK: FCB

For disk I/O, you must define an FCB in the Data Segment. The FCB contains descriptive information about the file and its records. The following describes the entries in the FCB. You must initialize bytes 0-15 and 32-36; DOS sets bytes 16-31.

Byte	Purpose
0	Disk drive. Code 01 for drive A and code 02 for drive B.
1-8	Filename. The name of the file, left-adjusted with trailing blanks (if any). The entry may be a reserved filename such as LPT1 for line printer, without a colon.
9-11	Filename extension. A subdivision of filename for further identification of the file, such as DTA or FLE. If less than three characters, left-adjust. DOS stores the filename and extension in the Directory.
12-13	Current block number. A block consists of 128 records. Read and write operations use the current block number and current record number (byte 32) to locate a particular record. The number is relative to the beginning of the file, where the first block is 0, the second is 1, and so forth. An open operation sets this entry to zero.
14-15	Logical record size. An open operation initializes the record size to 128 (hex 80). After the open and before any read or write, you may set this entry to your own required record size.
16-19	File size. When a program creates a file, DOS calculates and stores the size of the file (number of records times record size) in the Directory. An open operation subsequently extracts the file size from the Directory and stores it in this field. Your program may read this field but should not change it.
20-21	Date. DOS records the date in the Directory when the file was created or last updated. An open operation extracts the date from the Directory and stores it in this field.
22-31	Reserved by DOS.
32	Current record number. This entry contains the current record number (0-127) within the current block (see bytes 12-13). The system uses the current block/record to locate records in the disk file. Although the usual initial record number is 0, you may set this field to begin sequential processing at any number between 0 and 128.
33-36	Relative record number. For *random* read/write, this entry must contain a relative record number. For example, in order to randomly read record 25, set this entry to hex 19000000. To access a record randomly, the system automatically converts the relative record number to current block/record. Because there is a limit to the maximum size of a file (1,073,741,824 bytes), a file with a short record size can contain more records and consequently may have a higher maximum relative record number. If the record size is greater than 64, byte 36 always contains 00.

Remember that numeric values in words and doublewords are stored in reversed byte sequence.

There is also an extended FCB that you can use to search in the disk Directory for files with special attributes. Details are available in the DOS manual.

CREATING A DISK FILE UNDER DOS

For each disk file that a program references, the program must contain a properly defined File Control Block. All disk I/O operations require the address of the FCB in the DX register and use this address to access fields within the FCB by means of DS:DX registers.

On initialization, the program must "create" a new file using the function call hex 16 and DOS interrupt 21H as follows:

```
LEA     DX,FCBname      ;Create
MOV     AH,16H          ; disk
INT     21H             ; file
```

DOS searches the Directory for a filename that matches the entry in the FCB. If found, DOS reuses the space in the Directory, and if not found, DOS searches for a vacant entry. The operation then initializes the file size to 0 and "opens" the file. The open step checks for available disk space and sets the AL register as follows:

> 00 —Space is available.
> FF—No space is available.

Open also initializes the FCB current block number to 0 and sets a default value in the FCB record size of 128 (hex 80) bytes. Before writing a record, you may override this default with your own record size.

The Disk Transfer Area (DTA) is the start of the definition of your output record, in any format. Since the FCB contains the record size, the DTA does not require a delimiter to indicate the end of the record. Prior to any write operation, supply DOS with the address of the DTA using function call hex 1A. There may be only one DTA active at any time. The following initializes the address of the DTA:

```
LEA     DX,DTAname      ;Set
MOV     AH,1AH          ; address
INT     21H             ; of DTA
```

Note that if a program processes more than one disk file, it needs to initialize the DTA only once for the entire execution. If a program processes more than one file, it must initialize the appropriate DTA immediately before *each* read or write.

To write a sequential disk record, use function call hex 15:

```
LEA    DX,FCBname    ;Write
MOV    AH,15H        ; record
INT    21H           ; sequentially
```

The write operation uses the information in the FCB and the address of the current DTA. If the record is the size of a sector, the operation writes the record. Otherwise, the operation fills records into a buffer area that is the length of a sector and writes the buffer when full. For example, if each record is 128 bytes long, the operation fills the buffer with four records (4 × 128 = 512) and writes the buffer into an entire disk sector.

On a successful write, DOS increments the FCB file size field (by adding the record size to it) and increments the current record number by 1. When the current record number exceeds 128, the operation sets it to 0 and increments the FCB current block number. The operation then returns a code to the AL register:

00—The write was successful.
01—The disk is full.
02—There is no space in the disk transfer segment for one record.

On completion of writing all the records, *close* the file using function call hex 10:

```
LEA    DX,FCBname    ;Close
MOV    AH,10A        ; the
INT    21H           ; file
```

The operation writes on disk any partial data still in the DOS disk buffer and updates the Directory with the date and the file size. The following codes are returned to the AL register:

00 — The write was successful.
FF — The file was not in the correct position in the Directory
(perhaps caused by the user changing the diskette).

PROGRAM: CREATING A DISK FILE

The program in Figure 13-2 creates a disk file of names that a user enters through the keyboard. The FCB, named FCBREC in the example, contains the following entries:

FCBDRIV	The program is to create a file on a diskette in drive 2 (or B).
FCBNAME	The name of the file is NAMEFILE.
FCBEXT	The file extension is TST.
FCBBLK	The current block number is initialized to 0.
FCBRCSZ	The record size is undefined because the open operation sets this entry to 128.
FCBSQRC	The current record number is initialized to 0.

Figure 13-2 Creation of a Disk File.

```
         page    60,132
TITLE    CREATDSK - Create disk file of names
; ---------------------------------------------------
STACKSG SEGMENT PARA STACK 'STACK'
        DW      80 DUP(?)
STACKSG ENDS
; ---------------------------------------------------
DATASG  SEGMENT PARA 'DATA'
RECLEN  EQU     32
NAMEPAR LABEL   BYTE                    ;Start of Name parameter list
MAXNLEN DB      RECLEN                  ;Max. length of name
ACTNLEN DB      ?                       ;No. chars entered, incl. carr. return
NAMEFLD DB      RECLEN DUP(' '),'$' ;Disk Transfer Area (DTA)

FCBREC  LABEL   BYTE                    ;FCB for disk file
FCBDRIV DB      02                      ;Disk drive B
FCBNAME DB      'NAMEFILE'              ;File name
FCBEXT  DB      'TST'                   ;Extension
FCBBLK  DW      0000                    ;Current block#
FCBRCSZ DW      ?                       ;Logical record size
FCBFLSZ DD      ?                       ;DOS file size
        DW      ?                       ;DOS date
        DT      ?                       ;DOS reserved
FCBSQRC DB      00                      ;Current record #
        DD      ?                       ;Relative record #

ERRCDE  DB      00
OPNMSG  DB      '*** Open error ***','$'
PROMPT  DB      'Name?','$'
WRTMSG  DB      '*** Write error ***','$'
DATASG  ENDS
; ---------------------------------------------------
CODESG  SEGMENT PARA 'CODE'
BEGIN   PROC    FAR
        ASSUME  CS:CODESG,DS:DATASG,SS:STACKSG,ES:DATASG
        PUSH    DS
        SUB     AX,AX
        PUSH    AX
        MOV     AX,DATASG
        MOV     DS,AX
        MOV     ES,AX
        CALL    Q10CLR                  ;Clear screen
        CALL    C100PEN                 ;Open file, set DTA
        CMP     ERRCDE,00               ;Available space?
        JZ      A20LOOP                 ;Yes - continue
        RET                             ;No  - return to DOS
```

```
        A20LOOP:
                CALL    D10PROC
                CMP     ACTNLEN,00      ;End of input?
                JNE     A20LOOP         ;No  - continue
                CALL    G10CLSE         ;Yes - close,
                RET                     ;   return to DOS
        BEGIN   ENDP
        ;               Open disk file:
        ;               --------------
        C10OPEN PROC    NEAR
                MOV     AH,16H          ;Request create
                LEA     DX,FCBREC
                INT     21H
                CMP     AL,00           ;Available space?
                JNZ     C20             ;No - error

                MOV     FCBRCSZ,RECLEN  ;Record size (EQU)
                LEA     DX,NAMEFLD      ;Set address of DTA
                MOV     AH,1AH
                INT     21H
                RET
        C20:
                LEA     DX,OPNMSG       ;Error message
                CALL    X10ERR
                RET
        C10OPEN ENDP
        ;               Accept input:
        ;               ------------
        D10PROC PROC    NEAR
                MOV     DX,0000         ;Set cursor to 00,00
                CALL    Q20CURS
                MOV     AH,09           ;Request display
                LEA     DX,PROMPT       ;Display prompt
                INT     21H

                MOV     AH,0AH          ;Request input
                LEA     DX,NAMEPAR      ;Accept name
                INT     21H
                CALL    Q10CLR
                CMP     ACTNLEN,00      ;No name? (indicates end)
                JNE     D20
                RET                     ;If so, return to A20LOOP
        D20:
                MOV     BH,00           ;Replace return char
                MOV     BL,ACTNLEN
                MOV     NAMEFLD[BX],' ' ;Store blank
                CALL    F10WRIT         ;Call write routine

                CLD
                LEA     DI,NAMEFLD      ;Clear
                MOV     CX,RECLEN / 2   ; name
                MOV     AX,2020H        ; field
                REP STOSW
                RET
        D10PROC ENDP
        ;               Write disk record:
        ;               -----------------
        F10WRIT PROC    NEAR
                MOV     AH,15H          ;Request write
                LEA     DX,FCBREC
```

```
                INT     21H
                CMP     AL,00           ;Valid write?
                JZ      F20             ;  -yes
                LEA     DX,WRTMSG       ;  -no,
                CALL    X10ERR          ;    call error routine
                MOV     ACTNLEN,00
F20:
                RET
F10WRIT ENDP
;                       Close disk file:
;                       ---------------
G10CLSE PROC    NEAR
                MOV     AH,10H          ;Request close
                LEA     DX,FCBREC
                INT     21H
                RET
G10CLSE ENDP
;                       Clear screen:
;                       ------------
Q10CLR  PROC    NEAR
                MOV     AX,0600H        ;Request scroll
                MOV     BH,07
                MOV     CX,0000
                MOV     DX,184FH
                INT     10H
                RET
Q10CLR  ENDP
;                       Set cursor acc'g to DX:
;                       ----------------------
Q20CURS PROC    NEAR
                MOV     AH,02           ;Request set
                MOV     BH,00           ;  cursor
                INT     10H
                RET
Q20CURS ENDP
;                       Disk error routine:
;                       ------------------
X10ERR  PROC    NEAR
                MOV     AH,09           ;DX contains
                INT     21H             ;  address of message
                RET
X10ERR  ENDP

CODESG  ENDS
        END     BEGIN
```

The program is organized as follows:

BEGIN	Initializes the Segment registers and calls C10OPEN to create the file and to set the DTA address for DOS.
A20LOOP	Calls D10PROC for accepting input. If there is no more input, the routine calls G10CLSE and terminates.
C10OPEN	Creates an entry for the file in the Directory, sets the size of the record to 32 (hex 20), and initializes the address of the DTA.

D10PROC	Prompts and accepts input of names from the terminal and calls F10WRIT to write the entered name on disk.
F10WRIT	Writes names onto the disk file
G10CLSE	Closes the file.
X10ERR	In the event of an invalid create or write operation, displays an error message on the screen

Each write operation automatically adds 1 to FCBSQRC (the current record number) and hex 20 (the record size) to FCBFLSZ (the file size). Since each record is 32 bytes long, the operation fills the buffer with 16 records and then physically writes the entire buffer onto a disk sector.

DTA: |curr rec|

Buffer: |rec 00|rec 01|rec 02| ... |rec 15|

If a user enters 25 names, the record count increments from 1 to 25 (hex 19). The file size is therefore

$$25 \times 32 \text{ bytes} = 800 \text{ bytes, or hex } 320$$

The close operation writes the remaining nine records in the buffer onto a second sector and updates the Directory for date and file size. The size is stored with reversed bytes as 20030000.

Buffer: |rec 16|rec 17| ... |rec 24| | | |...

For simplicity, the program creates records that contain only one field. Most records, however, contain various alphabetic and binary fields and just require defining the record in the DTA.

To make a program more flexible, consider allowing the user to specify which drive contains the disk file. At the start, the program could display a message for the user to enter the disk drive number and could then change the first byte of the FCB.

SEQUENTIAL READING OF A DOS DISK FILE

A program that reads a disk file must contain a File Control Block that defines the file exactly how it was created. On initialization, the program must open the file using the function call hex 0F:

```
LEA    DX,FCBname    ;Open
MOV    AH,0FH        ; the
INT    21H           ; file
```

The open operation checks that the Directory contains an entry with the filename and extension defined in the FCB. If the entry is not in the Directory, the operation sets the AL to hex FF. If the entry is present, the operation sets the AL to 00, the actual file size in the FCB, the FCB current block number to 0, and the FCB record size to hex 80. After the open, you may override this default with your own record size.

The DTA is the start of the definition of the input record, according to the format that was used to create the file. Set the address of the DTA just as for creating a disk file, using the function call hex 1AH:

```
LEA    DX,DTAname    ;Set
MOV    AH,1AH        ; address
INT    21H           ; of DTA
```

To read a disk record sequentially, use function call hex 14:

```
LEA    DX,FCBname    ;Read
MOV    AH,14H        ; record
INT    21H           ; sequentially
```

The read operation uses the information in the FCB to deliver the disk record beginning at the address of the DTA. The operation then sets the AL register as follows:

00 — The read was successful.
01 — End-of-file, no data in record.
02 — Not enough space in the disk transfer segment to read one record.
03 — End-of-file, has read a partial record filled out with zeros.

The first read operation reads an entire sector into the DOS buffer. The operation determines the record size from the FCB and delivers to the DTA the first record from the buffer. Subsequent read operations cause the remaining records (if any) to be delivered until the buffer contains no more records. At this point, the operation determines the address of the next sector and reads its contents into the buffer.

On a successful read, the operation automatically increments the current record number in the FCB. On completion of sequential reading, the program recognizes the end-of-file for which you should test. Because the Directory would be unchanged, it is not necessary to close an input file.

DOS 2.0 provides a number of additional function calls, hex 2F through hex 57, used with INT 21H that are relevant to processing diskettes and hard disks. See the manual for details.

PROGRAM: READING A DISK FILE

The program in Figure 13-3 reads the file that the previous program created and displays the input names on the screen. Both programs contain an identical FCB. Although the names of the entries need not be the same, the *operands* for filename and extension must be identical.

Figure 13-3 Reading a Disk File.

```
          page     60,132
TITLE     SEQREAD - Read disk records created by CREATDSK
; -------------------------------------------------------
STACKSG SEGMENT PARA STACK 'STACK'
        DW      80 DUP(?)
STACKSG ENDS
; -------------------------------------------------------
DATASG  SEGMENT PARA 'DATA'
FCBREC  LABEL   BYTE               ;FCB for disk file
FCBDRIV DB      02                 ;Disk drive B
FCBNAME DB      'NAMEFILE'         ;File name
FCBEXT  DB      'TST'              ;Extension
FCBBLK  DW      0000               ;Current block#
FCBRCSZ DW      0000               ;Logical record size
        DD      ?                  ;DOS file size
        DW      ?                  ;DOS date
        DT      ?                  ;DOS reserved
FCBSQRC DB      00                 ;Current record#
        DD      ?                  ;Relative record#

RECLEN  EQU     32                 ;Record length
NAMEFLD DB      RECLEN DUP(' '),'$'

ENDCDE  DB      00
OPENMSG DB      '*** Open error ***$'
READMSG DB      '*** Read error ***$'
ROWCTR  DB      00
DATASG  ENDS
;--------------------------------------------------------
CODESG  SEGMENT PARA 'CODE'
BEGIN   PROC    FAR
        ASSUME  CS:CODESG,DS:DATASG,SS:STACKSG,ES:DATASG
        PUSH    DS
        SUB     AX,AX
        PUSH    AX
        MOV     AX,DATASG
        MOV     DS,AX
        MOV     ES,AX
        CALL    Q10CLR             ;Clear screen
        CALL    Q20CURS            ;Set cursor
        CALL    E100PEN            ;Open file, set DTA
        CMP     ENDCDE,00          ;Valid Open?
```

```
            JNZ      A90             ;No - terminate
A20LOOP:
            CALL     F10READ         ;Read disk record
            CMP      ENDCDE,00       ;Normal read?
            JNZ      A90             ;No  - exit
            CALL     G10DISP         ;Display name
            JMP      A20LOOP         ;Continue
A90:        RET                      ;Terminate
BEGIN  ENDP
;                    Open disk file:
;                    ---------------
E10OPEN PROC     NEAR
            LEA      DX,FCBREC
            MOV      AH,0FH          ;Request open
            INT      21H
            CMP      AL,00           ;File found?
            JNZ      E20             ;No - error

            MOV      FCBRCSZ,RECLEN  ;Set record length (EQU)
            MOV      AH,1AH
            LEA      DX,NAMEFLD      ;Set address of DTA
            INT      21H
            RET
E20:
            MOV      ENDCDE,01       ;Error message
            LEA      DX,OPENMSG
            CALL     X10ERR
            RET
E10OPEN ENDP
;                    Read disk record:
;                    ----------------
F10READ PROC     NEAR
            MOV      AH,14H          ;Request read
            LEA      DX,FCBREC
            INT      21H
            CMP      AL,00           ;Normal read?
            JZ       F90             ;Yes - exit
            MOV      ENDCDE,01       ;No:
            CMP      AL,01           ;End-of-file?
            JZ       F90             ;Yes
            LEA      DX,READMSG      ;Invalid read
            CALL     X10ERR
F90:
            RET
F10READ ENDP
;                    Display name:
;                    ------------
G10DISP PROC     NEAR
            MOV      AH,09           ;Request display
            LEA      DX,NAMEFLD
            INT      21H
            CALL     Q20CURS
            RET
G10DISP ENDP
;                    Clear screen:
;                    ------------
Q10CLR  PROC     NEAR
            MOV      AX,0600H        ;Request scroll
            MOV      BH,07
            MOV      CX,0000
            MOV      DX,184FH
            INT      10H
```

```
                RET
     Q10CLR  ENDP
     ;                    Set cursor:
     ;                    ----------
     Q20CURS PROC    NEAR
             MOV     AH,02           ;Request set
             MOV     BH,00           ;  cursor
             MOV     DH,ROWCTR
             MOV     DL,00
             INT     10H
             INC     ROWCTR
             CMP     ROWCTR,25       ;Bottom of screen?
             JNE     Q90             ;No - bypass
             MOV     ROWCTR,00       ;Reset row#
     Q90:    RET
     Q20CURS ENDP
     ;                    Disk error routine:
     ;                    -------------------
     X10ERR  PROC    NEAR
             MOV     AH,09           ;DX contains address
             INT     21H             ;  of message
             RET
     X10ERR  ENDP

     CODESG  ENDS
             END     BEGIN
```

The program is organized as follows:

BEGIN	Initializes the Segment registers and calls E10OPEN to open the file and set the DTA.
A20LOOP	Calls F10READ to read a disk record. If end-of-file, the program terminates. If not the end, the program calls G10DISP.
E10OPEN	Opens the disk file, sets the record size to the correct length of 32 (hex 20), and initializes the address of the DTA.
F10READ	Reads disk records sequentially. The read operation automatically increments the FCB current record number.
G10DISP	Displays the input name on the screen.
X10ERR	In the event of an invalid open or read operation, displays an error message on the screen.

The open operation checks that the filename and extension (NAMEFILE TST) exist in the Directory. If so, the operation automatically sets the FCB entries for file size (hex 320), date, and record size (hex 80). The first read, which references current record number 00, accesses disk and reads a full sector (16 records) into the buffer. It then delivers the first record to the DTA and increments the current record number in the FCB from 00 to 01:

Buffer: |rec 00|rec 01|rec 02| . . . |rec 15|

DTA: |rec 00|

The second read that the program executes does not have to access disk. Since the required record is already in the buffer, the operation simply transfers current record 01 from the buffer to the DTA and increments the current record number to 02. Each read operation continues in this manner until all 16 records have been processed.

An attempt to read current record 16 causes the operation to physically read the entire next sector into the buffer. In this case, there are only nine records remaining, numbered 16 through 24. The read operations then transfer each record successively from the buffer to the DTA. An attempt to "read" current record 25 causes the operation to signal an end-of-file condition that sets the AL to hex 01.

FILE ALLOCATION TABLE (FAT)

The purpose of the File Allocation Table (FAT) is to allocate disk space for files. If you create a new file or revise an existing file, DOS revises the FAT entries according to the location of the file on disk. Under DOS 1.0 and 1.1, the FAT is stored on track 0, sector 2 (0:2) and is duplicated in sector 3 (0:3). Under DOS 2.0, the Boot record and FAT vary in length, but the general concept is the same. FAT contains an entry for each cluster on the disk from track 0, sector 6 (0:6) through track 39, sector 8 (39:8). A cluster on single-sided diskettes is one sector and on dual-sided diskettes is an adjacent pair of sectors. As a consequence, a dual-sided diskette can reference twice the data with the same number of FAT entries.

Track 0: | Boot | FAT1 | FAT2 | Directory | |
Sector: 1   2   3   4   5   6   7   8

The first two FAT entries define disk locations 0:6 and 0:7 in order to provide indication of the size and format of the Directory. Since 0:6 is the first sector the FAT references, 0:6 is relative sector 000, 0:7 is relative sector 001, 0:8 is relative sector 002, 1:1 is relative sector 003, and so forth.

Each FAT entry consists of three hex digits (12 bits) to indicate the use of a particular sector in the following format:

000 — The referenced sector is currently unused.
FFF — The sector is the last one of a file (see also the DOS 2.0 manual).
nnn — The relative sector number of the next sector for a file.

For example, assume that a single-sided diskette contains only one file named PAYROLL.ASM on 0:8, 1:1, and 1:2 (relative sectors 002, 003, and 004). The Directory entry for this file contains the filename PAYROLL, extension ASM, hex 00 to indicate a normal file, the creation date, 002 for the first relative sector of the file, and an entry for file size in bytes. The FAT would appear as follows:

```
FAT entry:        |xxx|xxx|003|004|FFF|000|000|. . .|000|
Relative sector:    0   1   2   3   4   5   6 . . . 314
```

The first two FAT entries reference the Directory on relative sectors 000 and 001. In order to enter this file into memory, the system takes the following steps:

1. DOS accesses the diskette and searches the Directory for the filename PAYROLL and extension ASM.
2. DOS then extracts from the Directory the location of the first relative sector (002) of the file and delivers the contents of this sector to its buffer in main memory.
3. DOS then accesses the entry in the FAT that represents relative sector 002. From the diagram, this entry contains 003, meaning that the file continues on relative sector 003. DOS delivers the contents of this sector to the buffer in main memory.
4. DOS next accesses the entry in the FAT that represents relative sector 003. This entry contains 004, meaning that the file continues on relative sector 004. DOS delivers the contents of this sector to the buffer in main memory.
5. The FAT entry for relative sector 004 contains hex FFF to indicate that there is no more data for this file.

From the foregoing, you can see that all files must begin on a sector boundary. Also, what may not be so immediately clear is that a file need not be contained on adjacent sectors, but could be scattered on the diskette in various sectors.

Under DOS 2.0, the first byte of the FAT indicates whether disk is fixed or is single- or dual-sided diskette with eight or nine sectors per track. Check the DOS manual for the actual layout.

DOS FILES

The preceding examples created files and read them. But you may also want to process files that DOS or CP/M have created. All you need to know are the organization of the Directory and the FAT and the way in which the system stores data in a sector. DOS stores your data in an ASM file, for example, exactly the way that you key it, including the characters for tab (hex 09), return (hex 0D), and line feed (hex 0A). However, to conserve disk space, DOS does not store blanks that appear on the screen immediately preceding a tab character nor blanks on a line to the right of a return character. The following illustrates an Assembler instruction entered on the screen:

<tab>MOV<tab>   AH,09<return>

For the above, the contents of the DOS file would be

094D4F560941482C30390D0A

When TYPE or EDLIN read the file, the tab, return, and line feed characters automatically adjust the data on a screen or a printer.

Let's now examine the program in Figure 13-4 that reads and displays the file, SEQREAD.ASM (the example from Figure 13-3), one sector at a time.

Figure 13-4 Reading a DOS File.

```
            page    60,132
    TITLE   DOSREAD - Read disk records created by DOS
    ;
    STACKSG SEGMENT PARA STACK 'STACK'
            DW      80 DUP(?)
    STACKSG ENDS
    ; -------------------------------------------------
    DATASG  SEGMENT PARA 'DATA'
    FCBREC  LABEL   BYTE                ;FCB for disk file
    FCBDRIV DB      02                  ;Disk drive B
    FCBNAME DB      'SEQREAD '          ;File name
    FCBEXT  DB      'ASM'               ;Extension
    FCBBLK  DW      0000                ;Current block#
    FCBRCSZ DW      0000                ;Logical record size
            DD      ?                   ;DOS file size
            DW      ?                   ;DOS date
            DT      ?                   ;DOS reserved
    FCBSQRC DB      00                  ;Current record#
            DD      ?                   ;Relative record#

    RECLEN  EQU     512                 ;Record length
    SECTOR  DB      RECLEN DUP(' '),'$'

    ENDCDE  DB      00
    OPENMSG DB      '*** Open error ***$'
    READMSG DB      '*** Read error ***$'
    ROWCTR  DB      00
    DATASG  ENDS
    ; -------------------------------------------------
    CODESG  SEGMENT PARA 'CODE'
    BEGIN   PROC    FAR
            ASSUME  CS:CODESG,DS:DATASG,SS:STACKSG,ES:DATASG
```

```
                PUSH    DS
                SUB     AX,AX
                PUSH    AX
                MOV     AX,DATASG
                MOV     DS,AX
                MOV     ES,AX
                CALL    Q10CLR          ;Clear screen
                CALL    Q20CURS         ;Set cursor
                CALL    E10OPEN         ;Open file, set DTA
                CMP     ENDCDE,00       ;Valid Open?
                JNZ     A90             ;Yes - continue
A20LOOP:
                CALL    F10READ         ;Read disk record
                CMP     ENDCDE,00       ;Normal read?
                JZ      A30             ;Yes - continue
                CMP     ENDCDE,03       ;End-file, some data?
                JNZ     A90             ;No - exit
A30:
                CALL    G10DISP         ;Display sector
                CMP     ENDCDE,03       ;End-of-file?
                JNZ     A20LOOP         ;No - continue
A90:    RET                             ;Yes - terminate
BEGIN   ENDP
;                       Open disk file:
;                       ---------------
E10OPEN PROC    NEAR
                LEA     DX,FCBREC
                MOV     AH,0FH          ;Request open
                INT     21H
                CMP     AL,00           ;File found?
                JNZ     E20             ;No - error

                MOV     FCBRCSZ,RECLEN  ;Set record length (EQU)
                MOV     AH,1AH
                LEA     DX,SECTOR       ;Set address of DTA
                INT     21H
                RET
E20:
                MOV     ENDCDE,01       ;Error message
                LEA     DX,OPENMSG
                CALL    X10ERR
                RET
E10OPEN ENDP
;                       Read disk sector:
;                       -----------------
F10READ PROC    NEAR
                MOV     AH,14H          ;Request read
                LEA     DX,FCBREC
                INT     21H
                CMP     AL,00           ;Normal read?
                JZ      F90             ;Yes - exit
                MOV     ENDCDE,AL       ;No:
                CMP     AL,01           ;End-of-file?
                JZ      F90             ;Yes - exit
                CMP     AL,03           ;End-of-file?
                JZ      F90             ;Yes - exit
                LEA     DX,READMSG      ;Invalid read
                CALL    X10ERR
```

```
F90:
            RET
F10READ  ENDP
;                   Display sector:
;                   ---------------
G10DISP  PROC       NEAR
            MOV     AH,09               ;Request display
            LEA     DX,SECTOR
            INT     21H
            CALL    Q20CURS
            RET
G10DISP  ENDP
;                   Clear screen:
;                   -------------
Q10CLR   PROC       NEAR
            MOV     AX,0600H            ;Request scroll
            MOV     BH,07
            MOV     CX,0000
            MOV     DX,184FH
            INT     10H
            RET
Q10CLR   ENDP
;                   Set cursor:
;                   -----------
Q20CURS  PROC       NEAR
            MOV     AH,02               ;Request set
            MOV     BH,00               ;  cursor
            MOV     DH,ROWCTR
            MOV     DL,00
            INT     10H
            INC     ROWCTR
            CMP     ROWCTR,25           ;Bottom of screen?
            JNE     Q90                 ;No -- exit
            MOV     ROWCTR,00           ;Set row to top
Q90:        RET
Q20CURS  ENDP
;                   Disk error routine:
;                   -------------------
X10ERR   PROC       NEAR
            MOV     AH,09               ;DX contains address
            INT     21H                 ;  of message
            RET
X10ERR   ENDP

CODESG   ENDS
            END     BEGIN
```

If you keyed and tested SEQREAD already, you can easily copy it to a new name such as DOSREAD.ASM and make the following minor changes:

1. Change FCBNAME to 'SEQREAD ' (including the rightmost blank!)
2. Change RECLEN from 32 to 512, the length of a sector.
3. Change the end-of-file test in F10READ to check for both return codes 01 and 03. Code 01 means that DOS has recognized the end of data and code 03 means that the last record (sector) contains some data (less than 512 bytes).

Actually, the program performs the same functions as DOS TYPE. But what you can do for fun and profit is to run DOSREAD under DEBUG. After each disk input, display the contents of the input area and see how DOS has formatted your records. Further, just after initializing the Segment registers, you could enter a different file name, such as one with an EXE extension, and examine the way in which DOS stores an object file.

You could enhance this program's versatility by the following:

1. Prompt a user to enter the filename and file extension.
2. Clear each screen line prior to displaying. (You will notice that data is left on the screen, and each new line may or may not replace all of the previous contents.)

ABSOLUTE DISK I/O UNDER DOS

You can also process disk directly using DOS 25H and 26H for absolute reads and writes. In this case, you lose the advantages of the features that DOS INT 21H provides: Directory handling and blocking/deblocking of records.

Since DOS 25H and 26H treat all records as the size of a sector, you must perform your own blocking, if any. These operations directly access a whole sector or block of sectors. Disk addressing is in terms of "logical record number" (absolute sector). That is, to determine a logical record number on single-sided diskettes, count each sector from track 0, sector 1, as follows:

Track	Sector	Logical Record Number
0	1	0
0	2	1
1	1	8
1	8	15
2	8	23

A convenient formula for single-sided diskettes is

$$\text{Logical record number} = (\text{sector\#} \times 8) + (\text{track} - 1)$$

For example, the logical record number for track 2, sector 8, is

$$(2 \times 8) + (8 - 1) = 16 + 7 = 23$$

The operations are INT 25H for absolute disk read and INT 26H for absolute disk write. The required coding is the following:

MOV	AL,drive#	;0 for A, 1 for B, etc.
MOV	BX,addr	;Transfer address
MOV	CX,sectors	;No. of sectors to read/write
MOV	DX,record#	;Beginning logical record no.
INT	25H or 26H	;DOS absolute read or write

An absolute disk read/write operation destroys all registers except the Segment registers. It sets the CF Flag to indicate if the operation was successful (0) or unsuccessful (1). If unsuccessful, the AL is set to describe the error:

AL	Reason
10000000	Attachment failed to respond
01000000	Seek operation failed
00100000	Controller failure
00010000	Bad CRC on diskette read
00001000	DMA overrun on diskette read
00000100	Requested sector not found
00000011	Attempt to write on write-protected diskette
00000010	Address mark not found

The INT operation pushes the flags onto the Stack. On return, the original flags are still on the Stack and should be popped.

BIOS DISK I/O

You can code directly at the BIOS level, although BIOS supplies no automatic use of the Directory or blocking and deblocking of records. The BIOS disk operation INT 13H treats all "records" as the size of a sector. Disk addressing is in terms of actual track number and sector number.

For disk read, write, and verify, you have to initialize the following registers:

AH	The operation to perform: read, write, verify, or format.
AL	The number of sectors, 1–8.
CH	Track number, 0–39.
CL	Starting sector number, 1–8.
DH	Head number, 0 or 1 (0 if one-sided diskette).
DL	Drive number, 0–3 (0 = drive A, 1 = drive B).
ES:BX	The address of the I/O buffer in the Data Segment (except for verify operations).

BIOS INT 13H requires a code in the AH register to identify the operation.

AH = 00: Reset the diskette system. This operation performs a hard reset to the NEC diskette controller and requires only hex 00 in the AH for INT 13H to execute.

AH = 01: Read the Diskette Status. This operation returns to the AL the *status* from the last diskette I/O operation (see STATUS BYTE below). Execution requires only hex 01 in the AH register.

AH = 02: Read Sectors. The operation reads a specified number of sectors into memory. The following example reads one sector into an area named INP_AREA:

```
MOV   AH,02              ;Request read
MOV   AL,01              ;One sector
LEA   BX,INP_AREA        ;Input buffer
MOV   CH,05             ;Track no. 5
MOV   CL,03             ;Sector no. 3
MOV   DH,00             ;Head no. 0
MOV   DL,01             ;Drive no. 1
INT   13H               ;Call BIOS
```

On return, the AL contains the number of sectors that the operation actually reads. The DS, BX, CX, and DX registers are preserved.

For most situations, a program would not specify an actual number for each disk I/O. Rather, it would initialize the CH and CL and would increment them to read or write sectors sequentially. Note that when the sector number reaches 09 (or 10 for tracks with nine sectors), you have to reset it to 01 and increment the track number, or change from side 0 to side 1 for dual-sided diskettes. When the track number reaches 40, you are either finished or have to begin another diskette – perhaps set for the next drive number – and then reset the side/track/sector numbers.

AH = 03. Write Sectors. This operation writes a specified area from memory (presumably 512 bytes or a multiple of 512) onto a designated sector or sectors. You load registers and handle processing just as for reading disk. On return, the AL contains the number of sectors that the operation actually wrote. The DS, BX, CX, and DX registers are preserved.

AH = 04: Verify Sector. This operation specifies the sectors that are to be verified. You could use it after a write (code 03) to verify that the data was written correctly. This feature does ensure more reliable output at a cost of more I/O time. On return, the AL contains the number of sectors actually verified. The DS, BX, CX, and DX registers are preserved.

AH = 05: Format Tracks.   You can use this operation to format a designated number of tracks according to one of four different sizes (the standard for the PC system is 512). Read/write operations require the format information to locate a requested sector. For this operation, the ES:BX registers must contain an address that points to a group of address fields for the track. For each sector on a track there must be one four-byte entry of the form T/H/S/B, where

    T = track number
    H = head number
    S = sector number
    B = bytes per sector (00 = 128, 01 = 256, 02 = 512, 03 = 1024)

For example, if you format track 03, head 00, and 512 bytes per sector, then the first of eight entries for the track is hex 03000102. Remaining entries for this track increment the sector from 01 through 08.

STATUS BYTE

For all AH codes 02, 03, 04, and 05, if the operation is successful, the CF Flag and the AH are set to 0. If the operation fails, the CF Flag is set to 1 and the AH contains a diskette status identifying the cause. (This is the same status that AH code 01 returns to the AL.)

AH:	Reason:
00000001	Bad command was passed for diskette I/O.
00000010	Could not find address mark on disk.
00000011	Attempted to write on protected disk.
00000100	Could not find required sector.
00001000	Operation overran DMA (Direct Memory Access)
00001001	Attempted to DMA across a 64K boundary.
00010000	Encountered a bad CRC on a read.
00100000	Failure by the NEC diskette controller.
01000000	Seek operation failed.
10000000	Attachment failed to respond.

If the interrupt operation returns an error, the usual action is to reset the diskette (AH code 00) and to retry the operation three times. If there is still an error, display a message and give the user a chance to change the diskette.

PROGRAM EXAMPLE USING BIOS

Now let's examine the program in Figure 13-5 that reads sectors from diskette using the BIOS input instruction INT 13H. The program is based on the example in Figure 13-4 with the following changes:

```
┌─────────────────────────────────────┐
│ Figure 13-5 Reading a Disk File      │
│ with BIOS.                           │
└─────────────────────────────────────┘
```

```
          page     60,132
TITLE     BIOREAD - Read disk sectors via BIOS
STACKSG SEGMENT PARA STACK 'STACK'
          DW       80 DUP(?)
STACKSG ENDS
; --------------------------------------------------
DATASG  SEGMENT PARA 'DATA'
RECDIN  DB       512 DUP(' '),'$'
;
ENDCDE  DB       00
READMSG DB       '*** Read error ***$'
CURADR  DW       0004H           ;Beginning tr/sector
ENDADR  DW       0501H           ;Ending track/sector
ROWCTR  DB       00
DATASG  ENDS
; --------------------------------------------------
CODESG  SEGMENT PARA 'CODE'
BEGIN   PROC     FAR
          ASSUME  CS:CODESG,DS:DATASG,SS:STACKSG,ES:DATASG
          PUSH    DS
          SUB     AX,AX
          PUSH    AX
          MOV     AX,DATASG
          MOV     DS,AX
          MOV     ES,AX
          CALL    Q10CLR          ;Clear screen
          CALL    Q20CURS         ;Set cursor
A20LOOP:
          CALL    C10ADDR         ;Calculate disk address
          MOV     CX,CURADR
          MOV     DX,ENDADR
          CMP     CX,DX           ;At ending sector?
          JE      A90             ;Yes - exit
          CALL    F10READ         ;Read disk record
          CMP     ENDCDE,00       ;Normal read?
          JNZ     A90             ;No  - exit
          CALL    G10DISP         ;Display name
          JMP     A20LOOP         ;Repeat
A90:      RET                     ;Terminate
BEGIN   ENDP
;                 Calculate next disk address:
;                 ----------------------------
C10ADDR PROC     NEAR
          MOV     CX,CURADR       ;Get track/sector
          CMP     CL,09           ;Past last sector?
          JNE     C90             ;No - exit
          MOV     CL,01           ;Set sector to 1
          INC     CH              ;Increment track
          MOV     CURADR,CX
C90:      RET
C10ADDR ENDP
;                 Read disk sector:
;                 -----------------
F10READ PROC     NEAR
          MOV     AL,01           ;No. of sectors
```

```
                MOV     AH,02           ;Request read
                LEA     BX,RECDIN       ;Address of buffer
                MOV     CX,CURADR       ;Track/sector
                MOV     DH,00           ;Side 0
                MOV     DL,01           ;Drive B
                INT     13H             ;Request input
                CMP     AH,00           ;Normal read?
                JZ      F90             ;Yes - exit
                MOV     ENDCDE,01       ;No:
                LEA     DX,READMSG      ;Invalid read
                CALL    X10ERR
F90:
                INC     CURADR          ;Increment sector
                RET
F10READ ENDP
;                       Display sector:
;                       --------------
G10DISP PROC    NEAR
                MOV     AH,09           ;Request display
                LEA     DX,RECDIN
                INT     21H
                CALL    Q20CURS
                RET
G10DISP ENDP
;                       Clear screen:
;                       ------------
Q10CLR  PROC    NEAR
                MOV     AX,0600H        ;Request scroll
                MOV     BH,07
                MOV     CX,0000
                MOV     DX,184FH
                INT     10H
                RET
Q10CLR  ENDP
;                       Set cursor:
;                       ----------
Q20CURS PROC    NEAR
                MOV     AH,02           ;Request set
                MOV     BH,00           ;  cursor
                MOV     DH,ROWCTR
                MOV     DL,00
                INT     10H
                INC     ROWCTR
                CMP     ROWCTR,25       ;Bottom row?
                JNE     Q90             ;No -- exit
                MOV     ROWCTR,00       ;Yes - set to zero
Q90:
                RET
Q20CURS ENDP
;                       Disk error routine:
;                       ------------------
X10ERR  PROC    NEAR
                MOV     AH,09           ;DX contains address
                INT     21H             ;  of message
                RET
X10ERR  ENDP

CODESG  ENDS
        END     BEGIN
```

1. There is now no FCB definition or open routine.

2. The program has to calculate each disk address. After each read, it increments the sector number. In C10ADDR, when the sector reaches 9, the routine increments the track number and resets the sector to 1. For 9-sectored diskettes, test for reaching 10 sectors. For dual-sided diskettes, you also have to provide for flip-flopping between sides. For example, on reading all the sectors for side 0, track 1, set the side to 1, leave the track at 1, and set the sector to 1. On reading all the sectors for side 1, track 1, set the side to 0, increment the track to 2, and set the sector to 1. You can flip-flop the side number in C10ADDR as follows:

       SIDE   DB   00
               ...
               XOR   SIDE,01

3. CURADR contains the beginning track/sector (which the program increments) and ENDADR contains the ending track/sector. You could enhance the program by prompting a user for starting and ending track/sector.

Suggestion: Run this program under DEBUG. Trace through the instructions that initialize the Segment registers and then adjust the start and end sectors to the location of the FAT (its location varies by operating system version). Use G (go) to execute and then examine the input area for the FAT and Directory entries.

To avoid using DEBUG, you could also convert the ASCII characters in the input area to their hex equivalents and display the hex values just as DEBUG does (see the program back in Figure 12-5). In this way, you could examine the contents of any sector (even "hidden" ones). You could even allow a user to enter changes and write the changed sector back onto diskette!

SUMMARY

This chapter provides the basic material for processing files on disk. Sequential processing is adequate for creating a file, for printing the contents of an entire file, and for making changes to small files. However, you may occasionally have to update a file with new data. A program restricted only to sequential processing would have to perform the following steps: Read each record, change the specified ones, and write the records into another file (it could use the same DTA but would require a different FCB). A common practice is to read the input file from disk A and to write the updated file onto disk B. (Note that you cannot store two files on a diskette with the same filename and extension.) The advantage of this method is that it does provide an automatic backup file.

Quite often, however, you may want to access a particular record. For example, a user may need to request the information for a few employees or stock part numbers, or need to change the contents of a few records. It is possible to initialize the current block/record numbers—if you happen to know the location of the records in the file—and issue a sequential read command. However, DOS has a system that facilitates random processing—but that's a topic for the next exciting chapter.

DOS absolute disk read/write and BIOS INT 13H also can be used for random processing. Indeed, they are more suitable for that purpose since neither supplies automatic end-of-file handling.

KEY POINTS TO REMEMBER

□   Regardless of their size, all files begin on a sector boundary.

□   The Directory contains an entry for each file on the diskette and indicates the filename, extension, file attribute, time, date, starting sector, and file size.

□   A program using DOS INT 21H for disk I/O must define a File Control Block (FCB) for each file that it accesses.

□   A block consists of 128 records. In the FCB, the current block number combined with the current record number indicates the disk record that is to be processed.

□   The entries in the FCB for current block, record size, file size, and relative record number are stored in reversed byte sequence.

□   All programs that reference a file must define the FCB similarly.

□   The Disk Transfer Area (DTA) is the location of the record that is to be written or read. You have to initialize each DTA in a program prior to a write or read operation.

□   The open operation sets the FCB entries for filename, extension, record size (hex 80), file size, and date. The program should change the record size to the correct value.

□   A program using DOS INT 21H for writing a file must close it at the end in order to write the records (if any) in the buffer and to complete the Directory entries.

□   On reads and writes under DOS INT 21H, the system automatically updates the current record number in the FCB.

□   A DOS INT 21H read operation first checks the buffer for the required record, and if not present, performs a disk access.

- □ DOS INT 25H and 26H provide absolute disk read/write operations.
- □ BIOS INT 13H provides direct access to track and sector.
- □ DOS INT 25H and 26H and BIOS INT 13H do not supply automatic Directory handling, end-of-file operations, and blocking and deblocking of records.

QUESTIONS

13-1. What is the content of track 0, sectors 1 through 7, under DOS 1-1?

13-2. How many files may a diskette contain on one side?

13-3. What is the relative sector number for track 1, sector 4?

13-4. What is the additional effect on a diskette when you format with FORMAT /S?

13-5. Assume that the size of a file is 2890 bytes:

(a) Where does the system store the size?

(b) What is the size in hexadecimal format?

(c) Show the value as the system stores it.

13-6. Provide the DOS hex function calls for the following operations: (a) create, (b) set the DTA, (c) sequential write, (d) open, (e) sequential read.

13-7. A program uses the record size to which the open operation defaults:

(a) How many records would a sector contain?

(b) How many records would a diskette contain, assuming one side of a diskette and formatted without /S.

(c) If the file in (b) is being read sequentially, how many physical disk accesses will occur?

13-8. Write a program that creates a disk file containing part number (five characters), part description (12 characters), and unit price (one word). Allow a user to enter these values on the terminal. Remember to convert the quantity from ASCII to binary.

13-9. Write a program that displays the contents of the file created in Question 13-8.

13-10. Code the instructions for BIOS INT 13H to write three sectors using memory address OUT_DSK, drive 0, head 0, track 8, and sector 1.

14

DISK PROCESSING II:
ADVANCED

Objective:
To examine the programming
requirements for more advanced
processing of disk files including
random accessing.

INTRODUCTION

Quite often there is a need for accessing a particular record in a file. If it is the 300th record, sequential processing could involve reading through the preceding 299 records before delivering the 300th (although technicaly the system could begin at a specific current block/record number). DOS provides a method of random processing that facilitates directly accessing records in a file.

Chapter 13 provides the basic material for disk processing. Indeed, although you may create a file sequentially, you may access records sequentially or randomly. The requirements for random processing simply involve inserting the required record number in the FCB relative record field and issuing a random read or write command. Indeed, it is even possible to read or write an entire file with one random block command, subject to sufficient space in the program for all the records.

For random accessing, DOS requires a number in the FCB relative record field. However, for many applications, it is difficult for a user to know the relative location of disk records. This chapter introduces a technique of indexing. A user may enter, for example, an actual inventory part number. By means of a table, or index, the program can convert the part number to a relative record number which is used to randomly locate the required record on disk.

Random processing uses the relative record number (bytes 33-36) in the FCB. The value is a doubleword, stored in reverse sequence. To locate the random record, the system automatically converts the relative record number to current block (bytes 12-13) and current record (byte 32) numbers.

RANDOM READING

Some computer applications require accessing particular records in a file. For example, to directly access relative record number 05, insert the number 05 into the FCB field for relative record number and issue the instructions for random read. If successful, the operation returns the contents of the record to the DTA.

The open operation and the setting of the DTA are the same for both sequential and random processing. To read a disk record randomly, store the required relative record number in the FCB and use the function call hex 21:

```
LEA     DX,FCBname      ;Read record
MOV     AH,21H          ;  randomly
INT     21H             ;Call DOS
```

The read operation converts the relative record number to current block/record. It uses this value to locate the required disk record, delivers the record to the DTA, and sets the AL register as follows:

00 — The read was successful.
01 — No more data is available.
02 — Terminated transfer because of insufficient room in the disk transfer segment.
03 — Has read a partial record filled with zeros.

As you can see, there is no end-of-file condition as such. If you are seeking a particular record which is supposed to exist, the only valid response is 00. You can cause invalid responses by various means, such as setting an invalid relative record number and failing to initialize the correct address in the DTA or in the FCB. Since these errors are easy to make, it is a good idea after a random read to test the AL for a nonzero code.

When a program first requests a random record, the operation uses the Directory to locate the sector where the record resides, reads the entire sector from disk into the buffer, and delivers the record to the DTA. For example, assume that records are 128 bytes long and four to a sector. A request for random record number 23 causes the following four records to be read into the DTA:

| rel rec #20 | rel rec #21 | rel rec #22 | rel rec #23 |

When the program requests the next random record—for example, number 23—the operation first checks the buffer. Since the record is in the buffer, it is transferred directly to the DTA. If the program requests a record such as number 35 that is not in the buffer, the operation uses the Directory to locate the record, reads the entire sector into the buffer, and delivers the record to the DTA.

You can see that it is more efficient to request random record numbers that are close together—for example, in ascending sequence. However, if records are the size of a sector (512 bytes), every read will involve a disk access.

RANDOM WRITING

You can also write records randomly. For example, you may want to update items in an inventory file. Your program could randomly read an inventory item, change the quantity on hand, and write the record back into the same disk location. With the relative record number initialized in the FCB, a *random write* uses the function call hex 22 as follows:

```
LEA     DX,FCBname      ;Write record
MOV     AH,22H          ; randomly
INT     21H             ;Call DOS
```

The write operation sets the AL as follows:

00 — The write was successful.
01 — The disk is full.
02 — Transfer ended because of insufficient space to write the record in the disk transfer segment.

You could get a nonzero return code when randomly creating a new file. But if you have read a record randomly and are now rewriting an updated record in the *same* disk location, you would expect the return code to be only 00.

Note: The random relative record number in the FCB is a doubleword (four bytes) stored in reversed sequence. If the file is small, you may have to initialize only the leftmost byte or two. But for large files, setting the record number for three or four bytes requires a bit of care.

PROGRAM: READING A DISK FILE RANDOMLY

The program in Figure 14-1 reads the same file created earlier in Figure 13-2. By keying in a relative record number that is within the bounds of the file, a user can request any record to display on the screen. If the file contains 25 records, then the valid record numbers are 00 through 24. Any number entered from the keyboard is in ASCII format, and in this case will be only one or two digits.

```
┌─────────────────────────────────────────────┐
│  Figure 14-1  Random Reading of Disk Records.│
└─────────────────────────────────────────────┘
```

```
TYPE B:RANREAD.ASM
          page    60,132
TITLE    RANREAD - Random read of records created by CREATDSK
; -----------------------------------------------------------
STACKSG SEGMENT PARA STACK 'STACK'
        DW      80 DUP(?)
STACKSG ENDS
; -----------------------------------------------------------
DATASG  SEGMENT PARA 'DATA'
RECDPAR LABEL   BYTE                ;Parameter list
MAXLEN  DB      3                   ;
ACTLEN  DB      ?                   ;
RECDNO  DB      3 DUP(' '),'$'      ;

RECLEN  EQU     32                  ;Record length
NAMEFLD DB      RECLEN DUP(' '),'$' ;Disk Transfer Area (DTA)

FCBREC  LABEL   BYTE                ;FCB for disk file
FCBDRIV DB      02                  ;Disk drive B
FCBNAME DB      'NAMEFILE'          ;File name
FCBEXT  DB      'TST'               ;Extension
FCBBLK  DW      0000                ;Current block#
FCBRCSZ DW      0000                ;Logical record size
        DD      ?                   ;DOS file size
        DW      ?                   ;DOS date
        DT      ?                   ;DOS reserved
        DB      00                  ;Current record#
FCBRNRC DD      00000000            ;Relative record#

OPENMSG DB      '*** Open error ***$'
READMSG DB      '*** Read error ***$'
PROMPT  DB      'Record number?$'
ROWCTR  DB      00
```

```
ENDCDE   DB      00
DATASG   ENDS
; -----------------------------------------------
CODESG   SEGMENT PARA 'CODE'
BEGIN    PROC    FAR
         ASSUME  CS:CODESG,DS:DATASG,SS:STACKSG,ES:DATASG
         PUSH    DS
         SUB     AX,AX
         PUSH    AX
         MOV     AX,DATASG
         MOV     DS,AX
         MOV     ES,AX
         CALL    Q10CLR          ;Clear screen
         CALL    Q20CURS         ;Set cursor
         CALL    C100PEN         ;Open file, set DTA
         CMP     ENDCDE,00       ;Valid Open?
         JZ      A20LOOP         ;Yes - continue
         RET                     ;No  - terminate
A20LOOP:
         CALL    D10RECN         ;Request record #
         CMP     ACTLEN,00       ;No more requests?
         JE      A40             ; - exit
         CALL    F10READ         ;Random read
         CMP     ENDCDE,00       ;Normal read?
         JNZ     A30             ;No  - bypass
         CALL    G10DISP         ;Call Display routine
A30:     JMP     A20LOOP
A40:     RET                     ;Terminate
BEGIN    ENDP
;                Open disk routine:
;                ------------------
C100PEN  PROC    NEAR
         MOV     AH,0FH          ;Request open
         LEA     DX,FCBREC
         INT     21H
         CMP     AL,00           ;Valid open?
         JNZ     C20             ;No - error

         MOV     FCBRCSZ,RECLEN  ;Record size (EQU)
         MOV     AH,1AH
         LEA     DX,NAMEFLD      ;Set address of DTA
         INT     21H
         RET
C20:
         MOV     ENDCDE,01       ;Error message
         LEA     DX,OPENMSG
         CALL    X10ERR
         RET
C100PEN  ENDP

;                Get record number:
;                ------------------
D10RECN  PROC    NEAR
         MOV     AH,09H          ;Request display
         LEA     DX,PROMPT
         INT     21H

         MOV     AH,0AH          ;Request input
         LEA     DX,RECDPAR
         INT     21H
```

```
                CMP       ACTLEN,01        ;Check length 0, 1, 2
                JB        D40              ;Length 0, terminate
                JA        D20
                SUB       AH,AH            ;Length 1
                MOV       AL,RECDNO
                JMP       D30
        D20:
                MOV       AH,RECDNO        ;Length 2
                MOV       AL,RECDNO+1
        D30:
                AND       AX,0F0FH         ;Clear ASCII 3's
                AAD                        ;Convert to binary
                MOV       WORD PTR FCBRNRC,AX
        D40:    RET
        D10RECN ENDP
        ;                 Read disk record:
        ;                 ----------------
        F10READ PROC      NEAR
                MOV       ENDCDE,00        ;Clear indicator
                MOV       AH,21H           ;Random read
                LEA       DX,FCBREC
                INT       21H
                CMP       AL,00            ;Normal read?
                JZ        F20              ;Yes - exit
                MOV       ENDCDE,01        ;No:
                LEA       DX,READMSG       ; invalid read
                CALL      X10ERR           ;Call error routine
        F20:
                RET
        F10READ ENDP
        ;                 Display name:
        ;                 ------------
        G10DISP PROC      NEAR
                MOV       AH,09            ;Request display
                LEA       DX,NAMEFLD
                INT       21H
                CALL      Q20CURS
                RET
        G10DISP ENDP
        ;                 Clear screen:
        ;                 ------------
        Q10CLR  PROC      NEAR
                MOV       AX,0600H         ;Request scroll
                MOV       BH,07
                MOV       CX,0000
                MOV       DX,184FH
                INT       10H
                RET
        Q10CLR  ENDP
        ;                 Set cursor:
        ;                 ----------
        Q20CURS PROC      NEAR
                MOV       AH,02            ;Request set
                MOV       BH,00            ;  cursor
                MOV       DH,ROWCTR
                MOV       DL,00
                INT       10H
```

```
                INC     ROWCTR
                RET
    Q20CURS ENDP
    ;                   Disk error routine:
    ;                   -------------------
    X10ERR  PROC    NEAR
                MOV     AH,09           ;DX contains address
                INT     21H             ;  of message
                RET
    X10ERR  ENDP

    CODESG  ENDS
                END     BEGIN
```

The program is organized as follows:

C10OPEN   Opens the file, sets the record size to 32, and sets the address of the DTA.

D10RECN   Accepts a record number from the keyboard and converts it to binary format in the FCB relative record field. An improvement in the routine would be to check that the number is valid, that is, a *number* between 00 and 24.

F10READ   Uses the relative record number in the FCB to deliver a record to the DTA.

G10DISP   Displays the record on the screen.

The routine D10RECN accepts a record number from the keyboard and checks its length in the parameter list. There are three possible lengths:

00—End of processing requested.
01—A one-digit request, stored in the AL.
02—A two-digit request, stored in the AX.

The routine has to convert the ASCII number to binary. Since the value is in the AX register, the AAD instruction works nicely for this purpose. The contents of the AX, now in binary, are moved to the leftmost two bytes of the FCB relative record field. As an example, if the entered number is ASCII 12, then the AX would contain 3132. AND converts this to 0102 and AAD further converts it to 000C. The result in the FCB random record field is C0000000.

RANDOM BLOCK PROCESSING

If you have sufficient space in your program you can with one *random block* operation write an entire file from the DTA onto disk, and can read the entire file from disk into the DTA. This feature is especially useful for storing tables on disk which other programs can read into memory for processing.

Technically, you may begin with any valid relative record number and any number of records, although the block must be within the file's range of records. You still must first open the file and initialize the DTA.

For a *random block* write, initialize the required number of records in the CX register, set the starting relative record number in the FCB, and use function call hex 28:

```
MOV     CX,records      ;Initialize no. of records
LEA     DX,FCBname      ;Random
MOV     AH,28H          ; block
INT     21H             ; write
```

The operation converts the FCB relative record number to current block/record. It uses this value to determine the starting disk location, and sets a code in the AL register:

00—Successful write of all records.

01—No records written because of insufficient disk space.

The operation sets the FCB relative record field and the current block/record fields to the next record number. That is, if it wrote records 00 - 24, the next record is 25 (hex 19).

For *random block* read, initialize the required number of records in the CX and use function call hex 27:

```
MOV     CX,records      ;Initialize no. of records
LEA     DX,FCBname      ;Random
MOV     AH,27H          ; block
INT     21H             ; read
```

The read operation returns a code to the AL register:

00—Successful read of all records.

01—Has read to end of file and last record is complete.

02—Read as many records as possible in the disk transfer segment.

03—Has read to end of file and last record is partial.

The operation stores in the CX the actual number of records read and sets the FCB relative record field and current block/record fields to the next record.

You may want to read an entire file but are uncertain of the number of records. Since the open operation initializes the FCB file size field, simply divide this value by the record length. For example, if the file size is hex 320 (800) and the record length is hex 20 (32), then the number of records would be hex 19 (25).

PROGRAM: READING A RANDOM BLOCK

The program in Figure 14-2 performs a block read of the file created earlier in Figure 13-2. The program initializes the starting relative record number to 00 and the CX to 25 records and displays the entire DTA on the screen (just to show that it really works!). Other variations could involve initializing at a record other than 00 and reading fewer than 25 records.

Figure 14-2 Reading a Random Block.

```
          page    60,132
TITLE    RANBLOK - Random block read of name file
; ------------------------------------------------
STACKSG SEGMENT PARA STACK 'Stack'
        DW      80 DUP(?)
STACKSG ENDS
; ------------------------------------------------
DATASG  SEGMENT PARA 'Data'
DSKRECS DB      1024 DUP(?),'$' ;DTA for block of records

FCBREC  LABEL   BYTE            ;FCB for disk file
FCBDRIV DB      02              ;Disk drive B
FCBNAME DB      'NAMEFILE'      ;File name
FCBEXT  DB      'TST'           ;Extension
FCBBLK  DW      0000            ;Current block #
FCBRCSZ DW      0000            ;Logical record size
FCBFLZ  DD      ?               ;DOS file size
        DW      ?               ;DOS date
        DT      ?               ;DOS reserved
        DB      00              ;Current record #
FCBRNRC DD      00000000        ;Relative record #

ENDCODE DB      00
NORECS  DW      25              ;Number of records
OPENMSG DB      '*** Open error ***$'
READMSG DB      '*** Read error ***$'
ROWCTR  DB      00
DATASG  ENDS
; ------------------------------------------------
CODESG  SEGMENT PARA 'Code'
BEGIN   PROC    FAR
        ASSUME  CS:CODESG,DS:DATASG,SS:STACKSG,ES:DATASG
        PUSH    DS
        SUB     AX,AX
        PUSH    AX
        MOV     AX,DATASG
        MOV     DS,AX
        MOV     ES,AX
```

```
            CALL    Q10CLR
            CALL    Q20CURS
            CALL    E100PEN        ;Open file, set DTA
            CMP     ENDCODE,00     ;Valid Open?
            JNZ     A30            ;No - terminate
            CALL    F10READ        ;Read records
            CALL    G10DISP        ;Call display
A30:        RET                    ;No  - terminate
BEGIN   ENDP
;                   Open disk file:
;                   --------------
E100PEN PROC    NEAR
            LEA     DX,FCBREC
            MOV     AH,0FH         ;Request open
            INT     21H
            CMP     AL,00          ;Valid open?
            JNZ     E20            ;No - error

            MOV     FCBRCSZ,0020H  ;Record size
            MOV     AH,1AH
            LEA     DX,DSKRECS     ;Set address of DTA
            INT     21H
            RET
E20:
            MOV     ENDCODE,01     ;Error message
            LEA     DX,OPENMSG
            CALL    X10ERR
            RET
E100PEN ENDP
;                   Read disk block:
;                   --------------
F10READ PROC    NEAR
            MOV     AH,27H         ;Random Block read
            MOV     CX,NORECS      ;No. of records
            LEA     DX,FCBREC
            INT     21H
            MOV     ENDCODE,AL     ;Save return condition
            RET
F10READ ENDP
;                   Display disk block:
:                   ------------------
G10DISP PROC    NEAR
            MOV     AH,09          ;Request display
            LEA     DX,DSKRECS
            INT     21H
            RET
G10DISP ENDP
;                   Clear screen routine:
;                   --------------------
Q10CLR  PROC    NEAR
            MOV     AX,0600H       ;Request scroll
            MOV     BH,07
            MOV     CX,0000
            MOV     DX,184FH
            INT     10H
            RET
Q10CLR  ENDP
;                   Set cursor routine:
;                   ------------------
Q20CURS PROC    NEAR
            MOV     AH,02          ;Request set cursor
```

```
            MOV     BH,00
            MOV     DH,ROWCTR
            MOV     DL,00
            INT     10H
            INC     ROWCTR
            RET
Q20CURS  ENDP
;                   Disk error routine:
;                   ------------------
X10ERR   PROC     NEAR
            MOV     AH,09          ;DX contains address
            INT     21H            ;  of message
            RET
X10ERR   ENDP

CODESG   ENDS
            END     BEGIN
```

The program is organized as follows:

E10OPEN   Opens the file, sets the FCB record size to 32, and sets
            the address of the DTA.

F10READ   Initializes the number of records to 25 and performs the
            block read.

G10DISP   Displays the block on the screen.

The read operation converts the FCB relative record number 00 to current block 00 and current record hex 00. At the end of the read operation, the FCB current record number contains hex 19 and the relative record number contains hex 19000000.

INDEXES

One drawback to the random processing method that you probably noticed is that a user is unlikely to know the relative number for a particular record. Presumably, the user could have a list such as the following:

Part number	Relative record
023	0
024	1
027	2
049	3
114	4
...	

However, since a computer supposedly can do almost anything, the user may wonder why it is not possible to key in the actual part number. Then the computer could figure out the location of the required record. Indeed it can, and that's just what we'll do next.

Assume that a disk file contains the following records:

```
Part#  Price   Description
|023 |00315 |Assemblers  |
|024 |00430 |Linkages    |
|027 |00525 |Compilers   |
|049 |00920 |Compressors |
|114 |11250 |Extractors  |
|117 |00630 |Haulers     |
|122 |10520 |Lifters     |
|124 |21335 |Processors  |
|127 |00960 |Labellers   |
|232 |05635 |Bailers     |
|999 |00000 |            |
```

The method requires that the particular keys (part numbers in this case) are set up in a special table known as an *index*. In its simplest form, there is one index entry for each key in the file. The index for the preceding table of part numbers could contain just the part numbers:

Index: |023|024|027|049|114|117|122|124|127|232|999|

The location of a key in the index indicates the relative record. For example, entry 023 means that the record with key 023 is relative record 00, entry 024 means relative record 01, and so forth. A program that defines the index accepts requests from a user in the form of part number. The program compares the user part number successively against each key in the index. For each unequal compare, the program adds 1 to the relative record number (initially 00). On an equal compare, the relative record number specifies the required disk record.

Ideally, an index is stored as a separate file on disk and is available to any program. An extremely large file may require a more sophisticated indexing method. For example, the file may be too large for a random block read, or an entry for every record may cause the index to be too large.

Assume that the records in a file are 64 bytes long. The system stores eight of these records per sector. Just for illustrative purposes, let's assume that the file is on only three sectors. In the following example, the key numbers represent each record:

Sector 1: | 20 | 25 | 27 | 28 | 30 | 35 | 37 | 40 |
Sector 2: | 47 | 49 | 53 | 58 | 63 | 66 | 69 | 74 |
Sector 3: | 82 | 83 | 85 | 87 | 88 | 92 | 99 | |

The index for this file could contain the high key for each sector, as

|40|74|99|

A program could have a copy of this index, either defined or loaded from disk. If a user requests key number 87, the program compares this key against each index entry as follows:

87:40   High—try the next entry.
87:74   High—try the next entry.
87:99   Low—record is located.

The record—if it exists at all—should be on sector 3. Note that sector 1 begins with relative record 00, sector 2 with relative record 08, and sector 3 with relative record 16. For each unequal compare in the index, the search can add 8 to the relative record number (initially 0).

Other methods of determining the relative record number are (1) incrementing 1 for each unequal compare and, on reaching an equal, multiplying the sum by 8 and (2) storing the number along with the key in the index. As an example of the latter, the following index contains the high key and relative record number of the last record for each sector:

Index: | 40 00 | 74 08 | 99 16 |

PROGRAM: DISK PROCESSING USING AN INDEX

The program in Figure 14-3 illustrates the use of an index for randomly locating disk records. Assume that another program has already created a part file with records containing part number, price, and description, as described in the previous section. This program defines an index (named INDEX) containing the key (part number) for each record.

Figure 14-3 Use of an Index for Accessing Disk.

```
          page    60,132
TITLE    RANDPAR - Use of an index for random read
; -------------------------------------------------
STACKSG SEGMENT PARA STACK 'STACK'
        DW      80 DUP(?)
STACKSG ENDS
; -------------------------------------------------
```

```
                DATASG  SEGMENT PARA 'DATA'
                PARTPAR LABEL   BYTE                ;Parameter list
                MAXLEN  DB      4                   ;
                ACTLEN  DB      ?                   ;
                PARTNO  DB      3 DUP(' '),'$'      ;

                PARTREC DB      3 DUP(' ')          ;Disk Transfer Area
                PARTPRC DB      5 DUP(' ')          ;
                PARTDSC DB      24 DUP(' '),'$'     ;

                FCBREC  LABEL   BYTE                ;FCB for disk file
                FCBDRIV DB      02                  ;Disk drive B
                FCBNAME DB      'PARTFILE'          ;File name
                FCBEXT  DB      'TST'               ;Extension
                FCBBLK  DW      0000                ;Current block#
                FCBRCSZ DW      0000                ;Logical record size
                        DD      ?                   ;DOS file size
                        DW      ?                   ;DOS date
                        DT      ?                   ;DOS reserved
                        DB      00                  ;Current record #
                FCBRLRC DD      00000000            ;Relative record #

                INDEX   DB      '023','024','027','049'
                        DB      '114','117','122','124'
                        DB      '127','232','999'

                ENDCDE  DB      00
                ERRMSG  DB      'Part # not in table$'
                OPENMSG DB      '*** Open error ***$'
                PROMPT  DB      'Part number?$'
                READMSG DB      '*** Read error ***$'
                RECLEN  EQU     32                  ;Record length
                ROWCTR  DB      00
                DATASG  ENDS
                E30:
                        LEA     DX,ERRMSG           ;Display error
                        CALL    X10ERR              ; message
                        MOV     CX,'**'             ;Set error indicator
                E40:
                        RET
                E10SRCH ENDP
                ; ------------------------------------------------------
                CODESG  SEGMENT PARA 'CODE'
                BEGIN   PROC    FAR
                        ASSUME  CS:CODESG,DS:DATASG,SS:STACKSG,ES:DATASG
                        PUSH    DS
                        SUB     AX,AX
                        PUSH    AX
                        MOV     AX,DATASG
                        MOV     DS,AX
                        MOV     ES,AX
                        CALL    Q10CLR              ;Clear screen
                        CALL    Q20CURS             ;Set cursor
                        CALL    C100PEN             ;Open file, set DTA
                        CMP     ENDCDE,00           ;Valid Open?
                        JZ      A20LOOP             ;Yes - continue
                        RET                         ;No  - terminate
                A20LOOP:
                        CALL    D10RECN             ;Request record #
                        CMP     ACTLEN,00           ;No more requests?
                        JE      A40                 ; - exit
                        CMP     CX,'**'             ;Invalid part# entered?
                        JZ      A30                 ; yes - bypass disk read
                        CALL    F10READ             ;Random read
                        CMP     ENDCDE,00           ;Normal read?
                        JNZ     A30                 ;No  - bypass
                        CALL    G10DISP             ;Display record
                A30:
                        CALL    Q20CURS
                        JMP     A20LOOP
                A40:    RET                         ;No  - terminate
                BEGIN   ENDP
                ;               Open disk file:
                ;               --------------
                C100PEN PROC    NEAR
                        MOV     AH,0FH              ;Request open
                        LEA     DX,FCBREC
                        INT     21H
                        CMP     AL,00               ;Valid open?
                        JNZ     C20                 ;No - error

                        MOV     FCBRCSZ,RECLEN      ;Record size (EQU)
                        LEA     DX,PARTREC          ;Set address of DTA
                        MOV     AH,1AH
                        INT     21H
                        RET
                C20:
                        MOV     ENDCDE,01           ;Error message
                        LEA     DX,OPENMSG
```

```
            CALL    X10ERR
            RET
C100PEN ENDP
;               Get part number:
;               ----------------
D10RECN PROC    NEAR
            MOV     AH,09H
            LEA     DX,PROMPT       ;Display prompt
            INT     21H

            MOV     AH,0AH
            LEA     DX,PARTPAR      ;Accept part
            INT     21H
            CMP     ACTLEN,00       ;If length = 0,
            JZ      D40             ; terminate
            CALL    E10SRCH         ;Search index
D40:        RET
D10RECN ENDP
;               Search index:
;               -------------
E10SRCH PROC
            MOV     WORD PTR FCBRLRC,00 ;Clear rel rec.#
            CLD
            LEA     DI,INDEX
E20:
            LEA     SI,PARTNO
            MOV     CX,03
            MOV     DX,DI           ;Save index address
            REPE CMPSB              ;Compare part# : index
            JB      E30             ;Not in index - error
            JE      E40             ;Found
            INC     WORD PTR FCBRLRC ;Incr't rel record #
            MOV     DI,DX           ;Restore index address
            ADD     DI,03           ;Add for next index
            JMP     E20
;               Read disk record:
;               ---------------##
F10READ PROC    NEAR
            MOV     ENDCDE,00
            MOV     AH,21H          ;Random read
            LEA     DX,FCBREC
            INT     21H
            CMP     AL,00           ;Normal read?
            JZ      F20             ;Yes - exit
            MOV     ENDCDE,01       ;No:
            LEA     DX,READMSG      ;Invalid read
            CALL    X10ERR
F20:
            RET
F10READ ENDP
;               Display record:
;               ---------------
G10DISP PROC    NEAR
            MOV     AH,09           ;Set display
            LEA     DX,PARTREC
            INT     21H
            RET
G10DISP ENDP
;               Clear screen:
;               ------------
Q10CLR  PROC    NEAR
            MOV     AX,0600H        ;Set scroll
            MOV     BH,07
            MOV     CX,0000
            MOV     DX,184FH
            INT     10H
            RET
Q10CLR  ENDP
;               Set cursor:
;               ----------
Q20CURS PROC    NEAR
            MOV     AH,02
            MOV     BH,00
            MOV     DH,ROWCTR
            MOV     DL,00
            INT     10H
            INC     ROWCTR
            RET
Q20CURS ENDP
;               Error routine:
;               -------------
X10ERR  PROC    NEAR
            MOV     AH,09           ;DX contains address
            INT     21H             ; of message
            RET
X10ERR  ENDP

CODESG  ENDS
            END     BEGIN
```

The program is organized as follows:

A10LOOP	Calls D10RECN to request a part number; calls F10READ to randomly read the record; calls G10DISP to display the record.
C10OPEN	Opens the file, establishes the record length, and initializes the DTA, PARTREC.
D10RECN	Displays a prompt and accepts a part number; calls E10SRCH to search the index.
E10SRCH	Searches the index for the requested part number; displays an error message if not found.
F10READ	Reads the disk record randomly.
G10DISP	Displays the record on the screen.

Note that the preceding discussion uses DOS INT 21H for disk accessing. The advantage is that this method provides some automatic features. However, for direct accessing, you can also use DOS INT 25H and 26H or BIOS INT 13H.

FIXED DISK

DOS 2.0 supports one or more fixed disk drives with (at the time of this writing) up to 10 megabytes of storage.

Each fixed disk drive has two platters, with a total of four surfaces;
Each surface has 306 tracks;
Each track has 17 sectors; and
Each sector has 512 bytes.

Programming for fixed disk is similar to that for diskette, although the Directory necessarily requires more features. See the manual, especially Chapters 4, 5, 9, 10, and Appendixes A, G, and I.

KEY POINTS TO REMEMBER

☐ Random processing requires a record number in the relative record number entry in the FCB. Prior to performing a read or write, the system converts the number to current block/record.

☐ The eight bytes (doubleword) of the relative record number are stored in reversed sequence.

☐ If a required random record is already in the buffer, the system transfers it directly to the DTA. Otherwise, the operation accesses disk and reads into the buffer the entire sector containing the record.

☐ Where there is sufficient space in a program, a random block read or write is more efficient. This feature is especially useful for loading tables in a program.

☐ The use of an index can greatly facilitate random processing.

QUESTIONS

14-1. Determine the current block/record for the following random record numbers: (a) 45, (b) 73, (c) 150, (d) 260.

14-2. How does the random record number (decimal) 2652 appear in the FCB relative record field?

14-3. Provide the hexadecimal function calls for the following operations: (a) random write, (b) random read, (c) random block write, (d) random block read.

14-4. Write the instructions to determine the number of records in a file. Assume that the open operation has already occurred. The name of the file size is FCBFLSZ and record size is FCBRCSZ.

14-5. Use the program from Question 13-9 to create part number, price, and description using the data in the section "Indexes" from this chapter. Write a program that performs one block read for this file and displays each record down the screen.

14-6. Revise the programs in Questions 13-9 and 14-5 so that price is stored in the disk record as a binary value.

14-7. Modify the program in Figure 14-5 so that

(a) it performs a random read,

(b) a user can enter part number and quantity, and

(c) it calculates and displays value (quantity times price).

14-8. Revise the program in Figure 14-7 so that the index contains the high key for each sector. Generate enough records to cause the file size to exceed a sector.

15

MACRO WRITING

Objective:
To explain the definition and use of
Assembler macro-instructions.

Note: The small (64K) Assembler version does not support the macro facility. Assembling a program that defines and uses a macro instruction requires the large (96K) Assembler and the MASM command. Also, the material in this chapter applies specifically to PC-DOS and MS-DOS.

INTRODUCTION

For each coded instruction, the Assembler generates one machine language instruction. But for each coded statement, a compiler language such as Pascal or PL/M generates one or more (often many) machine language instructions. In this regard, you can think of a compiler language as consisting of macro statements.

Assembler language also has macro facilities, but you—as the programmer—must define the macros. You define a specific name for the macro, the Pseudo-op MACRO, the various Assembler instructions that the macro is to generate, and terminate the macro definition with the MEND Pseudo-op. Then, whenever you need to execute that particular block of code in the program, simply code the name of the macro. The Assembler generates the defined instructions.

Macros are useful for the following purposes:

☐ To simplify and to reduce the amount of coding.
☐ To streamline an Assembler program to make it more readable.
☐ To reduce errors caused by repetitive coding.

Examples of possible macros could be input/output operations that initialize registers and perform INT instructions, conversion of ASCII and binary data, multiple-word arithmetic operations, string handling routines such as MOVS, and divide by subtraction.

Macros may be "nested"—a macro definition can use a macro name that has already been defined. Only the size of available memory limits the the number of nested macros.

This chapter covers most of the features in the macro facility, including explanations of features that the Assembler manual does not make clear. However, you should still refer to the Assembler manual for some of the less-used operations and for occasional updates in new releases of the Assembler.

A SIMPLE MACRO DEFINITION

Let's examine a simple *macro definition* that initializes the Segment registers. A macro definition must appear before the Stack, Data, and Code Segments. The macro defintion, in this example named INIT1, appears as follows:

```
INIT1  MACRO                                                ;Define macro
       ASSUME    CS:CODESG,DS:DATA,SS:STACK,ES:DATA   ; }
       PUSH      DS                                   ; } Body
       SUB       AX,AX                                ; } of
       PUSH      AX                                   ; } the
       MOV       AX,DATA                              ; } macro
       MOV       DS,AX                                ; } defin'n
       MOV       ES,AX                                ; }
       ENDM      ;End macro
```

The Pseudo-operation MACRO tells the Assembler that the following instructions—up to ENDM—are to be part of a macro definition. The name of the macro is INIT1, although any other unique valid Assembler name is acceptable. The Pseudo-op ENDM terminates the macro definition. The seven instructions between MACRO and ENDM comprise the *body* of the macro definition.

The names referenced in the macro definition, CODESG, DATA, and STACK, must be defined elsewhere in the program. You use the macro-instruction INIT1 in the Code Segment where you want to initialize the registers. When the Assembler encounters the instruction INIT1, it scans a table of symbolic instructions, and failing to find an entry, checks for macro-instructions. Since the program contains a definition of the macro INIT1, the Assembler substitutes the body of the definition, generating the instructions—the *macro expansion*. This particular macro-instruction would be used only once in a program, although other macros are designed to be used any number of times, and each time the Assembler generates the same macro expansion.

Figure 15-1 provides the assembled program. Note that the listing shows the macro expansion with a plus (+) sign to the left of each instruction to indicate that a macro-instruction generated it. Also, the ASSUME Pseudo-op does not list in the macro expansion because it generates no object code.

Figure 15-1 Simple Assembled Macro-Instruction.

```
                                          page      60,132
                             TITLE   MACRO1  Simple macro to initialize
                             ; --------------------------------------------
                             INIT1  (MACRO)                    ;Define a macro
                                    ASSUME  CS:CSEG,DS:DATA,SS:STACK,ES:DATA
                                    PUSH    DS
                                    SUB     AX,AX
                                    PUSH    AX
                                    MOV     AX,DATA
                                    MOV     DS,AX
                                    MOV     ES,AX
                                    ENDM                       ;End of the macro
                             ; --------------------------------------------
0000                         STACK   SEGMENT PARA STACK  'Stack'
0000      20 [  ????  ]              DW      32 DUP(?)
0040                         STACK   ENDS
                             ; --------------------------------------------
0000                         DATA    SEGMENT PARA 'Data'
0000    54 65 73 74 20 6F    MESSGE  DB       'Test of macro-instruction','$'
        66 20 6D 61 63 72
        6F 2D 69 6E 73 74
        72 75 63 74 69 6F
        6E 24
001A                         DATA    ENDS
                             ; --------------------------------------------
0000                         CSEG    SEGMENT PARA 'Code'
0000                         START   PROC    FAR
                                     INIT1                     ;Macro-instruction
0000   1E                    +       PUSH    DS
0001   2B C0                 +       SUB     AX,AX
0003   50                    +       PUSH    AX
0004   B8   ---- R           +       MOV     AX,DATA
0007   8E D8                 +       MOV     DS,AX
0009   8E C0                 +       MOV     ES,AX
```

```
000B  8D 16 0000 R              LEA      DX,MESSGE       ;Display message
000F  B4 09                     MOV      AH,09
0011  CD 21                     INT      21H
0013  CB                        RET
0014               START        ENDP

0014               CSEG         ENDS
                                END      START
```

Macros:
```
                       N a m e                      Length
INIT1. . . . . . . . . . . . . . .                  0004
```

Segments and groups:
```
                       N a m e                      Size    align   combine class
CSEG . . . . . . . . . . . . . .                    0014    PARA    NONE    'CODE'
DATA . . . . . . . . . . . . . .                    001A    PARA    NONE    'DATA'
STACK. . . . . . . . . . . . . .                    0040    PARA    STACK   'STACK'
```

Symbols:
```
                       N a m e                      Type     Value   Attr
MESSGE . . . . . . . . . . . . .                    L BYTE   0000    DATA
START. . . . . . . . . . . . . .                    F PROC   0000    CSEG    Length =0014
```

A later section, "INCLUDES from a Macro Library," discusses how to catalog macros in a library and how to include them automatically into any program.

USE OF PARAMETERS IN MACROS

The previous macro definition requires fixed names for the Segments: CODESG, DATA, and STACK. To make a macro more flexible so that it can accept any name for the Segments, define their names in the macro as *dummy arguments:*

```
INIT2   MACRO    CSNAME,DSNAME,SSNAME        ;Dummy arguments
        ASSUME   CS:CSNAME,DS:DSNAME,SS:SSNAME,ES:DSNAME
        PUSH     DS
        SUB      AX.AX
        PUSH     AX
        MOV      AX,DSNAME
        MOV      DS,AX
        MOV      ES,AX
        ENDM                                 ;End macro
```

The dummies in the macro definition tell the Assembler to match these names with any occurrence of the same names in the macro body. The three dummy arguments CSNAME, DSNAME, and SSNAME all occur in the ASSUME statement, and DSNAME occurs in a later MOV instruction. A dummy argument may have any valid Assembler name and need not be the same as a name defined in the Data Segment.

Now when using the macro-instruction INIT2, supply as *parameters* the actual names of the three Segments in the specified sequence. For example, the following macro-instruction contains three parameters that match the dummy arguments in the original macro definition:

Macro definition: INIT2 MACRO   CSNAME,DSNAME,SSNAME (arguments)

Macro-instruction: INIT2   CDSEG, DSSEG, SSSEG   (parameters)

The Assembler has already matched arguments in the original macro definition with statements in the body. It now substitutes the parameters of the macro-instruction entry for entry with the dummy arguments in the macro definition:

☐   Parameter 1 for argument 1: CDSEG matches with CSNAME in the macro definition. The Assembler substitutes CDSEG for each occurrence (one) of CSNAME.

☐   Parameter 2 for argument 2: DSSEG matches with DSNAME in the macro definition. The Assembler substitutes DSSEG for each occurrence (two) of DSNAME.

☐   Parameter 3 for argument 3: SSSEG matches with SSNAME in the macro definition. The Assembler substitutes SSSEG for each occurrence (one) of SSNAME.

The macro definition and the macro expansion are shown in Figure 15-2.

Figure 15-2 Use of Macro Parameters.

```
                    page     60,132
              TITLE  MACRO2  Use of Parameters
              ; ------------------------------------
              INIT2 (MACRO)  CSNAME,DSNAME,SSNAME
                    ASSUME   CS:CSNAME,DS:DSNAME,SS:SSNAME,ES:DSNAME
                    PUSH     DS
                    SUB      AX,AX
                    PUSH     AX
                    MOV      AX,DSNAME
                    MOV      DS,AX
                    MOV      ES,AX
                    ENDM                      ;End of the macro
              ; ------------------------------------
0000          STACK  SEGMENT PARA STACK 'Stack'
0000  20 [ ???? ]          DW       32 DUP(?)
0040          STACK  ENDS
```

```
                          ; --------------------------------------------
0000                      DATASG SEGMENT PARA 'Data'
0000   54 65 73 74 20 6F  MESSGE DB        'Test of macro','$'
       66 20 6D 61 63 72
       6F 24
000E                      DATASG ENDS
                          ; --------------------------------------------
0000                      CODESG SEGMENT PARA 'Code'
0000                      START  PROC     FAR
                                 INIT2    CODESG,DATASG,STACK
0000   1E                 +      PUSH     DS
0001   2B C0              +      SUB      AX,AX
0003   50                 +      PUSH     AX
0004   B8  ---- R         +      MOV      AX,DATASG
0007   8E D8              +      MOV      DS,AX
0009   8E C0              +      MOV      ES,AX
000B   8D 16 0000 R              LEA      DX,MESSGE        ;Display message
000F   B4 09                     MOV      AH,09
0011   CD 21                     INT      21H
0013   CB                        RET
0014                      START  ENDP

0014                      CODESG ENDS
                                 END      START
```

A dummy argument may have any legal Assembler name. Even if you use a register name such as CX as a dummy name, the Assembler replaces it with a parameter. As a consequence, register names and names defined in the Data Segment are not recognized as such by the macro definition. You may define a macro with any number of dummy arguments, separated by commas, up to column 120 of a line.

COMMENTS

Comments may appear in a macro definition in order to clarify its purpose. A COMMENT Pseudo-op or a semicolon indicates a comment line:

```
PROMPT   MACRO   MESSGE
;            This macro permits display of messages
         LEA      DX,MESSGE
         MOV      AH,09
         INT      21H
         ENDM
```

You may or may not want the comment to appear for each expansion of the macro-instruction. The Assembler's default is to list only instructions that generate object code. Therefore, the Assembler will not display the comment when the above macro definition is expanded. If you want the comment to appear with each expansion, use the listing Pseudo-op .LALL ("list all," including the leading period):

.LALL
PROMPT   MESSAG1

A macro definition could contain a number of comments, some of which you may want to list and some to suppress. Still use .LALL, but code double semicolons (;;) before comments that are always to be suppressed. The Assembler default is .XALL, which causes a listing only of instructions that generate object code. Finally, you may not want any of the Assembler code of a macro expansion to list, especially if the macro-instruction is used several times in a program. Code the listing Pseudo-op .SALL ("suppress all"). The use of .SALL reduces the size of the printed program, although it has no effect on the size of the object module.

A listing Pseudo-op holds effect throughout a program until another listing Pseudo-op is encountered. You can place them in a program to cause some macros to display comments, some to display the macro expansion, and some to suppress these.

The program in Figure 15-3 demonstrates the preceding features. The program defines the two macros, INIT2 and PROMPT, that were described earlier. The Code Segment contains the Listing Pseudo-op .SALL to suppress the expansion of INIT2 and the first expansion of PROMPT. For the second use of PROMPT, the Listing Pseudo-op .LALL causes the Assembler to print the comment and the expansion of the macro. Note, however, in the macro definition for PROMPT that the comment containing a double semicolon (;;) still does not print in this macro expansion.

> **Figure 15-3** Listing and Suppression of Macro Expansions.

```
                page    60,132
        TITLE   MACRO3  Use of .LALL & .SALL
        ; ---------------------------------------------------
        INIT2  (MACRO)  CSNAME,DSNAME,SSNAME
               ASSUME   CS:CSNAME,DS:DSNAME,SS:SSNAME,ES:DSNAME
               PUSH     DS
               SUB      AX,AX
               PUSH     AX
               MOV      AX,DSNAME
               MOV      DS,AX
               MOV      ES,AX
               ENDM
        ; ---------------------------------------------------
        PROMPT (MACRO)  MESSGE
        ;           This macro will display any message
        ;;          Generates code that links to DOS
               LEA      DX,MESSGE
               MOV      AH,09
               INT      21H
               ENDM
```

```
              ; ------------------------------------------------
0000            STACK   SEGMENT PARA STACK 'Stack'
0000  20 [  ????  ]             DW        32 DUP(?)
0040            STACK   ENDS
              ; ------------------------------------------------
0000            DATA    SEGMENT PARA 'Data'
0000  43 75 73 74 6F 6D  MESSG1 DB        'Customer name?','$'
      65 72 20 6E 61 6D
      65 3F 24
000F  43 75 73 74 6F 6D  MESSG2 DB        'Customer address?','$'
      65 72 20 61 64 64
      72 65 73 73 3F 24
0021            DATA    ENDS
              ; ------------------------------------------------
0000            CSEG    SEGMENT PARA 'Code'
0000            START   PROC    FAR
                        .SALL
                        INIT2   CSEG,DATA,STACK
                        PROMPT  MESSG1
                        .LALL
                        PROMPT  MESSG2
            +
            + ;         This macro will display any message
            +
0013  8D 16 000F R   +         LEA       DX,MESSG2
0017  B4 09          +         MOV       AH,09
0019  CD 21          +         INT       21H
001B  CB                       RET
001C            START   ENDP

001C            CSEG    ENDS
                        END     START
```

THE LOCAL PSEUDO-OP

Some macros require definition of a data field or of an instruction label. If you use the macro more than once in the same program, the Assembler defines the data field or label for each occurrence, and generates an error message because of duplicate names. As a consequence, you have to ensure that each generated name is unique. The LOCAL Pseudo-op is used for this purpose and must appear immediately after the MACRO statement, even before comments. Its general format is:

LOCAL   dummy-1, dummy-2, ...   ;One or more dummy arguments

Figure 15-4 illustrates the use of LOCAL. The purpose of the program is to perform division by successive subtraction (see details in Chapter 10). The routine subtracts the divisor from the dividend and adds 1 to the quotient until the dividend is less than the divisor. For this purpose, two labels are required: COMP, for the loop address, and OUT, for exiting on completion. Both COMP and OUT are defined as LOCAL and may have any legal Assembler names.

Figure 15-4 Use of LOCAL.

```
                      page      60,132
                TITLE    MACRO4   Use of LOCAL
                ; --------------------------------------------------------
                DIVIDE MACRO    DIVIDEND,DIVISOR,QUOTIENT
                       LOCAL    COMP
                       LOCAL    OUT
                ;        AX = div'd, BX = divisor, CX = quotient
                         MOV      AX,DIVIDEND       ;Set dividend
                         MOV      BX,DIVISOR        ;Set divisor
                         SUB      CX,CX             ;Clear quotient
                COMP:
                         CMP      AX,BX             ;Div'd < div'r?
                         JB       OUT               ;Yes - exit
                         SUB      AX,BX             ;Div'd - divisor
                         INC      CX                ;Add to quotient
                         JMP      COMP
                OUT:
                         MOV      QUOTIENT,CX       ;Store quotient
                         ENDM
                ; --------------------------------------------------------
0000            STACK    SEGMENT PARA STACK 'Stack'
0000 20 [ ???? ]         DW       32 DUP(?)
0040            STACK    ENDS
                ; --------------------------------------------------------
0000            DATA     SEGMENT PARA 'Data'
0000 0096       DIVDND DW       150                 ;Dividend
0002 001B       DIVSOR DW       27                  ;Divisor
0004 ????       QUOTNT DW       ?                   ;Quotient
0006            DATA     ENDS
                ; --------------------------------------------------------
0000            CSEG     SEGMENT PARA 'Code'
0000            START    PROC     FAR
                         ASSUME   CS:CSEG,DS:DATA,SS:STACK,ES:DATA
0000 1E                  PUSH     DS
0001 2B C0               SUB      AX,AX
0003 50                  PUSH     AX
0004 B8 ---- R           MOV      AX,DATA
0007 8E D8               MOV      DS,AX
                         .LALL
                         DIVIDE   DIVDND,DIVSOR,QUOTNT
              + ;        AX = div'd, BX = divisor, CX = quotient
              +
0009 A1 0000 R +         MOV      AX,DIVDND         ;Set dividend
000C 8B 1E 0002 R +      MOV      BX,DIVSOR         ;Set divisor
0010 2B C9     +         SUB      CX,CX             ;Clear quotient
0012           + ??0000:
0012 3B C3     +         CMP      AX,BX             ;Div'd < div'r?
0014 72 05     +         JB       ??0001            ;Yes - exit
0016 2B C3     +         SUB      AX,BX             ;Div'd - divisor
0018 41        +         INC      CX                ;Add to quotient
0019 EB F7     +         JMP      ??0000
001B           + ??0001:
001B 89 0E 0004 R +      MOV      QUOTNT,CX         ;Store quotient
001F CB                  RET
0020            START    ENDP

0020            CSEG     ENDS
                         END      START
```

Now note the macro expansion: the generated symbolic label for COMP is ??0000 and for OUT is ??0001. If the DIVIDE macro-instruction were used again in the same program, the symbolic labels for the next macro expansion would become respectively ??0002 and ??0003. In this way, the LABEL facility ensures that generated labels are unique.

INCLUDES FROM A MACRO LIBRARY

It may seem rather pointless to take the trouble to define a macro such as INIT1 or INIT2 and then use it just once in a program. It's easier simply to code the initialization instructions the usual way. A better approach is to catalog all your macros in a library. Simply store them all (using a line or text editor) under any descriptive name, such as MACRO.LIB:

```
INIT        MACRO   CSNAME,DSNAME,SSNAME
              .
              .
            ENDM
PROMPT   MACRO   MESSGE
              .
              .
            ENDM
```

Now when you want to use any of the catalogued macros, instead of the MACRO definition at the start of the program, use an INCLUDE Pseudo-op:

```
INCLUDE  B:MACRO.LIB
              .
              .
    INIT        CSEG,DATA,STACK
```

The Assembler accesses the file named MACRO.LIB (in this case) presumably on disk B, and includes both macro definitions INIT and PROMPT into the program. In this example, only INIT is actually required. As coded, the assembled listing will contain a copy of the macro definition indicated by the letter C in column 30 of the LST file. Following the macro-instruction is the expansion of the macro along with its generated object code indicated by a + in column 31.

Now, since the assembly is a two-pass operation, you can cause the INCLUDE to occur only on pass 1 (instead of both passes) using the following statements:

IF1
INCLUDE B:MACRO.LIB
ENDIF

IF1 and ENDIF are Conditional Pseudo-ops. IF1 tells the Assembler to access the named library only on pass 1 of the assembly. ENDIF terminates the IF logic. Now the copy of the macro definition does not appear on the listing—a saving of both time and space.

The program in Figure 15-5 contains the above IF1, INCLUDE, and ENDIF statements, although on the LST file the Assembler lists only the ENDIF. The two macro-instructions used in the Code Segment, INIT and PROMPT, are both catalogued in MACRO.LIB. They were simply recorded together as a disk file under that name using an Editor program.

The placement of an INCLUDE is not critical and works even if it appears at the start of the Code Segment. It must, however, appear before a macro-instruction that references the library entry.

Figure 15-5 Use of Library Include.

```
                              page    60,132
                      TITLE   MACRO5  Test of INCLUDE
                      ENDIF
                      ; -------------------------------------------
0000                  STACK   SEGMENT PARA STACK 'Stack'
0000   20 [ ???? ]            DW      32 DUP(?)
0040                  STACK   ENDS
                      ; -------------------------------------------
0000                  DATA    SEGMENT PARA 'Data'
0000   54 65 73 74 20 6F MESSGE DB     'Test of macro','$'
       66 20 6D 61 63 72
       6F 24
000E                  DATA    ENDS
                      ; -------------------------------------------
0000                  CSEG    SEGMENT PARA 'Code'
0000                  START   PROC    FAR
                              INIT    CSEG,DATA,STACK
0000   1E           +        PUSH    DS
0001   2B C0        +        SUB     AX,AX
0003   50           +        PUSH    AX
0004   B8   ---- R  +        MOV     AX,DATA
0007   8E D8        +        MOV     DS,AX
0009   8E C0        +        MOV     ES,AX

                              PROMPT  MESSGE

000B   8D 16 0000 R +        LEA     DX,MESSGE
000F   B4 09        +        MOV     AH,09
0011   CD 21        +        INT     21H
0013   CB                    RET
0014                  START   ENDP

0014                  CSEG    ENDS
                              END     START
```

Purge

An INCLUDE statement causes the Assembler to "include" all the macro definitions that are in the specified library. For example, a library contains the macros INIT, PROMPT, and DIVIDE, but a program requires only INIT. The PURGE Pseudo-op enables you to "delete" the unwanted macros PROMPT and DIVIDE from the current assembly:

```
IF1
          INCLUDE MACRO.LIB          ;Include full library
ENDIF
PURGE  PROMPT,DIVIDE                 ;Delete unneeded macros
    ...
INIT     CSEG,DATA,STACK             ;Use remaining macro
```

A PURGE operation only facilitates the assembly and has no effect on the macros still stored in the macro library.

CONCATENATION (&)

The ampersand (&) character indicates that the Assembler is to join (concatenate) text or symbols. The following MOVE macro provides for either MOVSB or MOVSW:

```
                    MOVE    MACRO    TAG
                            REP MOVS&TAG
                            ENDM
```

A user could code the macro-instruction either as MOVE B or as MOVE W. The Assembler concatenates the parameter with the MOVS instruction, as REP MOVSB or REP MOVSW. Admittedly, this example is somewhat trivial; it's for illustrative purposes and is not intended to be very useful!

REPETITION: REPT, IRP, AND IRPC

You can cause the Assembler to repeat a block of statements, terminated by ENDM. Technically, these Pseudo-ops do not have to be contained in a MACRO definition, but if they are, one ENDM is required to terminate the repetition and a second ENDM to terminate the MACRO definition.

REPT: Repetition

The REPT operation causes repetition of a block of statements up to ENDM according to the number of times in the expression entry:

REPT   expression

The following initializes the value N to 0, and then repeats generation of DB N five times:

```
N =      0
REPT     5
N =      N + 1
DB       N
ENDM
```

The result is five generated DB statements, DB 1 through DB 5. REPT could be used to define a table or part of a table. As another example, the following code

```
REPT     5
MOVSB
ENDM
```

generates five MOVSB instructions and is equivalent to REP MOVSB where the CX contains 05.

IRP: Indefinite Repeat

The IRP operation causes a repeat of a block of instructions up to the ENDM. The following is the general format:

IRP   dummy,<arguments>

The arguments, contained in angle brackets, are any number of legal symbols, string, numeric, or arithmetic constants. The Assembler generates a block of code for each argument. In the following example

```
IRP     N,<3,9,17,25,28>
DB      N
```

the Assembler generates DB 3, DB 9, DB 17, DB 25, and DB 28.

IRPC: Indefinite Repeat Character

The IRPC operation causes a repeat of the block of statements up to the ENDM. The following is the general format:

IRPC   dummy,string

The Assembler generates a block of code for each character in the "string." In the following example,

```
IRPC    N,345678
DW      N
ENDM
```

the Assembler generates DW 3 through DW 8.

CONDITIONAL PSEUDO-OPERATIONS

The Assembler supports a number of Conditional Pseudo-ops. We used one of them, IF1, earlier to include a library entry only during pass 1 of the assembly. Conditional Pseudo-ops are most useful within a MACRO definition but are not limited to that purpose. Every IF Pseudo-op must have a matching ENDIF to terminate the tested condition. Optionally, there may be one ELSE to provide an alternative action:

```
IFxx      (condition)
   .                     }
   .                     } conditional
[ELSE]    (optional)     }
   .                     } block
   .                     }
ENDIF     (end of IF)
```

Omission of ENDIF causes an error message: undetermined conditional. If the condition being examined is true, the Assembler executes the conditional block up to the ELSE, or if no ELSE up to the ENDIF. If the condition being examined is false, the Assembler executes the conditional block following the ELSE, or if no ELSE generates none of the conditional block.

The following explains the various conditional Pseudo-ops.

IF expression	If the Assembler evaluates the expression to non-zero, it assembles the statements within the conditional block.
IFE expression	If the Assembler evaluates the expression to zero, it assembles the statements within the conditional block.
IF1 (no expression)	If the Assembler is processing pass 1, it acts on the statements in the conditional block.
IF2 (no expression)	If the Assembler is processing pass 2, it acts on the statements in the conditional block.
IFDEF symbol	If the symbol is defined in the program or is declared as EXTRN, the Assembler processes the statements in the conditional block.
IFNDEF symbol	If the symbol is not defined or is not declared as EXTRN, the Assembler processes the statements in the conditional block.
IFB <argument>	If the argument is blank, the Assembler processes the statements in the conditional block. The argument requires angle brackets.
IFNB <argument>	If the argument is not blank, the Assembler processes the statements in the conditional block. The argument requires angle brackets
IFIDN <arg-1>,<arg-2>	If the argument-1 string is identical to the argument-2 string, the Assembler processes the statements in the conditional block. The arguments require angle brackets.
IFDIF <arg-1>,<arg-2>	If the argument-1 string is different from the argument-2 string, the Assembler processes the statements in the conditional block. The arguments require angle brackets.

Don't despair—examples are coming soon!

THE EXITM PSEUDO-OP

A MACRO definition may contain a Conditional Pseudo-op that tests for a serious condition. If the condition is true, the Assembler is to exit from any further macro expansion. The EXITM Pseudo-op serves this purpose:

```
IFxx      [condition]

  .
  .       (invalid condition)
  .
EXITM

  .
  .
ENDIF
```

If the Assembler encounters EXITM in its expansion, it discontinues the macro expansion and resumes after the ENDM Pseudo-op. You can also use EXITM to terminate REPT, IRP, and IRPC even if they are contained within a MACRO definition.

The next two sections illustrate the Conditional Pseudo-ops and EXITM.

MACRO USING IF AND IFNDEF CONDITIONS

The skeleton program in Figure 15-6 contains a MACRO definition named DIVIDE that generates a routine to perform division by successive subtraction. A user has to code the macro-instruction with parameters for dividend, divisor, and quotient, in that order. The macro uses IFNDEF to check if the program actually contains their definitions. For any entry not defined, the macro increments a field named CNTR. Technically, CNTR could have any legal name and is for temporary use in a MACRO definition. After checking all three parameters, the macro checks CNTR for nonzero:

```
      IF      CNTR
  ;           Macro expansion terminated
      EXITM
      ENDIF
```

If CNTR has been set to a nonzero value, the Assembler generates the comment and exits (EXITM) from any further macro expansion. Note that an initial instruction clears CNTR to 0, and also that the IFNDEF blocks need only to set CNTR to 1 rather than increment it.

Figure 15-6 Use of IF and IFNDEF.

```
              page      60,132
      TITLE   MACRO6    Test of IF and IFNDEF
  ; --------------------------------------------------
  DIVIDE (MACRO)  DIVIDEND,DIVISOR,QUOTIENT
              LOCAL     COMP
              LOCAL     OUT
              CNTR      = 0
```

```
                              ;           AX = div'nd, BX = div'r, CX = quot't
                                (IFNDEF)  DIVIDEND
                              ;           Dividend not defined
                              CNTR        = CNTR +1
                                ENDIF
                                (IFNDEF)  DIVISOR
                              ;           Divisor not defined
                              CNTR        = CNTR +1
                                ENDIF
                                (IFNDEF)  QUOTIENT
                              ;           Quotient not defined
                              CNTR = CNTR + 1
                                ENDIF
                                  (IF)    CNTR
                              ;           Macro expansion terminated
                                EXITM
                                ENDIF
                                MOV       AX,DIVIDEND      ;Set dividend
                                MOV       BX,DIVISOR       ;Set divisor
                                SUB       CX,CX            ;Clear quot
                              COMP:
                                CMP       AX,BX            ;Div'd < div'r?
                                JB        OUT              ;Yes - exit
                                SUB       AX,BX            ;Div'd - div'r
                                INC       CX               ;Add to quot
                                JMP       COMP
                              OUT:
                                MOV       QUOTIENT,CX      ;Store quot
                                ENDM
                              ; -------------------------------------------
0000                          STACK  SEGMENT PARA STACK 'Stack'
0000     20 [ ???? ]          DW         32 DUP(?)
0040                          STACK  ENDS
                              ; -------------------------------------------
0000                          DATA   SEGMENT PARA 'Data'
0000     0096                 DIVDND DW  150              ;Dividend
0002     001B                 DIVSOR DW  27               ;Divisor
0004     ????                 QUOTNT DW  ?                ;Quotient
0006                          DATA   ENDS
                              ; -------------------------------------------
0000                          CSEG   SEGMENT PARA 'Code'
0000                          START  PROC FAR
                                ASSUME   CS:CSEG,DS:DATA,SS:STACK,ES:DATA
0000     1E                     PUSH     DS
0001     2B C0                  SUB      AX,AX
0003     50                     PUSH     AX
0004     B8  ---- R             MOV      AX,DATA
0007     8E D8                  MOV      DS,AX
                                .LALL
                                DIVIDE   DIVDND,DIVSOR,QUOTNT
= 0000                        +  CNTR    = 0
                              + ;        AX = div'nd, BX = div'r, CX = quot't
                              +
                              +          ENDIF
                              +          ENDIF
                              +          ENDIF
                              +          ENDIF
0009     A1 0000 R            +          MOV    AX,DIVDND       ;Set dividend
000C     8B 1E 0002 R         +          MOV    BX,DIVSOR       ;Set divisor
0010     2B C9                +          SUB    CX,CX           ;Clear quot
0012                          + ??0000:
0012     3B C3                +          CMP    AX,BX           ;Div'd < div'r?
0014     72 05                +          JB     ??0001          ;Yes - exit
0016     2B C3                +          SUB    AX,BX           ;Div'd - div'r
0018     41                   +          INC    CX              ;Add to quot
0019     EB F7                +          JMP    ??0000
001B                          + ??0001:
```

```
001B  89 0E 0004 R     +          MOV      QUOTNT,CX        ;Store quot
                       +
                                  DIVIDE  DIDND,DIVSOR,QUOT
  = 0000               +          CNTR     = 0
                       + ;        AX = div'nd, BX = div'r, CX = quot't
                       +          IFNDEF   DIDND
                       + ;              Dividend not defined
  = 0001               +          CNTR     = CNTR +1
                       +          ENDIF
                       +          ENDIF
                       +          IFNDEF   QUOT
                       + ;              Quotient not defined
  = 0002               +          CNTR = CNTR + 1
                       +          ENDIF
                       +          IF       CNTR
                       + ;              Macro expansion terminated
                       +          EXITM
001F  CB                          RET
0020                   START      ENDP

0020                   CSEG       ENDS
                                  END      START
```

If the Assembler passes all the tests safely, it generates the macro expansion. In the Code Segment, the first DIVIDE macro-instruction contains an invalid dividend and quotient and generates only comments. The macro could be improved by testing that the divisor is nonzero and that the dividend and divisor have the same sign; for this purpose, use Assembler code rather than Conditional Pseudo-ops.

MACRO USING IFIDN CONDITION

The skeleton program in Figure 15-7 contains a MACRO definition named MOVIF that generates a MOVSB or MOVSW depending on a supplied parameter. A user has to code the macro-instruction with a parameter B (for byte) or W (for word) to indicate if the MOVS is to be MOVSB or MOVSW.

Figure 15-7 Use of IFIDN.

```
                       page     60,132
                TITLE  MACRO6   Tests of IFIDN
            ; ---------------------------------------

            MOVIF  MACRO    TAG
                   IFIDN    <&TAG>,<B>
                   REP MOVSB
                   EXITM
                   ENDIF
                   IFIDN    <&TAG>,<W>
                   REP MOVSW
                   ELSE
            ;      No B or W tag -- default to B
                   REP MOVSB
                   ENDIF
                   ENDM
```

```
                                 ; -----------------------------------------
      0000                       STACK   SEGMENT PARA STACK 'STACK'
      0000   20 [ ???? ]                 DW      32 DUP(?)
      0040                       STACK   ENDS
                                 ; -----------------------------------------
      0000                       DATA    SEGMENT PARA 'DATA'
      0000                       DATA    ENDS
                                 ; -----------------------------------------
      0000                       CSEG    SEGMENT PARA 'CODE'
      0000                       START   PROC    FAR
      0000   1E                          PUSH    DS
      0001   2B C0                       SUB     AX,AX
      0003   50                          PUSH    AX
      0004   B8  ---- R                  MOV     AX,DATA
      0007   8E D8                       MOV     DS,AX
      0009   8E C0                       MOV     ES,AX

                                         .LALL
                                         MOVIF   B
                              +          IFIDN   <B>,<B>
      000B   F3/ A4           +          REP MOVSB
                              +          EXITM

                                         MOVIF   W
                              +          ENDIF
                              +          IFIDN   <W>,<W>
      000D   F3/ A5           +          REP MOVSW
                              +          ENDIF

                                         MOVIF
                              +          ENDIF
                              +          ELSE
                              + ;        No B or W tag -- default to B
      000F   F3/ A4           +          REP MOVSB
                              +          ENDIF
      0011   CB                          RET
      0012                       START   ENDP
      0012                       CSEG    ENDS
                                         END     START
```

Note the first two statements of the MACRO definition:

```
        MOVIF   MACRO   TAG
        IFIDN  <&TAG>,<B>
```

The IFIDN conditional compares the supplied parameter (supposedly B or W) to the string B. If the two are identical, the Assembler generates REP MOVSB. The normal use of the ampersand (&) operator is for concatenation. However, the operand <TAG> without the ampersand does not work.

If the user supplies neither B nor W, the Assembler generates a comment and a default to MOVSB.

The examples in the Code Segment test MOVIF three times: for a B, for a W, and for invalid. Admittedly, the macro in this example is not very useful; its purpose is to illustrate the use of conditional Pseudo-ops in a simple manner. By this point, however, you should have sufficient direction to be able to code some large useful macros.

KEY POINTS TO REMEMBER

☐ The use of macros in Assembler programs can result in more readable and more productive code.

☐ A MACRO definition requires a MACRO Pseudo-op, a block of one or more statements known as the body that the MACRO definition is to generate, and an ENDM Pseudo-op to terminate the definition.

☐ A macro-instruction is the use of the macro in a program. The code that a macro-instruction generates is the macro expansion.

☐ The use of .SALL, .LALL, and .XALL controls the listing of comments and the generated object code in a macro expansion.

☐ The LOCAL Pseudo-op facilitates using names within a macro definition, and must appear immediately after the MACRO statement.

☐ The use of dummy arguments in a MACRO definition allows a user to code parameters for more flexibility.

☐ A macro library makes macros available to all your other Assembler programs.

☐ Conditional Pseudo-ops enable you to validate macro parameters.

QUESTIONS

15-1. Specify the required instructions:

(a) to suppress all instructions that a macro generates;

(b) to list only instructions that generate object code.

15-2. Code two macro definitions that perform multiplication:

(a) MULTB is to generate code that multiplies byte times byte;

(b) MULTW is to generate code that multiplies word times word.

Include the multiplicands and multipliers as dummy arguments in the macro definition. Test execution of the macros with a small program that also defines the required data fields.

15-3. Store the macros defined in Question 15-2 in a "macro library." Revise the program to INCLUDE the library entries during pass 1 of the assembly.

15-4. Write a macro named PRBIOS that uses BIOS INT 17H to print. The macro should include a test for status and should provide for any defined print line with any length.

15-5. Revise the macro in Figure 15-6 to test if the divisor is zero (bypass the divide).

16

LINKING TO SUBPROGRAMS

Objective:
To cover the programming techniques
involved in linking and executing
separately assembled programs.
   Note: The material in this chapter
applies specifically to PC-DOS
and MS-DOS.

INTRODUCTION

Up to this point, all the program examples have consisted of one assembly
step. It is possible, however, to execute a program module that consists
of more than one assembled "program." In such a case, you could look at
the program as consisting of a main program and one or more subprograms.
Reasons for organizing a program into subprograms include the following:

☐   Written as one module, the program could be too large for the Assembler to process.
☐   Parts of a program may be written by different teams who assemble
their modules separately.
☐   Because of the large size of an executable module, it may be necessary
to overlay parts of the program during execution.

☐   It may be desirable to link between languages—for example, to combine the computing power of a high-level language with the efficiency of Assembler.

Each program is assembled separately and generates its own unique object (OBJ) module. The LINK program then links the object modules into one combined executable (EXE) module. Typically, the main program routine is the one that begins execution, and it calls one or more subprograms. Subprograms in turn may call other subprograms. Figure 16-1 shows two examples of a hierarchy of a main program and three subprograms.

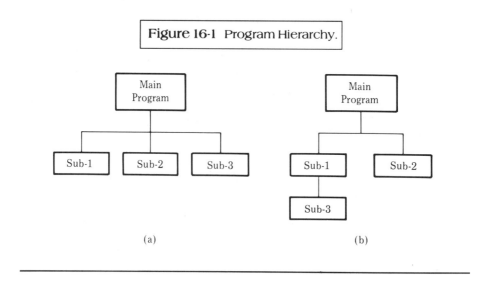

Figure 16-1 Program Hierarchy.

(a)   (b)

In Figure 16-1(a), the main program calls subprograms 1, 2, and 3. Technically, however, subprogram 1 could call subprogram 2 which in turn could call subprogram 3—this works as long as the RET instructions trace backwards through the same steps.

In Figure 16-1(b), the main program calls subprograms 1 and 2, and only subprogram 1 calls subprogram 3. Technically, however, both the main program and subprogram 2 could call subprogram 3.

There are numerous variations of subprogram organization and the Assembler has few specific rules. But you do have to organize your program so that it makes sense to the Linker and to execution. You also have to watch out for situations in which, for example, subprogram 1 calls subprogram 2, which calls subprogram 3, which in turn calls subprogram 1. This process is called *recursion*; although it can be made to work, if not handled carefully, recursion can cause some interesting execution bugs.

INTERSEGMENT CALLS

The CALL instructions used to this point have been *intrasegment calls*—that is, within the same Code Segment. An intrasegment CALL may be near (if within + 127 or − 128 bytes) or far (if exceeding these values). The operation pushes the IP register onto the Stack and replaces the IP with the offset of the destination address.

For example, an intrasegment CALL could consist of the following object code:

E8 2000

Hex E8 is the operation code for a conventional intrasegment CALL. The operation stores the 2000 as offset 0020 in the IP. The processor then combines the current address in the CS with the offset in the IP for the next instruction to execute. On exit from the called Procedure, the RET instruction pops the stored IP off the Stack and into the IP and returns to the instruction following the CALL.

A CALL outside of the Code Segment is an *intersegment CALL*. This operation first pushes the contents of the CS register onto the Stack and inserts an intersegment pointer into the CS. It then pushes the IP onto the Stack and inserts an offset address in the IP. In this way, both the address in the Code Segment and the offset are saved for the return from the called subprogram.

For example, an intersegment CALL could consist of the following object code:

9A 0002 AF04

Hex 9A is the operation code for an intrasegment CALL. The operation stores the 0002 as 0200 in the IP and stores the AF04 as 04AF in the CS. These combine to establish the address of the first instruction to execute in the called subprogram:

Code Segment	04AF0
Offset in IP	0200
Effective address	04CF0

On exit from the called Procedure, an intersegment RET pops both the original CS and IP addresses back into their respective registers and returns to the instruction following the CALL.

For CP/M-86: Use the CALLF instruction for intersegment calls, and return from the called routine with RETF.

THE EXTRN AND PUBLIC ATTRIBUTES

Let's consider a main program (MAINPROG) that calls one subprogram (SUBPROG). An intersegment CALL is required as shown in Figure 16-2.

Figure 16-2 Intersegment CALL.

```
                    EXTRN     SUBPROG:FAR
    MAINPROG:         .
                      .
                    CALL      SUBPROG
                      .
                      .

                    PUBLIC    SUBPROG
    SUBPROG:          .
                      .
                      .
                    RET
```

The CALL instruction in MAINPROG has to know that SUBPROG exists outside this Segment (or else the Assembler generates an error message that SUBPROG is an undefined symbol). An EXTRN Pseudo-op performs this function—it notifies the Assembler that any reference to SUBPROG is to a FAR label that is defined in another assembly. Because the Assembler has no way of knowing if this is true, it generates "empty" object code operands for the Linker to fill:

$$9A\ 0000\ ----\ E$$

SUBPROG contains a PUBLIC Pseudo-op that tells the Assembler and Linker that another module has to know the address of SUBPROG. In a later step, when both MAINPROG and SUBPROG are successfully assembled into object modules, they may be linked as follows:

LINK Prompt	Reply
Object Modules [.OBJ]:	B:MAINPROG + B:SUBPROG
Run File [filespec.EXE]:	B:COMBPROG (or any legal name)
List File [NUL.MAP]:	CON
Libraries [.LIB]:	[return]

The Linker matches EXTRNs in one object module with PUBLICs in the other and inserts any required offset addresses. It then combines the two object modules into one executable module. If unable to match references, the Linker supplies error messages—watch for these before attempting to execute.

The EXTRN Pseudo-op

The EXTRN Pseudo-op has the following format:

EXTRN name:type [, . . .]

You can define more than one name up to the end of the line, or code additional EXTRN statements. Another assembly module must define the name and identify it as PUBLIC. The type entry may be ABS, BYTE, DWORD, FAR, NEAR, WORD, or a name defined by an EQU, and must be valid in terms of the actual definition of name.

The PUBLIC Pseudo-op

The PUBLIC Pseudo-op tells the Assembler and Linker that the address of the specified symbol is to be available to other programs. The general format is

PUBLIC symbol [, . . .]

You can define more than one symbol up to the end of the line, or code additional PUBLIC statements. The symbol entry can be a label (including PROC labels), a variable, or a number. Invalid entries include register names and EQU symbols that define values greater than two bytes.

Let's now examine three different ways of linking programs.

PROGRAM: USE OF EXTRN AND PUBLIC FOR A LABEL

The program in Figure 16-3 consists of a main program, CALLMUL1, and a subprogram, DOMUL1. The main program defines a Stack Segment, a Data Segment, and a Code Segment. The Data Segment defines QTY and PRICE. The Code Segment loads the AX with PRICE and the BX with QTY and then calls the subprogram. An EXTRN in the main program defines the entry point to the subprogram as SUBMUL.

The subprogram contains a PUBLIC statement (after the ASSUME) that makes SUBMUL known to the Linker as the entry point for execution. This subprogram simply multiplies the contents of the AX (price) by the BX (quantity). The product is developed in the DX:AX pair as hex 002E 4000.

Since the subprogram does not define any data, it does not need a Data Segment; it could, but such data would be recognized only in this subprogram.

Figure 16-3 Use of EXTRN and PUBLIC.

```
                        page    60,132
                        TITLE   CALLMUL1 - Call Subprogram to multiply
                        EXTRN   SUBMUL:FAR
                        ; ------------------------------------------------
0000                    STACKSG         SEGMENT PARA STACK 'STACK'
0000   40 [ ????  ]                     DW      64 DUP(?)
0080                    STACKSG         ENDS
                        ; ------------------------------------------------
0000                    DATASG  SEGMENT PARA 'DATA'
0000   0140             QTY     DW      0140H
0002   2500             PRICE   DW      2500H
0004                    DATASG  ENDS
                        ; ------------------------------------------------
0000                    CODESG  SEGMENT PARA 'CODE'
0000                    BEGIN   PROC    FAR
                                ASSUME  CS:CODESG,DS:DATASG,SS:STACKSG
0000   1E                       PUSH    DS
0001   2B C0                    SUB     AX,AX
0003   50                       PUSH    AX
0004   B8   ---- R              MOV     AX,DATASG
0007   8E D8                    MOV     DS,AX
0009   A1 0002 R                MOV     AX,PRICE    ;Set up price
000C   8B 1E 0000 R             MOV     BX,QTY      ; & quantity
0010   9A 0000 ---- E           CALL    SUBMUL      ;Call Subprogram
0015   CB                       RET
0016                    BEGIN   ENDP

0016                    CODESG  ENDS
                        END     BEGIN
```

Segments and groups:

Name	Size	align	combine	class
CODESG	0016	PARA	NONE	'CODE'
DATASG	0004	PARA	NONE	'DATA'
STACKSG.	0080	PARA	STACK	'STACK'

Symbols:

Name	Type	Value	Attr	
BEGIN.	F PROC	0000	CODESG	Length =0016
PRICE.	L WORD	0002	DATASG	
QTY.	L WORD	0000	DATASG	
SUBMUL	L FAR	0000		External

```
                        page    60,132
                        TITLE   DOMUL1  Called subprogram, multiplies
                        ; ------------------------------------------------
0000                    CODESG  SEGMENT PARA 'CODE'
0000                    SUBMUL  PROC    FAR
                                ASSUME  CS:CODESG
                                PUBLIC  SUBMUL
0000   E8 0004 R                CALL    C10MUL  ;Call subroutine
0003   CB                       RET
0004                    SUBMUL  ENDP
```

```
                              ;            Multiply subroutine:
                              ;            --------------------
  0004                        C10MUL PROC     ;Price in AX, qty in BX
  0004   F7 E3                       MUL   BX ;Product in DX:AX
  0006   C3                          RET
  0007                        C10MUL ENDP

  0007                        CODESG ENDS
                                     END   SUBMUL
```

Segments and groups:

Name	Size	align	combine	class
CODESG	0007	PARA	NONE	'CODE'

Symbols:

Name	Type	Value	Attr			
C10MUL	N PROC	0004	CODESG	Length	=0003	
SUBMUL	F PROC	0000	CODESG	Global	Length	=0004

```
A>LINK
IBM Personal Computer Linker
Version 1.00 (C) Copyright IBM Corp 1981
Object Modules: B:CALLMUL1,B:DOMUL1
Run File: B:CALLMUL1
List File [B:CALLMUL1.MAP] :CON
Libraries [ ] : !

  Start   Stop    Length  Name            Class

  00000H  00015H  0016H   CODESG          CODE    ← 2 Code Segments
  00020H  00026H  0007H   CODESG          CODE
  00030H  00033H  0004H   DATASG          DATA
  00040H  000BFH  0080H   STACKSG         STACK

Program entry point at 0000:0000
```

The subprogram also does not define a Stack Segment. The CALL instruction does not change the address in the SS and SP registers. Therefore, when the subprogram pushes and pops the Stack, it references the *same* Stack addresses as the main program. As a consequence, the Stack defined in the main program is available to the subprogram. The Linker requires definition of at least one Stack, and the definition in the main program serves this purpose.

Now let's examine the Symbol Tables following each assembly. Notice that the Symbol Table for the main program shows SUBMUL as FAR and External. The Symbol Table for the subprogram shows SUBMUL as F (for FAR) and Global. This latter term implies that the name is known "globally" outside of this subprogram.

The Link Map listed at the end of the subprogram depicts the organization of the program in memory. Note that there are two Code Segments, one for each assembly, but at different starting addresses. These appear in the sequence that you enter when linking, and the main program is normally first. In this case, the main program starts at offset hex 00000, and the subprogram at hex 00020.

A trace of program execution discloses that CALL SUBMUL generates

9A 0000 B104

The machine code for an intersegment CALL is hex 9A. The operation pushes the IP register onto the Stack and loads the IP with 0000. It then pushes the CS register containing AF04 onto the Stack and loads the CS with hex B104. The next instruction to execute is now CS:IP, or hex 04B10 plus 0000. What is at 04B10? Well, the main program begins with the CS register containing hex AF04, or technically 04AF0. The Map shows that the subprogram begins at offset hex 00020. Adding these two values supplies the address of the Code Segment for the subprogram:

CS address	04AF0
IP offset	00020
Effective address	04B10

The Linker (clever fellow) determines this value just as we have and substitutes it in the CALL operand.

PROGRAM: USE OF PUBLIC IN THE CODE SEGMENT

Our next example in Figure 16-4 provides a variation on Figure 16-3. There is one change in the main program and one change in the subprogram. The change is the use of PUBLIC in the SEGMENT Pseudo-op for both Code Segments:

CODESG   SEGMENT   PARA PUBLIC   'CODE'

There is an interesting result in the Link Map and in the CALL object code.

> ### Figure 16-4 Code Segment Defined as PUBLIC.

```
                        page      60,132
                TITLE   CALLMUL2 - Call Subprogram to multiply
                        EXTRN    SUBMUL:FAR
                ; -----------------------------------------------
0000            STACKSG          SEGMENT PARA STACK 'STACK'
0000   40 [ ???? ]        DW     64 DUP(?)
0080            STACKSG          ENDS
                ; -----------------------------------------------
```

```
0000                          DATASG SEGMENT PARA 'DATA'
0000    0140          QTY     DW      0140H
0002    2500          PRICE   DW      2500H
0004                          DATASG ENDS
                      ; ---------------------------------------------
0000                          CODESG SEGMENT PARA (PUBLIC) 'CODE'
0000                          BEGIN  PROC    FAR
                              ASSUME CS:CODESG,DS:DATASG,SS:STACKSG
0000    1E                    PUSH    DS
0001    2B C0                 SUB     AX,AX
0003    50                    PUSH    AX
0004    B8  ---- R            MOV     AX,DATASG
0007    8E D8                 MOV     DS,AX
0009    A1 0002 R             MOV     AX,PRICE    ;Set up price
000C    8B 1E 0000 R          MOV     BX,QTY      ; & quantity
0010    9A 0000 ---- E        CALL    SUBMUL      ;Call Subprogram
0015    CB                    RET
0016                          BEGIN  ENDP

0016                          CODESG ENDS
                              END     BEGIN
```

Segments and groups:
```
                N a m e         Size    align   combine class

CODESG . . . . . . . . . . . .  0016    PARA    PUBLIC  'CODE'
DATASG . . . . . . . . . . . .  0004    PARA    NONE    'DATA'
STACKSG. . . . . . . . . . . .  0080    PARA    STACK   'STACK'
```

Symbols:
```
                N a m e         Type    Value   Attr

BEGIN. . . . . . . . . . . . .  F PROC 0000     CODESG  Length =0016
PRICE. . . . . . . . . . . . .  L WORD          0002    DATASG
QTY. . . . . . . . . . . . . .  L WORD          0000    DATASG
SUBMUL . . . . . . . . . . . .  L FAR           0000            External
```

```
                      page    60,132
                      TITLE   DOMUL2  Called subprogram, multiplies
                      ; ---------------------------------------------
0000                          CODESG SEGMENT PARA (PUBLIC) 'CODE'
0000                          SUBMUL PROC    FAR
                              ASSUME CS:CODESG
                              PUBLIC SUBMUL
0000    E8 0004 R             CALL    C10MUL  ;Call subroutine
0003    CB                    RET
0004                          SUBMUL ENDP
                      ;               Multiply subroutine:
                      ;               ------------------
0004                          C10MUL PROC    ;Price in AX,
0004    F7 E3                 MUL     BX      ;Qty in BX,
0006    C3                    RET             ;Product in DX:AX
0007                          C10MUL ENDP

0007                          CODESG ENDS
                              END     SUBMUL
```

Segments and groups:
```
                N a m e         Size    align   combine class
```

```
CODESG . . . . . . . . . . . . . 0007   PARA    PUBLIC  'CODE'

Symbols:
                    N a m e           Type   Value   Attr
C10MUL . . . . . . . . . . . . . N PROC 0004      CODESG  Length =0003
SUBMUL . . . . . . . . . . . . . F PROC 0000      CODESG  Global   Length =0004
```

```
A>LINK
IBM Personal Computer Linker
Version 1.00 (C) Copyright IBM Corp 1981
Object Modules: B:CALLMUL2,B:DOMUL2
Run File: B:CALLMUL2
List File [B:CALLMUL2.MAP] :CON
Libraries [ ] : !

Start   Stop    Length   Name                      Class
00000H 00026H 0027H   CODESG                     CODE   ← One Code Segment
00030H 00033H 0004H   DATASG                     DATA
00040H 000BFH 0080H   STACKSG                    STACK

Program entry point at 0000:0000
```

Note the Symbol Table following each assembly: The combine-type for DATASG is PUBLIC (in Figure 16-3 it is NONE). More interesting is the Link Map at the end: There is now only one Code Segment! The fact that both Segments have the same name (DATASG), same class ('CODE'), and same PUBLIC attribute has caused the Linker to combine the two logical Code Segments into one physical Code Segment. Further, a trace of machine execution shows that the CALL instruction in the subprogram is now the following:

$$9A\ 2000\ AF04$$

This instruction stores hex 2000 in the IP and hex AF04 in the CS register. Because the subprogram shares a common Code Segment with the main program, the CS register is set to the same starting address, hex 04AF. But there is now an offset of 0020:

CS address	04AF0
IP offset	0020
Effective address	04B10

The Code Segment of the subprogram therefore presumably begins at hex 04B10. Is this correct? The Link Map doesn't make this point entirely clear, but you can infer the address from the listing of the main program— its size ends at offset 0016. Since the Code Segment for the subprogram is defined as SEGMENT, it must begin on a Paragraph boundary (evenly divisible by hex 10, so that the rightmost digit is 0). The Linker sets the subprogram at the first Paragraph boundary immediately following the main program—and this offset address is 00020. Therefore, the Code Segment of the subprogram begins at 04AF0 plus 0020, or 04B10.

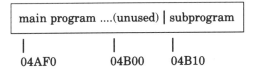

If the Linker is so clever, let's see if it can handle data defined in the main program and referenced in the subprogram.

PROGRAM: COMMON DATA IN SUBPROGRAMS

A common requirement is to process data in one assembly module that is defined in another assembly module. Let's modify the preceding examples so that although the main program still defines QTY and PRICE, the subprogram now inserts their values into the BX and AX.

Figure 16-5 gives the revised coding. The new changes are the following:

☐   The main program defines QTY and PRICE as PUBLIC. The Data Segment is also defined with the PUBLIC attribute. Note in the Symbol Table the Global attribute for QTY and PRICE.

Figure 16-5 Common Data in Subprograms.

```
                              page     60,132
                    TITLE   CALLMUL3 - Call Subprogram, multiplies
                          EXTRN    SUBMUL:FAR
                          PUBLIC   QTY,PRICE
                    ; --------------------------------------------
0000                STACKSG              SEGMENT PARA STACK 'STACK'
0000    40 [  ????  ]            DW      64 DUP(?)
0080                STACKSG              ENDS
                    ; --------------------------------------------
0000                DATASG SEGMENT PARA PUBLIC 'DATA'
0000    0140        QTY     DW      0140H
0002    2500        PRICE   DW      2500H
0004                DATASG ENDS
                    ; --------------------------------------------
```

```
0000                            CODESG SEGMENT PARA PUBLIC 'CODE'
0000                            BEGIN  PROC    FAR
                                       ASSUME  CS:CODESG,DS:DATASG,SS:STACKSG
0000   1E                              PUSH    DS
0001   2B CO                           SUB     AX,AX
0003   50                              PUSH    AX
0004   B8   ---- R                     MOV     AX,DATASG
0007   8E D8                           MOV     DS,AX
0009   9A 0000 ---- E                  CALL    SUBMUL     ;Call Subprogram
000E   CB                              RET
000F                            BEGIN  ENDP
000F                            CODESG ENDS
                                       END     BEGIN
```

```
Segments and groups:
                     N a m e              Size     align    combine class

CODESG . . . . . . . . . . . . . . 000F      PARA      PUBLIC    'CODE'
DATASG . . . . . . . . . . . . . . 0004      PARA      PUBLIC    'DATA'
STACKSG. . . . . . . . . . . . . . 0080      PARA      STACK     'STACK'

Symbols:
                     N a m e              Type    Value    Attr

BEGIN. . . . . . . . . . . . . . . F PROC 0000      CODESG    Length =000F
PRICE. . . . . . . . . . . . . . . L WORD          0002      DATASG    Global
QTY. . . . . . . . . . . . . . . . L WORD          0000      DATASG    Global
SUBMUL . . . . . . . . . . . . . . L FAR           0000                External
```

```
                                page   60,132
                         TITLE   DOMUL3  Called subprogram, multiplies
                         EXTRN   QTY:WORD,PRICE:WORD
                         ; ------------------------------------------
0000                            CODESG SEGMENT PARA PUBLIC 'CODE'
0000                            SUBMUL PROC    FAR
                                       ASSUME  CS:CODESG
                                       PUBLIC  SUBMUL
0000   E8 0004 R                       CALL    C10MUL   ;Call subroutine
0003   CB                              RET
0004                            SUBMUL ENDP
                                ;              Multiply routine:
                                ;              ----------------
0004                            C10MUL PROC
0004   A1 0000 E                        MOV    AX,PRICE
0007   8B 1E 0000 E                     MOV    BX,QTY
000B   F7 E3                            MUL    BX        ;Product in DX:AX
000D   C3                               RET
000E                            C10MUL ENDP

000E                            CODESG ENDS
                                       END     SUBMUL
```

```
Segments and groups:
                     N a m e              Size     align    combine class
```

```
CODESG . . . . . . . . . . . . . 000E   PARA    PUBLIC  'CODE'

Symbols:
                  N a m e          Type   Value   Attr

C10MUL . . . . . . . . . . . . . N PROC 0004     CODESG  Length =000A
PRICE. . . . . . . . . . . . . . V WORD          0000            External
QTY. . . . . . . . . . . . . . . V WORD          0000            External
SUBMUL . . . . . . . . . . . . . F PROC 0000     CODESG  Global  Length =0004
```

```
A>LINK
IBM Personal Computer Linker
Version 1.00 (C) Copyright IBM Corp 1981
Object Modules: B:CALLMUL3,B:DOMUL3
Run File: B:CALLMUL3
List File [B:CALLMUL3.MAP] :CON
Libraries [ ] : !

Start   Stop   Length  Name                Class

00000H 0001DH 001EH   CODESG              CODE
00020H 00023H 0004H   DATASG              DATA
00030H 000AFH 0080H   STACKSG             STACK

Program entry point at 0000:0000
```

- The subprogram defines QTY and PRICE as EXTRN, and both as WORD. This definition informs the Assembler as to the length of the two fields. The Assembler can now generate the correct operation code for the MOV instructions, but the Linker will have to complete the operands. Note in the Symbol Table that PRICE and QTY are External.

The Assembler lists the MOV instructions in the subprogram as

A1 0000 E	MOV AX,PRICE
8B 1E 0000 E	MOV BX,QTY

Object code hex A1 means move a word from memory to the AX, whereas hex 8B means move a word from memory to the BX (AX operations often require fewer bytes). Tracing execution reveals that the Linker has completed the object code operands as follows:

A1 0200

8B 1E 0000

The object code is now identical to that generated for the previous examples where the MOV instructions are in the calling program. This is a logical result because the operands in all three programs reference the same DS register and the same offset addresses.

The main program and the subprogram may define any other data fields, but only those defined as PUBLIC and EXTRN are known in common.

If you follow the general rules discussed in this chapter, you should be able to link a program consisting of more than two assembly modules and to make data known in all the modules. But watch out for the size of the Stack—for large programs, defining 64 words could be a wise precaution.

Chapter 18 provides additional features of Segments, including defining more than one Code or Data Segment in the same assembly module and the use of GROUP to combine these into a common Segment.

PASSING PARAMETERS

Another way of making data know to a called subprogram is to pass the data physically via the Stack. In this case, ensure that each PUSH references a word, either in memory or a register. The operation is known as *passing parameters*.

The program in Figure 16-6 pushes both PRICE and QTY prior to calling SUBMUL. After the CALL, the Stack appears as follows:

$$\ldots | \ 1600 \ | \ \text{AF04} \ | \ 4001 \ | \ 0025 \ | \ 0000 \ | \ 9\text{F04} \ |$$
$$6 \quad\quad 5 \quad\quad 4 \quad\quad 3 \quad\quad 2 \quad\quad 1$$

1. The initializing instruction PUSH DS pushed this address onto the Stack. This address may vary by operating system.
2. PUSH AX loaded the zero address onto the Stack.
3. A PUSH instruction loaded PRICE onto the Stack.
4. A PUSH instruction loaded QTY onto the Stack.
5. The CALL instruction pushed the contents of the CS register.
6. Since this is an intersegment CALL, the CALL also pushed the contents of the IP register.

Figure 16-6 Passing Parameters.

```
                          page    60,132
                 TITLE    CALLMUL4 - Call Subprogram, pass parameters
                 EXTRN    SUBMUL:FAR
                 ; --------------------------------------------
0000             STACKSG           SEGMENT PARA STACK 'STACK'
0000  40 [ ???? ]         DW       64 DUP(?)
0080             STACKSG           ENDS
                 ; ---------------------------------ι-----------
0000             DATASG SEGMENT PARA 'DATA'
0000  0140       QTY      DW       0140H
0002  2500       PRICE    DW       2500H
0004             DATASG ENDS
                 ; --------------------------------------------
0000             CODESG SEGMENT PARA PUBLIC 'CODE'
0000             BEGIN  PROC       FAR
                 ASSUME   CS:CODESG,DS:DATASG,SS:STACKSG
0000  1E                 PUSH     DS
0001  2B C0              SUB      AX,AX
0003  50                 PUSH     AX
0004  B8   ---- R        MOV      AX,DATASG
0007  8E D8              MOV      DS,AX
0009  FF 36 0002 R       PUSH     PRICE
000D  FF 36 0000 R       PUSH     QTY
0011  9A 0000 ---- E     CALL     SUBMUL     ;Call Subprogram
0016  CB                 RET
0017             BEGIN  ENDP

0017             CODESG ENDS
                 END      BEGIN

Segments and groups:
                 N a m e        Size    align    combine class

CODESG . . . . . . . . . . . . 0017    PARA    PUBLIC  'CODE'
DATASG . . . . . . . . . . . . 0004    PARA    NONE    'DATA'
STACKSG. . . . . . . . . . . . 0080    PARA    STACK   'STACK'

Symbols:
                 N a m e        Type    Value   Attr

BEGIN. . . . . . . . . . . . . F PROC 0000     CODESG  Length =0017
PRICE. . . . . . . . . . . . . L WORD          0002    DATASG
QTY. . . . . . . . . . . . . . L WORD          0000    DATASG
SUBMUL . . . . . . . . . . . . L FAR           0000            External


                          page    60,132
                 TITLE    DOMUL4  Called subprogram, multiplies
                 ; --------------------------------------------
0000             CODESG SEGMENT PARA PUBLIC 'CODE'
0000             SUBMUL PROC       FAR
                 ASSUME   CS:CODESG
                 PUBLIC   SUBMUL
0000  55                 PUSH     BP
0001  8B EC              MOV      BP,SP
0003  8B 46 08           MOV      AX,[BP+8]   ;Price
0006  8B 5E 06           MOV      BX,[BP+6]   ;Quantity
0009  F7 E3              MUL      BX          ;Product in DX:AX
000B  5D                 POP      BP
```

```
000C   CA 0004                      RET      4
000F           SUBMUL ENDP

000F                  CODESG ENDS
                      END
```

```
Segments and groups:
                N a m e           Size    align    combine class

CODESG . . . . . . . . . . . . . 000F    PARA     PUBLIC   'CODE'

Symbols:
                N a m e           Type    Value    Attr

SUBMUL . . . . . . . . . . . . . F PROC 0000      CODESG   Global   Length =000F
```

```
A>LINK
IBM Personal Computer Linker
Version 1.00 (C) Copyright IBM Corp 1981
Object Modules: B:CALLMUL4,B:DOMUL4
Run File: B:CALLMUL4
List File [B:CALLMUL4.MAP] :CON
Libraries [ ] : !

Start  Stop   Length  Name                    Class

00000H 0002EH 002FH   CODESG                   CODE
00030H 00033H 0004H   DATASG                   DATA
00040H 000BFH 0080H   STACKSG                  STACK

Program entry point at 0000:0000
```

The called program requires the use of the BP to access the parameters in the Stack. Its first action is to save the contents of the BP for the calling program by pushing it onto the Stack. In this case, the BP happens to contain zero, and it is stored to the left of word number 6 in the Stack.

The program then inserts the contents of the SP into the BP because the BP is usable as an index register (but not the SP). The operation loads the BP with the value 0072. Initially, the SP contained the size of the Stack—hex 80. Each word pushed onto the Stack decrements the Stack by 2:

0000	1600	AF04	4001	0025	0000	9F04

SP: 72   74   76   78   7A   7C   7E

Because the BP now also contains 0072, then the price parameter is at BP + 8 and the quantity parameter is at BP + 6. The routine moves these values from the Stack to the AX and BX, respectively, and performs the multiplication.

On returning to the calling program, the routine pops the BP (returning the zero address to the BP) and increments the SP by 2, from 72 to 74.

The last instruction is a far return to the calling program. The RET instruction performs the following:

□   Pops the word now at the top of the Stack (1600) to the IP.
□   Increments the SP by 2, from 74 to 76.
□   Pops the word now at the top (AF04) onto the CS.
□   Increments the SP by 2, from 76 to 78.

This operation returns correctly to the calling program—but there is one remaining explanation. The instruction is coded as

RET   4

The 4, known as a *pop-value*, contains the number of bytes in the passed parameters (two one-word parameters in this case). The RET operation also adds the pop-value to the SP, correcting it to 7C.

In effect, because the parameters in the Stack are no longer required, they are discarded. Be especially careful restoring the SP register—errors can create very interesting results.

LINKING BASIC AND ASSEMBLER

The BASIC manual for the IBM PC provides methods of linking BASIC with Assembler routines. Two reasons for linking these languages are to make use of BIOS interrupt routines through Assembler and to generate a more efficient program. The purpose of this section is to give a general overview of the linkage requirements; the technical details in the BASIC manual need not be repeated here.

For linking to BASIC, you have to code the Assembler routine separately and assemble and link it. You have a choice of allocating space for the machine language subroutine either inside or outside the 64K memory area to which BASIC is restricted. Space requirements for the various routines are the following:

DOS	12K
BASIC interpreter	10
DEBUG	6
Available to BASIC program and machine code	36
Total space	64K

If the BASIC program exceeds 36K in size, you will have to load the machine code subroutine outside the 64K area and in effect will need at least 96K of memory.

There are two ways of loading a machine code subroutine into memory. You can either use the BASIC POKE statement or combine an edited linked module with the BASIC program.

Use of the BASIC POKE Statement

Although the simplest method, it is suitable only for very short subroutines. First determine the object code of the Assembler routine either through the LST file or through DEBUG. Code the hex values directly in the BASIC program as DATA statements. A BASIC READ statement reads each hex byte successively, and a BASIC POKE plugs each byte into memory for execution.

Linked Assembler Modules

A larger Assembler subroutine will normally be easier to handle if it is assembled and linked as an execute module. You then have to organize the BASIC program and the executable module into a working program. Use BSAVE (BASIC save) to store the program permanently, and use BLOAD to load it for execution.

Before coding the BASIC and Assembler programs, decide which of two ways you want to interface them. The two BASIC methods are USR (user) function and the CALL statement. For both methods:

☐ On entry, the DS, ES, and SS registers contain the address of BASIC's address space. The CS contains the current value that the latest DEF SEG (if any) specified. The SP references a Stack of only eight words, so you may need to set up a Stack within the subroutine; if so, on entry save the location of the current Stack, and on exit restore it.

☐ On exit, restore Segment registers and the SP and return to BASIC with an intersegment RET.

You have to link your assembled object file so that it is at the HIGH end of memory; the sixth prompt from the LINK program handles this requirement. Use DEBUG to load the EXE subroutine and use R to determine the values in the CS and IP registers: these supply the starting address of the subroutine. While still in DEBUG, name (N) BASIC and load (L) it.

There are two ways of linking your BASIC program to your EXE subroutine: by use of USRn and by CALL. During the DEBUG session you determined the starting address of the EXE subroutine; insert this address either in the BASIC USRn or in the BASIC CALL statement. The IBM BASIC manual (Appendix C) provides details of the USRn function and the CALL statement, along with various examples.

Program: Linking BASIC and Assembler

Let's now study a simple example that links a BASIC program with an Assembler subprogram. In this example, the BASIC program prompts for input of hours and rate and displays the product (wage). A FOR/NEXT loop provides for five entries of hours and rate and then terminates. All that we are going to do is get the BASIC program to link to an Assembler module that clears the screen.

Figure 16-7 shows the original BASIC program and Assembler subprogram. Note the following features in the BASIC program:

Figure 16-7 BASIC Main Program and Assembler Subprogram.

```
LOAD"B:BASTEST.BAS"
Ok
LIST
10        CLEAR ,32768!
20        ' for BLOAD later
30        ' for DEF SEG
40        ' for entry-point for CALL
50        ' to CALL asm module
60        FOR N = 1 TO 5
70        INPUT "Hours"; H
80        INPUT "Rate"; R
90        W = H * R
100       PRINT "Wage = " W
110       NEXT N
120       END
Ok
```

```
TYPE B:LINKBAS.ASM
        page    60,132
TITLE   LINKBAS - Link BASIC & Assembler
;
CODESG  SEGMENT PARA 'CODE'
        ASSUME  CS:CODESG
CLRSCRN PROC    FAR
        PUSH    BP              ;Save BP
        MOV     BP,SP           ;Set base param list
        CALL    Q10CLR          ;Clear screen
        POP     BP
        RET                     ;Terminate
CLRSCRN ENDP
;
;               Clear screen:
;               ------------
Q10CLR  PROC    NEAR
        MOV     AX,0600H        ;Request scroll
        MOV     BH,07
        MOV     CX,0000
        MOV     DX,184FH
        INT     10H
        RET
Q10CLR  ENDP

CODESG  ENDS
        END
```

- ☐ Statement 10 clears 32K bytes of memory.
- ☐ Statements 20, 30, 40, and 50 temporarily contain comments. Later, we will insert BASIC statements to facilitate linking to an Assembler module.

You could test this program right now. Enter the command BASIC and key in each numbered statement just as it appears on the example. Then press F2 to run the program. Remember to save it using

SAVE "B:BASTEST.BAS"

Note the following features in the Assembler subprogram:

- ☐ There is no Stack Segment (BASIC supplies it); this subprogram is not intended to be run alone, and indeed it cannot.
- ☐ The subprogram saves the contents of the BP register on the Stack and stores the SP register in the BP.
- ☐ The subprogram only clears the screen, although you could revise it to perform other features, such as scroll up or down or set the cursor.

Now all that's left is to link these programs together. The following assumes that your DOS diskette is in drive A and working programs are in drive B:

1. Key in the Assembler subprogram, save it as B:LINKBAS.ASM, and assemble it.
2. Use LINK to generate an object module that will load in the high portion of memory:

LINK B:LINKBAS,B:LINKBAS/HIGH,CON;

3. Use DEBUG to load the BASIC compiler: DEBUG BASIC.COM.
4. Use the DEBUG R command to display the registers. Record the contents of the SS, CS, and IP registers.
5. Now name and load the linked assembly module as follows

N B:LINKBAS.EXE
L

6. Use the R command to display the registers. Record the contents of the CX, CS, and IP registers.
7. Change the contents of the SS, CS, and IP registers to the values from step 4 (use R SS, R CS, and R IP for this purpose).

8. Enter the DEBUG G (go) command in order to transfer control to BASIC. At this point, the screen should show the BASIC prompt.

9. In order to save the Assembler module, enter the following commands (with no statement numbers):

        DEF SEG = &Hxxxx   (value in CS from step 6)
        BSAVE "B:CLRSCRN.MOD",0,&Hxx   (value in CX from step 6)

The first entry supplies the address in memory where the module is to load for execution. The second entry identifies the name of the module, the relative entry point, and the size of the module. At this point, the system should write the module onto drive B.

10. Now you have to modify the BASIC program for the linkage. You could load it right now while still in DEBUG, but instead, key in SYSTEM to exit from BASIC and key in Q to exit from DEBUG. The DOS prompt should now appear on the screen.

11. Enter the comand BASIC, load the BASIC program, and display it:

                    BASIC
                    LOAD "B:BASTEST.BAS"
                    LIST

12. Change statements 20, 30, 40, and 50 as follows:

        20 BLOAD "B:CLRSCRN.MOD"
        30 DEF SEG = &Hxxxx   (value in CS from step 6)
        40 CLRSCRN = 0   (entry point to subprogram)
        50 CALL CLRSCRN   (invoke subprogram)

13. List, run, and save the revised BASIC program.

If you have entered the correct BASIC and Assembler instructions and the correct hex values from registers, the linked program should immediately clear the screen and display prompts for hours and rate. Figure 16-8 provides a printout of the steps, but watch out—the values differ for versions of operating system and memory size.

The example is intentionally simple to illustrate linkage. You could perform more advanced techniques by passing parameters from the BASIC program to the Assembler subprogram using

            CALL subprogram (parameter-1, parameter-2, ...)

```
┌─────────────────────────────────────────────────────┐
│ Figure 16-8 Steps in Linking BASIC and Assembler.   │
└─────────────────────────────────────────────────────┘
```

```
A>LINK B:LINKBAS,B:LINKBAS/HIGH,CON;

IBM Personal Computer Linker
Version 1.10 (C)Copyright IBM Corp 1982

Warning: No STACK segment

 Start  Stop   Length  Name                    Class
 00000H 00015H 0016H   CODESG                  CODE

There was 1 error detected.

A>DEBUG BASIC.COM
-R
AX=0000  BX=0000  CX=2C80  DX=0000  SP=FFF0  BP=00Q0  SI=0000  DI=0000
DS=04B5  ES=04B5  SS=04B5  CS=04B5  IP=0100  NV UP DI PL NZ NA PO NC
04B5:0100 E9032A        JMP     2B06
-N B:LINKBAS.EXE
-L
-R
AX=0000  BX=0000  CX=0016  DX=0000  SP=0000  BP=0000  SI=0000  DI=0000
DS=04B5  ES=04B5  SS=3FFE  CS=3FFE  IP=0000  NV UP DI PL NZ NA PO NC
3FFE:0000 55           PUSH    BP
-R SS
SS 3FFE
:04B5
-R CS
CS 3FFE
:04B5
-R IP
IP 0000
:0100
-G

Direct statement in file
Ok
DEF SEG = &H3FFE
Ok
BSAVE "B:CLRSCRN.MOD",0,&H16
Ok
SYSTEM

Program terminated normally
-Q

A>BASIC

Version D1.10 Copyright IBM Corp. 1981, 1982
61371 Bytes free
Ok
LOAD"B:BASTEST.BAS"
Ok
20      BLOAD "B:CLRSCRN.MOD"
30      DEF SEG = &H3FFE
40      CLRSCRN = 0
50      CALL CLRSCRN
LIST
10      CLEAR ,32768!
20      BLOAD "B:CLRSCRN.MOD"
30      DEF SEG = &H3FFE
40      CLRSCRN = 0
50      CALL CLRSCRN
60      FOR N = 1 TO 5
70      INPUT "Hours"; H
80      INPUT "Rate"; R
90      W = H * R
100     PRINT "Wage = " W
110     NEXT N
120     END
Ok
```

The Assembler subprogram can access these parameters by using the BP register as [BP], just as Figure 16-3 did earlier. You also have to supply a pop-value in the RET operand to account for the parameter addresses on the Stack. For example, if CALL delivers three parameters, code RET 6.

LINKING PASCAL TO ASSEMBLER

Although Pascal is a powerful high-level language, it does not (at this time) support good screen handling. However, you can easily link Pascal to Assembler to take advantage of Assembler's interrupt capability.

As an example, the program in Figure 16-9 shows a simple Pascal program that links to an Assembler subprogram. The Pascal program is compiled to produce an OBJ module and the Assembler program is assembled to produce an OBJ module. The LINK program then links together these two OBJ modules into one EXE executable module.

Figure 16-9 Linking Pascal to Assembler.

```
program pascall ( input, output );

    procedure move_cursor( const row: integer;
                           const col: integer ); extern;
    var
        temp_row:       integer;
        temp_col:       integer;

    begin

        write( 'Enter cursor row: ' );
        readln( temp_row );

        write( 'Enter cursor column: ' );
        readln( temp_col );

        move_cursor( temp_row, temp_col );
        write( 'New cursor location' );

        end.
```

```
        page    60,132
TITLE   MOVCUR  Assembler subprogram called by PASCAL
        PUBLIC  MOVE_CURSOR
;--------------------------------------------------------------
;
;    MOVE_CURSOR  -  Set cursor on screen at passed location
;
;    Passed:     const row       -  row and column where
;                const col          cursor is to be moved
;
;    Returned:  nothing
;
;--------------------------------------------------------------
CODESEG SEGMENT PARA PUBLIC 'CODE'

MOVE_CURSOR PROC FAR
        ASSUME  CS:CODESEG

ROWPAR  EQU     8               ;Row parameter loc'n
COLPAR  EQU     6               ;Col parameter loc'n

        PUSH    BP              ;Save caller's BP register
        MOV     BP,SP           ;Point BP to parameters passed

        MOV     SI,[BP+ROWPAR]  ;SI points to row
        MOV     DH,[SI]         ;Move row to DH

        MOV     SI,[BP+COLPAR]  ;SI points to column
        MOV     DL,[SI]         ;Move column to DL
```

```
                MOV     AH,02           ;Move cursor
                SUB     BH,BH           ;Page #0
                INT     10H

                POP     BP              ;Return to caller
                RET     4
MOVE_CURSOR     ENDP

CODESEG ENDS
        END
```

```
        Start   Stop    Length  Name                    Class

        00000H  000C6H  00C7H   PASCALL                 CODE
        000D0H  000E6H  0017H   CODESEG                 CODE
        000F0H  00415H  0326H   MISGQQ                  CODE
        00416H  00D53H  093EH   ERREQQ_CODE             CODE
        00D60H  00D60H  0000H   INIXQQ                  CODE
        00D60H  00E26H  00C7H   ENTXQQ                  CODE
        00E28H  01ECAH  10A3H   FILUQQ_CODE             CODE
        01ECCH  02F18H  104DH   FILFQQ_CODE             CODE
        02F1AH  03080H  0167H   PASUQQ_CODE             CODE
        03082H  0365CH  05DBH   ORDFQQ_CODE             CODE
        0365EH  0368BH  002EH   MISOQQ_CODE             CODE
        0368CH  03EF9H  086EH   CODCQQ_CODE             CODE
        03EFAH  0401AH  0121H   UTLXQQ_CODE             CODE
        0401CH  043ACH  0391H   STRFQQ_CODE             CODE
        043AEH  0455EH  01B1H   HEAHQQ_CODE             CODE
        04560H  04605H  00A6H   MISHQQ_CODE             CODE
        04606H  046F5H  00F0H   MISYQQ_CODE             CODE
        04700H  04700H  0000H   HEAP                    MEMORY
        04700H  04700H  0000H   MEMORY                  MEMORY
        04700H  048FFH  0200H   STACK                   STACK
        04900H  04FD7H  06D8H   DATA                    DATA
        04FE0H  05711H  0732H   CONST                   CONST
        05720H  05720H  0000H   ??SEG

        Program entry point at 00D6:0000
```

The PASCAL program defines two items named temp_row and temp_col and accepts entries for row and column from the keyboard into these variables. It then sends the addresses of temp_row and temp_col as parameters to the Assembler subprogram to set the cursor to this location. The Pascal program defines the name of the Assembler subprogram in a procedure as move_cursor and defines the two parameters as extern. The statement in the Pascal program that "calls" the name of the Assembler subprogram and passes the parameters is

move_cursor(temp_row, temp_col);

Values pushed onto the Stack are the calling program's frame pointer, return segment pointer, return offset, and the addresses of the two passed parameters. The following shows the offsets for each entry in the Stack:

00 Caller's frame pointer
02 Caller's return segment pointer
04 Caller's return offset
06 Address of second parameter
08 Address of first parameter

Since the Assembler subprogram is going to use the BP register, you have to PUSH it onto the Stack in order to save its address for the return to the Pascal calling program. Note that the steps in the called subprogram are very similar to the example in Figure 16-6 earlier.

The SP register normally addresses entries in the Stack. However, you cannot use the SP to act as an index register. Therefore, the next step after pushing the BP is to move the address in the SP to the BP. This step enables you to use the BP as an index register to access entries in the Stack.

The next step is to access the addresses of the two parameters in the Stack. The first passed parameter, the row, is at offset 08 in the Stack and can be accessed by BP + 08. The second passed parameter, the column, is at offset 06 and can be accessed by BP + 06.

The two addresses in the Stack have to be transferred to one of the available index registers: BX, DI, or SI. This example has chosen the SI. It uses [BP+08] to move the address of the row to the SI and then uses [SI] to move the contents of the passed parameter to the DH register.

The column is transferred to the DL register in a similar way. Then the subprogram uses the row and column in the DX register to call BIOS to set the cursor. On exit, the subprogram pops the BP. The RET instruction requires an operand value that is two times the number of parameters—in this case, 2 × 2, or 4. Values are automatically popped off the Stack and control transfers back to the calling program.

If you use any Segment registers, be sure to PUSH them on entry and POP them on exit. Note also that you can use the Stack to pass values from a subprogram to a calling program.

Following the two programs is the MAP that the Linker generated. The first entry is for the Pascal program named PASCALL; the second entry is for the Assembler subprogram named CODESEG (the name of the Code Segment). Following are a "heap" of Pascal subroutines. This rather trivial program has resulted in hex 5720 bytes of memory—over 20K! A compiler language typically generates considerable overhead regardless of the size of the program.

KEY POINTS TO REMEMBER

☐ In a main program that calls a subprogram, define the entry point as

EXTRN; in the subprogram define the entry point as PUBLIC.

☐ Handle recursion carefully – that is, subprogram 1 calls subprogram 2, which in turn calls subprogram 1.

☐ If two Code Segments are to be linked into one Segment, define them with the same name, same class, and the PUBLIC combine-type.

☐ To simplify programming, begin execution with the main program. It is also generally easier (but not necessary) to define common data in the main program. The main program defines the common data as PUBLIC and the subprogram (or subprograms) define the common data as EXTRN.

QUESTIONS

16-1. Assume that a program named CALLSUB is to call a subprogram named SUBPROG.

(a) What instruction in CALLSUB tells the Assembler that the name SUBPROG is defined outside of its own assembly?

(b) What instruction in SUBPROG is required to make its name known to CALLSUB?

16-2. Assume that CALLSUB has defined variables named QTY as DB, VALUE as DW, and PRICE as DW. SUBPROG is to divide VALUE by QTY and is to store the quotient in PRICE.

(a) How does CALLSUB tell the Assembler that the three variables are to be known outside this assembly?

(b) How does SUBPROG tell the Assembler that the three variables are defined in another assembly?

16-3. Combine Questions 16-1 and 16-2 into a working program and test it.

16-4. Revise Question 16-3 so that CALLSUB passes all three variables as parameters. Note, however, that SUBPROG is to return the calculated price intact in its parameter.

16-5. Here's an exercise that should keep you busy for a while. Expand Question 16-4 so that CALLSUB permits a user to enter quantity and value on the keyboard; CALLSUB2 converts the ASCII amounts to binary; CALLSUB3 calculates the price; and CALLSUB4 converts the binary price to ASCII and displays the result.

BIOS AND INTERRUPTS

Objective:
To describe the full interrupt
functions of BIOS.

INTRODUCTION

BIOS is based in ROM and handles all interrupts for the system. We
have already used a number of interrupts for video display, memory size,
disk input/output, and printing. This chapter describes the various BIOS
interrupts and as a reference also lists the DOS interrupts. The complete
ROM listings of Assembler code are available in the IBM PC Technical
Reference manual.

An interrupt is an operation that interrupts the execution of a program
so that the system can take special action. There are two main reasons
for an interrupt: (1) an intentional request for such action as input from a
device and output to a device, and (2) an unintentional serious error such
as a divide overflow.

External devices signal for attention via an INTR pin on the processor.
The processor always responds to a request if the Interrupt Flag (IF) is
enabled (that is, contains 1). Under most circumstances, the processor

ignores an interrupt if the IF Flag is disabled (equals 0). The instruction for setting an interrupt is STI and for clearing an interrupt is CLI.

The operand of an interrupt instruction also contains an interrupt type that identifies the request. For example, INT 14H requests communications I/O. For each type, the processor maintains an address in a table beginning in memory location 0000. There are 256 entries, each four bytes long. Each address relates to an interrupt routine that handles the specific interrupt type. See Table 17-1 for a list of the interrupt table. As you can see, the address for INT 14H is hex 50 (hex 14 x 4 = hex 50).

An interrupt operation pushes on the Stack the contents of the Flags register, the CS, and the IP. An example of an interrupt is INT 12H that returns the memory size in the AX register. The table address of interrupt 12H is hex 0048 (hex 12 times 4 equals hex 48). The operation extracts the four-byte address from location 0048 and stores two bytes in the IP and two in the CS. It then executes the designated interrupt routine (which we traced away back in Chapter 2). The interrupt returns via an IRET (Interrupt Return) instruction that pops the Flags, CS, and IP from the Stack and returns to the instruction following the interrupt.

Table 17-1   Table of Interrupt Addresses.

Address (hex)	Interrupt (hex)	Function
0-3	0	Divide by zero
4-7	1	Single step (trace)
8-B	2	Nonmaskable interrupt (NMI)
C-F	3	Break point instruction ('CC'x)
10-13	4	Overflow
14-17	5	Print Screen
18-1F	6,7	Reserved
20-23	8	Timer
24-27	9	Keyboard interrupt
28-37	A,B,C,D	Reserved
38-3B	E	Diskette interrupt
3C-3F	F	Reserved
40-43	10	Video screen I/O
44-47	11	Equipment check
48-4B	12	Memory size check
4C-4F	13	Diskette I/O
50-53	14	Communications I/O
54-57	15	Cassette I/O
58-5B	16	Keyboard input

5C-5F	17	Printer output
60-63	18	ROM Basic entry code
64-67	19	Bootstrap loader
68-6B	1A	Time of day
6C-6F	1B	Get control on keyboard break
70-73	1C	Get control on timer interrupt
74-77	1D	Pointer to video initialization table
78-7B	1E	Pointer to diskette parameter table
7C-7F	1F	Pointer to table for graphics characters ASCII 128-255.
80-83	20	DOS program terminate
84-87	21	DOS function call
88-8B	22	DOS terminate address
8C-8F	23	DOS Ctrl/Break exit address
90-93	24	DOS fatal error vector
94-97	25	DOS absolute disk read
98-9B	26	DOS absolute disk write
9C-9F	27	DOS terminate, fix in storage
A0-FF	28-3F	Reserved for DOS
100-1FF	40-7F	Not used
200-217	80-85	Reserved by BASIC
218-3C3	86-F0	Used by BASIC interpreter
3C4-3FF	F1-FF	Not used

Note: Interrupts 00-1F are BIOS and 20-FF are DOS and BASIC.

BIOS INTERRUPTS

This section covers most of the interrupts supported by BIOS.

INT 05H: Print the Screen. This operation causes the contents of the screen to print. It is activated externally by pressing the Ctrl/PrtSc keys and internally by issuing INT 05H. The operation enables interrupts (STI) and saves the cursor position.

INT 10H: Video Display I/O. Chapter 7 describes the 16 INT 10H operations in detail.

INT 11H: Equipment Determination. This operation determines the optional devices on the system and returns a value in the AX:

Bit	Device
15,14	Number of printers attached.
12	Game I/O attached.
11-9	Number of RS232 cards.

Bit	Device
7,6	Number of diskette devices, only if bit 0 = 1: 00 = 1, 01 = 2, 10 = 3, and 11 = 4.
5,4	Initial video mode: 00 = unused. 01 = 40 x 25 BW using a color card. 10 = 80 x 25 BW using a color card. 11 = 80 x 25 BW using a BW card.
3,2	Size of RAM in the System Board: 00 = 16K, 01 = 32K, 10 = 48K, and 11 = 64K.
1	Unused.
0	A value of 1 indicates that the system contains one or more diskette devices and is to load the operating system from diskette (IPL = initial program load).

INT 12H: Memory Size Determination. The operation returns in the AX the size of memory in terms of 1K bytes, such that 64K memory is hex 40. This operation is useful to software programmers who want to adjust program size according to available memory.

INT 13H: Diskette Input/Output. This operation provides for diskette I/O. Chapter 13 covers the six interrupt operations.

INT 14H: Communications Input/Output. This operation provides byte stream I/O to the RS232 communication port. The DX should contain the number of the RS232 adapter (0 or 1). There are four calls established through the AH register.

AH = 00: Initialize the communications port. Set the AL with the following parameters:

Baud Rate 7 − 5	Parity 4 − 3	Stopbit 2	Word Length 1 − 0
000 = 110	00 = none	0 = 1	10 = 7 bits
001 = 150	01 = odd	1 = 2	11 = 8 bits
010 = 300	10 = none		
011 = 600	11 even		
100 = 1200			
101 = 2400			
110 = 4800			
111 = 9600			

The operation returns the status of the communications port (see AH = 03 for details).

AH = 01:   Transmit a character. Load the AL with the character that the routine is to send over the communications line. On return, the operation sets the port status in the AH (see AH = 03). If the operation is unable to transmit the byte, it also sets bit 7 of the AH.

AH = 02:   Receive a character. The operation accepts a character from the communications line into the AL. It also sets the AH with the port status (see AH = 03) for error bits 7, 4, 3, 2, and 1. Thus, a nonzero value in the AX indicates an input error.

AH = 03:   Return the status of the communications port. The operation sets the AH with the line control status and sets the AL with the modem status:

AH = line control status:	AL = modem status:
7 = Time out	Received line signal detect
6 = Trans shift reg empty	Ring indicator
5 = Trans hold reg empty	Data set ready
4 = Break detect	Clear to send
3 = Framing error	Delta receive line signal detect
2 = Parity error	Trailing edge ring detector
1 = Overrun error	Delta data set ready
0 = Data ready	Delta clear to send

INT 15H: Cassette Input/Output. The operation provides four operations for cassette I/O according to the code in the AH register:

AH = 00:   Turn on the cassette motor.

AH = 01:   Turn off the cassette motor.

AH = 02:   Read one or more 256-byte blocks. Set the ES:BX with the pointer address of the input buffer and the CX with the number of bytes to be read. On return, the operation sets the ES:BX to the address of the last byte read plus 1, the DX to the number of bytes actually read, and the Carry Flag to 1 if an error occurred. In the event of an error (CF = 1), the AH provides the diagnosis:

01 = Detection of a CRC error.

02 = Lost data transitions.

04 = No data located.

AH = 03: Write one or more 256-byte blocks. Set the ES:BX with the pointer address of the output buffer and the CX with the number of bytes to be written. On return, the operation sets the ES:BX with the address of the last byte written plus 1 and the CX to 00.

Setting the AH to any other value causes INT 15H to set the CF Flag to 1 and the AH to hex 80.

INT 16H: Keyboard Input.   The operation provides three keyboard input commands according to the code in the AH:

AH = 00: Read a character. The operation reads into the AL the next ASCII character entered from the keyboard and sets the scan code in the AH.

AH = 01: Determine if a character is available. The operation sets the Zero Flag to indicate if a character is available for reading. ZF = 0 means that a character is available; the next character to be read is in the AX, and the entry remains in the buffer.

AH = 02: Return the current shift status. The operation returns the status of keyboard shift in the AL:

Bit	Bit
7 Insert state is active	3 Alt shift pressed
6 Caps lock state toggled	2 Ctrl/Shift pressed
5 Numeric lock state toggled	1 Left shift pressed
4 Scroll lock state toggled	0 Right shift pressed

INT 17H: Printer Output.   Chapter 7 discusses printing in detail.

INT 18H: ROM Basic Entry.

INT 19H: Bootstrap Loader.   If a diskette device is available (see also INT 11H), the operation reads track 0, sector 1, into the boot location in memory, Segment 0, offset 7C00 and transfers control to this location. If there is no diskette drive, the operation transfers to the cassette entry point via INT 18H (ROM Basic Entry).

INT 1AH: Time of Day.   This operation enables setting and reading of the clock according to the value in the AH. Counts occur at about 18.2 per second. Set a code in the AH according to the required operation:

AH = 00:   Read the clock. The operation sets the CX to the high portion of the count and the DX to the low portion. If the time has passed 24 hours since the last read, the operation also sets the AL to nonzero.

AH = 01:   Set the clock. Set the CX with the high portion of the count and the DX with the low portion.

INT 1FH: Pointer to Graphics Table.   Video graphics mode offers direct access only to the first (bottom) 128 ASCII characters. This interrupt enables you to access the top 128 characters in a 1K table containing eight bytes per character.

DOS INTERRUPTS

DOS supplies two modules, IBMBIO.COM and IBMDOS.COM, to facilitate using BIOS. Since the DOS modules provide much of the additional required testing, the DOS operations are generally easier to use than their BIOS counterparts. Both IBMBIO.COM and IBMDOS.COM are on the DOS diskette but do not display when you request DIR.

IBMBIO.COM provides a low-level interface to BIOS. This is an I/O handler program that facilitates reading data from external devices into memory and writing data from memory onto external devices.

IBMDOS.COM contains a file manager and a number of service functions such as blocking and deblocking disk records. When a user program requests input/output, the operation delivers to IBMDOS high-level information via the contents of registers and control blocks. To complete the request, IBMDOS.COM translates the information into one or more calls to IBMBIO.COM. The following shows the logical relationship:

User	High level	Low level	ROM	External
Program	DOS	DOS		
request <-->	IBMDOS.COM <-->	IBMBIO.COM <-->	BIOS <-->	Device
for I/O				

As Table 17-1 showed earlier, interrupt types hex 20 through hex 3F are reserved for DOS operations which are listed below.

INT 20H: Program Terminate.   A FAR RET instruction that terminates execution and returns to DOS generates this interrupt.

INT 21H: Function Request. This operation requires a function code in the AH and information in other registers according to the request:

00	Program terminate
01	Keyboard input
02	Display output
03	Auxiliary (asynchronous communications adapter) input
04	Auxiliary (asynchronous communications adapter) output
05	Printer output
06	Direct console input
07	Direct console input without echo
08	Console input without echo
09	Display string
0A	Buffered keyboard input
0B	Check keyboard status
0C	Clear keyboard buffer and invoke input
0D	Disk reset
0E	Select disk
0F	Open file
10	Close file
11	Search for first disk entry
12	Search for next disk entry
13	Delete file
14	Sequential read
15	Sequential write
16	Create file
17	Rename file
19	Determine the default disk drive
1A	Set disk transfer address
1B	Determine allocation table information
21	Random read
22	Random write
23	Determine file size
24	Set random record field
25	Set interrupt vector
26	Create a new program segment
27	Read random disk block
28	Write random disk block
29	Parse filename
2A	Get date
2B	Set date
2C	Get time
2D	Set time

2E   Set/reset verify switch
2F-57   DOS 2.0 functions – see the DOS manual

INT 22H: Terminate address.

INT 23H: Ctrl/Break Address.

INT 24H: Critical Error Handler Vector.

INT 25H: Absolute disk read.

INT 26H: Absolute disk write.

INT 27H: Terminate But Stay Resident.

Previous chapters have covered some of the interrupt operations. Since the DOS manual provides a detailed description of each operation, it need not be repeated here.

PORTS

What connects the processor to the external world is ports. Through a port a processor receives a signal—for example, from a user at a terminal—and through a port the processor can send a signal to the display screen. Although it seems rather extravagant, the processor can handle up to 65,536 ports. Each port has a unique number beginning with port 0.

Although the interrupt (INT) method is the normal way to handle I/O, it is possible to handle I/O directly at the port level. The Assembler instruction for reading data from an input port is IN, and for writing data to output ports is OUT.

☐   IN transfers data from an input port to the AL if byte and AX if word. The general format is

IN accum-reg,port

☐   OUT transfers data to an output port from the AL if a byte and from the AX if a word. The general format is

OUT port,accum-reg

You can specify a port number in one of two ways, statically or dynamically:

1. Statically. The first way is directly as an operand from 0 through 255 such as

Input:	IN AL,port#	;Input one byte
Output	OUT port#,AX	;Output one word

2. Dynamically. The second way is indirectly by the contents of the DX register – 0 through 65,535. This method would be suitable in a system that increments the DX in order to process consecutive port numbers. The following gives an example of using I/O port 10H:

MOV AL,byte	;Byte to output
MOV DX,10H	;I/O port hex 10
OUT DX,AL	;Send byte

Following is a listing of some port numbers, shown in hex:

60	Accepts input from the keyboard.
61	Controls the speaker (bits 0 and 1).
3B0-3BF	Controls the monochrome display and parallel printer adapter (3B8 initializes the monochrome display adapter).
3D0-3DF	Controls the color/graphics adapter.
3F0-3F7	Operates the disk controller (3F5 transmits data to and from disk drives).

For example, when a program requests input from the keyboard, it issues an interrupt instruction INT 16H. The system links to a routine in BIOS that issues an IN instruction to access a character from port hex 60.

For further examples of the IN and OUT instructions, examine the BIOS listings in the IBM PC Technical Reference Manual.

GENERATING SOUND

The PC generates sound by means of a builtin 2-1/4" permanent magnet speaker. You can either select one of two ways to drive the speaker or combine both ways. (1) Use bit 1 of port 61H to activate the Intel 8255A-5 Programmable Peripheral Interface (PPI) chip. (2) Use the gating of the Intel 8353-5 Programmable Interval Timer (PIT). The clock generates a 1.19318 Mhz signal. The PPI controls gate 2 at bit 0 of port 61H.

Let's examine the program in Figure 17-1 that generates a series of notes in ascending frequency. The Data Segment defines two words: DURTION provides the length of each note and TONE determines its frequency. Note that initially the program accesses port 61H and saves the value that the operation delivers. A CLI instruction clears the Interrupt flag in order

to permit a constant tone. The interval timer generates a clock tick of 18.2
ticks per second that (unless you code CLI) interrupts execution of your
program and causes the tone to wobble.

Figure 17-1 Generating Sound.

```
          page     60,132
TITLE     SOUND - Produce sound from speaker
STACK     SEGMENT PARA STACK 'Stack'
          DW       32 DUP(?)
STACK     ENDS
;
DATASG    SEGMENT PARA 'Data'
DURTION   DW       1000              ;Length of tone
TONE      DW       256H              ;Frequency
DATASG    ENDS
;
SOUNSEG   SEGMENT PARA 'Code'
START     PROC     FAR
          ASSUME   CS:SOUNSEG,DS:DATASG,SS:STACK
          PUSH     DS
          SUB      AX,AX
          PUSH     AX
          MOV      AX,DATASG
          MOV      DS,AX

          IN       AL,61H            ;Get port data
          PUSH     AX                ; and save
          CLI                        ;Clear interrupts
          CALL     B10SPKR           ;Produce sound
          POP      AX                ;Reset
          OUT      61H,AL            ;  port value
          STI                        ;Reset interrupts
          RET
START     ENDP
;
B10SPKR   PROC     NEAR
B20:
          MOV      DX,DURTION        ;Set duration of sound
B30:
          AND      AL,11111100B      ;Set bits 0 & 1 off
          OUT      61H,AL            ;Transmit to speaker
          MOV      CX,TONE           ;Set length
B40:
          LOOP     B40               ;Time delay
          OR       AL,00000010B      ;Set bit 1 on
          OUT      61H,AL            ;Transmit to speaker
          MOV      CX,TONE           ;Set length
B50:
          LOOP     B50               ;Time delay
          DEC      DX                ;Reduce duration
          JNZ      B30               ;Continue?
          SHL      DURTION,1         ;Increase length
          SHR      TONE,1            ;change frequency
          JNZ      B20               ;Now zero?
          RET                        ;Yes -- exit
B10SPKR   ENDP
;
SOUNSEG   ENDS
          END      START
```

The contents of TONE determines its frequency; high values cause low frequencies and low values cause high frequencies. After the routine B10SPKR plays each note, it increases the frequency of TONE by means of a right shift of 1 bit (effectively halving its value). Since decreasing TONE in this example also reduces how long it plays, the routine also increases DURTION by means of a left shift of 1 bit (effectively doubling its value).

The program terminates when TONE is reduced to 0. The initial values in DURTION and TONE don't have any technical or mystical significance. You can experiment with other values and even try execution without the CLI instruction. You could also revise the program to generate notes that decrease in frequency; initialize TONE to 01 and DURTION to a high value. On each loop, increase the value in TONE, decrease the value in DURTION, and terminate when DURTION equals 0.

You could use any variation of the logic in Figure 17-1 to play a sequence of notes. For example, you may want to draw a user's attention to enter data or to respond to an error.

18

ASSEMBLER PSEUDO-OP
REFERENCE

Objective:
To describe in detail Assembler operators
and Pseudo-operations.

INTRODUCTION

At first glance, the various Assembler features tend to be somewhat over-whelming. But once you have become familiar with the simpler and more common features described in the earlier chapters, you should find the descriptions in this chapter more easily understood and a handy reference.

We'll examine indexed memory, the attribute operators, value- return-ing operators, and data Pseudo-ops. This chapter reviews the more important features. The supplier's Assembler manual contains a few other marginally useful features.

INDEXED MEMORY

For a *direct* memory reference, one operand of an instruction specifies the name of a defined variable, as shown in the following examples:

```
            MOV CX,COUNT
            MOV VALUE,AX
```

During execution, the processor locates the specified variable in memory by adding the offset value of the variable to the address in the Data Segment.

For indexed memory, an operand references a base or index register, constants, offset variables, and variables. Square brackets indicate indexed memory operands and act like a plus (+) sign. You can use the following:

1.   Base register BX as [BX] in association with the DS segment register and base register BP as [BP] in association with the SS segment register.
2.   Index register DI as [DI] and index register SI as [SI], both in association with the DS segment register.
3.   [constant] containing an immediate number or name in square brackets.
4.   + or − displacement used with an indexed operand.

You may combine these operands in any sequence, but cannot combine two base registers [BX + BP] or two index registers [DI + SI]. Valid examples follow:

```
1.      MOV   CX,[BX]              ;Base register
2.      MOV   AX,[SI+4]            ;Index register + constant
3.      MOV   [BX+SI+8],AX         ;Base + index + constant
4.      MOV   DX,8[DI][4]          ;Displacement + index + constant
```

Example 1 uses the offset address in the BX (combined with the Segment address in the DS register) and moves the referenced item to the CX.
Example 2 combines the address in the DS, the offset address in the SI, plus the value 4, and moves the referenced item to the AX.
Example 3 combines the DS address, the BX offset, the SI offset, plus the constant 4, and moves the the contents of the AX to the referenced address.
Example 4 combines the DS address, the displacement 8, plus the DI offset, and moves the referenced item to the DX.

There is really no difference between the use of a constant or a displacement. A typical use of indexed addresses is in references to tables (or arrays) of data in which items are not named and the program calculates their location.

ASSEMBLER OPERATORS

There are three types of Assembler operators: *attribute operators*, *value-returning* operators, and *record-specific* operators. This section covers the first two types; the record-specific operators, MASK, shift count, and WIDTH, are associated with the RECORD Pseudo-op, covered in a later section.

LENGTH

The LENGTH operator returns the number of entries defined by a DUP operand. The following MOV instruction returns the length 10 (hex 0A) to the CX:

<pre>
      TABLEX   DW   10 DUP(?)
                ...
                MOV   CX,LENGTH TABLEX
</pre>

If the operand does not contain a DUP entry, the operator returns the value 01. See also SIZE and TYPE in this section. Under CP/M-86, LENGTH returns the actual number of bytes that the variable defines.

OFFSET

The OFFSET operator returns the offset address of a variable or label (that is, the relative address within the Data Segment or Code Segment). The general format is

OFFSET variable or label

The following MOV instruction returns the offset address of TABLEX (note that LEA would return the same value without using OFFSET):

MOV   DX,OFFSET TABLEX

PTR

The PTR operator uses BYTE, WORD, or DWORD to override the defined type (DB, DW, or DD) and uses NEAR and FAR to override implied distance. Its general format is

type PTR   expression

The type field is the new attribute such as BYTE. The expression refers to a variable or constant. The following are examples:

```
FLDW  DW    2532H                        ;Stored as 3225
FLDB  DB    17H
      DB    43H
      ...
      MOV   AH,BYTE PTR FLDW             ;Move first byte (32)
      ADD   BL,BYTE PTR FLDW+1           ;Add second byte (25)
      MOV   BYTE PTR FLDW,05             ;Move 05 to first byte
      MOV   AX,WORD PTR FLDB             ;Move two bytes (1743) to AX
      CALL  FAR PTR[BX]                  ;Call far procedure
```

Another Assembler feature that performs a similar function to PTR is the LABEL Pseudo-op, described in the next section.

SEG

The SEG operator returns the address of the Segment in which a specified variable or label is placed. This operator would most likely be used in programs that combine separately Assembler Segments. The general format is

SEG variable or label

The following MOV instructions return the address of the Segment in which they are defined:

```
      MOV   AX,SEG FLDW      ;Address of Data Segment
      MOV   AX,SEG A20       ;Address of Code Segment
```

SHORT

The purpose of the SHORT operator is to modify the NEAR attribute of a JMP destination if it is within $+127$ and -128 bytes.

JMP SHORT label

The Assembler reduces the machine code operand from two to one byte. However, a JMP in a Procedure within the near range generates only a one-byte operand. A JMP to a Procedure defined as FAR generates a two-byte operand. In this case, if the label really is within the near range, specifying SHORT in the JMP would save one byte. But then a program should use CALL rather than JMP to transfer to a Procedure!

SIZE

The SIZE operator returns the product of LENGTH times TYPE and is useful only if the referenced variable contains the DUP entry. The general format is

SIZE variable

See TYPE for an example. CP/M-86 does not contain a SIZE Directive.

TYPE

The TYPE operator returns the number of bytes according to the definition of the referenced variable:

Definition	Number of bytes
DB	1
DW	2
DD	4
DQ	8
DT	10
STRUC	Number of bytes defined by STRUC
NEAR label	Hex FFFF
FAR label	Hex FFFE

The general format of TYPE is

TYPE variable or label

The following example illustrates TYPE, LENGTH, and SIZE:

```
FLDB    DB    ?
TABLEX  DW    10 DUP(?)              ;Define 10 words

        ...
        MOV    AX,TYPE FLDB         ;AX = 0001
        MOV    AX,TYPE TABLEX       ;AX = 0002
        MOV    CX,LENGTH TABLEX     ;CX = 000A (10)
        MOV    DX,SIZE TABLEX       ;DX = 0014 (20)
```

Since TABLEX is defined as DW, the TYPE operator returns 0002. The LENGTH operator returns hex 000A based on the DUP entry. The SIZE operator returns type times length, or hex 14 (20). At the time of this writing, the use of TYPE with a FAR label returns hex FFFE. However, TYPE used with a NEAR label does not appear to assemble correctly. Also, two other operators, HIGH and LOW, do not appear to work the way the Assembler manual describes.

ASSEMBLER PSEUDO-OPERATIONS

This section describes most of the Assembler Pseudo-operations. The Pseudo-ops for defining data (DB, DW, etc.) are covered in detail in Chapter 4.

ASSUME

The purpose of ASSUME is to enable the Assembler to associate Segments with segment registers. Valid segment registers are CS, DS, ES, and SS. The general format is

ASSUME seg-reg:name [, ...]

Valid names are the names of segment registers, of Groups, and a SEG expression. You may assign up to four segment registers (in any sequence) with one ASSUME statement, as follows:

ASSUME CS:CODESG,DS:DATASG,SS:STACK,ES:DATASG

The use of the keyword NOTHING cancels any previous ASSUME for the specified segment register as follows:

ASSUME ES:NOTHING

Suppose that you do not assign the DS register or use NOTHING to cancel it. Then in order to reference a data item in the Data Segment, an instruction operand must make a specific reference to the DS register as follows:

```
MOV     AX,DS:[BX]      ;Use indexed address
MOV     AX,DS:FLDW      ;Move contents of FLDW
```

Of course, the DS register must contain a valid address! Note: CP/M-86 Assembler does not require an ASSUME Directive.

EXTRN

The purpose of the DOS EXTRN Pseudo-op is to inform the Assembler of variables and labels that this assembly references but that another assembly defines. The general format is

EXTRN name:type [, ...]

Chapter 16, "Subprograms," covers EXTRN in detail.

GROUP

A program may contain a number of Segments of the same type (Code, Data, Stack). The purpose of the DOS GROUP Pseudo-op is to collect them under one name so that they reside within a 64K Segment. The general format is

```
        name       GROUP       seg-name [, ...]
```

The following GROUP combines SEG1 and SEG2 in the same assembly module:

```
        GROUPX    GROUP       SEG1, SEG2
        SEG1      SEGMENT     PARA 'CODE'
                  ASSUME      CS:GROUPX
                  ...
        SEG1      ENDS
        ;
        SEG2      SEGMENT     PARA 'CODE'
                  ASSUME      CS:GROUPX
                  ...
        SEG2      ENDS
```

INCLUDE

You may have sections of assembly code or macro-instructions that various programs use. You can store these in separate disk files available for use by any program. Let's say that a routine that converts ASCII code to binary is stored on disk B in a file named CONVERT.LIB. To access the file, insert an INCLUDE statement such as

INCLUDE B:CONVERT.LIB

at the location in the source program where you would normally code the ASCII conversion routine. The Assembler locates the file on disk and includes the statements in with your own program. (If the Assembler cannot find the file, it issues an error message and ignores the INCLUDE.)

For each included line, the Assembler prints a C in column 30 of the LST file (column 33 begins the source code).

Chapter 15 on Macros gives a practical example of INCLUDE and explains how to include only for pass 1 of an assembly.

LABEL

The DOS LABEL Pseudo-op enables you to redefine the attribute of a defined name. The general format is

name   LABEL   type

You can use the type entry as BYTE, WORD, or DWORD to redefine data fields and the names of Structures and Records. You can also use LABEL to redefine executable code as NEAR or FAR. LABEL enables you, for example, to define a field as both DB and DW. The following illustrates the use of BYTE and WORD types:

```
      REDEFB   LABEL   BYTE
      FIELDW   DW      2532H
   ;
      REDEFW   LABEL   WORD
      FIELDB   DB      25H
               DB      32H
               ...
1.             MOV     AL,REDEFB    ;Move 1st byte
2.             MOV     BX,REDEFW    ;Move 2 bytes
```

The first MOV instruction moves the first byte of FIELDW only. The second MOV moves the two bytes beginning at FIELDB. The PTR operator also performs a similar function.

NAME

The DOS NAME Pseudo-op provides another way to assign a name to a module, coded as

NAME name

The Assembler selects the module name according to the following sequence:

1. If NAME is present, its operand becomes the name.
2. If NAME is not present, the Assembler uses the first six characters from TITLE, if any.
3. If neither NAME nor TITLE is present, the name of the source file becomes the module name.

The Assembler passes the selected name to the Linker. Since most programs likely use TITLE, the NAME Pseudo-op seems only marginally useful.

ORG

The Assembler uses a Location Counter to account for its relative position in a Data Segment or Code Segment. Assume that the Assembler is processing a Data Segment with the following definitions:

Offset	Name	Oper'n	Operand	Location Counter
00	FLDA	DW	2542H	02
02	FLDB	DB	36H	03
03	FLDC	DW	212EH	05
05	FLDD	DD	00000705H	09

Initially, the Location Counter is set to 00. Since FLDA is two bytes, the Location Counter is incremented to 02 for the location of the next item. Since FLDB is one byte, the Location Counter is incremented to 03, and so forth. You can use the ORG Pseudo-op to change the contents of the Location Counter and accordingly the location of the next defined items. The general format is

ORG   expression

The expression may be an absolute number, not a symbolic name, and must form a two-byte absolute number. Consider the following data items defined immediately after FLDD above:

Offset	Name	Oper'n	Operand	Location Counter
		ORG	0	00
00	FLDX	DB	?	01
01	FLDY	DW	?	02
03	FLDZ	DB	?	04
		ORG	$+5	09

The first ORG sets the Location Counter back to 00. The variables that follow, FLDX, FLDY, and FLDZ, define the same memory locations as FLDA, FLDB, and FLDC:

```
Offset:|   0   |   1   |   2   |   3   | 4 |   5   | 6 | 7 | 8 |
            |       |           |       |       |
          FLDA              FLDB    FLDC        FLDD
            |       |                   |
          FLDX    FLDY                FLDZ
```

An operand containing the dollar symbol ($) as in the second ORG above refers to the current value in the Location Counter. The operand $+5 therefore sets the Location Counter to 04 + 5, or 09, which is the same setting after the definition of FLDD.

A reference to FLDC is to a one-word field at offset 03, and a reference to FLDZ is to a one-byte field at offset 03:

```
MOV     AX,FLDC     ;One word
MOV     AL,FLDZ     ;One byte
```

You can use this ORG feature to redefine memory locations. But be sure that ORG sets the Location Counter back to the correct value and that you account for all redefined memory locations. Also, the redefined variables should not contain defined constants – these would overlay constants on top of the original constants. Note that you cannot use ORG within a STRUC definition.

PROC

A Procedure is a block of code that begins with the DOS PROC Pseudo-op and terminates with ENDP. A typical use is for a subroutine within the Code Segment.

Although technically you can enter a Procedure in-line or by a JMP instruction, the normal practice is to enter with CALL and to exit with RET.

A Procedure that is in the same Segment as the calling Procedure is a NEAR Procedure:

```
proc-name     PROC     [NEAR]
```

An omitted operand defaults to NEAR. If a Procedure is external to the calling Segment, you should use only CALL and the called Procedure must be declared as PUBLIC. Further, if the called Procedure is under a different ASSUME CS value, it must have the FAR attribute:

```
              PUBLIC     proc-name
proc-name     PROC       FAR
```

If you CALL a Procedure, be sure to use RET to exit from it.

PUBLIC

The purpose of the DOS PUBLIC Pseudo-op is to inform the Assembler that the identified symbols in an assembly are to be referenced by other assembly modules. The general format is

PUBLIC   symbol [, ...]

Chapter 16, "Subprograms," covers PUBLIC in detail.

RECORD

The DOS RECORD Pseudo-op enables you to define patterns of bits. One purpose would be to define switch indicators either as one bit or as multibit. The general format is:

record-name RECORD field-name:width[= exp] [, ...]

The record name and field names may be any unique valid identifiers. Following each field name is a colon (:) and a "width" — the number of bits. The range of the width entry is 1 to 16 bits:

No. of defined bits	Default size
1 - 8	8
9 - 16	16

Any length up to 8 becomes 8 bits, and 9 to 16 becomes 16, right-adjusted if necessary. The following example defines a Record:

BITREC RECORD BIT1:3,BIT2:7,BIT3:6

BIT1 defines the first 3 bits of BITREC, BIT2 defines the next 7, and BIT3 defines the last 6. The total is 16 bits, or one word.

You can initialize values in a RECORD as follows:

BITREC2 RECORD BIT1:3 = 101B,BIT2:7 = 0110110B,BIT3:6 = 011010B

Let's say that the definition of a RECORD is in front of the Data Segment. Within the Data Segment there should be another statement that allocates storage for the Record. Define a unique valid name, the record name, and an operand consisting of angle brackets (the less than, greater than symbols):

DEFBITS BITREC <>

The above allocation generates object code hex AD9A (stored as 9AAD) in the Data Segment.

The angle brackets may also contain entries that redefine BITREC. The program in Figure 18-1 illustrates defining BITREC as RECORD, but without initial values in the record fields. In this case, an allocation statement in the Data Segment initializes each field as shown within angle brackets.

Record-specific operators are WIDTH, shift count, and MASK. The use of these operators permits you to change the Record definition without having to change the instructions that reference the Record.

WIDTH

The WIDTH operator returns a width as the number of bits in a Record or in a Record field. For example, in Figure 18-1 following A10 are two examples of WIDTH. The first MOV returns the width of the entire Record BITREC (16 bits); the second MOV returns the width of the record field BIT2 (7 bits). In both cases, the Assembler has generated an immediate operand for the width.

> **Figure 18-1** Use of the RECORD Pseudo-op.

```
                       page    60,132
                 TITLE   TRECORD - Test of Record Pseudo-op
                 BITREC  RECORD  BIT1:3,BIT2:7,BIT3:6     ;Define record
                 ;-----------------------------------------------------
0000             STACKSG SEGMENT PARA STACK 'STACK'
0000  20 [ ???? ]        DW      32 DUP(?)
0040             STACKSG ENDS
                 ;-----------------------------------------------------
0000             DATASG  SEGMENT PARA 'DATA'
0000  9A AD      DEFBITS BITREC  <101B,0110110B,011010B> ;Init'ze record
0002             DATASG  ENDS
                 ;-----------------------------------------------------
0000             CODESG  SEGMENT PARA 'CODE'
0000             BEGIN   PROC    FAR
                         ASSUME  CS:CODESG,DS:DATASG,SS:STACKSG
0000  1E                 PUSH    DS
0001  2B C0              SUB     AX,AX
0003  50                 PUSH    AX
0004  B8   ---- R        MOV     AX,DATASG
0007  8E D8              MOV     DS,AX
0009             A10:                                    ;Width:
0009  B7 10              MOV     BH,WIDTH BITREC         ;  of record (16)
000B  B0 07              MOV     AL,WIDTH BIT2           ;  of field (07)
000D             B10:                                    ;Shift count:
000D  B1 0D              MOV     CL,BIT1                 ;  hex 0D
000F  B1 06              MOV     CL,BIT2                 ;       06
0011  B1 00              MOV     CL,BIT3                 ;       00
0013             C10:                                    ;Mask:
0013  B8 E000            MOV     AX,MASK BIT1            ;  hex E000
0016  BB 1FC0            MOV     BX,MASK BIT2            ;      1FC0
0019  B9 003F            MOV     CX,MASK BIT3            ;      003F
001C             D10:                                    ;Isolate BIT2:
001C  A1 0000 R          MOV     AX,DEFBITS              ;  get record
```

```
001F   25 1FC0              AND    AX,MASK BIT2    ;   clear BIT1 & 3
0022   B1 06                MOV    CL,BIT2         ;   get shift 06
0024   D3 E8                SHR    AX,CL           ;   shift right
0026              E10:                             ;Isolate BIT1:
0026   A1 0000 R            MOV    AX,DEFBITS      ;   get record
0029   B1 0D                MOV    CL,BIT1         ;   get shift 13
002B   D3 E8                SHR    AX,CL           ;   shift right
002D   CB                   RET
002E              BEGIN      ENDP

002E              CODESG     ENDS
                             END    BEGIN
```

Structures and records:

	Name	Width	# fields		
		Shift	Width	Mask	Initial
BITREC		0010	0003		
BIT1		000D	0003	E000	0000
BIT2		0006	0007	1FC0	0000
BIT3		0000	0006	003F	0000

Segments and groups:

	Name	Size	align	combine	class
CODESG		002E	PARA	NONE	'CODE'
DATASG		0002	PARA	NONE	'DATA'
STACKSG.		0040	PARA	STACK	'STACK'

Symbols:

	Name	Type	Value	Attr	
A10.		L NEAR	0009	CODESG	
B10.		L NEAR	000D	CODESG	
BEGIN.		F PROC	0000	CODESG	Length =002E
C10.		L NEAR	0013	CODESG	
D10.		L NEAR	001C	CODESG	
DEFBITS.		L WORD	0000	DATASG	
E10.		L NEAR	0026	CODESG	

Shift Count. A direct reference to a record field such as

MOV   CL,BIT2

does not refer to the contents of BIT2 (indeed, that would be rather difficult). Instead, the Assembler generates an immediate operand that contains a "shift count" to help you isolate the field. The immediate value represents the number of bits that you would have to shift BIT2 to right-adjust it. In

Figure 18-1, the three examples following B10 return the shift count for BIT1, BIT2, and BIT3.

MASK

The MASK operator returns a "mask" of 1-bits representing the specified field, and in effect defines the bit positions that the field occupies. For example, the MASK for each of the fields defined in BITREC are:

Field	Binary	Hex
BIT1	1110000000000000	E000
BIT2	0001111111000000	1FC0
BIT3	0000000000111111	003F

In Figure 18-1, the three instructions following C10 return the MASK values for BIT1, BIT2, and BIT3.

The instructions following D10 and E10, respectively, illustrate isolating BIT2 and BIT1 from BITREC. D10 gets the Record into the AX register and then ANDs it using a MASK of BIT2:

Record	101 0110110 011010
AND MASK BIT2:	000 1111111 000000
Result:	000 0110110 000000

The effect is to clear all bits except those of BIT2. The next two instructions cause the AX to shift six bits so that BIT2 is right-adjusted:

    0000000000110110   (hex 0036)

The example following E10 gets the Record into the AX, and because BIT1 is the leftmost field, the routine simply uses its shift factor to shift right 13 bits:

    0000000000000101   (hex 0005)

SEGMENT

A Segment is required for the Stack, for data definition, and for executable code. Any assembly module consists of one or more Segments, part of a Segment, or even parts of several Segments. The general format under PC-DOS and MS-DOS is

```
seg-name    SEGMENT [align] [combine] [class]
                    .
                    .
                    .
seg-name    ENDS
```

All operands are optional. The following describes the entries:

align: Indicates the starting boundary for the Segment, where x represents a hex digit:

PAGE = xxx00
PARA = xxxx0 (default boundary)
WORD = xxxxe (even)
BYTE = xxxxx

combine: Indicates the way the Linker is to handle the Segment.

NONE (default): The Segment is to be logically separate from other Segments, although it may end up to be physically adjacent. The Segment is presumed to have its own base address.

PUBLIC: Link loads PUBLIC Segments of the same name and class adjacent to one another. There is presumed to be one base address for all such PUBLIC Segments.

STACK: The Linker treats STACK the same as PUBLIC. There must be at least one STACK defined in a linked program. If there is more than one Stack, the Stack Pointer (SP) is set to the starting address of the first Stack Segment.

COMMON: If COMMON Segments have the same name and class, the Linker gives them the same base address. For execution, the second Segment overlays the first one. The largest Segment determines the length of the common area.

AT paragraph-address: The Paragraph must be previously defined. The entry facilitates defining labels and variables at fixed offsets within fixed areas of memory, such as ROM or the interrupt table in low memory. For example, the code in ROM defines the location of the video display buffer as:

VIDEO_RAM SEGMENT AT 0B800H

'class':   This entry may contain any legal name, contained in single quotes. The Linker uses it to relate Segments that have the same name and class. Typical examples are 'STACK' and 'CODE'.

The Linker combines the following two Segments into one physical Segment. The two Segments form one Segment under the same segment register:

Assembly module 1	SEG1	SEGMENT PARA PUBLIC 'CODE' ASSUME CS:SEG1
		...
	SEG1	ENDS
Assembly module 2	SEG2	SEGMENT PARA PUBLIC 'CODE' ASSUME CS:SEG1
		...
	SEG2	ENDS

You may nest Segments provided that the nested Segment is completely nested within the other:

```
SEG1   SEGMENT
          ...          SEG1 begins
SEG2   SEGMENT
          ...          SEG2 area
SEG2   ENDS
          ...          SEG1 resumes
SEG1   ENDS
```

For combining Segments into Groups, see the GROUP Pseudo-op. CP/M note: Each Segment requires a unique Directive: CSEG, DSEG, and SSEG.

STRUC

The DOS STRUC (not supported by the small Assembler) Pseudo-op facilitates defining related fields within a "Structure." Its general format is

```
struc-name STRUC
     ...
[ defined fields ]
     ...
struc-name ENDS
```

A Structure begins with its name and the Pseudo-op STRUC and terminates with the structure name and the Pseudo-op ENDS. The Assembler stores the contained defined fields one after the other from the start of the Structure. Valid entries are DB, DW, DD, DQ, and DT definitions with optional field names.

Refer now to Figure 18-2. The STRUC defines a parameter list named PARLIST for input of a name from the keyboard. The Data Segment contains an entry that allocates storage for the Structure:

PARAMS   PARLIST   <>

The allocate statement makes the Structure addressable within the Data Segment. The angle brackets (less than, greater than symbols) in the operand are empty in this example, but you may use them to redefine ("override") data within a Structure.

Figure 18-2 Example Structure.

```
                        page    60,132
                        TITLE   TSTRUC  Definition of a Structure
                        ;-------------------------------------------------
                        PARLIST STRUC                       ;Parameter list
0000 19                 MAXLEN  DB      25                  ;
0001 ??                 ACTLEN  DB      ?                   ;
0002 19 [ 20 ]  ]       NAMEIN  DB      25 DUP(' ')         ;
001B 24                         DB      '$'                 ;
001C                    PARLIST ENDS                        ;
                        ;-------------------------------------------------
0000                    STACKSG SEGMENT PARA STACK 'STACK'
0000 20 [ ???? ]                DW      32 DUP(?)
0040                    STACKSG ENDS
                        ;-------------------------------------------------
0000                    DATASG  SEGMENT PARA 'DATA'
0000 19                 PARAMS  PARLIST <>                  ;Allocate structure
0001 ??
0002 19 [   20   ]
001B 24
001C 57 68 61 74 20 69 PROMPT  DB      'What is name?','$'
     73 20 6E 61 6D 65
     3F 24
002A                    DATASG  ENDS
                        ;-------------------------------------------------
0000                    CODESG  SEGMENT PARA 'CODE'
0000                    BEGIN   PROC    FAR
                                ASSUME  CS:CODESG,DS:DATASG,SS:STACKSG
0000 1E                         PUSH    DS
0001 2B C0                      SUB     AX,AX
0003 50                         PUSH    AX
0004 B8   ---- R                MOV     AX,DATASG
```

```
0007 8E D8                          MOV     DS,AX
0009 E8 0013 R                      CALL    B10PROM
000C E8 001C R                      CALL    C10INPT
000F A0 0001 R                      MOV     AL,PARAMS.ACTLEN   ;Length of input
                         ;          ...
0012 CB                             RET
0013                     BEGIN      ENDP
                         ;                  Display prompt message:
                         ;                  -----------------------
0013                     B10PROM PROC
0013 8D 16 001C R                   LEA     DX,PROMPT          ;Prompt
0017 B4 09                          MOV     AH,09              ;Set display function
0019 CD 21                          INT     21H                ;Call DOS
001B C3                             RET
001C                     B10PROM ENDP
                         ;                  Accept input name:
                         ;                  ------------------
001C                     C10INPT PROC
001C 8D 16 0000 R                   LEA     DX,PARAMS          ;Addr of parameter
C020 B4 0A                          MOV     AH,0AH             ;Set input function
0022 CD 21                          INT     21H                ;Call DOS
0024 C3                             RET
0025                     C10INPT ENDP

0025                     CODESG  ENDS
                                 END     BEGIN
```

```
Structures and records:
                  N a m e             Width # fields
                                      Shift  Width   Mask    Initial

PARLIST. . . . . . . . . . . . .  001C   0004
    MAXLEN . . . . . . . . . . . .  0000
    ACTLEN . . . . . . . . . . . .  0001
    NAMEIN . . . . . . . . . . . .  0002

Segments and groups:
                  N a m e             Size   align   combine class

CODESG . . . . . . . . . . . . .  0025   PARA    NONE    'CODE'
DATASG . . . . . . . . . . . . .  002A   PARA    NONE    'DATA'
STACKSG. . . . . . . . . . . . .  0040   PARA    STACK   'STACK'

Symbols:
                  N a m e             Type   Value   Attr

B10PROM. . . . . . . . . . . . .  N PROC  0013   CODESG  Length =0009
BEGIN. . . . . . . . . . . . . .  F PROC  0000   CODESG  Length =0013
C10INPT. . . . . . . . . . . . .  N PROC  001C   CODESG  Length =0009
PARAMS . . . . . . . . . . . . .  L 001C  0000   DATASG
PROMPT . . . . . . . . . . . . .  L BYTE  001C   DATASG
```

Instructions in the Code Segment may reference the Structure name directly. However, to reference fields within a Structure, instructions must qualify them by using the allocate name of the Structure (PARAMS in the example) followed by a period that connects it with the field name as follows:

MOV   AL,PARAMS.ACTLEN

You can use the allocate statement to redefine the contents of fields within a Structure. For the rules of this practice, see the manual for your Assembler version.

19

DOS PROGRAM LOADER

Objective:
To describe the DOS requirements
for loading an executable module into
memory for execution.

INTRODUCTION

This chapter describes the general DOS organization and the steps that DOS takes in loading an executable module into memory for execution. DOS consists of four programs each of which provides a particular service:

    1. The Boot Record. The FORMAT command copies the boot record onto track 0, sector 1, of your diskette. When you initiate the system (assuming that the DOS diskette is in drive A), the system automatically loads the boot record from disk into memory. This program then loads the rest of DOS (the three programs described next) from disk into memory.

    2. IBMBIO.COM. This program loads in memory beginning at hex 00600 and is a low-level interface to the BIOS routines in ROM. On initiation, IBMBIO.COM determines device and equipment status and then loads COMMAND.COM. IBMBIO.COM handles input/output between main memory and external devices such as the video monitor and diskette.

3. IBMDOS.COM. This program loads into memory beginning at hex 00B00 and is a high-level interface to programs. IBMDOS.COM manages the Directory and files on diskette, handles blocking and deblocking of disk records, handles INT 21H functions, and also contains a number of other service functions.

4. COMMAND.COM. This program handles the various commands that you enter and runs requested programs. COMMAND.COM consists of three parts: a resident portion, an initialization portion, and a transient portion. These portions are loaded into high memory in separate areas. COMMAND.COM, covered in detail in the next section, is of particular interest because it is responsible for loading executable programs from diskette into memory.

Table 19-1 shows a map of the various interrupt and DOS programs in memory.

Table 19-1 Map of DOS in Memory.

Beginning address:	Program:
00000	Interrupt vector table (details in Chapter 17)
00400	ROM communication area
00500	DOS communication area
00600	IBMBIO.COM

XXXX0	IBMDOS.COM:
	    Directory buffer
	    Disk buffer
	    Drive parameter block/file allocation
	    table (FAT, one for each disk drive)

XXXX0	Resident portion of COMMAND.COM
XXXX0	External command or utility (COM or EXE files)
XXXX0	User Stack for COM files (256 bytes)
XXXX0	Transient portion of COMMAND.COM, stored in the highest portion of memory.

COMMAND.COM

The system loads the three portions of COMMAND.COM into memory either permanently during a session or temporarily as required. The following describes the three parts of COMMAND.COM in detail.

1. The Resident Portion is loaded immediately following IBMDOS.COM (and its data areas), where it resides during processing. The Resident portion handles all errors for disk I/O and the following types of interrupts:

INT 22H	Terminate address
INT 23H	Ctrl/Break handler
INT 24H	Error detection on disk read/write or a bad memory image of the File Allocation Table (FAT).
INT 27H	Terminate but stay resident.

2. The Initialization Portion immediately follows the resident portion and contains the AUTOEXEC file processor setup. After you start up the system, this portion initially takes control and performs the following:

□   Prompts for the date.

□   Determines the Segment address where the system is to load programs for execution.

None of these initialization routines is required again during a session. Consequently, the first command that you enter causes a program to load from disk and to overlay this section of memory. This area is known as the Program Segment.

3. The Transient Portion is loaded into the highest area of memory. "Transient" implies that DOS loads various routines into this area as required. Other than a small permanent "kernel" routine, the system overlays one program with another.

This portion of COMMAND.COM displays the A› prompt, reads requests, and executes them. It contains routines to load COM and EXE files from disk into memory for execution.

```
----------------------
```
COMMAND.COM
(resident)
```
----------------------
```
Program
Segment
Prefix
```
----------------------
```
Executable
program
```
----------------------
```

COMMAND.COM contains a relocation loader facility that determines where your program is to load in memory for execution. When you request execution of a program, the transient portion constructs a Program Segment Prefix (PSP) immediately following the resident portion of COMMAND.COM. It then loads your requested executable program from disk into offset hex 100 of the Program Segment, sets exit addresses, and gives control to your loaded program.

On completion of execution, your program executes an RET which causes a return to COMMAND.COM. Now let's examine the Program Segment Prefix in detail.

PROGRAM SEGMENT PREFIX

COMMAND.COM constructs a Program Segment Prefix (PSP) for each program that is to execute. The PSP is 256 (hex 100) bytes in size.

COMMAND.COM loads the program that is to execute immediately following the PSP. The Program Segment Prefix contains the following fields:

Relative hex Position:	Contents:
0	An INT 20H instruction.
2	Total size of memory, as xxxx0. For example, 64K is indicated as hex 1000 instead of hex 10000
4	Reserved
6	Long call to DOS for dispatcher Terminate address Ctrl/Break address (IP)
10	Ctrl/Break exit address (CS)
12	Reserved
5C	Formatted parameter area 1 (formatted as standard unopened FCB)
6C	Formatted parameter area 2 (formatted as standard unopened FCB; overlaid if FCB at hex 5C is opened)
80-FF	Default buffer for Disk Transfer Area (DTA)

LOADING A PROGRAM

The Linker produces an EXE module that consists of the following two parts:

1. A header record containing control and relocation information.
2. The actual load module.

The header record contains information about the size of the executable module, where it is to be loaded in memory, the address of the SS register, and relocation offsets to be inserted into incomplete machine addresses. The header contains the following fields:

Relative Hex Position:	Field:
00	Hex 4D5A. The Linker inserts this code to identify the file as a valid EXE file
02	Reserved
04	Size of the file including the header, in 512-byte increments ("pages")
06	Number of relocation table items following the formatted portion of the header
08	Size of the header in 16-byte increments. The purpose of this field is to help locate the start of the executable module that follows this header
0A	Reserved
0C	High/low loader switch. You decide at the start of LINK whether your program is to load for execution at a low (the usual) or a high memory address. Hex 0000 indicates high and hex FFFF indicates low
0E	Offset location in the executable module of the Stack Segment
10	Address that the Loader is to insert in the SP register when transferring control to the executable module
12	Checksum value – the sum of all the words in the file (ignoring overflows) used as a validation check for lost data
14	The offset that the Loader is to insert in the IP register when transferring control to the executable module
16	The offset location in the executable module of the Code Segment

Relative Hex Position:	Field:
18	The offset of the first relocation item in this file
1A	Reserved
1B	Relocation table containing a variable number of relocation items, as identified at offset 06

Position 06 of the header indicates the number of items in the executable module that are to be relocated. Each relocation item (beginning at header position 1B) consists of a two-byte offset value and a two-byte segment value.

The system constructs the Program Segment Prefix following the resident portion of COMMAND.COM which performs the load operation. The following are the steps that COMMAND.COM performs:

□ Reads the formatted part of the header into memory.
□ Calculates the size of the executable module (total file size in position 04 minus header size in position 08) and reads the module into memory at the start segment.
□ Reads the relocation table items into a work area and adds the value of each table item to the stack segment value (position 0E).
□ Sets the SS and SP registers to the values in the header and adds the start segment value to the SS.
□ Sets the DS and ES registers to the segment address of the Program Segment Prefix.
□ Adds the segment value to the CS value in the header (position 16) and then uses the value in the CS and the IP to give control to the executable EXE module. At this point, your program begins to execute.

EXAMPLE EXECUTABLE PROGRAM

Let's assume that the MAP for a linked program appears as follows:

Start	Stop	Length	Name	Class
00000H	00013H	0014H	CSEG	CODE
00020H	0003DH	001EH	DSEG	DATA
00040H	0013FH	0100H	STACK	STACK

Program entry point at 0000:0000

The MAP provides the relative location (not the actual) of each of the three Segments. The H following each value indicates hexadecimal format. Note that the Linker arranges these Segments in a sequence that may differ from the sequence in which you coded them.

According to the MAP, the Code Segment, named CSEG, is to start at 00000 – its relative location is the beginning of the executable module, and its length is hex 0014 bytes. The next Segment, named DSEG, begins at hex 00020. This is the first address following CSEG that aligns on a Paragraph boundary (evenly divisible by hex 10). The length of DSEG is hex 001E. The last Segment, STACK, begins at hex 00040, the first address following DSEG that aligns on a Paragraph boundary.

When the program was loaded under DEBUG, the registers contained the following:

$$SP = 0040 \quad DS = 049F \quad ES = 049F$$
$$SS = 04B3 \quad CS = 04AF \quad IP = 0000$$

For EXE modules, the Loader sets the DS and ES to the address of the Program Segment Prefix and sets the CS, IP, SS, and SP to values from the header record.

SP Register

The Stack Pointer is initialized to the length of the Stack. In this example, the Stack was defined as 32 DUP(?), that is, 32 two-byte fields = 64, or hex 40. The SP points to the current top of the Stack.

CS Register

According to the DS register in the MAP, the address of the Program Segment Prefix is at hex 049F(0). Since the PSP is hex 100 bytes long, the executable module follows immediately at hex 49F0 + 100 = 4AF0—you can see that address in the CS register. The CS register indicates the starting address of the code portion (CSEG) of the program. You can use the DEBUG dump command

D CS:0000

to view the machine code in memory and note that it is identical to the Assembler LST printout (other than operands tagged as R).

SS Register

The Loader has also set the SS register correctly:

Start address (see DS in the map)	49F0	
Length of Program Segment Prefix	100	
Offset of the Stack (see the map)	40	
Address of the Stack	4B30	(4B3 in map)

DS Register

The Loader used the DS register to establish the starting point for the Program Segment Prefix. This address is not suitable for your executable program. Technically, the Loader appears to be able to set up the correct segment address based on the following values:

Start address	49F0
Length of PSP	100
Start position on map	20
Address of DS	4B10

One reason why the Loader requires you to initialize the DS register is because a program may define more than one Data Segment. Consequently, you have to load the DS yourself, as follows:

```
0004 B8 ---- R    MOV AX,DSEG
0007 8E D8        MOV DS,AX
```

The Assembler has left unfilled the machine address of DSEG – this address becomes an entry in the Relocation Table in the header, discussed earlier. DEBUG shows the completed instruction as

B8 B104

B104 loads into the DS as 04B1. This address happens to be the same one we derived earlier. The address is stored in the DS register without the rightmost zero. For an exercise, you could trace any of your linked programs through DEBUG and note the changed values in the registers:

Instruction		Register Changed
PUSH	DS	IP and SP
SUB	AX,AX	IP and AX (if already nonzero)
PUSH	AX	IP and SP
MOV	AX,DSEG	IP and AX
MOV	DS,AX	IP and DS

After this point, the DS contains the correct address of the Data Segment. You can now view the contents of DSEG by using

D DS:00

And by the same procedure, you could view the contents of the Stack Segment by any of the following commands:

D SS:00
D CS:40   (Stack is hex 40 bytes from CSEG)
D DS:20   (Stack is hex 20 bytes from DSEG)

20

INSTRUCTION REFERENCE

Objective:
To explain machine code and to provide
a description of the instruction set.

INTRODUCTION

This chapter explains the machine code of the 8086/8088 instruction set
and provides an alphabetic listing of every symbolic instruction with an
explanation of its purpose.

Many instructions have a specific purpose so that a one-byte instruction code is adequate. The following are examples:

Obj. code:	Symbolic instruction:	
40	INC AX	;Increment the AX
50	PUSH AX	;Push the AX
C3	RET (short)	;Short return from a Procedure
CB	RET (far)	;Far return from a Procedure
FD	STD	;Set Direction Flag

None of the above instructions makes a direct reference to a memory location. Other instructions that specify an immediate operand, an eight-bit register, two registers, or a reference to memory require more complex machine code.

REGISTER NOTATION

Instructions that reference a register may have to indicate which register, and whether it is 8-or 16-bit. The instruction may contain three bits that indicate the particular register and a "w" bit that signifies if the "width" is byte or word. Also, only certain instructions may access the segment registers. Table 20-1 shows the complete register notations.

Table 20-1 Register Notation.

General, Bits	Base, and Index Registers: w = 0	w = 1	Bits:	Segment register:
000	AL	AX	00	ES
001	CL	CX	01	CS
010	DL	DX	10	SS
011	BL	BX	11	DS
100	AH	SP		
101	CH	BP		
110	DH	SI		
111	BH	DI		

Let's examine a MOV instruction that has a one-byte immediate operand:

MOV AH,00   10110 100 00000000
         w reg = AH

In this case, the first byte of machine code indicates a width of one byte (w = 0) and refers to the AH register (100). Here's a MOV instruction that contains a one-word immediate operand:

MOV AX,00   10111 000 00000000 00000000
         w reg = AX

The first byte of machine code indicates a width of one word (w = 1) and refers to the AX register (000). But don't generalize too much from these examples—for other instructions, w and reg may occupy different positions.

ADDRESSING MODE BYTE

The *mode byte*, where it exists, always occupies the second byte of machine code and consists of the following three elements:

1. mod   A two-bit mode, where 11 refers to a register and 00, 01, and 10 reference a memory location.

2. reg   A three-bit reference to a register.

3. r/m   A three-bit reference to register or memory, where r signifies which register and m indicates a memory address.

As well, the first byte of machine code may contain a "d" bit that indicates the direction of flow between operand 1 and operand 2.

Here's an example of adding the AX to the BX:

ADD BX,AX   00000011   11   011   000
                 dw   mod   reg   r/m

In this example, d = 1 means that mod (11) and reg (011) describe operand 1 and r/m (000) describes operand 2. Since w = 1, the width is a word. Therefore, the instruction is to add the AX (000) to the BX (011).

The second byte of the object instruction indicates most modes of addressing memory. The next section examines the addressing mode in more detail.

The MOD Bits

The two mod bits distinguish between addressing of registers and memory. The following explains their purpose:

00   Indicates that the r/m bits supply the exact addressing option, and there is no offset byte.

01   Indicates that the r/m bits supply the exact addressing option, and there is one offset byte.

10   Indicates that the r/m bits supply the exact addressing option, and there are two offset bytes.

11   Indicates that the r/m specifies a register. The "w" bit (in the operation code byte) determines if a reference is to an 8- or 16-bit register.

The REG Bits

The 3 reg bits, in association with the w bit, determine the actual register, either 8- or 16-bit.

The R/M Bits

The 3 r/m (register/memory) bits, in association with mod, determine the addressing mode, as shown in Table 20-2.

Table 20-2 The r/m Bits.

r/m	mod = 00	mod = 01	mod = 10	mod = 11 w = 0	mod = 11 w = 1
000	BX + SI	BX + SI + disp	BX + SI + disp	AL	AX
001	BX + DI	BX + DI + disp	BX + DI + disp	CL	CX
010	BP + SI	BP + SI + disp	BP + SI + disp	DL	DX
011	BP + DI	BP + DI + disp	BP + DI + disp	BL	BX
100	SI	SI + disp	SI + disp	AH	SP
101	DI	DI + disp	DI + disp	CH	BP
110	Direct	BP + disp	BP + disp	DH	SI
111	BX	BX + disp	BX + disp	BH	DI

EXAMPLE TWO-BYTE INSTRUCTIONS

The first example adds the AX to the BX:

ADD   BX,AX   0000 0011   11   011 000
                    dw   mod   reg r/m

d   1 implies that reg plus w describe operand 1 (BX), and mod plus r/m plus w describe operand 2 (AX).

w   1 indicates that the width is word.

mod   11 means that operand 2 is a register.

reg   011 means that operand 1 is the BX register.

r/m   000 means that operand 2 is the AX register.

The second example multiplies the AL by the BL:

        MUL   BL   11110110   11   100 011
                                    w   mod reg r/m

The MUL instruction assumes that the AL contains the multiplicand. The width (w = 0) is byte, mod references a register, and the register is the BL (011). Reg = 100 is not meaningful here.

EXAMPLE THREE-BYTE INSTRUCTION

The following MOV instruction generates three bytes of machine code:

        MOV   mem,AX   10100001 dddddddd dddddddd

A move from the accumulator (AX or AL) needs to know only if the operation is byte or word. In this example, w = 1 means word, and the 16-bit AX is understood. Use of AL in operand-2 would cause the w bit to be 0. Byte-2 and byte-3 contain the offset to the memory location. Note that instructions using the accumulator often generate shorter and more efficient machine code.

EXAMPLE FOUR-BYTE INSTRUCTIONS

For MUL, the processor assumes that the multiplicand is in the AL if byte and in the AX if word.

        MUL   mem_byte   11110110   00   100   110
                                        w   mod   reg   r/m

For this instruction, reg is always 100. Mod = 00 indicates a memory reference, and r/m = 110 means a direct reference to memory. The machine instruction also contains two bytes following which provide the offset to this memory location.

The second example illustrates the LEA instruction, which always specifies a word address.

        LEA   DX,mem   10001101   00   010 110
                            LEA   mod reg r/m

Reg = 010 designates the DX register. Mod = 00 and r/m = 110 indicate a direct reference to a memory address. Two following bytes provide the offset to this location.

These are only some random examples of how to interpret machine code. If you are interested in other examples, refer to the machine code of any of your programs and relate it to the explanation of the mode byte.

INSTRUCTIONS IN ALPHABETICAL SEQUENCE

This section covers the complete instruction set of the 8086/8088 processors in alphabetic sequence. Some instructions such as shift and rotate are grouped together for brevity. In addition to the preceding discussion of the mode byte and the width bit, the following abbreviations are relevant:

addr	Address of a memory location.
addr-high	The rightmost byte of an address.
addr-low	The leftmost byte of an address.
data	An immediate operand (8-bit if $w = 0$ and 16-bit if $w = 1$).
data-high	The rightmost byte of an immediate operand.
data-low	The leftmost byte of an immediate operand.
disp	Displacement (offset value).
reg	A reference to a register.

AAA: ASCII Adjust for Addition

Purpose: Corrects addition of two ASCII bytes.

Function: The AL would contain the sum of two ASCII bytes. If the rightmost four bits of AL have a value greater than 9 or if the AF Flag is set to 1, AAA adds 1 to the AH and sets the AF and CF Flags. The instruction always clears the leftmost four bits of the AL. AAA has no operands.

Flags: Affects AF and CF (OF, PF, SF, and ZF are undefined).

Object code: 00110111

AAD: ASCII Adjust for Division

Purpose: Corrects for division of ASCII values.

Function: Use AAD before dividing into an unpacked decimal value in the AX (the ASCII 3's should be stripped out). AAD corrects the dividend to a binary value in the AL for a subsequent binary divide. It multiplies the AH by 10, adds the product to the AL, and clears the AH. AAD has no operands.

Flags: Affects PF, SF, ZF (AF, CF, and OF are undefined).

Object code: |11010101|00001010|

AAM: ASCII Adjust for Multiplication

Purpose: Corrects the product generated by multiplying two unpacked decimal values.

Function: Use AAM after multiplying two unpacked decimal values. AAM divides the AL by 10 and stores the quotient in the AH and the remainder in the AL. AAM has no operands.

Flags: Affects PF, SF, and ZF (AF, CF, and OF are undefined).

Object code: |11010100|00001010|

AAS: ASCII Adjust for Subtraction

Purpose: Corrects subtraction of two ASCII bytes.

Function: The AL would contain the result of subtracting two ASCII numbers. If the rightmost four bits of the AL have a value greater than 9 or if the CF Flag is set to 1, AAS subtracts 6 from the AL, subtracts 1 from the AH, and sets the AF and CF Flags. The instruction always clears the leftmost four bits of the AL. AAS has no operands.

Flags: Affects AF and CF (OF, PF, SF, and ZF are undefined).

Object code: 00111111

ADC: Add with Carry

Purpose: Typically used in multiword binary addition to carry an over-flowed 1-bit into the next stage of arithmetic.

Function: If the CF Flag is set, ADC first adds 1 to operand 1. The instruction always adds operand 2 to operand 1, just as ADD does.

Flags: Affects AF, CF, OF, PF, SF, and ZF.

Object code (three formats):

```
Reg/mem with reg: |000100dw|modregr/m |
Immed to accum'r: |0001010w|data        |data if w = 1|
Immed to reg/mem:| 100000sw|mod010r/m| ---data---- |data if sw = 01|
```

ADD: Add Binary Numbers

Purpose: Adds two binary numbers.

Function: ADD adds byte or word values in memory, register, or immediate to a register, or adds byte or word values in a register or immediate to memory.

Flags: Affects AF, CF, OF, PF, SF, and ZF.

Object code (three formats):

```
Reg/mem with reg: |000000dw|modregr/m |
Immed to accum'r: |0000010w|--data--    |data if w = 1|
Immed to reg/mem:|100000sw|mod000r/m| ---data----  |data if sw = 01|
```

AND: Logical AND

Purpose: Performs a logical AND operation on bits of two operands. See also OR, XOR, and TEST.

Function: The two operands are both bytes or both words in a register or memory; operand 2 may be immediate. AND matches the two operands bit for bit. If both matched bits are 1, AND sets the operand 1 bit to 1; otherwise it is set to 0.

Flags: Affects CF, OF, PF, SF, and ZF (AF is undefined).

Object code (three formats):

```
Reg/mem with reg: |001000dw |modregr/m  |
Immed to accum'r: |0010010w |--data--      |data if w = 1|
Immed to reg/mem:|10100000w|mod 100 r/m| ---data----   |data if w = 1|
```

CALL: Call a Procedure

Purpose: Calls a near or far Procedure for subroutine linkage. The normal practice is to return from the Procedure using RET.

Function: CALL decrements the SP by 2 and pushes the address of the next instruction (in the IP) onto the Stack. It then loads the IP with the destination offset address. A subsequent RET instruction undoes these steps on return. There are four types of CALL instructions for transferring within and between Segments. If an intersegment CALL, the instruction first decrements the SP, pushes the CS onto the Stack, and loads an intersegment pointer onto the Stack.

Flags: None.

Object code (four formats):

> Direct within Segment:|11101000| disp-low |disp-high|
> Indir. within Segment: |11111111|mod010r/m|
> Indirect intersegment: |11111111|mod011r/m|
> Direct intersegment:
> > |10011010|offset-low|offset-high|seg-low |seg-high|

CBW: Convert Byte to Word

Purpose: Extends a one-byte arithmetic value to a word. See also CWD.

Function: The byte value should be in the AL. CBW duplicates the sign (bit 7) of the AL through the AH. Thus, a 0-bit or 1-bit extends through each of the bits in the AL. CBW has no operands.

Flags: None.

Object code: 10011000

CLC: Clear Carry Flag

Purpose: Clears the Carry (CF) Flag. The effect is that an ADC, for example, does not add a 1-bit. See also STD.

Function: Clears the CF Flag to 0. CLC has no operands.

Flags: CF (becomes 0).

Object code: 11111000

CLD: Clear Direction Flag

Purpose: Clears the Direction (DF) Flag. The effect is to cause string operations such as CMPS and MOVS to process from left to right. See also STD.

Function: CLD clears the DF Flag to 0. CLD has no operands.

Flags: DF (becomes 0).

Object code: 11111100

CLI: Clear Interrupt Flag

Purpose: Disables maskable external interrupts which appear on the processor's INTR line. See also STI.

Function: Clears the IF Flag to 0. CLI has no operands.

Flags: IF (becomes 0).

Object code: 11111010

CMC: Complement Carry Flag

Purpose: Complements the Carry (CF) Flag.

Function: CMC reverses the CF bit value – 0 becomes 1 and 1 becomes 0. CMC has no operands.

Flags: CF (reversed).

Object code: 11110101

CMP: Compare

Purpose: Compares the contents of two data fields.

Function: CMP internally subtracts operand 2 from operand 1, but does not change the values. Operands should be either both byte or both word. CMP may compare register, memory, or immediate to a register, or compare register or immediate to memory.

Flags: Affects AF, CF, OF, PF, SF, and ZF.

Object code (three formats):

```
Reg/mem with reg: |001110dw|modregr/m |
Immed to accum'r: |0011110w|---data----  |data if w = 1|
Immed to reg/mem:| 100000sw|mod111r/m|---data----   |data if sw = 0|
```

CMPS/CMPSB/CMPSW: Compare Byte or Word String

Purpose: Compares strings of any length.

Function: These instructions are normally used with a REPE prefix, for example as REPE CMPSB. CMPSB compares bytes and CMPSW compares words in memory. The DS:SI registers address operand 1 and the ES:DI registers address operand 2. If the DF Flag is 0, the operation compares from left to right and increments the SI and DI. If the DF is 1, the operation compares from right to left and decrements the SI and DI.

Flags: Affects AF, CF, OF, PF, SF, and ZF.

Object code: 1010011w

CWD: Convert Word to Doubleword

Purpose: Extends a one-word arithmetic value to a doubleword. See also CBW.

Function: CWD duplicates the sign (bit 15) of the AX through the DX, typically to generate a 16-bit dividend. CWD has no operands.

Flags: None.

Object code: 10011001

DAA: Decimal Adjust for Addition

Purpose: Corrects the result of adding two BCD (packed decimal) fields. See also DAS.

Function: The AL would contain the sum of two BCD bytes. If the rightmost four bits of the AL have a value greater than 9 or the AF Flag is 1, DAA adds 6 to the AL and sets the AF. If the AL contains a value greater than hex 9F or the CF Flag is 1, DAA adds hex 60 to the AL and sets the CF Flag. DAA has no operands.

Flags: Affects AF, CF, PF, SF, and ZF (OF undefined).

Object code: 00100111

DAS: Decimal Adjust for Subtraction

Purpose: Corrects the result of subtracting two BCD (packed- decimal) fields. See also DAA.

Function: The AL would contain the result of subtracting two BCD bytes. If the rightmost four bits of the AL have a value greater than 9 or the AF is 1, DAS subtracts hex 60 from the AL and sets the CF Flag. DAS has no operands.

Flags: Affects AF, CF, PF, SF, and ZF.

Object code: 00101111

DEC: Decrement by 1

Purpose: Decrements a value by 1. See also INC.

Function: DEC subtracts 1 from a byte or word in a register or memory, used for example as DEC CX.

Flags: Affects AF, OF, PF, SF, and ZF.

Object code (two formats):

Register: |01001reg |
Reg/memory:|1111111w | mod001r/m|

DIV: Divide

Purpose: Divides an unsigned dividend (16 or 32-bit) by an unsigned divisor (8-or 16-bit).

Function: DIV treats a leftmost 1-bit as a data bit, not a minus sign. A 16-bit dividend is in the AX and its 8-bit divisor is in a register or memory, coded, for example, as DIV BH. The quotient is generated in the AL and the remainder in the AH. A 32-bit dividend is in the DX:AX and its 16-bit divisor is in a register or memory, coded, for example, as DIV CX. The quotient is generated in the AX and the remainder in the DX.

Flags: Affects AF, CF, OF, PF, SF, and ZF (all undefined).

Object code: |1111011w|mod110r/m|

ESC: Escape

Purpose: Facilitates use of coprocessors to perform special operations.

Function: Although the 8086/8088 processors have a large instruction repertoire, there are some operations that require the use of a coprocessor such as the 8087 NDP for floating point. The coprocessor scans the instructions that the 8086/8088 are to execute. An ESC instruction provides the coprocessor with an instruction and operand for execution.

Flags: None.

Object code: |11011xxx|modxxxr/m|(x-bits are not important)

HLT: Enter Halt State

Purpose: Causes the processor to enter its halt state while waiting for an interrupt.

Function: HLT is usually associated with interrupts. It causes the processor to terminate with the CS and IP registers pointing to the instruction following the HLT. When an interrupt occurs, the processor pushes the CS and IP on the Stack and executes the interrupt routine. On its return the IRET instruction pops the Stack and processing resumes following the original HLT. HLT has no operands.

Flags: None.

Object code: 11110100

IDIV: Integer (Signed) Division

Purpose: Divides a signed dividend (16 or 32-bit) by a signed divisor (8-or 16-bit). See also DIV.

Function: IDIV treats a leftmost 1-bit as a negative sign. A 16-bit dividend is in the AX and its 8-bit divisor is in a register or memory, coded, for example, as IDIV DL. The quotient is generated in the AL and remainder in the AH. A 32-bit dividend is in the DX:AX and its 16-bit divisor is in a register or memory, coded, for example, as IDIV BX. The quotient is generated in the AX and the remainder in the DX. See CBW and CWD to extend the length of a signed dividend.

Flags: AF, CF, OF, PF, SF, and ZF.

Object code: |1111011w|mod111r/m|

IMUL: Integer (Signed) Multiplication

Purpose: Multiplies a signed multiplicand (8-or 16-bit) by a signed multiplier (8-or 16-bit). See also MUL.

Function: IMUL treats a leftmost 1-bit as a negative sign. For 8-bit multiplication, the multiplicand is in the AL and the multiplier is in a register or memory, coded, for example, as IMUL BL. The product is developed in the AX. For 16-bit multiplication, the multiplicand is in the AX and the multiplier is in a register or memory, coded, for example, as IMUL BX. The product is developed in the DX:AX.

Flags: Affects CF and OF (AF, PF, SF, and ZF are undefined).

Object code: |1111011w|mod101r/m|

IN: Input Byte or Word

Purpose: Accepts data from a port. See also OUT.

Function: IN transfers from an input port a byte to the AL or a word to the AX. You can code the port as a fixed numeric operand (as IN AX,port#) or as a variable in the DX (as IN AX,DX).

Flags: None.

Object code (two formats):

> Variable port: | 1110110w |
> Fixed port: | 1110010w | --port-- |

INC: Increment by 1

Purpose: Increments a value by 1. See also DEC.

Function: INC adds 1 to a byte or word in a register or memory, coded, for example, as INC CX.

Flags: Affects AF, OF, PF, SF, and ZF.

Object code (two formats):

> Register: | 01000reg |
> Reg/memory: | 1111111w | mod000r/m |

INT: Interrupt

Purpose: Interrupts processing of a program and transfers control to one of the 256 interrupt (vector) addresses.

Function: INT performs the following: (1) Decrements the SP by 2, pushes the Flags onto the Stack, and resets the IF and TF Flags; (2) Decrements the SP by 2, pushes the CS onto the Stack, and places the high-order word of the interrupt vector in the CS; and (3) decrements the CS by 2, pushes the IP onto the Stack, and fills the IP with the low-order word of the interrupt vector.

Flags: Affects IF and TF.

Object code: | 1100110v | --type-- | (if v = 0 type is 3)

INTO: Interrupt on Overflow

Purpose: Causes an interrupt if an overflow has occurred. See also INT.

Function: If the OF Flag is set to 1, INTO performs an INT 4. The interrupt address is at location hex 10H. Processing is similar to that for INT. INTO has no operands.

Flags: None.

Object code: 11001110

IRET: Interrupt Return

Purpose: Provides a return from an interrupt routine. See also RET.

Function: IRET performs the following: (1) Pops the word at the top of the Stack into the IP, increments the SP by 2, and pops the top of the Stack into the CS; (2) Increments the SP by 2 and pops the top of the Stack into the Flags register. This procedure undoes the steps that the interrupt originally took and performs a return. IRET has no operands.

Flags: Affects all.

Object code: 11001111

JA/JNBE: Jump Above or Jump if not Below/Equal

Purpose: Used after a test of unsigned data to transfer to another address.

Function: If the CF Flag is 0 (no carry) and the ZF Flag is 0 (nonzero), the instruction adds the operand offset to the IP and performs a jump.

Flags: None.

Object code: |01110111|--disp--|

JAE/JNB: Jump if Above/Equal or Jump if not Below

Purpose: Used after a test of unsigned data to transfer to another address.

Function: If the CF Flag is 0 (no carry), the instruction adds the operand offset to the IP and performs a jump.

Flags: None.

Object code: |01110011|--disp--|

JB/JNAE: Jump if Below or Jump if not Above/Equal

Purpose: Used after a test of unsigned data to transfer to another address.

Function: If the CF Flag is 1 (carry), the instruction adds the operand offset to the IP and performs a jump.

Flags: None.

Object code: |01110010|--disp--|

JBE/JNA: Jump if Below/Equal or Jump if not Above

Purpose: Used after a test of unsigned data to transfer to another address.

Function: If the CF Flag is 1 (carry) or the AF Flag is 1, the instruction adds the operand offset to the IP and performs a jump.

Flags: None.

Object code: |01110110|--disp--|

JC: Jump if Carry

Purpose: See JB/JNAE (identical operations).

JCXZ: Jump if CX is Zero

Purpose: For control over looping.

Function: JCXZ jumps to the specified address if the CX contains zero. JCXZ could be useful at the start of a loop.

Flags: None.

Object code: |11100011|--disp--|

JE/JZ: Jump if Equal or Jump if Zero

Purpose: Used after a test of signed or unsigned data to transfer to another address.

Function: If the Zero (ZF) Flag is 1 (zero condition), the instruction adds the operand offset to the IP and performs a jump.

Flags: None.

Object code: |01110100|--disp--|

JG/JNLE: Jump if Greater or Jump if not Less/Equal

Purpose: Used after a test of signed data to transfer to another address.

Function: If the ZF Flag is 0 (nonzero) and the SF Flag equals the OF Flag (both 0 or both 1), the instruction adds the operand offset to the IP and performs a jump.

Flags: None.

Object code: |01111111|--disp--|

JGE/JNL: Jump if Greater/Equal or Jump if not Less

Purpose: Used after a test of signed data to transfer to another address.

Function: If the SF Flag equals the OF Flag (both 0 or both 1), the instruction adds the operand offset to the IP and performs a jump.

Flags: None.

Object code: |01111101|--disp--|

JL/JNGE: Jump if Less or Jump if Greater/Equal

Purpose: Used after a test of signed data to transfer to another address.

Function: If the SF Flag is not equal to the OF Flag, the instruction adds the operand offset to the IP and performs a jump.

Flags: None.

Object code: |01111100|--disp--|

JLE/JNG: Jump if Less/Equal or Jump if not Greater

Purpose: Used after a test of signed data to transfer to another address.

Function: If the ZF Flag is 1 (zero condition) or if the SF Flag is not equal to the OF Flag, the instruction adds the operand offset to the IP and performs a jump.

Flags: None.

Object code: |01111110|--disp--|

JMP: Unconditional Jump

Purpose: To jump to a designated address under any condition.

Function: JMP replaces the IP with a destination offset address. There are five types of JMP operations for transferring control within Segments and between Segments. An intersegment jump also replaces the CS with a new segment address.

Flags: None.

Object code (five formats):

> Direct within Segment: |11101001|disp-low |disp-high|
> Direct within Seg short: |11101011|--disp--- |
> Indirect within Segment:|11111111|mod100r/m|
> Indirect intersegment: |11111111|mod101r/m|
> Direct intersegment:
> |11101010|offset-low|offset-high|seg-low|seg-high|

JNC: Jump no Carry

Purpose: See JAE/JNB (identical operations).

JNE/JNZ: Jump not Equal or Jump not Zero

Purpose: Used after a test of signed data to transfer to another address.

Function: If the ZF Flag is 0 (nonzero), the instruction adds the operand offset to the IP and performs a jump.

Flags: None.

Object code: |01110101|--disp--|

JNO: Jump No Overflow

Purpose: Used to jump to a designated address on a test for no overflow. See also JO.

Function: If the OF Flag is 0 (no overflow), the instruction adds the operand offset to the IP and performs a jump.

Flags: None.

Object code: |01110001|--disp--|

JNP/JPO: Jump No Parity or Jump Parity Odd

Purpose: Causes a jump to a designated address if an operation caused no (or odd) parity. Odd parity here means that an operation has caused the low order eight bits to be an odd number of bits. See also JP/JPE.

Function: If the PF Flag is 0 (odd parity), the instruction adds the operand offset to the IP and performs a jump.

Flags: None.

Object code: |01111011|--disp--|

JNS: Jump No Sign

Purpose: Causes a jump to a designated address if an operation caused the sign to be set to positive. See also JS.

Function: If the SF Flag is 0 (positive), JNS adds the operand offset to the IP and performs a jump.

Flags: None.

Object code: |01111001|--disp--|

JO: Jump if Overflow

Purpose: Causes a jump to a designated address if an operation caused an overflow. See also JNO.

Function: If the OF Flag is 1 (overflow set), JO adds the operand offset to the IP and performs a jump.

Flags: None.

Object code: |01110000|--disp--|

JP/JPE: Jump on Parity or Jump on Parity Even

Purpose: Causes a jump to a designated address if an operation caused even parity. Even parity here means that an operation has caused the low order eight bits to be an even number of bits. See also JNP/JPO.

Function: If the PF Flag is 1 (even parity), the instruction adds the operand offset to the IP and performs a jump.

Flags: None.

Object code: |01111010|--disp--|

JS: Jump on Sign

Purpose: Jumps to a designated address if an operation caused the sign to be set to negative.

Function: If the SF Flag is 1 (negative), JS adds the operand offset to the IP and performs a jump.

Flags: None.

Object code: |01111000|--disp--|

LAHF: Load AH from Flags

Purpose: Loads the Flags register into the AH. The instruction provides compatibility with the 8080 processor. See also SAHF.

Function: LAHF (coded with no operands) inserts the rightmost byte of the Flags register into the AH as follows:

$$S \; Z \; * \; A \; * \; P \; * \; C \; (* \text{ denotes an unused bit})$$

Flags: None.

Object code: 10011111

LDS: Load Data Segment Register

Purpose: Initializes the start address for the Data Segment and offset address of a variable so that succeeding instructions can access the variable.

Function: LDS transfers four bytes in memory containing an offset address and a segment address to a pair of destination registers. The segment address loads in the DS and the offset address transfers to any of the general, index, or pointer registers. The following example loads the offset address in the DI:

$$\text{LDS DI,memory-addr}$$

Flags: None.

Object code: |11000101|mod reg r/m|

LES: Load Extra Segment Register

Purpose: Initializes the start address for the Extra Segment and offset address of a variable so that succeeding instructions can access the variable.

Function: See LDS for similar processing (except that LES references the ES register).

Flags: None.

Object code: |11000100|mod reg r/m|

LOCK: Lock Bus

Purpose: Prevent other (co)processors from changing a data item at the same time.

Function: LOCK is a one-byte prefix that you may code immediately before any instruction. You could use it if you have an 8087 or other coprocessor. The operation sends a signal to the other processors to prevent them from using the data until the next instruction is completed.

Flags: None.

Object code: 11110000

LODS/LODSB/LODSW: Load Byte or Word String

Purpose: Loads the AL with a byte or the AX with a word from memory. One application could be for use with the OUT instruction.

Function: Although LODS is a string operation, there is no reason to use it repetitively with a REP prefix. The DS:SI registers address a byte (if LODSB) or a word (if LODSW) and load it from memory into the AL or AX. If the DF Flag is 0, the operation adds 1 (if byte) or 2 (if word) to the SI; otherwise it subtracts 1 or 2. The instruction has no coded operands.

Flags: None.

Object code: 1010110w

LOOP: Loop until Complete

Purpose: Controls executing a subroutine a specified number of times.

Function: The CX should contain a count before starting the loop. The LOOP instruction appears at the end of the loop and decrements the CX by 1. If the CX is nonzero, the instruction transfers to the operand address (adds the offset in the IP); otherwise it drops through to the next instruction.

Flags: None.

Object code: 11100010

LOOPE/LOOPZ: Loop if Equal or Loop if Zero

Purpose: Controls executing a subroutine a specified number of times or until the ZF Flag is set (to 1). See also LOOPNE/LOOPNZ.

Function: LOOPE/LOOPZ is similar to LOOP except that this operation terminates if the CX is 0 or if the ZF Flag is 0 (nonzero condition).

Flags: None.

Object code: |11100001|--disp--|

LOOPNE/LOOPNZ: Loop if not Equal or Loop if not Zero

Purpose: Controls executing a subroutine a specified number of times or until the ZF Flag is set (to 1). See also LOOPE/LOOPZ.

Function: LOOPNE/LOOPNZ is similar to LOOP except that this operation terminates if the CX is 0 or if the ZF Flag is set to 1 (zero condition).

Flags: None.

Object code: |11100000|--disp--|

MOV: Move

Purpose: Transfers a byte or word of data.

Function: MOV transfers data between two registers or between a register and memory, and transfers immediate data to a register or memory. MOV cannot transfer between two memory locations–see MOVS for that feature. There are seven types of MOV instructions.

Flags: None.

Object code (seven formats):

```
Reg/mem to/from reg: |100010dw | modregr/m |
Immed to reg/mem:    |1100011w | mod000r/m | ---data---|data if w = 1|
Immed to register:   |1011wreg |     ---data--| data if w = 1|
Mem to accumulator:  |1010000w |   addr-low | addr-high |
Accumulator to mem:  |1010001w |   addr-low | addr-high |
Reg/mem to seg reg:  |10001110 | mod0sgr/m | (sg = seg reg)
Seg reg to reg/mem:  |10001100 | mod0sgr/m | (sg = seg reg)
```

MOVS/MOVSB/MOVSW: Move Byte or Word String

Purpose: Moves data between memory locations.

Function: Normally used with the REP prefix, MOVSB moves any number of bytes and MOVSW moves any number of words between memory locations. ES:DI addresses operand 1 and DS:SI addresses operand 2. If the DF Flag is 0, the operation moves data from left to right in memory and increments the DI and SI. If the DF Flag is 1, the operation moves data from right to left in memory and decrements the DI and SI. There is no coded operand.

Flags: None.

Object code: 1010010w (no operand).

MUL: Multiply Unsigned

Purpose: Multiplies an unsigned multiplicand (8-or 16-bit) by an unsigned multiplier (8-or 16-bit). See also IMUL.

Function: MUL treats a leftmost 1-bit as a data bit, not a negative sign. For 8-bit multiplication, the multiplicand is in the AL and the multiplier is in a register or memory, coded as MUL CL. The product is developed in the AX. For 16-bit multiplication, the muliplicand is in the AX and the multiplier is in a register or memory, coded as MUL BX. The product is developed in the DX:AX.

Flags: Affects CF and OF (AF, PF, SF, and ZF are undefined).

Object code: |1111011w|mod100r/m|

NEG: Negate

Purpose: Reverses a sign from positive to negative and negative to positive.

Function: NEG provides two's complement of the specified operand: subtracts the operand from zero and adds 1.

Flags: Affects AF, CF, OF, PF, SF, and ZF.

Object code: |1111011w|mod011r/m|

NOP: No Operation

Purpose: Makes a program larger or slower! You could use one or more NOP instructions where you want to insert useful machine code later, or to delay execution for purposes of timing.

Function: Technically, NOP performs XCHG AX,AX which changes nothing. NOP has no operands.

Flags: None.

Object code: 10010000

NOT: Logical NOT

Purpose: Reverses the bit configuration of a byte or word.

Function: NOT simply changes 0-bits to 1-bits and vice versa. The operand is a byte or word in a register or memory.

Flags: None.

Object code: |1111011w|mod 010 r/m|

OR: Logical OR

Purpose: Performs logical OR on bits of two operands. See also AND and XOR.

Function: The two operands are both bytes or both words in a register or memory; operand 2 may be immediate. OR matches the two operands bit for bit. If either matched bit is 1, the operand 1 bit becomes 1, and is otherwise unchanged.

Flags: Affects CF, OF, PF, SF, and ZF (AF is undefined).

Object code (three formats):

Reg/mem with reg: |000010dw|modregr/m |
Immed to accum'r: |0000110w|---data-- |data if w = 1|
Immed to reg/mem:|1000000w|mod001r/m|---data---- |data if w = 1|

OUT: Output Byte or Word

Purpose: Transfers data to a port. See also IN.

Function: OUT transfers to an output port a byte from the AL or a word from the AX. You can code the port as a fixed numeric operand (as OUT port#,AX) or as a variable in the DX (as OUT DX,AX).

Flags: None.

Object code: Variable port: |1110111w| Fixed port: |1110011w|--port--|

POP: Pop Word off Stack

Purpose: Transfers a word (previously pushed on the Stack) to a specified destination. See also POPF and PUSH.

Function: The SP register points to the current word at the top of the Stack. POP transfers the word to the specified destination and increments the SP by 2. There are three types of POP instructions depending on whether the destination is a register, segment register, or memory word.

Flags: None.

Object code (three formats):

> Register: |01011reg|
> Segment reg:|000sg111| (sg implies segment reg)
> Reg/memory:|10001111|mod 000 r/m|

POPF: Pop Flags off Stack

Purpose: Transfers bits (previously pushed on the Stack) to the Flags register. See also PUSHF and POP.

Function: The SP register points to the current word at the top of the Stack. POPF (coded with no operand) transfers the bits from this word to the Flags register and increments the SP by 2. Normally a PUSHF instruction would have pushed the Flags onto the Stack, and POPF returns the Flag bits to the originating Flag positions as follows:

$$* * * * O D I T S Z * A * P * C$$

Flags: Affects all.

Object code: 10011101

PUSH: Push Word onto the Stack

Purpose: Saves a word value (address or data item) on the Stack for later use. See also POP and PUSHF.

Function: The SP register points to the current word at the top of the Stack. PUSH decrements the SP by 2 and transfers a word from the specified operand to the new top of the Stack. There are three types of PUSH instructions depending on whether the source is a register, a segment register, or a memory word.

Flags: None.

Object code (three formats):

> Register: |01010reg|
> Segment reg:|000sg110| (sg implies segment reg)
> Reg/memory:|11111111|mod 110 r/m|

PUSHF: Push Flags onto the Stack

Purpose: Preserves the contents of the Flags register on the Stack for later use. See also POPF and PUSH.

Function: The SP register points to the current word at the top of the Stack. PUSHF decrements the SP by 2 and transfers the Flags to the new top of the Stack.

Flags: Affects none.

Object code: 10011100

RCL AND RCR: Rotate Left through Carry and Rotate Right through Carry

Purpose: Rotates bits left or right through the CF Flag. See also ROL and ROR.

Function: The operation can act on a byte or word in a register or memory and can rotate bits left or right. Rotating one bit can specify an operand as 1; rotating more than one bit requires a reference to the CL containing a count. For RCL, the leftmost bit enters the CF Flag and the CF bit enters bit-0 of the destination; all other bits shift left. For RCR, bit-0 enters the CF Flag and the CF bit enters the leftmost bit of the destination; all other bits shift right.

Flags: Affects CF and OF.

Object code: RCL: |110100cw|mod010r/m| (if c = 0 shift is 1;
          RCR: |110100cw|mod011r/m| if c = 1 shift is in CL)

REP/REPE/REPZ/REPNE/REPNZ: Repeat String

Purpose: Repeats a String operation (CMPS, MOVS, SCAS, or STOS) a specified number of times.

Function: These are optional repeat prefixes coded before the String instructions CMPS, MOVS, SCAS, and STOS. Load the CX with a count prior to execution. The operation decrements the CX by 1 for each execution of the String instruction. For REP, the operation repeats until CX is 0. For REPE/REPZ, the operation repeats until CX is nonzero or until ZF is 0 (nonzero condition). For REPNE/REPNZ, the operation repeats until CX is 0 or until ZF is 1 (zero condition).

Flags: See the associated String instruction.

Object code: REP/REPNE: 11110010 REPE: 11110011

RET: Return from a Procedure

Purpose: Returns from a Procedure that was previously entered by a CALL. See also CALL.

Function: CALL can reference either a near or far Procedure. RET moves the word at the top of the Stack to the IP and increments the SP by 2. For an intersegment return, RET also moves the word now at the top of the Stack to the CS and again increments the SP by 2. If RET contains a numeric operand (a pop-value as RET 4), this is also added to the SP.

Flags: None.

Object code (four formats):

> Within a Segment: |11000011|
> Within a Segment with pop-value:
> > |11000010|data-low|data-high|
> Intersegment: |11001011|
> Intersegment with pop-value:
> > |11001010|data-low|data-high|

ROL and ROR: Rotate Left and Rotate Right

Purpose: Rotates bits left or right. See also RCL and RCR.

Function: The operation can act on a byte or word in a register or memory, and can rotate bits left or right. Rotating one bit can specify an operand as 1; rotating more than one bit requires a reference to the CL containing a count. For ROL, the leftmost bit enters bit-0 of the destination; all other bits shift left. For ROR, bit-0 enters the leftmost bit of the destination; all other bits shift right.

Flags: Affects CF and OF.

Object code: ROL: |110100cw|mod000r/m| (if c = 0 count = 1;
  ROR: |110100cw|mod001r/m| if c = 1 count is in CL)

SAHF: Store AH Contents in Flags

Purpose: SAHF provides compatibility with the 8080 processor for storing bits from the AH in the Flags. See also LAHF.

Function: SAHF transfers specific bits from the AH to the Flags register as follows:

$$S \; Z * A * P * C \; (* \text{ denotes unused bit})$$

Flags: Affects AF, CF, PF, SF, and ZF.

Object code: 10011110.

SAL, SAR, SHL, and SHR: Shift Left or Shift Right

Purpose: Shift bits left or right.

Function: The operation can act on a byte or word in a register or memory and can shift bits left or right. Shifting one bit can specify an operand as 1; shifting more than one bit requires a reference to the CL containing a count. SAR is an arithmetic shift that considers the sign of the referenced field. SHL and SHR are logical shifts that treat the sign bit as a data bit. SAL acts exactly like SHL.

SAL and SHL shift bits left a specified number and fill 0-bits in vacated positions to the right. SHR shifts bits to the right a specified number and fills 0-bits in vacated positions to the left. SAR shifts bits to the right a specified number and fills the sign bit (0 or 1) in vacated positions to the left. In all cases, bits shifted off are lost.

Flags: Affects CF, OF, PF, SF, and ZF (AF is undefined).

Object code: SAL/SHL: |110100cw|mod100r/m| (if c=0 count=1;
                        SAR: |110100cw|mod111r/m| if c=1 count in CL)
                        SHR: |110100cw|mod101r/m|

SBB: Subtract with Borrow

Purpose: Typically used in multiword binary subtraction to carry an overflowed 1-bit into the next stage of arithmetic. See also ADC.

Function: If the CF Flag is set, SBB first subtracts 1 from operand 1. SBB always subtracts operand 2 from operand 1, just as SUB does.

Flags: Affects AF, CF, OF, PF, SF, and ZF.

Object code (three formats):

Reg/mem with reg: | 000110dw | modregr/m |
Immed from accum'r: | 0001110w | ---data-- | data if w = 1|
Immed from reg/mem: | 100000sw | mod011r/m | ---data---- | data if sw = 01|

SCAS/SCASB/SCASW: Scan Byte or Word String

Purpose: Scans a string for a specified byte or word value.

Function: For SCASB load a value in the AL, and for SCASW load a value in the AX. ES:DI reference the string in memory that is to be scanned. The operations are normally used with a REPE/REPNE prefix. If the DF Flag is 0, the operation scans memory from left to right and increments the DI. If the DF Flag is 1, the operation scans memory from right to left and decrements the SI. There is no coded operand.

Flags: Affects AF, CF, OF, PF, SF, and ZF.

Object code: 1010111w

STC: Set Carry Flag

Purpose: Sets the Carry Flag. See also CLC.

Function: STC sets the CF Flag to 1. STC has no operand.

Flags: CF (becomes 1).

Object code: 11111001

STD: Set Direction Flag

Purpose: Sets the Direction Flag. This causes string operations such as MOVS and CMPS to process from right to left. See also CLD.

Function: STD sets the DF Flag to 1. STD has no operand.

Flags: DF (becomes 1).

Object code: 11111101

STI: Set Interrupt Flag

Purpose: Enables maskable external interrupts after execution of the next instruction. See also CLI.

Function: STI sets the IF Flag to 1. STI has no operand.

Flags: IF (becomes 1).

Object code: 11111011

STOS/STOSB/STOSW: Store Byte or Word String

Purpose: Stores a byte or word in memory. When used with a REP prefix, the operation duplicates a string value a specified number of times and would be suitable for such actions as clearing an area of memory.

Function: For SCASB load a byte in the AL, and for SCASW load a word in the AX. ES:DI reference a location in memory where the byte or word is to be stored. You would normally use REP with this instruction to repeat the byte or word through memory. If the DF Flag is 0, the operation stores in memory from left to right and increments the DI. If the DF Flag is 1, the operation stores in memory from right to left and decrements the DI. There is no coded operand.

Flags: None.

Object code: 1010101w

SUB: Subtract Binary Numbers

Purpose: Subtracts two binary numbers. See also SBB.

Function: SUB subtracts byte or word values in a register, memory, or immediate from a register or subtracts byte or word values in a register or immediate from memory.

Flags: Affects AF, CF, OF, PF, SF, and ZF.

Object code (three formats):

```
Reg/mem with reg:    |001010dw|modregr/m |
Immed from accum'r   |0010110w|---data--    |data if w = 1|
Immed from reg/mem:  |100000sw |mod101r/m|---data----    |data if sw = 01|
```

TEST: Test Bits

Purpose: Tests a byte or word for a specific bit configuration.

Function: TEST acts like AND but does not change the destination operand. The two operands are both bytes or both words in a register or memory; operand-2 may be immediate. The instruction sets Flags according to AND logic. See also AND.

Flags: Affects CF, OF, PF, SF, and ZF (AF is undefined).

Object code (three formats):

```
Reg/mem with reg:    | 1000010w | modregr/m |
Immed from accum'r   | 1010100w | ---data-- |data if w = 1|
Immed from reg/mem:  | 1111011w | mod101r/m | ---data---- |data if w = 1|
```

WAIT: Put Processor in Wait State

Purpose: Allows the processor to remain in a wait state until an external interrupt occurs. In this way the processor can be synchronized with external devices or with a coprocessor.

Function: The 8086/8088 processors wait until the external device (or coprocessor) finishes executing. They resume processing on receiving a signal in the TEST pin.

Flags: None.

Object code: 10011011

XCHG: Exchange

Purpose: Exchanges two bytes or two words.

Function: The instruction exchanges data between two registers (as XCHG AH,BL) or between a register and memory (as XCHG CX,word).

Flags: None.

Object code (two formats):

```
Reg with accumulator: |10010reg|
Reg/mem with reg:     |1000011w|mod reg r/m|
```

XLAT: Translate

Purpose: Translates bytes into a different format, such as lowercase to uppercase or ASCII to EBCDIC.

Function: You have to define a table and load its address in the BX. Load the AL with a byte that XLAT is to translate. The operation uses the AL value as an offset into the table, selects the byte from the table, and stores it in the AL. No operands need be coded.

Flags: None.

Object code: 11010111.

XOR: Exclusive OR

Purpose: Performs logical exclusive OR on bits of two operands. See also AND and OR.

Function: The two operands are both bytes or both words in a register or memory; operand 2 may be immediate. XOR matches the two operands bit for bit. If the matched bits are the same, XOR sets the operand 1 bit to 0, and if different to 1.

Flags: Affects CF, OF, PF, SF, and ZF (AF is undefined).

Object code (three formats):

```
Reg/mem with reg: |001100dw|mod reg r/m|
Immed to reg/mem:|1000000w|mod 110 r/m|---data----   |data if w=1|
Immed to accum'r: |0011010w|---data----   |data if w=1|
```

ASCII CHARACTER CODES

Dec	Hex	Char	Dec	Hex	Char	Dec	Hex	Char
000	00H	NUL	043	2BH	+	086	56H	V
001	01H	SOH	044	2CH	,	087	57H	W
002	02H	STX	045	2DH	−	088	58H	X
003	03H	ETX	046	2EH	.	089	59H	Y
004	04H	EOT	047	2FH	/	090	5AH	Z
005	05H	ENQ	048	30H	0	091	5BH	[
006	06H	ACK	049	31H	1	092	5CH	\
007	07H	BEL	050	32H	2	093	5DH	]
008	08H	BS	051	33H	3	094	5EH	^
009	09H	HT	052	34H	4	095	5FH	_
010	0AH	LF	053	35H	5	096	60H	'
011	0BH	VT	054	36H	6	097	61H	a
012	0CH	FF	055	37H	7	098	62H	b
013	0DH	CR	056	38H	8	099	63H	c
014	0EH	SO	057	39H	9	100	64H	d
015	0FH	SI	058	3AH	:	101	65H	e
016	10H	DLE	059	3BH	;	102	66H	f

Dec	Hex	Char	Dec	Hex	Char	Dec	Hex	Char
017	11H	DC1	060	3CH	<	103	67H	g
018	12H	DC2	061	3DH	=	104	68H	h
019	13H	DC3	062	3EH	>	105	69H	i
020	14H	DC4	063	3FH	?	106	6AH	j
021	15H	NAK	064	40H	@	107	6BH	k
022	16H	SYN	065	41H	A	108	6CH	l
023	17H	ETB	066	42H	B	109	6DH	m
024	18H	CAN	067	43H	C	110	6EH	n
025	19H	EM	068	44H	D	111	6FH	o
026	1AH	SUB	069	45H	E	112	70H	p
027	1BH	ESC	070	46H	F	113	71H	q
028	1CH	FS	071	47H	G	114	72H	r
029	1DH	GS	072	48H	H	115	73H	s
030	1EH	RS	073	49H	I	116	74H	t
031	1FH	US	074	4AH	J	117	75H	u
032	20H	SPACE	075	4BH	K	118	76H	v
033	21H	!	076	4CH	L	119	77H	w
034	22H	"	077	4DH	M	120	78H	x
035	23H	#	078	4EH	N	121	79H	y
036	24H	$	079	4FH	O	122	7AH	z
037	25H	%	080	50H	P	123	7BH	{
038	26H	&	081	51H	Q	124	7CH		
039	27H	'	082	52H	R	125	7DH	}
040	28H	(	083	53H	S	126	7EH	ã
041	29H	)	084	54H	T	127	7FH	DEL
042	2AH	*	085	55H	U			

Dec = decimal, Hex = Hexadecimal (H), Char = character.
LF = Feed, FF = Form Feed, CR = Carriage Return, DEL = Rubout

HEXADECIMAL AND DECIMAL CONVERSION

This appendix provides the steps in converting between hexadecimal and decimal formats. We will first show the steps to convert hex A4B6 to decimal 42,166 and then show the steps to convert decimal 42,166 back to hex A4B6.

CONVERTING HEXADECIMAL TO DECIMAL

How do you convert the hex number A4B6 to a decimal number? Starting with the leftmost hex digit (A), continuously multiply each hex digit and accumulate the results. Also, since multiplication is in decimal, convert hex digits A through F to decimal 10 through 15.

First digit: A (10)	10
Multiply by 16	$\times 16$
	160
Add next digit, 4	$+ \ 4$
	164

Multiply by 16	× 16
	2624
Add next digit, B (11)	+ 11
	2635
Multiply by 16	× 16
	42160
Add next digit, 6	+ 6
Decimal value	42166

You can also perform conversion by means of a table. For the hex number A4B6, think of the rightmost digit (6) as position 1, the next digit to the left (B) as position 2, the next digit (4) as position 3, and the leftmost digit (A) as position 4. Now refer to Table B-1 and locate the hex value in the table for each hex digit:

For position 1 (6), column 1 equals	6
For position 2 (B), column 2 equals	176
For position 3 (4), column 3 equals	1024
For position 4 (A), column 4 equals	40960
Decimal value	42166

HEXADECIMAL TO DECIMAL CONVERSION

How do you convert the decimal number 42,166 to hexadecimal? Using decimal arithmetic, continuously divide the decimal number 42,166 by 16. Develop the hex number from the remainders of each step of the division:

	Quotient	Remainder	Hex
42166 / 16	2635	6	6
2635 / 16	164	11	B
164 / 16	10	4	4
10 / 16	0	10	A

First divide the original number 42166 by 16; the remainder becomes the rightmost hex digit, 6. Next divide the new quotient 2635 by 16; the remainder, 11 or B, becomes the next hex digit to the left. Continue in this manner until the quotient is zero.

You can also convert decimal to hexadecimal by means of Table B-1. To convert the decimal number 42,166 to hex, locate in the table the number that is equal to or next smaller than 42,166. Note the equivalent hex number and its position in the table. Subtract the decimal value of that hex digit from 42,166, and locate the difference in the table. The procedure works as follows:

	Decimal	Hex
Starting decimal value	42,166	
Subtract next smaller number	40,960	A000
Difference	1,206	
Subtract next smaller number	1,024	400
Difference	182	
Subtract next smaller number	176	B0
Difference	6	6
Final hex number		A4B6

Table B-1 Hexadecimal to Decimal Conversion.

HEX	DEC	HEX	DEC	HEX	DEC	HEX	DEC	HEX	DEC	HEX	DEC	HEX	DEC	HEX	DEC
0	0	0	0	0	0	0	0	0	0	0	0	0	0	0	0
1	268,435,456	1	16,777,216	1	1,048,576	1	65,536	1	4,096	1	256	1	16	1	1
2	536,870,912	2	33,554,432	2	2,097,152	2	131,072	2	8,192	2	512	2	32	2	2
3	805,306,368	3	50,331,648	3	3,145,728	3	196,608	3	12,288	3	768	3	48	3	3
4	1,073,741,824	4	67,108,864	4	4,194,304	4	262,144	4	16,384	4	1,024	4	64	4	4
5	1,342,177,280	5	83,886,080	5	5,242,880	5	327,680	5	20,480	5	1,280	5	80	5	5
6	1,610,612,736	6	100,663,296	6	6,291,456	6	393,216	6	24,576	6	1,536	6	96	6	6
7	1,879,048,192	7	117,440,512	7	7,340,032	7	458,752	7	28,672	7	1,792	7	112	7	7
8	2,147,483,648	8	134,217,728	8	8,388,608	8	524,288	8	32,768	8	2,048	8	128	8	8
9	2,415,919,104	9	150,994,944	9	9,437,184	9	589,824	9	36,864	9	2,304	9	144	9	9
A	2,684,354,560	A	167,772,160	A	10,485,760	A	655,360	A	40,960	A	2,560	A	160	A	10
B	2,952,790,016	B	184,549,376	B	11,534,336	B	720,896	B	45,056	B	2,816	B	176	B	11
C	3,221,225,472	C	201,326,592	C	12,582,912	C	786,432	C	49,152	C	3,072	C	192	C	12
D	3,489,660,928	D	218,103,808	D	13,631,488	D	851,968	D	53,248	D	3,328	D	208	D	13
E	3,758,096,384	E	234,881,024	E	14,680,064	E	917,504	E	57,344	E	3,584	E	224	E	14
F	4,026,531,840	F	251,658,240	F	15,728,640	F	983,040	F	61,440	F	3,840	F	240	F	15
8		7		6		5		4		3		2		1	

Hexadecimal Positions

SOLUTIONS TO SELECTED QUESTIONS

1-1.   (a) 01001101; (b) 01101101; (c) 00111111; (d) 00110100.

1-2.   (a) 0111; (b) 1100; (c) 10011; (d) 11100.

1-3.   (a) 00100100; (b) 01100111; (c) 01000000.

1-4.   (a) 11110101; (b) 11100010; (c) 11100111.

1-5.   (a) 00110100; (b) 01100011; (c) 10000000.

1-6.   (a) 50; (b) 35; (c) 5C; (d) 6E.

1-7.   (a) 23C8; (b) 5200; (c) 8000; (d) 11182.

1-8.   (a) 11; (b) 22; (c) 57; (d) FF; (e) FFF; (f) F7C1.

1-9.   (a) Stack, Data, and Code.

(b) 64K

(c) Paragraph.

1-10. (a) AX, BX, CX, DX, DI, SI.

(b) CX primarily.

(c) AX and DX.

(d) CS, DS, ES, and SS.

(e) Flags.

(f) IP.

1-11. (a) ROM (read-only memory) is permanent and performs startup procedures and handles input/output.

(b) RAM (read-only memory) is temporary and is the area where programs and data reside when executing.

2-1. (a) B88752; (b) 056A03.

2-2. E CS:101 23

2-3. (a) The required instructions are the following:

MOV AX,5003

ADD AX,2000

RET

(b) Change to B8 50 03 05 20 00 CB

(c) R and IP to set the IP to 0.

3-1. TITLE and PAGE.

3-2. (a), (b), and (c) are valid.

(d) is invalid because it starts with a number.

(e) is valid only if it refers to the ES register.

3-3. The Stack Segment saves addresses for linking to subroutines and other programs; the Data Segment contains the data that a program defines; the Code Segment contains the instructions that execute.

3-4. (a) END; (b) ENDP; (c) ENDS.

3-5. A Pseudo-operation is a command to the Assembler to perform a particular action during assembly; an instruction is a command to the processor during program execution.

3-6. RET is an instruction that causes control to return to the operating system; END is a Pseudo-operation that tells the Assembler that there are no more instructions to assemble.

3-7. ASSUME CS:CDSEG,DS:DATSEG,SS:STKSEG.

3-8. PUSH DS
SUB AX,AX
PUSH AX

3-9. (a) MASM B:ASMSAMP,B:,B:,B:;
(b) B:ASM ASMSAMP,,,;

3-10. (a) DEBUG B:ASMSAMP.EXE

(b) B:ASMSAMP

3-11. (a) Contains the source program.
(b) Contains the assembled object file.
(c) Contains the assembled listing file with source and object code.
(d) Contains the cross-reference file.
(e) Contains the Link Map.
(f) Contains a backup of the source file.
(g) Contains the executable program module.

3-12. MOV AX,DATSEG
MOV DS,AX

3-13. The four instructions are
MOV AL,25H
SHL AL,1
MOV BL,15H
MUL BL

3-14. In the Data Segment:
FLD1 DB 25H
FLD2 DB 15H
FLD3 DW ?

In the Code Segment:
MOV AL,FLD1
SHL AL,1
MUL FLD2
MOV FLD3,AX

4-1. (a) 4; (b) 10; (c) 1; (d) 8; (e) 2.

4-2. TITLE1 DB 'Zolar Electronics'

4-3. (a) FLD1 DD 82H
(b) FLD2 DB 14H
(c) FLD3 DW ?
(d) FLD4 DB 00010100B
(e) FLD5 DW 15,18,19,26,40

4-4. (a) 3238 (ASCII); (b) 1C (hex).

4-5. (a) 25; (b) 7325; (c) 3A732500; (d) 3A73250000000000.

4-6. (a) MOV   AX,250
(b) CMP   FLD1,0
(c) ADD   CX,20H
(d) SUB   AX,20H
(e) SHL   FLD2,1   (or SAL)
(f) SHR   BH,1

5-1.   +127 and −128. The operand is a one-byte value allowing for hex 00 through 7F (0 through + 128) and hex 80 through FF (− 128 through − 1).

5-2.   (a) 45D; (b) 4B2; (c) 365 (convert 0D3 to two's complement).

5-3.   Following is an efficient solution, one of many possible solutions:

```
          MOV     AX,00
          MOV     BX,01
          MOV     CX,12
          MOV     DX,00
   B20:
          ADD     AX,BX    ;No. is in the AX
          MOV     BX,DX
          MOV     DX,AX
          LOOP    B20
```

5-4.   (a) CMP CX,DX   (b) CMP AX,BX   (c) JCXZ address
            JA address   JG address   or CMP CX,0
                                                              JZ address

        (d) JO address   (e) CMP AX,BX   (f) CMP CX,DX
                                  JLE or JNG   JBE or JNA

5-5.   (a) OF (1); (b) SF (1); (c) ZF (1);
        (d) TF (1); (e) DF (1).

5-6.   The next instruction immediately following CALL B10 would be CALL C10 in B10. The program would loop endlessly.

5-7.   The first (main) PROC must be FAR because the operating system links to its address for execution. A NEAR attribute means that the address is within this particular program (i.e., within the assembly).

5-8.   Although CALL is the recommended way, a program can JMP to a Procedure or can drop directly into it.

5-9.   Three (one for each CALL).

5-10. (a) 1001 1010; (b) 0110 0001; (c) 1111 1011;
        (d) 0000 0000; (e) 0001 1100.

5-12. (a) 0101 1100; (b) 0001 0111; (c) 1100 1000;
        (d) 1011 0010; (e) 0011 0111; (f) 1011 0011;
        (g) 0110 1001.

6-1.   27.

6-2.
```
   MOV     AH,02          ;Request move cursor
   MOV     BH,00          ;
   MOV     DH,15          ;Row 15
   MOV     DL,05          ;Column 5
```

```
        INT     10H
6-3.    MOV     AX,0600H        ;Request
        MOV     BH,07           ;clear
        MOV     CX,0A00H        ;screen
        MOV     DX,144FH
        INT     10H
```

6-4.   In the Data Segment:

MSSGE DB 'What is the date (mm/dd/yy)?',07H, '$'

In the Code Segment:
```
        MOV     AH,09           ;Request display
        LEA     DX,MSSGE        ; of date
        INT     21H
```

6-5.   In the Data Segment:
```
        DATEPAR     LABEL   BYTE
        MAXLEN      DB      9       ;Space for slashes and return
        ACTLEN      DB      ?
        DATEFLD     DB      9 DUP(' ')
                    DB      '$'
```

In the Code Segment:
```
                MOV     AH,0AH          ;Request accept input
                LEA     DX,DATEPAR      ; of date
                INT     21H
```

7-1.   (a) 1000 0001; (b) 0000 0111; (c) 0111 1000.

7-2.   (a)   MOV   AH,00   ;Request set mode
```
                MOV     AL,02           ; 80-column BW
                INT     10H
        (b)     MOV     AH,01           ;Request cursor type
                MOV     CH,05           ;Start line
                MOV     CL,12           ;End line
                INT     10H
        (c)     MOV     AH,060AH        ;Request scroll
                MOV     BH,07           ;Normal video
                MOV     CX,0000         ;Entire screen
                MOV     DX,184FH
                INT     10H
        (d)     MOV     AH,09           ;Request display
                MOV     AL,0B1H         ;Dot
                MOV     BH,00           ;Page #0
                MOV     BL,17H          ;Blink
                MOV     CX,10           ;Ten times
                INT     10H
```

7-3.   Eight colors for background, and 16 for foreground.

7-4.   (a) 0101 1011; (b) 0110 1110; (c) 1100 1000.

7-5.   Low resolution: four bits per pixel gives 16 colors. Medium resolu-
       tion: two bits per pixel gives 4 colors. High resolution: one bit per
       pixel gives 2 "colors" (BW).

7-6.
```
MOV   AH,09            ;Display
MOV   AL,04            ;Diamond
MOV   BH,00            ;Page #0
MOV   BL,01011100B     ;Light red on magenta
MOV   CX,05            ;Five times
INT   10H
```

7-7.
```
MOV   AH,11            ;Set color
MOV   BL,00             ;Background
MOV   BH,01            ;Blue
INT   10H
```

7-8.
```
MOV   AH,13            ;Read dot
MOV   CX,13            ;Column
MOV   DX,12            ;Row
INT   10H
```

8-1.   (a)
```
MOV   AH,05            ;Request print
MOV   DL,0CH           ;Form feed
INT   21H
```

       (b)
```
LEA   SI,NAMEFLD       ;Initialize name
MOV   CX,length        ; and length
B20:
MOV   AH,05            ;Request print
MOV   DL,[SI]          ;Character from name
INT   21H             ;Call DOS
INC   SI              ;Next character in name
LOOP  B20             ;Loop length times
```

       (c) You could code the line feed (hex 0A) in front of your address.
           The solution is similar to (b).
       (d) You could code the line feed (hex 0A) in front of your city/state.
       (e) Issue another form feed (hex 0C).

8-2.   Refer to Figure 8-3 as a guide for testing the printer status and for
       printing your name and address.

8-3.   You won't be able to use CX for looping five times because the loop
       that prints the name uses the CX. You could use the BX as follows:

```
                            MOV BX,05
                    C20:
                              .
                              .
                              .
                            DEC BX
                            JNZ C20
```

9-1. Be sure to set the DF for right-to-left move. For MOVSB, initialize at NAME1 + 9 and NAME2 + 9. For MOVSW, initialize at NAME1 + 8 and NAME2 + 8. The routine at H10SCAS can use

    MOV AX,'mb'

and use SCASW for the scan.

9-2. (a)
```
     CLD                            ;Left to right
     LEA       SI,TITLE1            ;Initialize
     LEA       DI,PRTLINE          ; to move
     MOV       CX,20               ; 20 bytes
     REP       MOVSB
```

    (b)
```
     STD                            ;Right to left
     LEA       SI,TITLE1 + 19      ;Initialize
     LEA       DI,PRTLINE + 19     ; to move
     MOV       CX,20               ; 20 bytes
     REP       MOVSB
```

    (c)
```
     CLD
     LEA       SI,TITLE1 + 2       ;Start at 3rd byte
     LODSW                         ;Load 2 bytes
```

    (d)
```
     LEA       DI,PRTLINE + 5      ;Initialize PRTLINE + 5
     STOSW                         ;Store AX
```

    (e)
```
     CLD                            ;Left to right
     MOV       CX,20               ;20 bytes
     LEA       SI,TITLE1           ;Initialize
     LEA       DI,PRTLINE          ; address
     REPE      CMPSB               ;Compare
```

    (f)
```
     CLD                            ;Left to right
     MOV       CX,20               ;20 bytes
     LEA       DI,TITLE1           ;Initialize address
     MOV       AL,' '              ; and blank
     REPNE     SCASB               ;Scan for blank
     JNE       F20                 ;Found?
     DEC       DI                  ;Correct address
     MOV       AH,[DI]             ;Yes–move to AH
```

9-3.   One solution is the following:

```
H10SCAS  PROC    NEAR
         CLD                           ;Left to right
         MOV     CX,10                 ;10 bytes
         LEA     DI,NAME1              ;Initialize address
         MOV     AL,'e'                ; & scan character
H20:
         REPNE   SCASB                 ;Scan
         JNE     H30                   ;Found?
         CMP     BYTE PTR[DI],'r'      ;Yes–next byte
         JNE     H20                   ; equals 'r'?
         MOV     AH,03
H30:
         RET
H10SCAS  ENDP
```

9-4.   In the Data Segment:

```
PATTERN DB 03H,04H,05H,20H
DISPLAY DB 80 DUP('   '),'$'
```

In the Code Segment:

```
         CLD                      ;Left to right
         LEA     SI,PATTERN       ;Initialize
         LEA     DI,DISPLAY       ; address
         MOV     CX,20            ;20 bytes
         REP     MOVSW            ;Move pattern
```

Then use INT 21H to display the variable DISPLAY on the screen.

10-1. (a) MOV AX,FIELDB
         ADD AX,FIELDA
         MOV FIELDB,AX
       (b) See Figure 10-2 for multiword addition.

10-2. STC sets the CF Flag. The sum is hex 0148 plus hex 0237 plus 1.

10-3. (a) MOV AX,FIELDA
           MUL FIELDB
       (b) See Figure 10-4 for multiplying a doubleword by a word.

10-4. Where a divisor causes a quotient that exceeds its available space.
       A one-byte divisor must be smaller than the AH, and a one-word
       divisor must be smaller than the DX.

10-5.   (a)   MOV   AX,FIELDA
                   MOV   BL,25
                   DIV   BL
           (b)   MOV   DX,FIELDA
                   MOV   AX,FIELDA + 2
```
```

```
            DIV      FIELDB
10-6.       MOV      CL,04           ;Shift factor
            SHR      AX,CL           ;Shift right AX 4 bits
            MOV      BL,DL           ;Save DL
            SHR      DX,CL           ;Shift right DX 4 bits
            SHL      BL,CL           ;Shift left BL 4 bits
            OR       AH,BL           ;Insert into leftmost 4 bits
```

11-1. (a) ADD generates hex 6C, and AAA generates hex 0102.
       (b) ADD generates hex 70, and AAA generates hex 0106.
       (c) SUB generates hex 02, and AAS has no effect.
       (d) SUB generates hex 2C, and AAS generates hex FF06.

11-2.
```
            LEA      SI,UNDEC   ;Initialize address of UNDER
            MOV      CX,04      ;Initialize 4 loops
       B20:
            OR       [SI],30H   ;Insert ASCII 3
            INC      SI         ;Increment for next byte
            LOOP     B20        ;Loop 4 times
```

11-3. Use Figure 11-2 as a guide, but initialize the CX to 03.

11-4. Use Figure 11-3 as a guide, but initialize the CX to 03.

11-5. (a) Convert ASCII to binary:

	Decimal	Hex
2 x 1 =	2	2
8 x 10 =	80	50
6 x 100 =	600	258
3 x 1000 =	3000	BC2
5 x 50000 =	50000	C350
		D1CC

(b) Convert binary to ASCII:

	Quotient	Remainder
D1CC / A =	14F8	2
14F8 / A =	218	8
218 / A =	35	6
35 / A =	5	3

ASCII number is 53682.

12-1. WKDAYS DB 'Sunday   '
                 'Monday   '
                 'Tuesday   '
                 'Wednesday'
                     ...

12-2. In the Data Segment:

```
          DAYNO     DB    ?
          DAYNAM    DB    9 DUP(?)
          NINE      DB    9
```

In the Code Segment:
```
          LEA     SI,WKDAYS      ;Address of table
          SUB     AH,AH          ;Clear AH
          MOV     AL,DAYNO       ;Day of week
          DEC     AL             ;Decrement day
          MUL     NINE           ;Gives location in table
          ADD     SI,AX          ;Add to address of table
          MOV     CX,09          ;Nine characters
          LEA     DI,DAYNAM      ;Address of destination
          REP     MOVSB            ;Move 9 characters from table
```

12-3. (a) ITEMNO   DB   '08','12','15' ,'22','25'
       (b) ITDESC   DB   'Videotape '
                     DB   'Receivers '
                     DB   'Modems '
                     DB   'Keyboards'
                     DB   'Diskettes '
       (c) ITPRICE DW   1395,7225,9067,6580,0385

12-4. A possible organization is into the following Procedures:
       Main Loop   Calls subroutines.
       B10READ   Displays prompt, accepts item number.
       C10SRCH   Searches table, displays message if
                         an invalid item number.
       D10MOVE   Extracts description & price from table.
       E10CONV   Converts quantity from ASCII to binary.
       F10CALC   Calculates value (quantity x price).
       G10CONV   Converts value from binary to ASCII.
       K10DISP   Displays description & value on screen.

12-5. In the Data Segment:

              SORTAB DB 5 DUP(9 DUP(?))

       In the Code Segment:

```
          LEA     SI,ITDESC      ;Initialize
          LEA     DI,SORTAB      ; table address,
          MOV     CX,45          ; and no. of characters
          CLD                    ;Left to right
          REP     MOVSB          ;Move
```

       The above routine moves the table. Refer to Figure 12-6 for sorting
       table entries.

13-1. Sector 1 is the boot record, 2-3 is the FAT, and 4-7 is the Directory.

13-2.   64.

13-3.   6.

13-4.   Records IBMBIO.COM on track 0, sector 8, through track 1, sector 3, and IBMDOS.COM on track 1, sector 4, through track 2, sector 8.

13-5.   (a) Positions 28-31 of the Directory.
        (b) Hex B4A.
        (c) 4A0B.

13-6.   All the function calls involve INT 21H:
        (a) 16H; (b) 1AH; (c) 15H; (d) 0FH; (e) 14H.

13-7.   (a) 4.
        (b) 1252 (one sector on track 0 plus 8 sectors for the remaining 39 tracks, times 4).
        (c) One access per sector, or 313 in all.

13-8.   Use Figure 13-2 as a guide for creating a disk file, and Figure 11-6 for conversion from ASCII to binary.

13-9.   Use Figure 13-3 as a guide for reading the disk file, and Figure 11-6 for conversion from binary to ASCII.

```
13-10. MOV   AH,03        ;Request write
       MOV   AL,03        ;3 sectors
       LEA   BX,OUT__DSK  ;Output area
       MOV   CH,08        ;Track 08
       MOV   CL,01        ;Sector 01
       MOV   DH,00        ;Head #0
       MOV   DL,00        ;Drive #0
       INT   13H
```

14-1.   (a) Block 0, record 44; (b) Block 0, record 72;
        (c) Block 1, record 21; (d) Block 2, record 3.

14-2.   Decimal 2652 is hex 0A5C, stored as 5C0A0000.

14-3.   All the function calls involve INT 21H:
        (a) 22H; (b) 21H; (c) 28H; (d) 27H.

14-4.   FCBFLSZ contains the size of the file in bytes (number of records times length of records), and FCBRCSZ contains the length of records. Divide FCBFLSZ (four bytes in the DX:AX) by FCBRCSZ (two bytes).

14-5.   Figure 14-2 provides an example of reading a block.

14-6.   Chapter 11 shows how to convert ASCII numbers to binary.

14-7.   You could use as guides Figure 14-1 for random reading and Figure 11-6 for conversion between ASCII and binary data.

14-8.   Use Figure 14-3 as a guide for using an index.

15-1. (a) .SALL; (b) .XALL (default).

15-2. (a) MULTB MACRO MULTPR,MULTCD
                      MOV   AL,MULTCD
                      MUL   MULTPR
                      ENDM
       (b) MULTW MACRO MULTPR,MULTCD
                      MOV   AX,MULTCD
                      MUL   MULTPR
                      ENDM

15-3. To include the macro in pass 1, code the following:

       IF1
            INCLUDE library-name
       ENDIF

15-4. The macro definition could begin with:

       PRBIOS MACRO PRTLINE,PRLEN

       PRTLINE and PRLEN are dummy arguments for the address and length of the line to be printed. Refer to Chapter 8 for using BIOS INT 17H to print.

15-5. Note that you cannot use a conditional IF to test for a zero divisor. A conditional IF works only during assembly, whereas the test must occur during program execution. You have to code Assembler instructions such as the following:

       CMP   DIVISOR,00   ;Zero divisor?
       JNZ   (bypass)   ;No - bypass
       CALL   (error message routine)

16-1. (a) EXTRN SUBPROG:FAR
       (b) PUBLIC SUBPROG

16-2. (a) PUBLIC QTY,VALUE,PRICE
       (b) EXTRN QTY:BYTE,VALUE:WORD,PRICE:WORD

16-3. Use Figure 16-5 as a guide.

16-4. Use Figure 16-6 as a guide for passing parameters. However, this question involves pushing three variables onto the Stack. The called program therefore has to access [BP + 10] for the third entry (PRICE) in the Stack. You can define your own standard for returning PRICE through the Stack. Watch also for the pop-value in the RET operand.

16-5. This program involves material in Chapter 6 (screen I/0), Chapter 11 (conversion between ASCII and binary), Chapter 10 (binary multiplication), and Chapter 16 (linkage to subprograms). Be especially careful of the Stack.

INDEX